LIBIDINAL ECONOMY

LIBIDINAL ECONOMY

Jean-François Lyotard

Translated by Iain Hamilton Grant

Continuum
The Tower Building
11 York Road
London SE1 7NX
www.continuumbooks.com

First published in Great Britain 1993 by
The Athlone Press Ltd
This edition 2004

First published in France 1974 by
Les Editions De Minuit, Paris
as *Economie Libidinale*
© 1974 by Les Editions de Minuit
English translation © 1993 The Athlone Press

Publisher's Note

The publishers wish to record their thanks to the French Ministry of
Culture for a grant towards the cost of translation.

British Library Cataloguing in Publication Data
A catalogue record for this book is available from the British Library

ISBN 08264 77003

Typeset by Interactive Science Ltd, Gloucester
Printed and bound by Antony Rowe, Chippenham, Wiltshire

Who knows not how to hide, knows not how to love.

Contents

Translator's Preface ix

Glossary xi

Introduction by Iain Hamilton Grant xix
A Shameless Immodest Provocation xix
Lyotard's Lyotards xx
One or Several Lyotards? xxii
Openings/Surroundings xxiii
The Libidinal Economics of Critical Philosophy xxvii
Critique and Crisis xxvii
Phantasy Island: Back to Kant xxxi

1: *The Great Ephemeral Skin* 1
    Opening the Libidinal Surface 1
    Pagan Theatrics 6
    Turning of the Bar 11
    Duplicity of Signs 15
    Deduction of the Voluminous Body 20
    Duplicity of the Two Pulsional Principles 24
    The Labyrinth, the Cry 31

2: *The Tensor* 42
    Semiotic Sign 42
    Dissimulation 48
    Intensity, the Name 53
    'Use Me' 59
    Simulacrum and Phantasm 64
    Syntax as Skin 73
    Exorbitant 79

CONTENTS

3: *The Desire named Marx*   94
    Libidinal Marx   94
    There Is No Subversive Region   102
    Every Political Economy Is Libidinal   107
    Every Political Economy Is Libidinal (contd)   112
    There Are No Primitive Societies   119
    Inorganic Body   125
    Edwarda and Little Girl Marx   132
    Force   139
    Tautology   145

4: *Trade*   156
    Nicomachean Erotics   156
    Lydian Eulogy   166
    Institutive Prostitution   173
    Outlet Payment   181
    War of Silver, Currency of Death: Mercantilist
    Politics   187

5: *Capital*   202
    Coitus Reservatus   202
    The Concentratory Zero   211
    Nihilist Theory of the Zero of Credit   216
    The Reproductive Use of Credit Money   223
    The Speculative Use of Credit Money: 1921   226
    The Speculative Use of Credit Money: 1929   232

6: *Economy of This Writing*   242
    Economy of the Figurative and the Abstract   242
    The Theoretical as Libidinal   247
    Bodies, Texts: Conductors   255

    Index   265

Translator's Preface

Lyotard's Long Sentences

The role of style in a text such as this immediately provides the translator with the problem of whether (a) to organize the material into a stylistically insensitive but comprehensible English, or (b) to attempt in vain to convey the rhythms and distortions of the original. Insofar as such a choice is possible, I have chosen the latter approach. For this reason, certain of Lyotard's most distinctive tempo-rhythmic structures pose certain problems for the reader, notably: a sentence will become a paragraph, with precious little punctuation, to be brought to a sudden halt by a short burst of extreme relief. The momentum built up by such constructions is lost if the long sentence is broken down into shorter ones, and perhaps more especially for this book than others, momentum, the rapid pressure of change, is crucial.

In recent years the 'question of style' has been posed, each new offering displacing the last of 'last year's lines'. Gilles Deleuze[1] writes of Nietzsche that, 'his masterful siege of the language permits him to transmit something uncodifiable: the notion of *style as politics*'. Lyotard partially confirms this approach in the present text, when he writes that 'our politics is of flight . . . like our style'. Furthermore, in one of the Welleck Library Lectures of 1986, Lyotard writes of *Libidinal Economy*: 'the dominant position given to writing or style could indicate nothing other than how impossible any argumentation, any debate over the so-called contents was.'[2]

But there is perhaps a further piece of evidence that may be drawn on to support such a wicked attempt at transmission as this. Lyotard has often cited Diderot's *Le Neveu de Rameau* as a text witnessing a vertiginous despair similar to some of the affects animating *Libidinal Economy*. These are chiefly manifest when Diderot's narrative gently relays the Nephew's 'colourful opinions' only to collapse under the general strain of attempting the expression of the Nephew's attempts at playing 'imaginary symphonies', feigning the entire corps of instruments and musicians.[3] It is at precisely these points of narrative breakdown (cata-hexes) that Lyotard's vertiginous text is articulated by the accelerating aleatory sweep of the tensor sign, sketching the very ephemerality of its ungraspable flight. Lyotard's sentences may be long, but they are intensive rather than extensive.

Translator's Notes

Insertions of translator's remarks have been kept to a minimum, but when they do occur they are indicated by an asterisk, located at the foot of the page and annotated '*tn*'. The superscripted numbers in the text refer to the notes which are found at the end of each chapter.

Acknowledgements

I should like to thank Karin Littau and David Wood of the University of Warwick for their generous help at many stages of the production of this translation.

Iain Hamilton Grant

Notes

1 Gilles Deleuze, '*Nomad Thought*' in D. B. Allison (ed), *The New Nietzsche* (Cambridge, Mass.: MIT Press, 1985), p. 143.
2 Jean-François Lyotard, *Peregrinations: Law, Form, Event* (New York: Columbia University Press, 1988), p. 13.
3 Denis Diderot, *Rameau's Nephew*, tr. Leonard Tancock (Harmondsworth: Penguin, 1966).

Glossary

1   **Concentrat/-ion/ary/-ed**: Lyotard's neologism *circonversion* does not
    lend itself to satisfactory transliteration into English. Several definitions
    are scattered throughout the text—'a furious force of concentration',
    'annulatory perversion', and so forth—all of which basically describe
    the centripetal movement of consolidation, or, more accurately, 'con-
    densation'. In one essay in *Des Dispositifs pulsionels*, Lyotard can be seen
    groping towards this term when he writes: 'What is important is rather
    the *fullness of circumscription*: the stable investment of energy.' All these
    aspects are covered by 'concentration'. (See point 15, *The Concentratory
    Zero*).

2   **Dispositif**: although this term is conventionally rendered as 'set-up',
    'apparatus' and the like, this gives a somewhat banal mechanistic picture
    of Lyotard's efforts. In *Des Dispositifs pulsionels*, we find the following
    passage: 'The positivity of these investments must be affirmed, rather
    than the disparity and exclusion they produce—the *positivity* rather than
    the *dis-* of *"dispositif"* . . . It is the production of new libidinal operators
    that is positive.' The *positif* is also a positing, an investment, the
    'dispositif' a disposition to invest, a cathexis. As such, the 'dispositif' is
    subject to economic movements and displacements, an aspect which the
    retention of the French term, by combining the dis-place with the dis-
    pose, movement with expenditure, helps to convey.

3   **Incompossibility**: 'compossibility' is a term used by Leibniz to indi-
    cate the relations between 'possible worlds'; many worlds are possible,

but not possible together, not *compossible*. It is left to God, therefore, to create the 'best of all possible worlds', which, since He is perfect, He cannot fail to do. Leibniz's definition of this perfection is profoundly economic: the less the expenditure the greater the perfection—God being perfect, His purse is never stretched. Lyotard's use of 'incompossibility', then, highlights not only, as is pointed out in the section entitled 'Turning of the Bar' (pp. 11–15), a logical violation, but an expensive and metamorphic economics.

4 **Investment**: I have translated *investissement* (the French translation of Freud's *Besetzung*) as 'investment' rather than 'cathexis' (James Strachey's translation of the same term for the *Standard Edition*) because the French is indifferently employed in libidinal and political economics, whereas Strachey's English term remains classical-libidinal.

5 **Jouissance**: French retained throughout, except where it is employed in a context where 'enjoyment' would serve better to indicate the political-legal sense of the word, i.e. the 'enjoyment of rights' or of property or wealth. For the verb *jouir* and the adjective *jouissif/-ve* I have used 'enjoy' and 'enjoyable', with the French following in brackets.

6 **Pouvoir/Impouvoir**: power and powerlessness. See point 8, *Puissance/Impuissance*.

7 **Pulsion-al**: *pulsion* is the French term for Freud's *Trieb*, which the *Standard Edition* translates as 'instinct', a move now widely condemned as inadequate, primarily because the same English word is used to translate both *Trieb* and *Instinkt*. The current term is 'drive', which I have sometimes used for reasons of euphony (death-pulsion reads horribly). To transliterate the French *pulsion*, however, seems preferable since it confers a less mechanistically dominated energetics than does 'drive'. These are the only two options used throughout the present text.

8 **Puissance/Impuissance**: Lyotard makes much of the distinction between (the gendered difference between) *la puissance* and *le pouvoir* throughout this work. Roughly, this can be rendered as the difference between 'force' and 'power', which are the main options used throughout the translation. Both words have, however, a range of uses which often blur the distinction: either word can be employed to designate 'power' (Nietzsche's *Wille zur Macht* (the Will-to-Power) is translated into French under the title *La Volonté de puissance*); the former has a use indicating 'potential', the latter 'capacity'; the former 'strength', the latter 'ability', and so on. Despite possible confusion arising over

another resultantly blurred distinction between the French *force* (which I have also translated as 'force') and its English counterpart, I deem this preferable to a confusion between *puissance* and the 'potentiality' Lyotard is keen to attack as the dawn of thought and other nihilistic products. I have, to guide the reader, inserted the French term in brackets following the word 'force'. Similarly, I have translated *impouvoir* as 'powerlessness' and *impuissance* as 'impotence'.

The following also merit a short gloss given the weight and importance accorded to them in Libidinal Economy.

9   **The Libidinal Band/Skin**: the band, which has, most importantly, neither an inside nor an outside, is most easily comparable to what Freud called the primary processes of the pulsions 'of' the psychical apparatus, and could be considered as a sort of analogical presentation of difference independent of the (secondary) orders of re-presentation in which identity, signification and reference are determined. Although the libidinal band allows Lyotard to show what is necessarily excluded by representational thinking, it is not to be considered to be 'descriptively' true (since the model would then collapse back into re-presentation) but as more forceful and more interesting and more inventive than previous totalizations of 'the real'. As a kind of persuasive fiction, the various descriptions of the band wish, nevertheless, to account for the closures and exclusions inherent to re-presentational thinking and suggest a 'pagan' manner of affirming the differences and singularities that run through the libidinal band in an aleatory and indeterminate fashion.

10 **The Bar**: if we imagine the libidinal band as having one surface, white-hot, labyrinthine and aleatory, then the bar is to be seen as the 'operator of disintensification' which, in slowing down, allows the displaceability and non-identity of the drives/pulsions and intensities to be arrested and given a designation and signification. It is through procedures of exclusion (notably negation and exteriorization) that the bar gives birth to the conceptual process, twisting the band into what Lyotard calls the theatrical 'volume'. Dividing up what takes place on the band into a 'this' and a 'not-this', the bar, as it cools down, 'accounts for' the series of conceptual frontiers which distinguish the ideal and the real, the authentic and the alienated, the useful and the exchangeable, the normal and the perverse, etc. It should be noted

that, for Lyotard, the bar and the band are nevertheless one and the same. When the bar rotates in a furious aleatory fashion, we have something like the libidinal band; when the bar slows down, we have something like the theatrical volume. Why the bar slows down is a question peculiar to representational thinking, itself an effect of the cooling bar.

11 **The Great Zero**: the name Lyotard gives to the instance informing a particular but insistent *dispositif* on the libidinal band. With the disintensification of the bar, the libidinal band is folded back into a theatrical volume which has an inside and an outside (appearance/essence, signs/the signified). The inside is then ultimately considered in terms of what is going on on the outside. One of the most important figurations of the outside is the great Zero which serves as a general term to cover the Platonic world of forms, God, the authentic mode of production, the phallus, etc. All these instances—and despite their differences—are effects of the slowing down of the bar, referring the intensities running through the band to an elsewhere which they appear to lack once they have been confined to the interiority of a volume. The great Zero is thus an empty centre which reduces the present complexity of what happens instantaneously on the band to a 'chamber of presence and absence'. In his description of the great Zero Lyotard wishes to show that all theories of signification are fundamentally 'nihilistic'.

12 **Intensities**: partly following Freud's description of the primary processes of the unconscious, Lyotard considers intensities as unbound excitations of force which are characterized by their displaceability, their instantaneity and their resistance to the temporal syntheses of memory. Lyotard radicalizes, however, Freud's understanding of psychic intensity, since libidinal intensities cannot be willed (even by the unconscious) and describe the forces running through the band as a whole (and not just a so-called part of it). It is through an organizing and regulatory central instance (e.g. the great Zero) that the singularity of an intensity becomes a communicable and exchangeble sign. If such a centre weakens intensities in this manner, it is nevertheless itself a particular arrangement of libidinal force: this will be important in Lyotard's description of capital.

13 **The Tensor**: it is in his description of the tensor that Lyotard combats most directly the nihilism he takes to be inherent in all semiotics (structuralism in particular). Signs form part of the theatrical *dispositif,* subordinating intensities (actions or emotions, for example) to a lack,

whether this lack be considered in terms of a signified or another signifier to which a sign refers in order to have a semiotic value. The sign refers or defers itself, to an elsewhere, constitutively replacing something (absent) for someone. Lyotard's wish to reintroduce into the sign a tension that prevents it from having either a unitary designation, meaning or caculable series of such designations or meanings (polysemia) is an attempt to block this movement of referral and remain as faithful as possible to the incompossible intensities informing and exceeding the sign. The tensor sign is a description of this attempt. The latter is not, therefore, a move 'beyond' re-presentation, the creation of an elsewhere outside the sign. For the idea of the tensor would then simply repeat the rules of the *dispositif* which organizes the possibility of signs in the first place. Signs are *also* tensors, 'indissociably singular, vain intensities in flight': signs dissimulate tensors.

14 **The Great Ephemeral Skin**: this is in many ways the most provocative figure in *Libidinal Economy*. It higlights the disruptive potential of the figure, a concern which occupied Lyotard from *Discours, figure* through his two 1973 collections of essays, *Dérive à partir de Marx et Freud* and *Des Dispositifs pulsionels*, to the present text. Freud's elaboration of the 'dream-work' (cf. *The Interpretation of Dreams*) provides Lyotard with an articulation of the connivance of the figural and the libidinal: the dream-work (condensation, displacement, secondary revision and considerations of representability) distorts figural materials which are constitutionally more plastic, or so Freud argues, than ideational materials (words, signs and ideas). In *Discours, figure*, Lyotard draws out the implications of the figural unconscious' plastic invasion into the realm of the conceptual conscious, the result of which invasion is not merely to demonstrate the inevitable confusion of the two realms, but to highlight difference in their respective organizations. Whereas the conceptual relies on rigid opposition, the figural works differences: concepts, in other words, utilize negation (the 'this' and the 'not-this' in the language of *Libidinal Economy*), isolating unit(ie)s as opposed entities, whereas figural difference, like the unconscious whose work it is, knows no negation. By the time of *Libidinal Economy*, the *difference* between opposition and difference is worked by the intensive unconscious: opposition, the bar (between conscious and unconscious), is itself the work of the unconscious, a simple disintensification, with positive difference a (disjunctive) synthetic intensification. The great ephemeral skin is the libidinal materialist (dis)solution

of figural difference and conceptual opposition as polymorphous (hence 'ephemeral'), material (hence 'skin') intensity.

15 **The Concentratory Zero**: the skin is subject to unlimited metamorphoses operated by many *dispositifs*, two of which Lyotard examines under the names of the 'great' and the 'concentratory' zeros. The first (see point 11, above) of these, the annexing regulative fore-quarters of the conqueror-centaur, as Lyotard has it, folds and hollows out the band into a site for regulated reproduction of the same. The second, however, the same monster's looting hind-quarters, 'puts the system of reproduction at risk' by jealously looting every over-excited intensity in order to plug them into the same circuits as established by the first zero, to the point of immobilizing the (in)organic body the zero produces, intensifying the concentratory process to the point of becoming fatal to the stability it serves. The two zeros dissimulate each other, they are not opposed, they are unclear and indistinct like the principal pulsions of Eros and Thanatos, life and death.

16 **Simulacrum/The Exorbitant**: the simulacrum is the name Lyotard gives to the exchangeable, the equivalent. Thus his analysis of Augustine's theory of simulacra establishes the generalized equivalence and exchangeability of signs for things due to the participation of the latter in a relation of similarity that subsists amongst all beings, such unity being guaranteed by (and guaranteeing) God's untity with natural things and the mirrorical unity of simulacra insofar as language, second-hand (or third-, for Plato) and representative, is used to display these relations. Exchangeability, then, is premissed on similarity. What then of dissimilarity? The exchangeability of money and goods in capitalism also operates a generalized equivalence which establishes the value of goods. Every good on the market has a price, but certain objects resist being turned into a good. Thus Klossowski has it that political economy can offer no equivalent for intensities, highlighting an asymmetrical relation between capital and libidinal economy. Political economy forecloses the libidinal, claiming, in conjunction with Augustine, that if a thing cannot be exchanged, it has no value and consequently does not exist, it is not on the market. According to Lyotard, every political economy is, however, libidinal. That intensity has no equivalent in currency does not rid the circuits of capital of the force of libidinal investment; on the contrary, intensive 'exchanges' are ignorant of the constitutive negation of both political economy and natural theology since the libido invests unconditionally. The libidinal

exchange in prostitution, for example, invests the prostitute's desire, a desire whose foreclosure capital (and the pimp) demands in order to profit from the prostitute's body. Beyond the circuits of capital as far as political economy is concerned, libidinal exchanges are exorbitant. The exorbitant, having no equivalent, is inevaluable and unaccountable. Moreover, the libido's metamorphic force, its polymorphousness, invests even these constitutive negations, for whatever intensities it can glean from it, it is prepared to sacrifice the most exorbitant 'price'.

Introduction

A Shameless, Immodest Provocation

Lyotard's *Economie libidinale* occupies a place in the history of contemporary French thought which many consider a minor and short-lived explosion of a somewhat naïve anti-philosophical expressionism, an aestheticizing trend hung over from a renewed interest in Nietzsche prevalent in the late 1960s. It is further held to be the philosophical expression of the political situationism experienced throughout Europe during the same period, just as short-lived, and just as much a 'dead end', as Peter Dews, echoing the maturity of contemporary wisdom, says in his *Logics of Disintegration* (London: Verso, 1987). To situate it more specifically in regard to its contemporaneous philosophical climate: it was written in 1974, two years after Deleuze and Guattari's *Anti-Oedipus* (Paris: Minuit, 1972; London: Athlone, 1984), with which it shares many thematic preoccupations; it is exactly contemporaneous with Luce Irigaray's *Speculum of the Other Woman* (Paris: Minuit, 1974; Ithaca: Cornell University Press, 1985), two years before Jean Baudrillard's *Symbolic Exchange and Death* (Paris: Gallimard, 1976; London: Sage, forthcoming, 1993), seven years after Derrida's *Of Grammatology* (Paris: Minuit, 1967; Baltimore: Johns Hopkins University Press, 1976; and it forms, with these other texts, a series of responses to the demise of structuralism as the dominant intellectual discourse, known collectively as poststructuralism. There is a major difference, however, in the trajectories of *Libidinal Economy* on the one hand, and the better-known Derridean response on the other; while the latter endlessly meditates on the end of metaphysics, the former will exploit and accelerate the movements of generalized disruption in a fundamentally affirmative manner, seeking to 'conduct' new and unheard-of intensities: 'We desire the effects of conduction and the conduction of effects' (*Libidinal Economy*, VI, p.259). Even when Derrida insists that *différance* be affirmed, in 'Nietzschean' fashion as he says, as nameless (but not aimless) amidst 'all the names of metaphysics', such affirmation remains 'simulated' and itself dissimulates a 'Heideggerian hope' that 'finally', anonymous *différance* will find its 'proper name' in the 'alliance of speech and Being'. The end of metaphysics is gained through a 'quest' beyond the 'other side of nostalgia'.[1] Deconstruction is not in quest for what it has lost, but 'hopes' for what it has never yet found, 'like an old beast awaiting its pasture', says Lyotard.

Libidinal Economy has in general drawn little critical response, save losing Lyotard many Marxist friends. Indeed, with a few exceptions, it is now only Lyotard himself who occasionally refers to the book, to pour new scorn on it, calling it his 'evil book, the book of evilness that everyone writing and thinking is tempted to do'.[2] By 1988, however, *Peregrinations'* narrated 'author' has passed from the fourfold 'yes' that ends *Libidinal Economy* to doing penance for this great work: 'The readers of this book—thank god they were very few—generally accepted the product as a rhetorical exercise and gave no consideration to the upheaval it required of my soul . . . Its rare readers disliked the book, which passed for a piece of shamelessness, immodesty and provocation.'[3] Ringing in Molly Bloom's desire-drunk ears, the yes becomes a death-knell: ' . . . the priest going by with the bell bringing the vatican to the dying . . . ' (James Joyce, *Ulysses* (Harmondsworth: Penguin, 1965), p.680).

Lyotard's Lyotards

From deep on the 'inside' of the academy (the Welleck Library Lectures) and in fitting confessional mode, the narratee exposes the academic's genealogy: piety, traditionalism and creativity. In a single trusting, good-humoured gesture at the opening to 'his' *Peregrinations*, Lyotard reveals that he had wanted to be (a) a monk; (b) an historian; (c) an artist; and (d) a novelist. In each case he was to meet with various frustrations, until 'in the end', as they say, he became a philosopher. In a sense, however, the respective modes of these never-to-be-attained 'professions' have haunted his career: instead of joining the Dominican order, he entered political brotherhoods ('Socialisme ou Barbarie' and 'Pouvoir Ouvrier') whose staunch and solemn intensity still rears its patriarchal head from time to time ('The sacrificial aspect of this commitment to political reflexion and praxis is obviously related to monastic obedience'. *Peregrinations*, p.17). Upon quitting this brotherhood, the historian performs the excommunicated's penance in extended meditations on Auschwitz and *Memorials for Marxism*.[4] The other faces making up this academic Hydra are the artist and the novelist, who contaminate the philosopher's purism, necessitating the 'naïve ideal' of attaining a 'zero degree style' in *The Differend* (Paris: Minuit, 1983; Manchester: Manchester University Press, 1988). To neutralize the effects of writing, reduce its material puissance, its opacity. As this minimalist desideratum brings style to zero, the paganism of *Libidinal Economy* yields to a Judaic monotheism respectfully attentive to writing as 'the word of the dead father',[5] as Lyotard says. So Lyotard offers a penitent's explanation for this act of stylistic contrition: 'I have schooled myself in [Wittgenstein's] *Philosophische Untersuchungen* in order to purge myself . . . Desolating my culture fecundated me.'[6] Monotheism and traditionalism depose the desolate hysteria of paganism.

Lyotard lays claim to the culture he desolates and to the fecundation it stimulates; a strange moment of appropriation, a strange difference between 'his' culture and 'his' me. The finally proper name, albeit not that of *différance*, concretizes around 'philosophical readings' of the 'great tradition',[7] whose latest mouthpiece is the penitent libidinalist. In *Libidinal Economy*, however, 'Lyotard' conducts an examination of the proper name as a tensor sign (see Glossary). As an exemplary case of the tensor sign, Lyotard selects Professor Dr Paul Emil Flechsig, who treated Judge Daniel Paul Schreber for paranoid psychosis.[8] Flechsig's name is no longer a depositing site for the stock-piled remnants of an identity, but functions as an unstable and unpredictable intense sign whose aleatory whirl traces labyrinthine paths into Judge Schreber's multi-sexed body, drawing, along with jurisprudential, psychiatric and theological phrases, even a libidinal-somatic semiotics, into its untraceable wake.

—Are you suggesting that 'Lyotard' is a paranoid psychotic, a Schreber, spoken by 'God's nerves' or some such thing? Surely he remains a writer, perhaps even a philosopher?

—Exactly how Schreber got out of hospital: he asked that his writing be taken as testimony of his sanity. Lyotard has 'himself' testified that *Economic libidinale* links paganism with hysteria: paganism has no one god who is removed from the civic, social or philosophical stage, but on the contrary, a multiplicity of gods who swarm over it. 'Hysterical anxiety', as Lyotard writes, 'signals not that the god is too far away but that he is too close . . . 'Intimacy with the gods without seeing their faces' would not be too far-fetched a description of *Libidinal Economy*'.[9] But this is not a sanity trial—we are interested in *writing*, and writing, says Lyotard, is *irresponsible*,[10] perhaps because it flies inevitably towards the multiple rather than homing in on the one? Perhaps we have the beginnings of an intensive theory of textuality, and with it, an hysterical rather than a penitent account of 'the evil book'. Is Lyotard then an author, even a responsible one? This is how he counters Van Den Abbeele's attempts to assess 'Lyotard's' responsibility for 'his works':

> If the heterogeneity of 'my' work 'passes by' [*dépasse*] the reader, it also 'passes by' me, insofar as I am my first reader. However, I am also the supposed 'author' of 'my' work, and you ask about my responsibility with regard to it. . . . We never publish anything except rough drafts . . . And in this sense, I can without lying plead limited responsibility. That is to say: a reader cannot incorrectly locate in a piece of writing an aspect which, according to me, is not there at all. (*D*, p.16)

'I can without lying plead limited responsibility': it is tempting to pursue a sanity trial, or even to subject 'Lyotard' or his 'work' to tensorial scrutiny. *Scandalous*. We shall momentarily shift our concern to the multiplicity of discourses in which 'Lyotard's texts' have engaged before and after the publication of *Libidinal Economy*.

One or Several Lyotards?

In the introduction to his book *Lyotard: Writing the Event* (hereafter cited as *LWE*), Geoffrey Bennington reports that 'Lyotard sees himself as having written three 'real' books (*Discours, figure, Economie libidinale* and *Le Différend*)' (*LWE*, p.2). Around these three texts are clusters of 'minor' works, collections of 'preparatory' essays, and suchlike. Despite the manifest heterogeneity of 'philosophical' works on libido theory, semiotics and the problem of justice, there are other works marking incursions into other realms of writing: a *récit Le Mur du Pacifique*; experimental essays, for example 'Désirévolution', in *Dérive* . . . ; texts from an experimental 'postmodern Crystal Palace'[11] exhibition; books which are the result of collaborations with contemporary artists, and so on.

After having adopted this device, however, Bennington indicates the problematics of inclusion/exclusion attendant upon it, electing finally to accept the homogenization his schema imposes. Succumbing to the 'temptation' of the same and universalizing this fall as the 'theology' of 'representation' (as Lyotard reminds us, reverence for the question of representation is a 'fall', a 'collapse', the 'weakening of intensities', necessary to 'philosophical discourse'[12]), Bennington goes on to fulfil the criteria of representation by constructing a *corpus*, a 'career', inscribing his discourse on the interior of the body of 'Lyotard's' oeuvre. We will not be the media perpetuating this 'general agonistics of the proper name' (Van Den Abbeele)[13], nor will we provide another bibliographical or biographical (nor even a *thanatographical*) account of Lyotard's work.[14] And rather than emphasize the obvious heterogeneity of 'Lyotard's' works (from the 'neutral place', as Judith Still says, of their unification under the logical ascetism of the 'rigid designator'[15] the function of which is to establish the inside and outside of the Bennington/Lyotard oeuvre), we emphasize that, far from designating an interiority, the proper name is a tensor. At low intensity: 'proper names have that property of attracting to themselves phrases belonging to different regimens and to heterogeneous genres of discourse' (*D*, p.20). High intensity: melting fragments that never were a totality into unheard-of configurations: to logicians and other nihilists, the tensor is the name of impropriety. *Scandal*. As Félix Guattari somewhat pompously snaps at Lyotard in particular and 'the Postmoderns' in general, 'I believe that this philosophy is no philosophy at all . . . [The postmodern] is nothing but a state of mind that happens to be in the air, a 'condition' of public opinion that gets its truths out of its surroundings . . . '[16]. Not 'philosophy'? Not critical, improper in that it refuses to stabilize into a proprietary inside and outside.

Openings/Surroundings

The opening event of *Libidinal Economy*: the anatomy of 'polymorphous perversion' undoes the libidinal investments and somatic folds that maintain the proper body. The volume implied in thinking the skin as the ego's boundary between the interior and the exterior (as Freud does[17]), spills into the folds and twists of the great ephemeral skin. The cold Kantian logic of Lyotard's 'Deduction of the Voluminous Body' contrasts with the extreme tension between life and death that is intensified with each cut in the skin of this 'body', in the little folds and their defences that constitute the organism, and the libido's indifference to such folds. Already faint rumours of Kant and Freud's complicity in this text can be discerned. Later chapters involve Marx, Machiavelli, Baudrillard[18] and Klossowski, to name but a few. Its immediate context, however, is most profitably explored in relation to Gilles Deleuze and Félix Guattari's *Anti-Oedipus: Capitalism and Schizophrenia Part 1* (hereafter cited as *Anti-Oedipus*). This work, as Vincent Descombes points out in his *Modern French Philosophy* (Cambridge: Cambridge University Press, 1980), continues the largely failed project of a synthesis of Freud and Marx in the work of Wilhelm Reich and the Frankfurt School theoreticians Herbert Marcuse and Erich Fromm. Deleuze and Guattari establish the site of this welding by industrializing the unconscious, hence *Anti-Oedipus'* 'desiring-machines' that constitute the various modes of unconscious investment. They attack Marxism for its derisory attitude towards the unconscious, and psychoanalysis for limiting its range to the individualized psychical apparatus. Just as Lyotard writes 'Every Political Economy Is Libidinal', so *Anti-Oedipus* has it that desiring-production 'machines', as they say, social material. We have, then, a libidinal, rather than a dialectical or historical, materialism.

But there is another main player in the cast of *Anti-Oedipus*: Kantian critique:

> In what he termed the critical revolution, Kant intended to discover criteria immanent to understanding so as to distinguish the legitimate and illegitimate uses of the syntheses of consciousness. In the name of transcendental philosophy (immanence of criteria), he therefore denounced the transcendent use of syntheses such as appeared in metaphysics. In like fashion we are compelled to say that psychoanalysis has its metaphysics—its name is Oedipus. And that a revolution—this time materialist—can proceed only by way of a critique of Oedipus, denouncing the illegitimate use of the syntheses of the unconscious as found in Oedipal psychoanalysis, so as to rediscover a transcendental unconscious defined by the immanence of its criteria, and a corresponding practice that we shall call schizoanalysis. (Gilles Deleuze and Félix Guattari, *Anti-Oedipus*, tr. Robert Hurley, Mark Seem and Helen Lane (London: Athlone, 1984), p.75)

Psychoanalysis claims, as did speculative metaphysics, to know desire, to identify its privileged forms. But everything psychoanalysis knows about desire it knows by injecting it into a certain schema called Oedipus, a closed, familial circuit wherein desire plays out its dramas of conflict, seduction, and anxiety with the figures of the child, the mother and the father. 'The imperialism of Oedipus' is such that any path sketched out by aberrant desire is immediately brought back to the fold. To produce the wolf-father out of the crowd of wolves in the Wolf-Man's phantasies, Freud turns the crowd into sheep so that the wolf-father may devour them. Hence: 'a schizophrenic out for a walk is a better model than a neurotic lying on the analyst's couch' (*Anti-Oedipus*, p.2). So rather than having discovered the 'true' paths of libidinal investment, the psychoanalyst uses his familial, Oedipal prejudice to engineer neurotics: 'yes, my boss is my father, and so is the Head of State, and so are you, Doctor', as they say (*Anti-Oedipus*, p.35). Schizoanalysis does not merely denounce Oedipus, as Kant denounces metaphysics' speculative attempts to prove or disprove God's existence, as an illusion, but critiques it as a structure in which the unconscious is trapped by psychoanalytic metaphysics. Schizoanalysis evokes the difference between the machine and the structure in terms of the immanence of the former to the unconscious. 'Everyone knows that the schizo is a machine' (*Anti-Oedipus*, p.381).

When Lyotard, therefore, writes in his review essay on *Anti-Oedipus*, 'Capitalisme énergumène',[19] that it 'is not a book of critique', but rather an 'energetic position inscribed in discourse, where negation of the adversary takes place not by means of the *Aufhebung* [sublation], but through forgetting' (*DP* p.10), it is at least difficult to reconcile this prima-facie oblivion of anti-Oedipal critique with the importance of the critical architecture of Deleuze and Guattari's text. What is important as regards Lyotard's (fundamentally Hegelian-Marxian) model of critique is the function and form of negation. In the above quote he establishes the divergence of the Hegelian *Aufhebung* and Nietzschean forgetting in this respect. Where Deleuze and Guattari, emphasizing the immanence of critique to the criticized characteristic of the Kantian model, establish the critical mechanism in a relation of immanence with the schizo-machines, Lyotard sees critique as irrevocably tied to the adversary's position. 'Get out immediately' is Lyotard's anti-critical response, 'forget immanence, it can only belong to the enemy'. This paranoia concerning the inside and the outside of enemy territory is apparently dispelled in *Libidinal Economy*: 'be inside *and* forget it, that's the position of the death drive' (*LE*, 1 p.3; emphasis added). Extreme critical tension: the alliance of Freud and Kant in the critical machinery.

The force of *Anti-Oedipus*, however, lies precisely in its libidinal materialist critique of psychoanalysis. Such a critique does not aim, as Reich's did, to produce a liberation of the unconscious or of sexuality, but to dissociate desire from lack, making desire a positive force, conditioning the social field in its entirety rather than being conditioned by a subject's lack or deprivation (such as Freud used to provide the psychoanalytic 'conception' of the female as 'lacking a penis'). Why then does Lyotard read *Anti-*

Oedipus as an acritical book? A certain loathing of critique resonates throughout what may be called Lyotard's 'libidinal period'. Indeed, despite the Freudo-Kantian axis mentioned above, critique remains the privileged object of rejection, a hated, isolated, despicable colony of virulent negativity at the hot core of *Libidinal Economy*.

The passage from pious and passionate critical activity to its denunciation and exile can be traced through Lyotard's two 1973 collections of essays. In the 1979 preface to the second edition of *Des Dispositifs pulsionels*, however, the postcritical libido is denounced as the speculative 'metaphysics of desire' (*DP*, Introduction to 2nd edn (1979), p.iii), marking a new shift where philosophy goes 'back to its beginnings in Kant' (*DP* p.iii) to a traditionalist, paranoiac and properly Kantian model of critique, where the libido now occupies the position of the exile. As this denunciation continues in Lyotard's works after 1979, it is accompanied by an increasing attachment to this conception of critique, leading Lyotard to pitch 'Kant against Freud' in an essay from 1984,[20] and to identify, in *L'Enthousiasme* (Paris: Galilée, 1986), critique with politics.

We have, then, a *libidinal hostility to critique and a critical hostility to the libidinal*. In the English-speaking world, we might perhaps be tempted to rush into identifying this situation as a 'differend' between the two parties. If so, it is a differend, a conflict, which Lyotard has been anxious to solve in one way or another. For example, in an interview with Willem van Reijen and Dick Veerman, he claims that '*Le Différend* remedies the shortcomings of *Economie libidinale*; it is an attempt *to say the same things* but without unloading problems so important as justice' (*I*, pp. 300–1; emphasis added). Again, in *Leçons sur L'Analytique du Sublime* (Paris: Galilée, 1991, p.183), Lyotard mentions an 'affective differend' ('*le différend affectuel*'). What this demonstrates is an ongoing critical attempt to recuperate the libido; the 'attempt to say the same things' constitutes a critical gesture according to Lyotard's reading of the *Aufhebung* as its privileged means, rather than the forgetting characteristic of the acritical mode of, as Lyotard sees it, *Anti-Oedipus*. How can the 'crisis of *Libidinal Economy*' (*Peregrinations*, p.16) be solved? Or: since the libido 'invests unconditionally', how does it invest [*bestetzen*] critique?

The Libidinal Economics of Critical Philosophy

Besetzung is Freud's German for what the *Standard Edition* gives as 'cathexis'. The French translation is *investissement*, 'investment', which is the fiscal sense of the German term. In the *New Introductory Lectures on Psychoanalysis* Freud plays with another of its senses. The superego has the arduous task of keeping the id in order, a task it accomplishes, writes Freud, by 'install[ing] a garrison [*Besetzung*] in the place where insurrection threatens' (*Standard Edition* Vol. 22, pp. 110–11). The superego occupies, takes up a position, counter-invests in the id's troubled areas. In this, psychoanalysis deploys a militarist ethic just as critique does, since for the latter conflict is the motor of its necessity. For example, in the *Critique of Pure Reason* (hereafter cited as *CPR*), Kant writes:

> To deny that the service which the Critique renders is positive in character, would thus be like saying that the police are of no positive benefit, inasmuch as their main business is merely to prevent the violence of which citizens stand in mutual fear. (*CPR*, Bxxv)

Both psychoanalysis and critique desire that the situation be stabilized; the former aims to stabilize the boundaries on the interior of the 'psychical apparatus' (Freud's name for the three agencies: idego-superego), through a 'dynamic equilibrium' being established by rival investments on the same territory by different agencies. Critique, on the other hand, hollows out a space on its own interior where the conflicts on which it feeds can be played out as 'mock combats', the deluded participants (speculative metaphysicians) supplying the 'peaceable onlooker' (the critical philosopher in his 'safe seat') with contributions to 'theoretical insight', a kind of surplus-value for pure reason (*CPR*, A747/B775).

Both orientations hollow out an interiority, stabilizing its borders through counter-insurrection manoeuvres or through annexation.[21] It is critique's function to redraw the borders of its territories and to strictly position reason within its proper field, the imagination in its proper field, and so on.[22] It is this positioning, this installation [*Besetzung*], which is the Freudian libidinal operator par excellence. And it is this function which Lyotard is concerned to analyse in *Libidinal Economy* in terms of the energetics of the bar and the band (see Glossary, points 9 and 10).

Critique and Crisis

Just as Schreber's name is linked up with God's nerves and with the Saxon judiciary, just as the skin can be operated on so as to produce the most *civilized* (the most *neurotic*) human being or the most intense and unchartable metamorphoses, so critique has an intensive range. We have seen the importance of military-fiscal-libidinal *Besetzungen* in the critical function, we must now follow its mutations across the range of displacements to which it is subjected by the various libidinal investments critique has filed under the name 'Lyotard'. We shall take three texts: 'On Theory: an Interview' (with Brigitte Devismes), 'Adrift'[23], and *Libidinal Economy* itself.

In 'On Theory' (which dates from 1970, before his first major book, *Discours, figure*) Lyotard retains a solidly Marxian view of critique:

> The function of theory is not only to understand, but also to criticize, i.e. to call into question and overturn a reality, social relationships, the relationships of men with things and other men, which are clearly intolerable. And as far as I am concerned, that is the dimension of politics. (*DPMF*, p. 210/*Driftworks*, p.19)

Lyotard repeats Marx's gesture: just as

> the critique of heaven turns into the critique of earth, the critique of religion into the critique of law and the critique of theology into the critique of politics . . . [C]riticism is not a passion of the head, but the head of passion. It is not a scalpel; it is a weapon.[24]

so theory is to pass from understanding to overturning situations which are 'clearly intolerable'. Intolerable to whom, or to what? To the exploited, the proletariat, a 'constant subject' subjected, in the classic example, by the Industrial Revolution to 'inhuman' conditions. The survival of the proletariat under these conditions is generally explained by the scope and effectiveness of the revolution: it was either that or die—they had to go from the country to the new urban environments, had to labour in factories, in mines, merely in order to survive. Such critique serves a supposed master, the oppressed, in the name of the future and of justice. Preparing for the scandal ('hang on tight and spit on me'), *Libidinal Economy* offers another analysis. It is never 'that or die', but always '*that and die*': the Industrial Revolution machines new 'inhuman' potentialities,[25] a different affective range, a generalized metamorphosis which sweeps away the pious, missionary fiction of the alienated and oppressed constant subject, displacing the orientation of this struggle from the 'white terror' of theory to the 'red cruelty' of acephalization.[26] The 'head of passion' is removed and there is nothing in its place:

> This trap consists quite simply in responding to the demand of the vanquished theory, and this demand is: put something in my place. The important thing is this place, however, not the contents of the theory. It is the place of theory that must be vanquished. And this can come about only through displacement and flight. (*Libidinal Economy*, p.104)

'Put something in my place', says vanquished theory. In the name of the future, of the revolution 'to come', obstacles are placed in the way of displacement and flight, repressions, we might say, like dams into rapids. Pressure brings out the libidinal in the theoretical: replace me, reinvest, make my position immortal, demands theory, ignorant of its own passing.

'Dérives' (1972) fully exposes the type of investment demanded by the critical and the theoretical.

> [Critique] . . . is deeply rational, deeply consistent with the system. Deeply reformist: the critic remains in the sphere of the criticized, he belongs to it, goes beyond one term of the position but does not alter the position of the terms. (*DPMF*, p.14/*Driftworks*, p.13)

Critique is defined by its maintenance of static forms, whether of the universal subject, the proletariat, or the forms of labour and exploitation; it even blocks its own issue in its almost Platonic commitment to retaining the system's position.[27] A sudden change of tack, a crisis. Must the critic labour at the interminable task presented by the deconstruction of accepted forms and stable positions ('Only form lends itself to expressing the movement of the revolution form is the revolution': *DPMF*, p.31)? Or does the morphic move inexorably into the metamorphic of itself? Is it now necessary to rewrite the 'critique of political economy', or of metaphysics, or even, as Lyotard suggests in 'Judiciousness in Dispute', a 'critique of critical reason' ('Judicieux dans le différend', in *La Faculté de juger*, ed., J.F. Lyotard, tr. Cecile Lindsay, in *The Lyotard Reader*, ed. Andrew Benjamin (Oxford: Blackwell, 1989), p.328). 'No need', says *Libidinal Economy*, 'just be inside and forget it, that's the position of the death drive' (p.3). Forget the stable positions/investments, forgetting rather than negativity, the acritical orientation Lyotard ascribes to *Anti-Oedipus*. This is the orientation adopted in 'Dérives':

> It is not true that . . . the *occupation* of a position necessarily entails its critique and compels us to adopt a position which will negatively contain and sublate the former. (*DPMF*, p.13/*Driftworks*, p.12; emphasis added)

The crisis does not entail a critical *denegation* of critique, there is no need to renew critique, to reinstate the head of passion (or 'the Queen of all the sciences', as Kant has it. *CPR*, Avii). Nor is it necessary that an anti-critique be formulated to right the wrongs of its predecessor. Taking up the lexical hint italicized in the above quote, Lyotard continues:

> There is a forgotten Freud in this reading, the one who dared to write that the
> libido never relinquishes one investment for a better one. (ibid.)

Freud continually emphasized that the unconscious has no capacity for negation. Unconscious libidinal investments are superimposed one upon the other, just as '[Rome's] ancient ruins . . . have provided the material for more recent structures' (*The Interpretation of Dreams*, VI, 1). Such investments are, in the language of *Libidinal Economy*, incompossible. They are 'blocked together', as Bill Readings says, drawing on a Lyotardian lexis from the time of 'Dérives . . . ', in his *Introducing Lyotard* (London: Routledge, 1991), without considerations of temporal or spatial order. Further, there is an extreme mobility of unconscious energies, a mobility which finds ingress, despite 'repression', into conscious organizations, by means of displacements: if the dam holds, the banks burst. Deformation, distortion:

> What follows does not belong to the drift from Marx and Freud, but to the drift
> which continues/discontinues it, adrift from this drift . . . *Derivatio* [diverting] is
> not simply leaving a shore, but diverting a *rivus* [stream], a course, a fluidity.
> Where It goes, we were not going [*Ça va ailleurs que là où l'on allait*]. What joy
> if *ripa* [shore] were derived from *rivus*, if this were the streaming which
> determined the shore! The shore of the stream, of the ocean, displaces itself
> along with it. (*DPMF* p.9)

The 'crisis' of *Libidinal Economy* is a perpetual displacement, an eternal turning rather than a splitting: 'drifting by itself is the end of all critique' (*DPMF*, p.15/*Driftworks*, p.13). Instead of fixing territories, setting up shields, or installing garrisons, libidinal investments traverse the entire metamorphic range of these unlimited displacements. The shores are disfigured and identities wrecked in this postcritical torrent which engulfs Kant's safe seat as much as the garrisons of the psychoanalytic superego.

Phantasy Island: Back to Kant

Jean-Luc Nancy opens his contribution to the 1985 Cérisy colloquium on Lyotard's work with a recognition of the latter's 'playing the stakes of Kantian resources'.[28] We have already mentioned Lyotard's turn to Kant, this turn being at Freud's expense. There is a distinct asymmetry here, an irreversibility in the critical *Besetzung*: while the libido 'invests uncondi-tionally', critique regroups to denounce the libido as a 'metaphysics of desire'. We have sketched an intensive range which runs through the term 'critique' in Lyotard's work, carrying it from the privileged tool of a rigid political agenda to a 'crisis', a krisis, a splitting. This splitting became at one point the focus of Lyotard's attention in the form of the differend, a radical and insoluble dispute whose demands for a justice can never be satisfied: the philosopher can only 'bear witness to the differend' in order to 'save the honour of thinking'.[29] In a sense *The Differend* exemplifies critical mechanisms: the return to a sense of the 'clearly intolerable', this time in a metaphysical-historical register (the classic example is Faurisson's question concerning the reality of the Holocaust), testified to by the occurrence of the differend which prevents the issue of a verdict, returns an object to the critical project—critique itself. The critical orbit is no longer a cycle from theoretical questioning to a real overturning and back, but a stuttering arc, ceaselessly failing to circumscribe its receding dominion, momentarily and provisionally linking up with other dominions, whether these be called 'language games', 'genres', or whatever else of this sort. These 'islands', or 'the Archipelago' as Lyotard terms this topography, these unconnected fragments no longer cry out for their reunification into a 'proper body', but constantly seek recognition of injustices perpetrated upon them. Injustice can merely be witnessed in the arc's flashes, to which the 'critical watchman' may bear testimony: fallout from the Enlightenment, burning fragments of the French Revolution and its Supreme Being[30] illuminate the crisis. No longer the concentric cycle with its fixed futural reference, nor the eccentric eternal turn of the libidinal band, but a penitent's attempt to return to the crisis at the end of critique.

More recently, there are perhaps signs that this return is no longer possible. In *L'Inhumain*, for example, this recognition:

> In this respect, even what may be most disturbing in Kant, which is not anthropological, but strictly transcendental, which in the *critical tension* goes to the point of shattering the more or less presupposed unity of the subject, as is the case, in exemplary fashion, it seems to me, in the analysis of the sublime or the historico-political writings, even that is expurgated, sanitized. Under the pretext of a return to Kant, we merely shelter humanist prejudice under his authority. (*L'Inhumain*, p.9; emphasis added)

With the sanitizing phantasy of a return to Kant's critical island dispelled, the 'critical tension' is building up again. The regulated cycles of revolutionary critique, and the stuttering arcs that mark its memorial, are themselves incompossible fragments of the duplicitous critical-libidinal *Besetzung*, displaced and disfigured along the libido's unaccountable flows. Is it a 'metaphysics of desire'?

> The question remained and has remained . . . is Being shameful . . . ? What about hysteria, especially hypochondria, as a mode in which Being or the law can be divined?' (*Peregrinations* p.14).

And the sublime, a tensor deployed in the rigid hierarchies of the faculties, intensifying critique, 'carr[ying] with it both pleasure and pain . . . which some would call neurosis or masochism'.[31] How to judge?

This is Lyotard's 'evil book', do not expect answers to the questions it generates, nor excuses or rationalizations of its scandals. Read impiously, brutally, through this divine and incompossible libidinal multiplicity, pagan like Nietzsche—'I am all the names in history'. If you must judge, then take this opportunity to 'judge without criteria', since never were there fewer, be the (hysterical) judge in the sanity trial we tempted you with, dear reader, add to the 'very few readers' of this 'honourable sinful offering'. To paraphrase Lyotard:

> A discourse at maximum intensity? This is much more than a critique, which is perhaps only a degenerate amusement.[32]

Notes

1 Jacques Derrida, 'Différance', in Peggy Kamuf (ed.), *A Derrida Reader* (New York: Columbia University Press, 1991), pp. 76–7.

2 Jean-François Lyotard, *Peregrinations* (New York: Columbia University Press, 1988), p.13; hereafter cited as *Peregrinations*.

3 ibid., p.14.

4 See Jean-François Lyotard, 'A Memorial of Marxism', tr. Cecile Lindsay, in ibid., pp. 45–76, for a detailed account of Lyotard's Marxist past. See also his *La Guerre des Algériens. Ecrits 1956–1963* (Paris: Galilée, 1989).

5 Jean-François Lyotard, 'Figure Foreclosed', in Andrew Benjamin (ed.), *The Lyotard Reader* (Oxford: Blackwell, 1989), p.96.

6 Georges Van Den Abbeele, 'Interview with Jean-François Lyotard', *Diacritics*, 14$_3$ (1984), p.17; hereafter cited as *D*.

7 Dick Veerman and Willem van Reijen, 'An Interview with Jean-François Lyotard', *Theory, Culture and Society*, 5 (1988), p.278; Hereafter cited as *I*.

8 Schreber's case is examined by Freud in 'Psychoanalytic Notes upon an Autobiographical Account of a Case of Paranoia (Dementia Paranoides)', in the *Standard Edition*, ed. James Strachy (London: Hogarth Press, 1953–74; hereafter cited as *SE*), Vol. 12, pp. 1–82. The basis of Freud's study is the 'Autobiographical Account': Daniel Paul Schreber, *Memoirs of my Nervous Illness*, ed. and tr. Ida Macalpine and Richard A. Hunter (Cambridge, Mass.: Harvard University Press, 1988).

9 *Peregrinations*, p.15. Lyotard's narrative continues to exploit the theme of piety: 'The monk I tried to become should have reminded himself that the polymorphic paganism of exploring and exploiting the whole range of intensive forms could easily be swept away into lawful permissiveness, including violence and terror. Of course, I had not yet recovered from the

temptation of indifference.' Lyotard's concern with paganism begins in *Libidinal Economy* with a section entitled 'Pagan Theatrics' (pp. 6–15). His two subsequent works continue this theme—*Rudiments païens* and *Instructions païennes*—and feed into the discussion of *Libidinal Economy* in *Just Gaming*.

10 Jean-François Lyotard, *Just Gaming*, tr. Wlad Godzich, Theory and History of Literature, Vol. 20 (Manchester: Manchester University Press, 1985), p.8; hereafter cited as *JG*.

11 Cf. John Rajchmann 'The Postmodern Museum', *Art in America*, 73$_1$0 (October 1985), and Kate Linker, 'A Reflection on Postmodernism', *Artforum*, 24$_1$ (September 1985).

12 Jean-François Lyotard, 'Notes sur le retour et le capital', in *Des Dispositifs pulsionels* (Paris: UGE, 1973; hereafter cited as *DP*), p.291; tr. Roger McKeon as 'Notes on the Return and Capital', *Semiotext(e)*, 3$_1$, (1978), p.44.

13 George Van Den Abbeele uses this term to describe Lyotard's politics in *D*, p.20.

14 For example, Eddie Yeghiayan's 'Checklist of Writings by and about Jean-François Lyotard' in *Peregrinations* is an excellent bibliography.

15 The 'rigidity' of Bennington's deployment of the designator 'Lyotard', of what is and is not proper to his name, is scrutinized by Judith Still in her 'Reacting to Lyotard', in *Paragraph* 12(3) (1989), pp. 239–48. She cites two overt examples of this *'pur et dur'* rigidity in its exclusive usage: Bennington's dismissal of *The Postmodern Condition* 'because, he explains, it is the least representative of Lyotard's work' (p. 248, n. 12); and the non-appearance of any mention of 'One of the Things at Stake in Women's Struggles' (tr. D. J. Clark, W. Woodhull and J. Mowitt, *Sub-Stance*, 20 (1978), an essay from *Rudiments païens* 'which does not figure in *Lyotard: Writing the Event*', p.247 n. 1), from which Still takes her opening quote. Covert examples of this usage are scattered throughout Still's text. Bennington's book is, she writes, 'impeccably faithful to the discipline (if only in the sense of rigorous training) of deconstruction' (p.239).

16 Félix Guattari, 'The Postmodern Dead End', tr. Nancy Blake in *Flash Art* 128 (1986), p.41.

17 See Freud, 'Beyond the Pleasure Principle', *SE*, Vol. 18. Cf. n.21 below.

18 Julian Pefanis explores the common roots, as he sees them, between Lyotard and Baudrillard in the work of Georges Bataille and Marcel Mauss. See Pefanis, *Heterology and the Postmodern: Bataille, Baudrillard, Lyotard* (London: Duke University Press, 1991), especially chapter 5, 'Lyotard and the *Jouissance* of Practical Reason'. For his part, Baudrillard is forever taking side-swipes at the libidinal Lyotard in particular. See, for example, Jean Baudrillard, *Symbolic Exchange and Death*, tr. I. H. Grant (London: Sage, forthcoming 1993) and 'The Precession of Simulacra', tr. Paul Foss and Paul Patton, in *Simulations* (New York: Semiotext(e), 1983).

19 *DP*, pp. 7–49. Tr. James Leigh as 'Energumen Capitalism', *Semiotext(e)* 2(3), (1977), pp. 11–26.

20 'La Peinture du secret à l'ère postmoderne: Baruchello', *Traverses* 30–1, (March 1984), p.96.

21 In *Beyond the Pleasure Principle*, however, Freud 'speculates' on the libido's involvement in pre-differentiated matter, producing the celebrated Eros —Thanatos couple, or the life drives and death drives to account for the development of life forms: libido theory becomes a transcendental account of the 'deduction of interiority', to paraphrase Lyotard, from undifferentiated libidinal pulsations, the complexification of life and death drives determining the development of the organism from its most primitive state (the single-celled amoeba) to its 'most developed' (human society). Psychoanalysis acquires, in Kantian terms, a libidinal noumenon.

22 Lyotard has recently devoted considerable quantities of energy to elaborating Kant's notion of the sublime ('philosophically' in *Le Différend, L'Enthousiasme*, and most recently in *Leçons sur L'Analytique du Sublime*; and 'aesthetically' in *L'Assassinat de l'expérience par la peinture, Monory* (Paris: Le Castor Astral, 1984), *Que Peindre* (Paris: Editions de la Différence, 1987), and in several shorter essays. As regards the current discussion, what is striking about the theory of the sublime is the improper admixture of the proper fields of the imagination and the understanding.

23 'On Theory: an Interview' and 'Adrift', tr. Roger McKeon, in Jean-François Lyotard, *Driftworks* (New York: Semiotext(e), 1984; hereafter cited as *Driftworks*), from 'Sur la théorie' and 'Dérives' in *Dérive à partir de Marx et Freud* (Paris: UGE, 1973 hereafter cited as *DPMF*).

24 Karl Marx, 'Contribution to the Critique of Hegel's Philosophy of Right: Introduction', in *The Portable Karl Marx*, ed. Eugene Kamenka (Harmondsworth: Penguin, 1983), pp. 116, 117.

25 The acephalus, the headless monster invented by Masson and celebrated by Bataille, turns up in the first section of *Libidinal Economy*. See section I, n. 3.

26 Lyotard's example in *Libidinal Economy* (repeated in *Les Transformateurs Duchamp* (Paris: Galilée, 1977; hereafter cited as *TD*), pp. 21–6) is an otological experiment by Tomatis concerning the auditory range of a worker neutralized by exposure to frequencies of 20,000 Hz. This, says Lyotard, is not a loss to a supposed proper body, but a 'contribution to the demensuration of what is taken to be human' (*TD*, p.23/ *Libidinal Economy*, p.110).

27 Critique's mechanisms of deferral, so strikingly similar to those of psycho-analysis, are read out like catechism in 'On Theory': 'Even if we managed to put an end to certain forms of exploitation and oppression, the deconstruction of what is written, taken for granted, connotated—habits, institutions, non-subverted phantasma—would be an interminable task.' (*DPMF*, p.225/*Driftworks*, p.32).

28 Jean-Luc Nancy, 'Dies Irae', in J.F. Lyotard, (ed.), *La Faculté de juger* (Paris: Minuit, 1985), p.12.

29 Jean-François Lyotard, *The Differend*, translated from *Le Différend* (Paris: Minuit, 1983) by George Van Den Abbeele (Manchester: Manchester University Press, 1988), pp. xiii, xii, respectively.

30 The occasion of the French Revolution affords Kant a sign of the 'progress of humanity towards the better' (see I. Kant, 'Is The Human Race Constantly Progressing?', in *Kant On History*, ed. Lewis White Beck (New York: Macmillan, 1963), pp. 137–154). Kant ignores the Terror (his essay was written in 1798, while the Terror began in winter 1793 with Robespierre's ascendancy after the trial and execution of the Girondins), concentrating instead on the 'enthusiasm' these events provoke in the spectators, which he reads as a sign of humanity's progress. The Differend contains a discussion of enthusiasm which adopts libidinal-economic terms. Enthusiasm, writes Lyotard, is 'a periodic unbridling . . . an energetic sign, a tensor of Wunsch' (p. 167).

31 Jean-François Lyotard, 'Answering the Question: What is Postmodernism?', tr. Régis Durand, in *The Postmodern Condition: A Report on Knowledge*, tr. Geoff Bennington and Brian Massumi, Theory and History of Literature, Vol. 10 (Manchester: Manchester University Press, 1984), p.77. 'Disturbing' aspects of Kant's historico-political texts are exposed in *The Differend* and *L'Enthousiasme*. Further, as has already been mentioned, Lyotard's latest analysis of the sublime is *Leçons sur L'Analytique du Sublime*.

32 'Notes sur le retour et le capital', *DP*, p.293/*Semiotext(e)* 3:1, p.45. I have placed 'critique' where Lyotard wrote 'deconstruction'.

1
The Great Ephemeral Skin

Opening the Libidinal Surface

Open the so-called body and spread out all its surfaces: not only the skin with each of its folds, wrinkles, scars, with its great velvety planes, and contiguous to that, the scalp and its mane of hair, the tender pubic fur, nipples, nails, hard transparent skin under the heel, the light frills of the eyelids, set with lashes—but open and spread, expose the labia majora, so also the labia minora with their blue network bathed in mucus, dilate the diaphragm of the anal sphincter, longitudinally cut and flatten out the black conduit of the rectum, then the colon, then the caecum, now a ribbon with its surface all striated and polluted with shit; as though your dress-maker's scissors were opening the leg of an old pair of trousers, go on, expose the small intestines' alleged interior, the jejunum, the ileum, the duodenum, or else, at the other end, undo the mouth at its corners, pull out the tongue at its most distant roots and split it, spread out the bats' wings of the palate and its damp basements, open the trachea and make it the skeleton of a boat under construction; armed with scalpels and tweezers, dismantle and lay out the bundles and bodies of the encephalon; and then the whole network of veins and arteries, intact, on an immense mattress, and then the lymphatic network, and the fine bony pieces of the

---

The great ephemeral skin (La grande pellicule éphémère): Lyotard later refers to the pellicule 'in the technical sense', meaning 'film'; I have chosen, in keeping with the imagery here, to take slight liberties and translate *pellicule* as 'skin'.—*tn*

wrist, the ankle, take them apart and put them end to end with all the layers of nerve tissue which surround the aqueous humours and the cavernous body of the penis, and extract the great muscles, the great dorsal nets, spread them out like smooth sleeping dolphins. Work as the sun does when you're sunbathing or taking grass.

And this is not all, far from it: connected onto these lips, a second mouth is necessary, a third, a great number of other mouths, vulvas, nipples. And adjoining the skin of the fingertips, scraped by the nails, perhaps there should be huge silken beaches of skin, taken from the inside of the thighs, the base of the neck, or from the strings of a guitar. And against the palm, all latticed with nerves, and creased like a yellowed leaf, set potter's clays, or even hard wooden handles encrusted with jewels, or a steering wheel, or a drifter's sail are perhaps required. Don't forget to add to the tongue and all the pieces of the vocal apparatus, all the sounds of which they are capable, and moreover, the whole selective network of sounds, that is, the phonological system, for this too belongs to the libidinal 'body', like colours that must be added to retinas, like certain particles to the epidermis, like some particularly favoured smells to the nasal cavities, like preferred words and syntaxes to the mouths which utter them and to the hands which write them. It is not enough, you see, to say, like Bellmer, that the fold in the armpit of the child, dreamily intent, her elbow on the table and chin in her hand, could *count as* [*valoir pour*] the folds of her groin, or even as the juncture of the lips of her sex. The question of 'counting as', don't urge us to ask it, far less to resolve it. It is not a part of the body, of what body?—the organic body, organized with survival as its goal against what excites it to death, assured against riot and agitation—not a part which comes to be *substituted* for another part, like, for example, in the case of this little girl, the fleshiness of the arm for that of the thighs and its faint fold for the vaginal slit; it is not this displacement of parts, recognizable in the organic body of *political economy* (itself initially assembled from differentiated and appropriated parts, the latter never being without the former), that we first need to consider. Such displacement, whose function is representation, substitution, presupposes a bodily unity, upon which it is inscribed through transgression. There is no need to begin with transgression, we must go immediately to the very limits of cruelty, perform the dissection of polymorphous perversion, spread out the immense membrane of the libidinal 'body' which is quite different to a frame. It is made from the most heterogeneous textures, bone, epithelium, sheets to write on, charged atmospheres, swords, glass cases, peoples, grasses, canvases to paint. All these zones are joined end to end in a band which has no back to it, a Moebius band which interests us not because it is closed, but because it is one-sided, a Moebian skin which, rather than being smooth, is on the contrary (is this topologically possible?) covered with roughness, corners, creases, cavities which when it passes on the 'first' turn will be cavities, but perhaps on the 'second', lumps. But as for what turn the band is on, no-one knows nor will know, in the eternal turn. The interminable band with variable geometry (for nothing requires that an excavation remain concave, besides, it is inevitably convex on the 'second' turn, provided it lasts) has not got two sides, but only one, and therefore neither exterior nor interior.

It is certainly not a libidinal theatre then, no density, intensities running here and there, setting up, escaping, without ever being imprisoned in the volume of the stage/auditorium. Theatricality and representation, far from having to be taken as libidinal givens, *a fortiori* metaphysical, result from a certain labour on the labyrinthine and Moebian band, a labour which prints these particular folds and twists, the effect of which is a box closed upon itself, filtering impulses and allowing only those to appear on the stage which come from what will come to be known as the *exterior*, satisfying the conditions of interiority. The representative chamber is an energetic *dispositif*. To describe it and to follow its functioning, that's what needs to be done. No need to do a critique of metaphysics (or of political economy, which is the same thing), since critique presupposes and ceaselessly creates this very theatricality; rather *be inside and forget it*, that's the position of the death drive, describe these foldings and gluings, these energetic vections that establish the theatrical cube with its six homogenous faces on the unique and heterogeneous surface. To go from the pulsion to representation, but without allowing oneself, in order to describe this implantation, this sedentarization of the influxes, without allowing oneself the suspect facility of lack, the trick facility of an empty Alterity, of a Zero whose silence is about to be shattered by the demand which disturbs it (demand, already speech then? and addressed already, and to something? yes, to this Other; and by something, which is therefore already able to speak? yes, whether in gestures, tears, fury, the infatuated suckling's torpor, interjections, as they say), so that with this trick of the demand and the Zero's silence, well, it remains only to inaugurate the theatre and power, and set them to work, the theatre of power where satisfactions will dupe the desire originating from this alleged lack itself. Quite the contrary, it is necessary, we will come to this later, to describe the business of the cube starting with the opened and exposed band of the libidinal body, according to the unique face without verso, the face which hides nothing.

We should not continue to confuse the closure of representation, that sarcastic discovery, that sham dropping of the scales from our eyes, by those thinkers who come and tell us: what is outside is really inside, there is no outside, the exteriority of the theatre is just as much its interiority—don't mix up this sad piece of news, this cacangelism which is only the other side of evangelism, this wretched news that the artefact-bearers running along their little wall behind the backs of slaves who are bound and seated at the bottom of their cave, do not even exist, or what amounts to the same: that they themselves are only shadows in the cave of the sunlit world, reduplication of sadness—don't go confusing this crestfallen message and this representation of an entirely closed theatre with our Moebian-labyrinthine skin, single-sided patchwork of all the organs (inorganic and disorganized) which the libido can traverse: for however well it is closed upon itself, it too, like a good Moebius band, is not at all closed in the sense of a volume, it is infinite, and contrary to the representative cube, intensities run in it without meeting a terminus, without ever crashing into the wall of an absence, into a limit which would be the mark of a lack, there is nothing the libido lacks in reality, nor does it lack regions to invest, the slender and very dark finger of her left hand which, in a conversation, the young woman, anxious because she is afraid of what she believes to be your erudition, passes over her eyebrow, while in the other hand she pulls at a cigarette—here is a real region to invest, one can die for it, one can give all one's organicity, one's ordered body, one's functional arrangement of organs, one's memory of organs, one's socio-professional status, one's supposed past and one's supposed future, one's agenda and one's intimate theatre, one can feel like paying very dearly, exorbitantly, for this finger which is like an engraver's stylus and the whole orbital space, cranial, vaginal, that it engenders around the eye. And it is not because it is prohibited that it is invested, not because it is represented, beyond a stage-set and because one hasn't the right to climb onto the stage—but because one desires to climb up there and *seize it*! The libido never fails to invest regions, and it doesn't invest under the rubric of lack and appropriation. It invests without condition. Condition is rule and knowledge. But the passage of emotion on the hand stroking the eyelid, what does it matter if it obeys rules, laws of emotion and other nonsense, what does it matter what causes the woman's shyness before your supposed personage (obviously paternal . . .), what does all this matter, this hotchpotch of words which will give an account and do the accounts? It is these words, which set about representing the gesture and produce it in the exteriority internal to all discourse, and the law that they invent in order to *explain* exteriority and the spectacle, it is their own law as knowledge.

Far from taking the great Zero as the ontological motif, imposed on desire, forever deferring, re-presenting and simulating everything in an endless postponement, we, libidinal economists, affirm that this zero is itself a figure, part of a powerful *dispositif*, wise like the god of the Jews and pale like the void of Lao-tzu, a concentratory *dispositif* [*dispositif de circonversion*] where, of course, several libidinal positions are affirmed together, which we make merry in disintricating and demonstrating with tact, in disengaging without shock, like Japanese, like blades enmeshed in a fencing match—and we will show not only that it is not necessary to pass through it in order to follow the course of intensities on the labyrinth, but moreover that the passage through the zero is itself a particular libidinal course, that the position of the Signifier or of the Other is, in the concentratory *dispositif*, itself an enjoyable [*jouissive*] position, that the 'rigour of the law' gives more than one person a hard-on, and that this Nothing is not a matter of ontological necessity, but of a religious fantasy, libidinal then, and as such, moreover, quite acceptable, that is, if it were not, alas, terroristic and deontic. We must model ourselves an affirmative idea of the Zero.

So we rebegin the critique of religion, so we rebegin the destruction of piety, we still seek atheism, terribly intelligent, we have understood that the reintroduction of the Zero, that is to say, of the negative, in the economy of desire, is quite simply that of accountancy in libidinal matters; it is political economy, that is, capital, carried even into the sphere of passions, and with this economy of capital, necessarily, and yet again, we have understood that it is piety that comes to take its course, the pulsional and passionate *dispositif* of religiosity, inasmuch as this is identified as the *force of lack*, capitalist religiosity, which is that of money engendering itself, *causa sui*. And therefore we 'are doing politics', we desire that the force of lack collapse, that it degenerate, we love and we want all that affirms that this zero not only does not engender itself, and no more is it engendered by another force (the force of labour, Marx supposes, but once again, exactly as lacking, effaced 'on the surface' of the social stage), but most of all that questions of engenderment are trapped, they bear within them knowledge and its 'answers', all of which strikes you as incredibly funny—no, we do not subordinate our anti-religious, that is to say, anti-capitalist, politics to knowing what the origin of meaning, that is to say, what surplus-value really is, not even to know that there really is no origin and that it does not lack any this or that, but is lacking as an origin, we want and do a dismembered, unaccountable politics, *godless* for politicians, and it is in this way that the *critique* of religion which we rebegin is no longer a critique at all, no longer remains in the *sphere* (that is to say, note, the theatrical volume) of what it critiques, since critique rests in turn on the force of lack, and that *critique is still religion.*

Pagan Theatrics

We desire the atheism of the libidinal band, and if it cannot be critical, that is to say religious, then it must be pagan, that is to say affirmative. We have therefore to leap over two frontiers, that which separates the political from the apolitical, but also that which separates the religious from the secular, we have to say, for example, that there is perhaps more atheism (affirmative) in that religion of the Low Empire which Augustine detested and ridiculed, this religion in which for the least hiccup, the least scandal, a copulation without issue, a birthing, a pee, a military decision, there was a god, a goddess, several gods and goddesses *attending* the act, the patient and the agent, not to double them in a pointless spectacle, as Augustine appeared to believe, and no more to divest the alleged subject, implied in the act in question, of his responsibility, but because in this way all these gestures, all these situations, in the life (ever since) called the everyday (as if there were another) on the one hand were valued as intensities, could not decay into 'utilities', and on the other hand did not have to be connected by a paradoxical, dialectical, arbitrary, terrorist link to an absent Law or Meaning, but on the contrary, being self-sufficient in their self-assertion, never failed to be affirmed as singularities. The *divine* was simply this self-assertion. Perhaps nothing is closer to what happens on the libidinal band than the *parody* that 'theatrical theology' makes of this popular religion, half sceptic, half stoic, of late Rome. It is in any case, even if we are unjust in its favour, much more atheist than the discourses of science, of politics and critique, of our contemporary liberators of desire, women, children, Blacks, Indians, spaces and the proletariat—liberators whom we love, and who, moreover, we *too* are.

Between theatrical theology and the Judaeo-Christian who today still governs the critique of religion and political economy, there is no opposition between a eulogy to the divine in the world and a hymn to God at the expense of the world and *in absentia*, there is the difference between two *dispositifs* of pathos. This is where Klossowski begins. On his advice, let us listen to Augustine discussing the disjunction made by Varro between a fabulous or mythic theology and a civil or political theology. The Christian takes the example of the nuptial coupling:

> And if Virginensis is among those present, to see to the untying of the virgin's girdle, and Subigus, to see that the bride is subdued to her husband, and Prema, to make sure that, when subdued, she is pressed tight, to prevent her moving—if they are there, what is the function of the goddess Pertunda? She should blush for shame and take herself off! Let the bridegroom have something to do for himself! It would be most improper for anyone but the husband to do what her name implies. But it may be that she is tolerated just because she is a goddess, not a god . . . But what am I talking about? Priapus is there as well, that all-too-male divinity. And the newly wed bride used to be told to sit on his phallus, that monstrous obscenity, following the most honourable and most religious custom of Roman matrons. So let our friends go and try to use all their subtlety to make a distinction between 'civil' and 'fabulous' theology, between the city and the theatre, the temple and the stage, priestly ceremonies and poets' verses—a supposed distinction between decency and obscenity, truth and falsehood, solemnity and frivolity, the serious and the farcical, between what is to be desired and what is to be rejected.[1]

And Augustine continues with a good apostle's argument: if Varro works in such a way that the respective representations of the divine on the theatrical stage and the social stage are after all indiscernible, it is because already the certainty fills this pagan that only natural theology is true, that of the philosophers, meaning Plato, and therefore that of Augustine, meaning Christ. All these simulacra, whether of actors or of priests, come to fall together on one side, on the side of the false, of the illusory, of the impure; the new limit is set up to separate all that, which is appearance, from the essential, which is pure and veridical. What is Augustine thereby doing? He believes he has finished with the theatre, he invents it, reinvents it after Plato and the others, restores what the adherents of Subigus, Prema and Pertunda had demolished, that is to say the devaluation of the here and now, its subordination to the Other, he reforms voluminous theatricality and repeats the *dispositif* by which the auditorium is ignored, in favour of the stage and the stage devoted to the representation of an Exteriority left behind at the doors to the theatre, and then judged non-theatrical once and for all.

But popular, Varronian theatrics did not present this distribution of functions in its scenography at all. If the young bridegroom provoked Virginensis to strip the girdle from the young woman he was about to deflower, how can it be imagined that it could be by indecency, foolishness and falsehood? Is it not obvious that Virginensis is the name borne by the impatience of the *vir desiderans* and the *virgo*, equally astonished and expectant, yet full of amazement; also the untying of the girdle in order that it be released, and superimposed, the formation of another knot in the process of being tied between her arms, her shoulders, stomach, thighs, her *introitus* and her *exitus?* Virginensis is a cry forced out by all this at once, a cry made of several incompossible cries: she opens up, he takes me, she resists, he squeezes, she gets loose, he starts and stops, she obeys and commands, this could happen, happen impossibly, supplication and order, oh the most powerful thing of all flowing through them, do what desire desires, be its slave, connect, I give you a name.

And for each connection, a divine name, for each cry, intensity and multiplication brought about by experiences both expected and unexpected, a little god, a little goddess, which has the appearance of being useless when one looks at it with globulous, sad, Platonic-Christian eyes, which in fact is of no use, but which is a name for the passage of emotions. Thus every experience gives rise to a divinity, every connection to an inundation of affects. But Augustine passed into the camp of the great Zero, and so already understands nothing of all this, he wants and calls for resignation, abandon the libidinal band, he says, only one thing merits affect, it is my own Zero, my Other, it is through him that all your emotions come, you must give them to him, go, leave them with him, render them unto him, he will buy them back from you, the redeemer. What does the Christian want? To bring connection into disrepute and almost to disconnect it: the *next*, what a joke of a word! The other is put into the atmosphere of an affective distance, then brought much nearer again by a particular and paradoxical effort, named *caritas** because it is expensive (one gives without return, one gives distances from a distance, it is the Zero who perceives them and fructifies them). As a result of this disconnection, more singularities. *Caritas* has an answer to everything. And

---

**Caritas* (*L.*): Christian love and charity; gift or payment; dearness, high price, esteem, affection.—*tn*

that is why everything which became the ancient god finds itself devalued, divided into its appearance, Virginensis, Priapus, fool, and into its essence, the new god, the central Zero, the stage-director [*metteur en scène*].

In its appearance, delirium or madness, and in its essence, divine intentions. Listen to the Father of the Church attempting to cleave intensities:

> They want to derive the name Liber from *Liberamentum* (deliverance), on the ground that through his assistance males are 'delivered' from semen in coition . . . Besides this they have women, as well as wine, assigned to Liber, with a view to provoking sexual desire, and in this way Bacchanalia were celebrated with all their limitless insanity; Varro himself admits that the Bacchants could not have performed their feats if their minds had not been deranged (*nisi mente commota* . . .). One thing is certain; such performances would never have taken place in the theatre; they had entertainment there, not raving madness. And yet to have gods who delight in such entertainments is similar to a kind of lunacy (*simile furoris*).[2]

That is how the excellent Father prepares the generalized closure of appearances under the name of symptoms. The devaluation of the given functions fully, that is to say emptily: the movement of forces becomes commotion of the spirit, and soon *dementia* and *amentia*. The pagans called it Dionysus and Bacchus, names of inestimable singularity. And note Augustine's paralogism, his faltering way of paying tribute, nevertheless, to the force of their theatrics: the Bacchants were prey to rage and madness; this cannot be seen in the theatre where one only acts; although theatre plays are such that they could please only the gods who were also seized by *furor*. The implication is direct, and pagan: *furor* is divine, the divine is *furor*, as much in sacred rites as in stage plays, there is nothing that does not enter the tracks of the impulses, under a singular name, and there is nothing that keeps itself outside this passage. We catch Augustine; here in the act of folding the libidinal band onto itself in order to produce within it a volume and a chamber of presence/absence. Intensities will need to be filtered and imparted to the active voice of the Zero, in order to balance all the accounts. And we see how he cannot succeed in doing this, how the difference between play and madness, simulacrum and truth, clowning and seriousness, is not successfully set up.

This, this affirmation of the band, this banditism, is written in a pain which makes the hand tremble. Let's listen to it, this is certainly more important than what is said. This pain is not a sadness or a loss of force, but the opposite. It is stamped with an expenditure of important quantities of energy, employed to make something bearable which is not bearable, perhaps this same accumulation of forces [*puissances*]. Crying, yelling are within the hand's capabilities. Figures—meanwhile the hand continues to advance its pen through Dionysus' groves—figures of life and death are accumulated, figures which are this same energy fixed for a moment and for an eternity, and which devour it, mistresses of wild beasts. Egyptian face, Negev hair, bistre-coloured androgyne, unmanageable girl-child.

With this pain, perhaps at the centre, this new event, truly awful: this same Egyptian face, staring into space with its impassive gaze, it has become yesterday evening, a *black* night. The figure of the young woman has become the death mask of a young man the cops had kept watch over and beaten up two years ago in an island prison bordering the African seaboard, and whose body had been buried after his father refused, having examined it, to admit their version of death by suicide. It is this same face, this same narrow forehead, big nose, a little crooked, and the third great identifying feature of the Abyssinian type, the same fineness of the jaw. And he spoke, all the time, while she kept silent, he yielded, escaping to his death and looking for it through floods of words, speaking like a Negro, multiplying the ambushes of words; but his speech was so soft and imperious that it was followed by visible effects, just like physical actions. If his death could have exploded as his words exploded, into palpable transformations, when he was his body! To make of his death his active body again, transformer. The anagrams of his *nomen* were Roma, Amor.

And this tension, above all difficulty and intolerance, is associated with the incompossibility of all these simultaneous figures. You would need to be one hundred per cent Christian and stupid to think that these Romans and Negros are libidinal idiots, innocents plunged in debauchery. This suffering through excess is that of the Bacchants, it proceeds from the *incompossibility* of figures, of masks which together occupy the same space-time and thereby reveal the libidinal band; for such an incompossibility where several parts, however different, of the alleged organic body, are affirmed at the same time, or even, if you prefer, where sections of the psychic and social apparatus which must only be affirmed separately or successively, are affirmed at the same time; it is unbearable. Is this because it is the dissolution of unity, of the supposed synthesis? What is engulfed in theatrical theology, for we who come long afterwards, having centuries, almost two millennia of disfiguring traditions upheld by religion, religions, metaphysics, capital, is identity. Is it possible that all intensity is suffering only because we are religious, are clergy of the Zero? Even to say this is perhaps a consolation.

Our danger, we libidinal economists, lies in building a new morality with this consolation, of proclaiming and broadcasting that the libidinal band *is good*, that the circulation of affects *is joyful*, that the anonymity and the incompossibility of figures *are great and free*, that all pain is reactionary and conceals the poison of a formation issuing from the great Zero—what I have just said. But it is not an ethics, this or another, that is required. Perhaps we need an *ars vitae*, young man, but then one in which we would be the artists and not the propagators, the adventurers and not the theoreticians, the hypothesizers and not the censors.

We do not even have to say: this great Zero, what crap! After all, it is a figure of desire, and from what position could we assume to deny it this quality? In what other, no less terrorist Zero? *One cannot assume a position* on the twisted, shock-ridden, electrified labyrinthine band. One's got to get this into one's head: the instantiation of intensities on an original Nothing, on an Equilibrium, and the folding back of complete parts onto the libidinal Moebian band, in the form of a theatrical volume, does not proceed from an error, from an illusion, from malice, from a counter-principle, but again from desire. One must realize that representing [*la mise en représentation*] is desire, putting on stage, in a cage, in prison, into a factory, into a family, being boxed in are desired, that domination and exclusion are desired; that extreme intensities are instantiable in these assemblages too. That the black Pharoah face has died, that the metamorphosis he was looking for had been the death that he was. We must succeed in hearing that without any rejection, for it is rejection, the exteriorization, which prolongs theatricality like a shadow cast over the libidinal band. This rejection is necessarily concomitant with the setting-up of a point of view on the Zero, on the empty centre, the place where everything is supposed to be visible and intelligible, the place of knowledge.

Turning of the Bar

Thus there is the pain of incompossibility. This pain is much older than the word incompossibility can indicate. This word could tend to produce the belief that the origin of pain is logic, the violation of the compossible, the simultaneous affirmation of the this and the not-this. There is certainly a bit of suffering, which the most acute mathematicians and logicians are well aware of, in these occupations of spaces previously reputed to be exclusive and carefully distinguished: one should recall the matter of imaginary numbers, of fuzzy sets, of the logic of individuals. Same thing with the painters, when Klee, for example, opens the perspectivist cube onto the plastic support as one, as ten dislocated boxes presented together from five or six points of view. A bit of suffering, but it is not, however, this pain, it is like its negative, it is this pain announced *a contrario* in the spaces of non-pain. Exactly where the concept had produced the strict delimitation of the this and the not-this, had crossed the limit, had thus determined a zone of points that were neither this nor not-this, neutralized points forming a frontier and forbidding confusion, a new 'labour' (as they say) of the concept displaces this series of points, unbound and rebound in another way, provoking the panic of a square negative, of a trivalent logic, or, in Lesnievski's hypothesis, the truth of a proposition like *the edge of the book is the book*.

Brief panic, one settles down again, one sedentarizes in another way, at least when we are in the grip of an obsession with the great Zero, when, at any cost, one wants to produce a discourse of so-called knowledge, when therefore one never ceases, after all these disturbances, to proclaim that now, this is it, one holds the true *dispositif* of the logic of propositions, of the theory of numbers, of whatever. The true, that is to say what the great Zero itself produces, and assumes. One soon stops nomadizing, one occupies and cultivates the earth, under the security of the True. But these disfigurations rarely take place, thank god, even today's scientists are starting out on the road to pain, letting their little sufferings subside, their little scandals, the petty dialectic and the wretched 'labour of the concept'. They know that this is deception itself, that what works is not the concept, that the concept is capital which pretends to work, but which determines the conditions of labour, delimits the outsides and insides, the authorized and the prohibited, selects and valorizes, invests, realizes, that the concept is trade, but that the movement, the strength of trade is not the concept, this wretched little suffering of the academic radical-socialist.

Our great mathematicians, those whom we love, our brothers in pain and joy, know very well that it is not even correct, that it is futile and almost base to say with a last smile: yes, all that we do is only a game, yes we quite understand that there is only the great Zero and that one can only turn about it, like a vast spectacle. They know as well as we do that it is *not at all* a question of a game, that one never leaves the sham seriousness of the concept for the fac-simile of the game. Roman pain and joy, pagan and stoic, are not games. The stage plays that Augustine despises (and adores) are in no way simulacra of another reality, the stage masks could not be the popular and political version of serious divinity; the Nothing with which the philosophers and priests have furnished us as the maximum and optimum of conciousness or knowledge or wisdom, and thanks to which the vivacious and deadly intensities that shoot across us shall be *discredited*, this Nothing, it is their desire that produces it, it is not it that produces their desire. These intensities do not in any way proceed from illusions of changing investment on the immobile circle that surrounds the Nothing; but on the contrary, they can engender this as the centre of a concentratory disposition also called the proper body, ego, society, universe, capital, the good lord. The thought of the game, of the great Game, game of desire and game of the world, is still a little sad thought, that is to say, a thought. It remains entirely instantiated on the Zero, and from there it makes this effort, supreme for thought, to say to itself: this, all that happens on the periphery, on the circle, is nothing but the transit of intensities, turn and eternal return; it says to itself: I am nothing but thought, that is, the Nothing and nothing, what is turns around outside, and so, to be, I have only to place myself as well on the circumference, turn with the intensities, act *as if* I loved, suffered, laughed, ran, fucked, slept, shat and pissed, I, thought. May this supreme effort of thought die, such is our wish as libidinal economists.

The pain of incompossibility does not refer to a delimiting, selective, orientating zero. Thought does not precede it. More often than not, what is called thought is what escapes it, is produced as a way out of it. The *dispositif* of confinement, that is to say of delimitation and conception, which will produce the exterior and the interior, which will enclose the extension of the concept, which will define *places* (of art, of culture, of production, of politics, of sexuality), this *dispositif* with its zero can only be engendered by disintensification.

The operator of disintensification is exclusion: either this, or not-this. Not both. The disjunctive bar. Every concept is therefore concomitant with negation, exteriorization. It is this exteriorization of the not-this that will give rise to theatricization: the outside 'will have to' *be conquered*, the concept 'will will' its own extension, to master what it had left at the gates of its territory, it will set off for war and for labour with Hegel, as previously with Augustine, towards the outside, in order to annex it. In reality it is pushed into this not only by the demon of confusion, by synchretism, by the *jouissance* of overthrowing, by the quest for intensities, but by flight in the face of this pain of incompossibility that we are talking about. What anguish in these limits, in these devaluations followed by exclusions! How they are loved, these exteriorities! Hence voyages, ethnology, psychiatry, pediatrics, pedagogy, the love of the excluded: enter, beautiful Negresses, charming Indians, enigmatic Orientals, dreamers, children, enter my work and the spaces of my concepts. All this is theatre; it is the white innocence of the West in expansion, base cannibalistic imperialism.

The little suffering is only the displacement of the disjunctive bar. The little suffering carried to the second degree, is the consciousness that this displacement is the rule, that there is always displacement. Little suffering that attains its acme in the thought of metaphor and of difference [*écart*]. But the pain we speak of is in no way bound to the displacement of the bar of the concept. This pain is not the depression that follows from the position of having one foot here and one foot there, one foot inside and one foot outside, of being *divided*. This pain has no relation to the little suffering of castration, which is the suffering of the concept, fissure and disfiguration ceaselessly deferred. Instead, this is how to imagine it, perfumed Mane of hair.

Take this bar which separates the this from the not-this. That is to say any segment at all. Place it in a neutral space, say three-dimensional to facilitate the imagination's highly crude intuition. Subject it to a movement of rotation around a point belonging to this segment, a movement yielding the following three properties: the rotation takes place on all the axes without exclusion, the central point is itself displaced over the segment in an aleatory way, finally it is equally displaced in the supposed neutral space. Thus a surface is engendered, which is nothing other than the labyrinthine libidinal band which was in question: this surface always has as its breadth the length of the segment, etc. But to describe the properties of the band is not the important thing. This segment which 'passes over' the whole landscape of 'corporeal' surfaces joined end to end as has been said (which in fact *engenders* this landscape point by point in the ungraspable time of its passage), the more quickly it turns on itself, the more energy it employs and expends, and heats the travelled zone. This passage may be absolutely immobile, the black sun of so-called hysterical *conversions*, or the so-called obsessional or paranoiac *fixations*, or conversely fulminating or ephemeral *ideas* of art, of science, of love. The ice that it leaves behind it is in proportion to the energy sucked up: extremely cold intensities. And every intensity, scorching or remote, is always *this and not-*

this, not at all through the effect of castration, of repression, of ambivalence, of tragedy due to the great Zero, but because intensity pertains to an asynthetic movement, more or less complex, but in any event so rapid that the surface engendered by it is, at each of its points, at the same time *this and not-this*. Of no point, of no region, however small, can one say what either is, because this region or this point has not only already disappeared when one claims to speak of it, but, in the singular or atemporal instant of intense passage, either the point or the region has been invested in from both sides at once.

When one says *at the same time*, one says *both together* (or *n* together), but one also says *one at a time*, in the singularity of the time, *della volta*. Only one turn, full of drifting affects. Not a matter of separation, but on the contrary, of movement, of displaceability on the spot. It is even necessary to imagine the monoface band as produced by this aleatory rotation, this mad segment acting as a matrix whose properties never stop changing and so unravelling the unpredictable ribbon of libidinal marks in its 'printout' [*sortie*]. But even this image needs to be corrected for it is modelled on an industrial machine, for example a wire drawing machine or a rolling mill, and with this model, it implies the category of an accumulation, of a stock-piling, of a material memory, and, what amounts to the same, of a diachrony. For example, you could, I think, modify in an incessant and arbitrary way the norms of extrusion or rolling, and you would still obtain bars or wires with necessarily variable properties. The fact remains that they *remain*, that the marks of variations are inscribed on these objects and transform them into monuments of a past activity, into means of determining an activity to come, they thus open the space of an upstream and a downstream in production, of a cumulative diachronic time, of a capitalizing history. And beware, because with the instrument, the machine, you are already right in the zero. When the whirls of the disjunctive segment in its libidinal journey, being singular, produce no memory, this segment only ever being where it is in an ungraspable time, *a tense*, and therefore what was 'previously' journeyed through does not exist: acephalia,[3] time of the unconscious.

Duplicity of Signs

See at once, grey-eyed Unkind One, where, once again, we intend to break off, we libidinal economists: we will no longer speak of *surfaces of inscription* (except inadvertently, count on it), of regions to invest, and other similar things. We are suspicious of the separation allowed between inscription and its site. It is necessary (very different, Nietzsche says, this *it is necessary* from the *you must*), it is necessary that we strengthen our imagination, our palpative potential [*puissance*] until—rather than to think, we are not thinkers—until we forge the idea of an intensity which far from setting itself up on a producer-body, determines it; the idea of a passage over nothing, which produces, one instant beyond countable time, the being of its proper passing, its *passage* (speaking like some others, but in quite another way). Therefore not a surface first, then a writing or inscription over it. But the libidinal skin of which, *after the event*, one will be able to say that it is made up of a patchwork of organs, of elements from organic and social bodies, the libidinal skin initially like the *track* of intensities, ephemeral work, useless like a jet trail in the thin air at an altitude of 10,000, with the exception that it be, as opposed to the trail, completely heterogeneous. But like it, being at the same time the surface crossed and the crossing. You will say: 'crossed' is a past, it is not the passage which produces the skin, but the past of the passage, not the intensity, but what it will have been [*son après coup*]; and the surface, the libidinal skin is thus already a memory of intensities, a capitalization, a localization of their passages, there is the intensity and what *remains* of it, and your comparison doesn't count since there is a *caput*,* a surface of inscription, a register, when its function was to render the acephalus visible.

I see you, Unkind One, smiling at the hoax played on me by the words of knowledge and capital, before I had even begun to speak. Let us love this farce, let us not fear it, let us say yes each time it *requires* us to (and it will require us to, and require us again) say what we have to say as libidinal economists, this farce will stuff our words with its old hash of nihilist sadness. Between the libidinal skin and a register of inscription, confusion will always be possible, as between Christ and the Antichrist, between matter and anti-matter. We haven't the *power*, thank god, to dissociate them, to isolate a region, precisely, a domain, precisely! which would be a good representation, precisely, of the libidinal band and would escape the management of the concept, its hard scepticism and its nihilism. There is no *affirmative region*, words which cancel each other out.

Freud said, marvellously: the death drives work in silence in the uproar of Eros. Eros and the death drives, incompossibles, are indissociable. And

---

Caput (L): a freeman as opposed to a slave; the head, the seat of the intellect; source (of a river); origin, beginning in time.—*tn*

so it is, all things being equal, for the passage of intensities and the surface of inscription. For this operates like memory, preserving the passage, it is that by means of which effervescence is recorded and conserved, it is the means of transforming the singular sign of nothing, which is intensity, into terms of presence/absence, the position, and thereby the value, of which will be assigned as the presence/absence of other terms, functioning as their recording, their place in a form, *Gestalt*, or composition. The surface of inscription is then the means of recording. And from the means of recording to the means of production there is but one thing to do, which the despot accomplishes, as Deleuze says, which the great Gestaltist accomplishes. We well know that this surface is *at the same time*, indiscernibly, the libidinal skin 'engendered' by the mad bar and the wise flat sheet of the account book. At the same time the juxtaposition of singular effects named Sarah, Birgit, Paul, faith, the left eye, the cold, hard neck, juxtaposition of punctual intensities, never assembled as a body, merely adjoined in the impossible idea of the pulsional band, which cannot be one surface of inscription, but rather *several* explosions, not even necessarily successive, ephemeral explosions of libidinal intensities—therefore at the same time this, and the index-sheet where, in the form of *lists*, of words, of registery offices, of notebooks, of indexes, under the double law of paradigm and syntagm, of the column and the line, where what remains of intensity is recorded, its trace, its writing.

There is the farce that words play with us, that intensities play with us and that our passion itself will play with us from one end to the other of this book: this fit of passion, reader, Unkind one, will reach you at *second hand*, reported, this sheet on which I write and which is in one moment, in bewilderment and impatience, a woman's skin caressed or the sheet of water in which I lovingly swim, this sheet, you receive it printed, the same thing repeated, reduplicated, you receive a recording sheet. Words burning the point of the pen, whipped like an inert herd by this point, making them run and trapping the most noble, the fastest, the strongest amongst them, in flight, you receive them as a lexicologist. And all the comparisons which may come to mind, they are damned in advance by the accumulation (*cum*) which they comprise and which subject them to procedures of weighing, thought, commensurability, good for the register and accountability, for ever incapable of yielding intensity in its *event*.

Do you believe that the gloomy declaration of this *differing* [*différer*] of writing dismays and depresses us? It interests us acutely and gives us new impetus. If there is a secret, it is this, its own: how does the impossible juxtaposition of intense singularities give way to the register and recording? How does the differing-displacement, beyond space-time, of the affective singularity give space and time to multiplicity, then to generality, then to universality, in the concept, in the frozen whole of the register, how does it give space-time to the differing-composition or co-placing? How does *force* [*puissance*] give rise to *power* [*pouvoir*]? How does searing affirmation become circumscribed around a zero which, inscribing it, annihilates it and assigns it meaning?

This is our great interest (political interest amongst others, since this is the entire political question). And the hows that we address to it are not *whys*. The *why* is galling, nostalgic, treacherous, always nihilistic. We do not deny the *reality*, libidinal of course, of this zero, of this register, we haven't the least intention of devaluing it *ex hypothesi*, to start saying: this zero is an evil despot, this zero represses us, this is what it is made for, etc., all *ressentiments* which are often used as a political means and which we take no part in. Once again, what interests us: the sign in the Klossowskian-Roman sense of *Subigus* and of *Pertunda*, the singular tensor with its mad multiplicity of directions, not contemplating its disintrication from the 'bad' nihilist sign, from Plato right up to Peirce and Saussure, with a view to placing it apart in a good place where one would be at last in the shelter of the great semiotic-semiotician's Zero, not therefore to dissociate and exteriorize it in relation to the bad sign, or—not even—to exteriorize the latter in relation to the former, to separate them and so ourselves become the Just, the Blessed, Sages, Equals, Brothers, Comrades; no, none of these settlements interests us, rather this: to become sufficiently refined where we are, in order to feel, *in* the baseness of exchangeable signs, the unrepeatable singularities of the passages of affect, sufficiently discriminatory and—I will say it as a provocation—sufficiently *Jesuitical* to seize, *in* the general movement of smoothing down and inscription on this Zero of capital, of the Signifier, the *this-sides* or the *beyonds* of this movement, the immobilities or the excitations which trail and betray this movement, to love inscription not because it communicates and contains, but through what its production necessitates, not because it channels, but because it drifts.

There is our problem, political and otherwise, there, at least, is its position: theatricality without reference, masks revealing no face, unless it is a mask in its turn, Names (beware the capital letter!) from a history which is not societies' memories, names which would be their amnesia —but always inseparable from this excess of the Apollinian appearance, the Dionysus inseparable from the great light, not as its opposite but as its nuclear night, the singularity always placed in the paranoiac order of the universal. And in this sense, it is not a revolution we need, it is one revolution, and one, and one more . . . *permanent* revolution if you like, but on condition that this word cease to denote continuity and mean: we will never be sufficiently refined, the (libidinal) world will always be *too beautiful*, there will always be too great an excess of mute vibrant trembling in the most ordinary nonsense or depression, we will never stop becoming disciples of its affects, the routes of the affects ceaselessly crossing and recrossing the signs of representation and tracing the most unheard of, the most audacious, the most disconcerting itineraries on them. And on condition that *permanent* also mean: we do not seek to produce a cartography, a memory, a register of our efforts at refinement, an organization, a party of the refined, an anti-society, a school for a framework of affects, an apparatus of refinement's officials, the permanence in question is not something that persists throughout a time identical to itself and from which could be distilled out of acquisitions, attainments, experiments and results, a knowledge in matters of intensities, on the contrary, all will be gradually lost (of what?), and will be so lost that in one sense we will never be able *to will* continually, to will in the sense of a sustained resolution, this refinement in the (dispossessing) seizures of signs, because power [*puissance*] (*Macht*) cannot be willed (*Willkür*), because desire cannot be assumed, accepted, understood, locked up in names = nomenclatured, because these intensities we desire horrify us, because we flee them, because we forget them. And it is in just such a way that there is a different revolution in each libidinal event, different to all others, incomparable (and always already comparable and still compared, as in the very words I have just employed); and no permanence at all: in fleeing *jouissance*-death, we *meet* it head on, unrecognizable, immediately recognized, *unheimlich* because *heimisch*, different, not willed by a deliberate decision, on the contrary avoided, fled from in panic and nostalgic terror, and therefore truly desired (*Wille*), unassumable. It will have to be forgotten every time, because it is unbearable, and then this forgetting means that it will be 'willed' in the sense of the *Wille*, produces displacement, the voyage of intensities, their return beyond identity. Our politics is of flight, primarily, like our style.

Deduction of the Voluminous Body

Caress ranging over the neck: place where the blouse stops, where the skin begins, or indeed the inverse, frontier or fissure? No, it is rather the region of transmutation from one skin into a different skin. The dark, flimsy cotton is a skin.—Elbow lodged like liquid in the palm, middle finger revolving and lightly effacing fold of the blue and white small of the arm. A fissure here again? No, zone of passage, of a change of surfaces. What is expressed in these regions? It is stupid to reduce them to a symbolism of the feminine sex. Are they imaginary *entries*, entries to the imaginary? The beginning of the theatre, the entry to the theatre, the theatricization of the libidinal surface?—No, at the outset one passes in front of the entry without going in, the long finger effaces the first illusion, that there is a fissure, thus an inside if it is penetrated. Yes, [you] are not a theatre in which my part will play, [you] are not a limit [*oui, n'es pas un théâtre dans lequel entre jouer ma pièce, n'es pas une limite*], penis sheathed in vagina is will be was a particular case of an incessant, maniacal and totally unforeseeable assemblage of parts of the great monoface skin. Force is amassed on these lines of contact which, thanks to its abundant investment, spread into new surfaces of so-called inscription. This afflux is the *event*.—Meanwhile, beneath the sleeve the hand cups the thoughtlessly folded elbow (by the action of this hand itself?), the gaze remains lost, but becomes dark and starts to look 'within'. This 'within' is this: the force which was lodged in the eyes escapes them and runs towards the small of the arm. Will this be to undo this contact with the digital skin, or to dash at and cross it? A third, busy speaking to him, sees nothing.

When, how does the ribbon start to become voluminous? Is it language which through its referential function gives it density and the presence of absence? Is it the eye that hollows surfaces into versos and immediately behind them, the continuity of their rectos? But what is 'language', what is 'the eye'? Entities of thought, concepts? What function can they have? So-called 'perverse' polymorphism, really simply diverse, is endlessly displaced from infancy over a surface without holes. There are no holes, only invaginations of surfaces. That is why when we cut open, we affirm only that which is, the vast coiled skin, where slits are not entries, wounds, gashes, openings, but the same surface following its course after a detour in the form of a pocket, front folded back almost against itself, as in Stalingrad. Diverse polymorphism is aware that there is no hole, no interior, no sanctuary to respect. 'The child', this western phantasm, the child, that is to say desire, is energetic, economic, non-representative.

Is it absence, rupture or breakage or loss or the disconnection of an ex-part of the libidinal skin which will give rise to a voluminous place, to the theatre, to the substitute sign, to interiority put in the place of exteriority, of the thing lost? This is what Freud says in *Jenseits*[4] with reference to his grandson. Such would be the origin of the theatre; the child had, in his pulsional skin [*pellicule*], just as one of the adjoining fragments makes this little skin [*peau*] infinite, his own theatre with his mother, the nipple on the tongue between his lips, the warm suppleness of the large breast under his blind fingers, his neck connected to her by the flesh of his shoulder, his eyes kept tight shut in pleasure, haughtily seeking his pleasure from her, in short, a very good multiple connection, diverse-perverse, he shits in his bed in the midst of sucking,—and that is how he 'loses' his mother, let's rather say: that this connection is undone, immense pain through lack, says Freud, unbearable distress, massive afflux from the drives to the outlet points, but everywhere impasses, gates shut, switches disconnected, breakdowns, stases, everything is going to explode. The theatre is set up, mama will be the bobbin, her loss will be repeated, '*o-o-o–o*'—'gone'! '*da*'—'there she is'! the distress will be *bound*, to find a way out for these menacing masses of displaceable energy that rumble at the threshold of the body, these gates will be opened onto its substitute, the bobbin theatre.

Pain, then, inaugurates the theatre, intensity insofar as it is deadly, Freud says. But note: the nipple, the swelling breast, the shoulder, arm and eyes, already had to be instantiated on a *person*, a *unity*, the mother, in order that this present-absent bobbin could take her place, substitute itself for her. Then the child could in fact suffer from the loss of an instance, but then he would no longer be the polymorphous perversity which interests us, Freud and us. There is the possibility of a pain through lack, even the possibility of an absence, only because it had been previously supposed that there was the presence of a mother, of *someone*. And this constitutes a *petitio principii*, a formal vice without weight for people like us whose discourse makes no claim to consistency, refusing to buy it when an explanation is attempted: as soon as there is someone, an instance which passes for the place of totalization, the unification of several singularities, of several libidinal intensities, one is already in the great Zero, one is already in the negative; and one is already in distress, since this instance onto which these singular *jouissance*-deaths will be beaten down, the mother or whatever equivalent, is on the one hand never *given*, there is never a connection *onto her*, there are only scraps, partial metamorphoses, and thus nostalgia begins with the production of this unitary instance; and on the other hand, such an instance devalues, annihilates, inevitably cleaves the intense signs that are libidinal commutations, disaffects the adjoining lips-tongue-nipple, the connections neck-shoulder, fingers-breast, since *instead* of being passages of abundant intensity, these metamorphoses become metaphors of an impossible coupling, these commutations just so many allusions to an elusive ability to enjoy [*pouvoir-jouir*], these incomparable, fiercely singular signs just so many common, universal signs of a lost origin.

Our question is: who suffers in pain? Freud's response is: the child, thus an already constituted subject, formed in the object-mother's gaze, in symmetry with her, already, then, there is the specular partition between them, already the auditorium-side and the stage-side, already the theatre; and the theatre the child constructs with the edge of his bed as the footlights, and the thread attached to the bobbin as curtain and scenery, governs entries and exits, this prosthesis-theatre is of the same type as that already hollowed out within him, it is the replica in 'exteriority' of the hollow volume in which the two poles of his own body and that of his mother, theatrical counterparts, non-existent poles, capture, secure in their field, dominate every event of the libidinal band. Pain as caesura, as fissure, split and disconnection, only hurts unitary totality. In conceiving pain as the motor of theatricality, Freud gives it the metaphysical consistency of the negative, he is therefore a victim of that theatricality, since only representation of a unitarist calling is hurt by fissure and disconnection, only through the already proper, proprietary body is loss felt as aggression, only for an already organized conciousness is death a horror. If one wants to explain the birth of the theatre, its secret must not be sought in the pain of a loss, for there is loss only for a memory, and, the said polymorphous perversion being acephallic, loss is or is not for it an occasion of pleasure-pain, that is all. Not even suffering on the one hand, pleasure on the other: this dichotomy belongs to the order of the organic body, of the supposed unified instance, it requires the labour of decision, of *Verneinung*, which satisfies the pleasure principle in spitting out what harms and admitting only that which does good; the pleasure principle being just as much the reality principle since to spit out is to separate the painful, expelled into exteriority, and the pleasurable, conserved in interiority. We must sweep aside all these wonderful little fables which presuppose what they are intended to explain, the formation of the duality, of the substitute sign, of the interior theatre redoubling an exterior reality (and reciprocally) and therefore also the formation of the caesura, wound, fissure which made their way to the interior; all these fables, in *Jenseits*, in *Die Verneinung*[5] are already placed in the duality of the Zero (of the One, of the proper person, object or subject, of the Ego . . .) and of intensity (of *jouissance*, of pain, of both together). It is necessary that the attempt be made to describe the circumscription of a theatre where there had been flat skin, affirmatively, energetically, without presupposing lack, when this would be under the name of pain.

Now imagine this, ermine gash. The turning bar slackens its pace, the mad, aleatory movement which engenders the libidinal band is sufficiently checked so that the this and the not-this, confused by its extremely high speed in all the points of the field, now distinct, are sometimes the this, sometimes the not-this, here it is, now it's gone, here it is, *fort/da*. The bar becomes a frontier, not to be crossed on pain of confusion, sin against the concept, transgression, stupidity, madness, primitive thought. The bar becomes a boundary, the boundary of a stage: over there the not-this, here the this. End of dissimulation, beginning of value, and of ambivalence. For to go from the not-this to the this, it will now be necessary to pay: it will cost a great deal to have the not-this over there. To pay to enter the over there, to get on stage. To have: the manner of being what one is not, prosthesis which supposes negation. And *time* also begins with this abatement: now this, now that, repetition, and so also memory, synthesis of the now, of the no longer, of the already more, always to be renewed since the temporal poles are 'from now on' held in exteriority, in relation to each other, at the same time that they are co-posed, composed on either side of what separates them. Montage and the stage and narrative time.

What is this abatement? A cooling? A lowering of intensity? A withdrawal of investment? Yes, all that. Influxes are displaced, the bar will turn 'further off', it is not the mother which the child loses, it is the lips-nipple connection which now appears as a connection, from now on as a paradoxical juncture of two zones, of a this and a not-this, when this was never a synthesis, but an intense libidinal zone. The child loses nothing, he gains a mother, and the mother a child, the this and the not-this are put in place under the name of *complementarities* whereas the movement of the segment, by slowing down, sediments them, centrifuges them. The concept, time, negation, ambivalence, come with the weakening of intensities. Representation supposes that the stars are not dead, but indifferent.

de-siderium, the constellations do not shatter,* nostalgic desire, the wish, the *Wunsch*, begins with the decline of libidinal economy.

Duplicity of the Two Pulsional Principles

Why does the movement of the bar slow down? We know nothing of this, there is no answering the question why, which implies precisely nihilism and thought. We turn this question around, we say: when it is turning intensely, no why; your why itself results from it turning less strenuously, it is recuperative and nostalgic. The movement of the bar slows down *because*, and then this *because* . . . is intensified. Then the not-this will start to be advanced to account for the this. Then the space of the nihilism of reasons is opened up. (For example, those I have just given?)

Thus the theatre comes with the concept. The bar stops turning; on the contrary, it circumscribes. The intense sign which engenders the libidinal body abandons this vast Moebian skin to the significative sign, the singularity of a passage or a voyage of affects is herded, closed up into a communicable trace. Whether this trace is communicable, or whether this sign is amenable to systematization, or whether the opposition which conceals (but in what space-time?) the irrelevant difference is permanent, all this refers to the duplicity of signs, already noted. But this deserves a much more refined analysis. First, that means that there is no notable difference between a libidinal formation and a discursive formation, insofar as they are both formations, *Gestaltungen*. A libidinal *dispositif*, considered, precisely, as a stabilization and even a stasis or group of energetic stases, is, examined formally, a structure. Conversely, what is essential to a structure, when it is approached in economic terms, is that its fixity or consistency, which allows spatio-temporal maintenance of identical denominations between a this and a not-this, work on pulsional movement as would dams, sluices and channels. One can, therefore, step twice, and even innumerable times, into the same river, if the river is located by its slope, its banks, its direction, its flow, as it is by any discriminating mind-body; but one never steps twice into the same river, quite simply because *there is no river*, that is what is said by the madman,

---

**De-siderium: les sidera ne sidèrent pas* . . . : *desiderium* (L.): petition, sense of loss, longing, want; *sidera* (L.): constellations, skies, destinies. Lyotard's splitting of *de-siderium* effectively means a 'de-shattering', the 'indifference' of the stars/constellations to death, and the suspension constitutive of the wish.—*tn*

lover of singularities, be his name Proust, Sterne, Pascal, Nietzsche, Joyce, a madman determined to judge a given swim as *unexchangeable* for any other, *in spite* of its generic name, a madman ready to want a proper name, a divine name, for each intensity, and thus to die with each of them, to lose even his memory (river-bed and course), and certainly his own identity. Madness of pathos; but recognize, Unkind one, back to back with this madness, that of the structuralist, who made himself incapable of hearing, in the silence, the crackling masses of flux which circulate in the system, and which are, however, the 'final cause' of their operativity.

This confusion of formations, *Gestaltungen*, which render libidinal *dispositifs* identical in principle to formal structures; it is Freud who is their victim. The confusion forms a barrier to his project or to his idea of a libidinal economy.

If ebbing intensities stabilize themselves into configurations, if affects are distributed according to the vast matrix-*dispositifs*, along with what Klossowski calls phantasma, into *voluminous bodies*, into *simulacra*, and equally, therefore, into fixed organizations of elements of the 'formerly' libidinal skin become organism, psychic apparatus, or whatever you like of this kind of thing, then it is certain that Eros can live happily together with Logos. And when I say Eros, it is still too simplistic, as we shall see: it is just as much the death drives whose deregulation or deregulating, when its effect is the fixation of impulsions, produces quite as many configurations, stases, economic rigidities which will pass (in silence . . .) for formal structures. Who can distinguish what is sick from what is therapeutic in conversion hysteria (to speak like nosographists)? It has become banal, following Freud, to consider neurosis as a compromise formation, as a stabilization which fulfils desire in its double dimension, erotic and deadly. That the two dimensions are undecidable in the symptom, then, is almost in its nature. But no less certain is the quasi-communicative, logical function of the symptom; every energetic configuration, because it rests on disjunctions and synthetic recoveries of the disjoined elements, is a structure. The symptom, or at least the syndrome, will be able to be *read*, analysed and reconstituted as a structure, a stable composition of elements; intense passages, tensors, are then no longer singularities, they take on value, as elements, from their continuation, from their opposition, from a metonymy without end. The unconscious is structured like a language, let's speak of it in this way, that's all it *demands*. It is in fact, and is only so when intensities are in decline, when the incandescence of the bar makes way for the glow of what is discriminating, when the dream is exchanged for the dream-narrative, when the traveller has just lain down and sold images for an ear which would relieve him of them.

To discriminate instances of Eros from those of death by specific effects is to believe that to one of these instances, the life drive, one function would be attached, that of collection and binding, whereas the other would only disperse, expend, draw out impulsions for the greatest death of organisms. This is once again to presume too much of binarism; it is to accept the return of the concept in the midst of its dissolution: if *one* and only one function is assignable to each instance, both instances, of life *and of death*, will always be identifiable by their functions, by effects which will always be instantiated, precisely, sometimes on life, sometimes on death, but always in an unequivocal way. Although one might well protest that the signs from which these inductions or instantiations are brought about are equivocal or at least polysemic, and that on them the rivalry, or just as much the connivance, of death and life is played out, it would still be the case that one concede in principle the essential in admitting for each instance the unicity of its function, and again therefore the possible identification of the instance by its function. But in terms of what the 1920 text says, if Freud introduced the instance of the death drives, it is precisely in order to keep not only such a sign, but libidinal economy in its entirety, in the shelter of the concept and of binarist discrimination. It is not at all a matter of *cleaving* the instances *in two*, this is the so-called 'labour' of the concept, it is, on the contrary, a matter of rendering their confusion always possible and menacing, of rendering insoluble the question of knowing whether a particular *Gestaltung* is an effect of life rather than death, if a particular flood, pulsional unbinding, is suicidal rather than therapeutic from the point of view of the apparatus which endures it, whether, on the contrary, a particular stasis, a particular fixation, a particular crystallization of a stable *dispositif* is amenable to palliative orthopaedics or mortiferous entropy.

Silence is a single line stretched over the brows and curving in on each side in such a way as to envelop the cheekbones, as the lover's hand, in Khajuraho's sculptures, envelops the obliging mistress's breast; next it widens into a deltoid surface and rises to form the narrow flanks of the nose. Around the Mediterranean, in Umbria, in Provence, one finds these strange *slopes*, calm and inflexible, sometimes cultivated, sometimes deserts, according to its aspect, always smooth; strange because the terrain, far from being constructed of hills and valleys, flows like a liquid body; and it flows as much towards the top as towards the bottom, it does not flow in the way that a wash-basin leaks, it slides in both, in all directions at once, displaying an inclined space without limit while being clearly delimited.

A fixed gaze turns into a smile, the eyelid system remains immobile, it is only the matter of a modification of the cornea's brightness, perhaps of the iris, of the diameter of the pupil, something to be grasped in a 'time' less than that of a blink of the eye. It is silence itself that calls up the influx, the abyss. What is blockage, stasis of forces, immobilization and sudden damming of impulsions (and which could be described accordingly as inhibition, neurosis), gives rise to other tracks and grows in force. This is why it is intolerable that one should pretend to cure this silence, to bring its meaning, supposedly sayable in words, to light. Excessive domination of the *dispositif* of knowledge over every silence, as if, in the scientist's, the philosopher's, or the analyst's discourse (and not only in that of the ideologist), it was no longer silence, silence left behind it by the drip by drip of the tap of well-weighed words, the track of desire which they extract, which produces its strength! Were the doctor to bend over the abyss of silence, were he to hear with one ear (the third), as in an anechoic chamber, the noise and the frenzy of blood pounding against artery walls and of nervous influxes coursing along the fibres of the trigeminus . . . from his 'own body'—good luck to him!

What have we to cure? I do not exactly know, but at least and first this: the disease of the will to cure. And the *talking cure* is not to be privileged over physical-chemical methods: the one is of a pair with the other, domination everywhere, occupation by all means, words or substances, of regions allegedly attacked and their sanitization. 'The formation of the Super-ego', says Freud, 'which attracts dangerous aggressive tendencies is equivalent, so to speak, to the installation of troops in the place where sedition threatens.'[6]

Gaze of an eye, slow, thoughtless, fixed, then in a flash the head pivots so that there is no more than a profile, Egypt. The silence which settles around it extends to large patches of the libidinal band which, it appears, are the property of its own body. These zones are also silent, this means that heavy flood-tides continuously, noiselessly, surge towards 'their' own regions or come from these same regions, along the length of the inclines. No need to try to land. This silence is not blind and does not require that one make certain of what comes about through a language, even one of hands or skins. We love the language of hands and skins, but here it would be unsubtle. To resort to it here would be to obey the ideology of sexuality.

To suggest to someone: let's fuck, would truly be to treat oneself as *representing* the sexual liberation movement. Same domination as from the doctor, this time from the militant. Same gross preterition of the libidinal labyrinth, in which, if it is true that language is nothing, sex is not all. There then, plugging into a sort of pain and joy, joy of the flood breaking up so many dams, pain of such a drift, entire regions coming undone drifting towards other regions, and pain moreover because everything does not leave, impatience that investments still resist, that the abyss does not call loudly enough.

But then why and how can the two principles, of life and death, be assumed if they cannot be discerned through their two functions, if bound wholes can be as congenial to life (organisms, statutes, institutions, memories of all kinds) as to death (neuroses and psychoses, paranoiac confinements, lethal stable disorders of organic functions), if unbinding is as much for the relief of bodies—orgasm and the release of semen, drunkenness and the blurting out of words, the dance and loosening of the muscles—as for their destruction: the mad laugh which sends the asthmatic's respiratory rhythm into disorder and asphyxiates him, the panic which distorts the joy of youthful demonstrations, the centrifugal impotence which annihilates the strength of those who do not wish to hold any power, the wandering to death of the schizophrenic who is in fact bedridden? What good are two principles if every effect can be related to both, together? Is it not contrary to the rule of economy in hypotheses and of impoverishment in concepts which controls the elaboration of theoretical systems?

Freud was well aware of these formal demands. If he introduced the principle which he names Nirvana, it is in order that his libidinal economy escapes the thermodynamic and, more generally, mechanical analogy, and so that this thought of the unconscious does not precisely close up into a theoretical system; so close to Nietzsche in this respect. Libidinal economy is a disorder of machines, if you will; but what *for ever* prevents the hope of producing the systematization and functionally complete description of it, is that, as opposed to dynamics, which is the theory of systems of energy, the thought—but this is still to say too little—the *idea* of libidinal economy is all the time rendered virtually impossible by the indiscerniability of the two instances. This 'duality' is not at all that of the dialogue, it sets no dialectic in motion, it does not accept a dualism, since the two instances are indiscernible *a priori*, and it is only by examining a particular effect with patient, almost infinite care (as Proust does with a gait, a smile, a taste, contact with a field, the lamplight on a staircase, each event inexchangeable, and therefore lost for the memory), that it will be possible, bit by bit, to attribute a particular *Gestaltung* to life and the conservation of a particular organized whole, a particular unbinding and disruption rather to death through excess or lack. What may pass for a superabundance of concepts has therefore nothing whatever to do with any failure *vis-à-vis* the rules of formation of a theoretical system: it is not a matter of concepts, since even if we could *think* the instances of life and death (for example, in the manner of cyberneticians, the first being the memory which in a homeostatic whole relates the system thrown into disorder by some event to its unit of reference, the second then being something like the loss of this memory, amnesia), since, in spite of these thoughts, we cannot grasp, predict, control, effects, affects, with the help of the thought of instances: therefore very little of the conceptual . . . Freud wants, we want, some ideas which would be in their 'order', that is to say for the scrap of the libidinal skin which they invest, what one solemnly calls the theoretical field!—which would be just as, almost as, impossible as is the effect of the passage of the turning bar described previously.

This effect is not of duality, but of duplicity. In the 'theoretical order' it will be necessary to proceed in this way, like this duplicitous bar, not through an anxiety over mimeticism or *adaequatio*, but because thought is itself libidinal, because what counts is its force (its intensity) and because it is this that it is *necessary* to overlook in words, this interminable worry, this incandescent duplicity. It is therefore necessary that what one thinks can be always assignable to a theoretical ensemble (semantic, formal, it matters little), and shown equally to despair of such an assignation. It is necessary to alter the course of the destiny that pushes thought towards the concept, otherwise one will manufacture a libidinal economy which will resemble a trivial political economy, that is to say an ideology with the pretension to order, incapable of grasping the *duplicity* of the said economic movements. It is necessary to let the alleged theoretical field be swept by the tumult of intensities, even the most difficult to accept 'theoretically'. No-one can say that he will be up to such a task, everyone seeks to flee these intensities and their undecidability in the direction of the system and its binary ideal. It is true that the price to pay for these *ideas* is extraordinarily inflated, and renders the business hardly *profitable*, when it is compared to this rich man's activity which is the labour of the concept, which makes sense of the least scrap of material and whose process of accumulation appears infallible. With the hypothesis (but this is not a hypothesis, evidently, it is not discussed, and one need not wait for the alleged *facts* in order that it be falsified or remain acceptable), with the position of the two instances, one is plunged into fallibility precisely because one thinks without criteria of falsification, because the criterion of true and false is irrelevant to the idea when this latter is an intensely spun top. And one is plunged into the greatest anguish, for really, sirs, radical-socialists of the concept, we are not stupid, we are well aware of what profile can be seen on the horizon of thought as libido, the same scarecrow which you get out of your pockets and wave above your fleshy ears each time that an intensity goes past and we jump, crazy with joy and fear, into its whirl: the scarecrow of *fascism*; the same as the one you were waving in '68 in France, in Germany, in Italy. You don't have to be pushed very hard before you come right out with it: idea-force is fascism. You will always confuse *power and force* [*pouvoir et puissance*], you will always call the violence which threatens your power power-terror.

We know this, we know that between force [*puissance*] and power there is, for crass eyes, a sort of indiscernibility . . . we will not respond to this because we do not enter into dialogue with the radical-socialist concept ('communism' included), having learned that to begin this dialogue is already to concede the essential, that is the position of the concept itself and its consequences of the 'repressive' order. You should raise your soul to the following idea: we are certain, absolutely certain of what we are saying (without this being certainty in the slightest, in the sense that you habitually understand it), and at the same time, at the same instant, completely deprived of all security;—certain, magisterially certain of the points when, as we 'think', the libido attains intensity, because we are educated and refined enough in matters of *jouissance* and pain to have acquired this *pyromaniac* flair; but stripped once and for all of the protection of the concept, thrown out of the sanitary cordon of the thought of systems, and thus fragile like children, suspects, the insane, stupidity awaits us, close to us, drawing us out from it and throwing us into your arms, men of the concept, days when the fire is too intense, when we may fear that in our words and ideas, this is no more than the death drive busy consuming everything, and when we no longer dare to breathe above the surfaces which you would have divided up, frightened to be swept along with it.

The Labyrinth, the Cry

The labyrinth is a flint desert exposed to the Near-Eastern sun, without wall, door, or window, a chalk surface. We recognize its model: a labyrinth which, in his mania for knowledge, one of our professors constructed for the instruction of a wingless insect. Made from an immaculate box, fully lit by an arc-lamp, the white terror which it was supposed to communicate to the beast had to impel it to go all the way through this labyrinth, without error. In this way the acquisition of habits is studied, and the animal's intelligence evaluated by the number of attempts necessary to achieve a faultless crossing. The cut-up box rested on a sheet of water, which also frightened the insect. The beast, expelled from the dark shelter where it was kept, runs in all directions, an almost imperceptible silver thread, terrified. It never learns this labyrinth.

Terror in the labyrinth is such that it precludes the observation and notation of identities: this is why the labyrinth is not a permanent architectural construction, but is immediately formed in the place and at the moment (on what map, according to what calendar?) where there is terror. The labyrinth, then, does not exist, but there are as many labyrinths 'in it' as terrifying emotions, whether or not they are felt. Each encounter gives rise to a frantic voyage towards an outside of suffering. The suppression of this could only result in an identical repetition of the encounter. One flees perhaps to learn, to rediscover the encountered property, because through repeating it one hopes to be able to localize it, to set up its situation, to inscribe it in a time. But since this terror produces its own, singular, labyrinth, there are other corridors, other corners than those which the flight, and the fleer, are able to delineate: that is why the beast learns nothing, it multiplies incomparable labyrinths.

A similar feature justifies the strange behaviour of one of my Italian friends, which he recounted to me while acknowledging his inability to account for it. A researcher, he had left his laboratory very late, exhausted, and he had gone to a reception given by one of his friends, a cultural director in one of the town's big museums. This reception was held in some of the rooms of the museum itself, it was celebrating the museum's renovation and new organization, more appropriate for doing justice to modern artworks; but it also marked the end, for my friend's friend, of the contract by which for several years the town had charged him with the creation and presentation of pictorial, musical and cinematographic activities. When my narrator entered the museum, the crowd of his friend's friends was scattered throughout all the open rooms, which form a closed chain: groups everywhere chat, scream, laugh, ask each other questions, smoke, drink, eat, recognize each other, around the buffets, the two pop groups, the gallons of flowing wine, in armchairs, or sit on the floor. All the faces make it seem that my friend might know them.

His tiredness and his isolation happen, so to speak, to balance each other, alleviated and aggravated. He takes to eating, drinking, without meeting anyone, goes round the circuit of rooms, examines the retrospectives that they exhibit, the years of work; certain works are restored; others are present only in the form of photographic reproductions; but all of them, silent in the tumult, were still there simply in order to bear witness to past activities, like traces before effacement. The rooms diametrically opposite the buffet and the bandstand are almost empty, he flees them, returns to the swollen belly of the crowd, crosses and waves to his friend the curator, drinks again, begins the circuit again, examining the faces as much as the walls, prey to a growing agitation, which he notices nevertheless.

It is on this second circuit that he recognizes on a wall, a face, recently photographed at the time of a Warhol exhibition, in front of the series entitled *Marilyn*. A mediocre *cliché* in black and white, like a line drawing, exaggerating the harshest values. In front of the grid formed by the series of the actress's portraits, themselves just a painted cliché, he is brought to a halt by the face of a woman who, some years previously, had been his mistress; she is turning towards the lens, with affected surprise, her mouth half open, as if the photographer had called to her just when she looked at the picture. The hair, the eyebrows, the make-up on her eyelids and lips are here coal black; the glistening of the irises and pupils is faithfully rendered.

The photograph is pinned up by four drawing pins, amongst others which illustrate the same period of the museum's activity. An old suffering, for which this woman was certainly responsible, loses no time in reawakening, he sets off to lose himself in the crowd, he hopes to find someone he knows. But his circumnavigation of the retrospective leads him back in front of the photo. What to do? He sets off a fourth time, stops for a long while in front of the *Prose du transsibérien* illustrated by Sonia Delaunay, in an almost deserted room, more through discipline than genuine interest, however, preoccupied by the menace emanating from the photograph. He drank again. It is very late, it will soon be closed, groups disperse, the bands are packing up, the guards begin to empty the rooms, starting from the point opposite the great entrance hall, where the *cliché* is, and slowly advancing along the two semicircles which lead there.

My friend finds himself once more in front of the image, still incognito in the anonymous jostling. Taking advantage of the disruption, he prises the pins out with his nails, he places the photo under his jacket, in the hollow of his armpit, and leaves, having stolen it. He gets into his car, and heads towards his home; but he takes the road for the apartment of this woman, whom he hasn't seen since the break-up. The apartment is situated at the top of a large building, which can be reached from the top floor only by means of a spiralling metal staircase hanging over empty space, from which one can see what is happening in the front room. It is lit, he sees silhouetted movement, he slips the photograph under the door, runs quickly down the spiral stair, takes the lift, gets back into his car, and waits with all the lights off. He was followed, he hears his pursuer's footsteps in the humid, deserted street, it is the woman's boyfriend. My friend sets off without knowing if he has been identified. Some weeks later, she calls him up, saying that she doesn't understand what he was doing bringing the photo, waits for an explanation. He feigns astonishment: what photo is she talking about, she knows very well he hasn't any of her? She cannot contradict him.

The hero of this story tells me that he was not aware of what he was doing, but he acknowledges the importance of having felt so possessed by something which dictated his conduct. We know no better than he; but the effect of powerlessness must be remembered. If one wants to eliminate it, the theft and the 'restitution' will be interpreted as significative signs: for example, my friend wants to suppress even the duplicata of a past suffering; and also: in delivering this fac-simile to the woman, he wants to start up with her again. It will then be said: this is ambivalent, that is why it was intense. We seek no why, and judge ambivalence a little platitude.

In the labyrinth of the museum, my friend, the wingless insect, had an encounter. He began the circuit over and again, several times; each time, he loses his way in front of the photo; he learns nothing. He flees the image, but finally takes it with him; the image opens a second labyrinth, that of the town streets, the corridors and staircases of buildings. The second encounter takes place in this other labyrinth which grows disconcertingly from the encounter in the first. The delivery of the photo puts an end to the second labyrinth and to the suffering of which it is the effect, and which was encountered in the first. The ironic denial on the telephone marks the dissolution of the third labyrinth, originating somewhere (perhaps in this woman) from the relocation of the photograph. A fourth labyrinth may then be opened, onto the listener, but no, nothing of the sort happened, it appears. Unless the fact that my friend had told me of this event and that I am publishing it would have to be considered as a third encounter, opening a labyrinth of which I am ignorant even of the material from which it might be made; in any case, none of this can be decided.

No-one has the power to draw up the map of the great film; this, seen from the outside (but it has no outside) would be some kind of monstrous beast whose constitutive parts would change according to unforeseeable modulations, would appear and disappear with the same terrifying ease as virtual images on a screen. It would still be necessary to imagine that the succession and nature of these images were not determined by real images inscribed on the film [*pellicule*] (in a technical sense). More generally, let's imagine that neither the so-called contents nor the technical procedures permit the synthesis into a story, into a doctrine, into a style, of the fragments of the film joined end to end; it would then be impossible to construct a single time to contain and organize the monster of images; even the recurrences suggested by certain schemes would remain ignored, each occurrence would be experienced as a present and innocent effect. And there would be nothing monstrous about this assemblage, which would exist for neither a mind nor an eye.

When my Roman friend passes from one labyrinth to another, he is not moving through a spatio-temporal grid. The labyrinths which for convenience's sake (in the inevitable tribute paid to the order of the reasonable) I called first, second, etc., in no way form an ordered series. They do not belong to a structure of carrying over [*structure de report*]; nothing of the one is rediscovered in the other, at least as long as each is formed as a sort of cyclone around a heart which is the encounter, whose effects he prolongs and which he flees. Each of these mazes is closed, at the same time as it is in undecidable expansion; closed in that it has no crossover point, nor any part in common, with the other terrifying cyclones; as to its expansion, this would be in proportion to the effective force [*puissance d'effet*] of the encounter.

It must not be said that the encounter takes place in the labyrinth; the labyrinth issues from the encounter. There are only encounters, each tracing at full speed around itself a multitude of transparent walls, secret thresholds, open grounds, empty skies in which each encounter flees from itself, overflows itself, is forgotten,—or is repeated, ceasing then to be an encounter. This latter does not return, does not reproduce itself; the insect's terror is unique, new every time; nothing is inscribed; a complete layout of the unconscious needs to be constructed in order to succeed in imputing to it the responsibility for the return of the same; it must be supposed that its effects are subordinated to a system on which identities or—what amounts to the same thing—differences could be identified. The pulsions are stupid exactly to the extent that they do not repeat the same effects, therefore they invent. Invention is a triviality of time.

In 'The Theologians', Borgès imagines two heresies by non-repetition; one is the act of certain sects called Histrions, of whom he writes: 'They reasoned that the world would end when the number of its possibilities was exhausted; since there can be no repetitions, the righteous should eliminate (commit) the most infamous acts, so that these will not soil the future and will hasten the coming of the kingdom of Jesus.' The other heretics, belonging to the diocese of Aurelian, 'affirmed that time does not tolerate repetitions . . . The admonitions of this new doctrine ("Do you want to see what human eyes have never seen? Look at the moon. Do you want to hear what ears have never heard? Listen to the bird's cry. Do you want to touch what hands have never touched? Touch the earth. Verily I say that God must create the world anew.") were much too affected and metaphorical to be transcribed.'[7]

So the labyrinth ceaselessly invents and effaces itself. The first heretics he cites profess and practise the impatience to have done with it; but however much they affirm that nothing repeats itself, if they can hope to precipitate the coming of the promised result in committing (and thus eliminating) the most infamous acts, it is that they think that the quantity of evils is not innumerable and that a backwards count may be taken up somewhere else, at the end of which the truth will be attained; their ethics is an algebra of the primacy of the negative (Jouhandeau would belong to this heresy). But can both the heresy of singularity and the heresy of acceleration be sustained at the same time? Does this latter not require a sort of memory, a catamnesia? But the heresy of singularity must exclude even catamnesia, which supposes that there is an end already assigned to history, and that the future exhausts itself entirely in manoeuvres proper to removing whatever delays this end. These manoeuvres are not perverse since their infamy is at last concentrated [*circonvertie*], into the negative, on the immaculate mystical body of Jesus. Such a theology we say to be as wretched as Hegel's; it remains within the dialectic of good and evil, hardly caricatured and rendered amusing: the *Phenomenology of Mind* has 96 images per second, a 33 rpm record of the *Phaedre* switched to 78.

But that the earth must always be touched for the first time, the moon be seen, the bird be heard, as the other heresy professes, that is harsh in another way. My Italian friend would adhere to this sad innocence, as would my friend the insect: great fears, great loves are not inscriptions on a spatio-temporal register, and continuity or fidelity play no part in them since there is nothing permanent from one encounter to another, only the singular intensity, opening its own labyrinth each time. Always lost, even when we believe we make some sense of it, when, for example, we attribute such an emotion to an underlying support [*suppôt*], to ourselves, to a person.

This does not entail that fidelity or continuity may not give rise to an intense encounter; but this is *as ephemera*. There are labyrinths of continuity just as there are labyrinths of treachery and interruption. Let us endeavour not to subordinate anything to anything else, neither permanence to discontinuity, nor the encounter to reliability. This is the strangest thing.

I see the theology of the Historians, which I said was wretched, as an indirect, vicious subordination of the ephemeral to the permanent. Octave's relation to Roberte, in Klossowski's work, would belong to this subordination. The laws of hospitality permit, through the prostitution of the mistress of the house to her hosts, the measure of her worth in her husband's eyes. Even if this price is priceless, it necessitates an appreciation, an estimation, the reduction of each strong suffering and sensual pleasure onto a standard of measurement.

Let's listen to the pleas of an unfaithful husband: 'The cry', he is saying, 'that lacerates my wife's plexus, which I never cease to love, every time she believes she sees my eyes gaze lovingly at another face, which takes the ground from under her; this cry is what I seek most in the world, like death, the only certainty, it is this to which I have sacrificed and will sacrifice every face, every head of hair, every fissure and fold encountered and touched. My desire is for precisely such a sacrifice, it is that, for this cry, whole populations of cries remain for ever unheard, unfailingly and deliberately, populations of pain and pleasure simply abandoned, from one day to the next. This must suggest that the true libidinal relation of my treachery is not that my beloved wife be sacrificed to my pleasures, but that, on the contrary, my eyes, hands, lips are only laid upon other surfaces and muscles in order that the unbearable pain in her plexus attain the intensity without any equivalent for my body; only to draw these intensities, certainly not small, back towards her plexus in order that they throw her about like a lightning strike, incomparable to any orgasm.'

This is a bad peroration if the litigant leaves it there; it develops the Sadean's position, the proprietor's: priceless implying a comparative calculation. It is also the position of the Histrion heretics: each one of my infamies takes place only to hasten my meeting up again with truth and life, love for my beloved male or female Jesus; I deceive only to gain. But who can say without shame (and without ridicule) that the suffering which he spreads is a means and even a proof of love, and that he maintains power over the direction of intensities? And then, the lightning strike of which the unfaithful one speaks, if he is not a little pimp who can be reassured by procuring, negative ethics and political economy, and who can find in the comparative valuations of pleasures and pains something to stabilize his pitiful ego, this lightning strike not only hits the body of a victim, an exploited body, it is the blind deaf immobile belly of a labyrinth in accelerated expansion, without issue. The zone struck is not just his wife's body, the torment is not only her own, not even both of theirs, it is the product of several pieces of the pulsional film heated to white-hot anonymity.

Borgès tells the story of a duel to the death between two drunken men, rivals in competition; they have never learned to fight; they choose their weapons from their host's armoury by chance, one a dagger with a U-shaped hilt, the other a short-bladed knife whose wooden handle is decorated with a tree; to the witnesses' surprise, the struggle proves to be conducted with a knowing precision, not the indiscriminate butchery that was expected, but a meticulous chess game played on bodies, right up till the final blow. Much later the narrator learns that these weapons from the duel had belonged to two rivals, gauchos famous for their courage and ability to kill; he concluded that it was indeed *they who were fighting*, inspiring their bearers.[8]

The anonymity of these latter does not exclude, but implies their proper names. It would be only with regard to a central instance, that of a great Armourer keeping archives of all the murders committed by his weapons, that of a Pimp keeping books on all the *jouissances* he allots to the prostitute-bodies—that another anonymity would creep into the pulsional band, and that in place of proper names and insane mazes which they signal one could put register numbers, consequently allowing subjects at work to be located: imperceptible, but immense, slipping, from tensorial anonymity to productive prostitutive bureaucratic anonymity.

Add this besides to your first, 'unfaithful' plea: 'My wife's cry is not the effect of any cause, whether the dishonour, incurred from falling from her position as a person, that I subject her to through my infamies, as is the case with a Sadean, an Octave. I am not the producer, the archivist, the knower, of this cry. I do not calculate it. It shrieks over my body at the same time as it does over hers, not only when I say to her: this is how this other woman is in pleasure, not only when on her express will I make her imagine my eyes and my palms stroking fine excited areas, but also moreover at that suspended moment when the glans receives the distant pulsing coming from the depths of the other's womb. Even there it screams of cruelty, and in this violence there is my wife's pain. This presence is not obtained by comparison, trade, the interplay of the price and the priceless, it presupposes no monetary-mnemonic instance, of the general equivalent and the possible rescinder of debts, it is not comparative and written into the accounts-book. How this is possible, I do not know.'

This presence is not therefore that of the same, an instance of neither reference nor difference (be it accelerated by crimes). There is no permanent cry. The permanent is silent because it repeats itself; its abjection and its cop's or political commissioner's intelligence result from its repeating itself. The cry of your torture victim is not *a* cry: she cries every time, her cries open as many labyrinths. If you hear her crying—no, that is not even it: if the cry resonates throughout the labyrinth in which you are lost, it is not because it is at the end, like a perverse result. The problem of jealousy must cease to be posed in terms of exteriority, of triangular formation, of penis-envy and homosexual identification. *There could be a pulsional jealousy*, far simpler, more singular, concerning libidinal economy alone, a jealousy itself dissimulated, for example, in the highly coded jealousy that novelists, psychologists and common sense are acquainted with, that belonging to whatever topic, coming under whatever instance, and ending up of course in political economy, for example, in mercantilism and in all imperialism.

The jealousy of the cry is not, or not only, that of an instance held up to ridicule; it is the relation of every piece of the libidinal band with that piece which desire elects, when they are in affinity. This jealousy is a pulsional call; force investing itself here wrests a cry, an exhalation, from there, nearby, it seizes all surrounding force, it sucks up all surrounding energy. Jealousy is the whistling made by the leap of force [*puissance*] suddenly beating down onto an area (or inventing it); and the labyrinth is formed by its flows (but the centre is ephemeral like the eye of a tornado). The vulva is jealous of the thoroughly kissed mouth, so is the mistress of the book her lover writes, the man of the young man's future, the sun of the closed shutters behind which your imagination lets itself go in adventures of reading. The cry which resounds in your helplessness, unfaithful one, is not your wife's, nor yours, it's true: it is the noise made on the band by the incompossibility of several co-present intensities. The ancient gods were jealous of each other; this Olympus full of their cries, it is the great film (a little simplified) turning and returning on itself following its labyrinths like a monster attacked in several places at once.

There is no intensity without a cry and without a labyrinth. The force which strikes a given surface of the great skin (that is to say which invents it) exhausts its surroundings by making it scream, and opens the maze of its flows. If infidelity makes the infidel cry as it does the man or woman to whom he is related, it is because their bodies, fragments of their bodies, never cease haunting the areas surrounding the points on which force [*puissance*] beats down. Your body itself, unfaithful one, is jealous of the intensities which your infidelity brings it, it too cries from the energy taken from it, and if it cries at the same time as your lover, it is because they belong to the same pulsional surroundings.

It is necessary to hear the cry of the insect thrown under the glare of 500 watts, and fleeing into the maze. Every labyrinth is traced as flight towards an outlet. There is no outlet: either one grows accustomed to it, as the professor waited for the beast to do, the way of being accustomed that is depression and inhibition; or else through an encounter, in a new cry, another labyrinth, another time opens up, but nobody is the master of encounters. Love is not giving what one does not have; it is having to cry near to areas struck by lightning.

My examples are of suffering; they could have been of elation. There are labyrinths of joy, the latter no less mad than suffering, very close to it. Around the armchair from the *Marriage of Figaro*, Beaumarchais traces some dazzling mazes, where pieces of bodies expelled from their shelters flee and get lost, but by laughing. Joy is constructive, concentratory; it is an elevation around a supreme addressee, but incredulous and insolent joy is the laughter of metamorphoses that awaits no-one's recognition and enjoys only its ductility. It is a horizontal laugh, without assent. But, you say, the encounter in joy engenders no line of flight, on the contrary, it seeks to maintain itself, doesn't it produce the very permanence you detest?—No, flight is not only from terror, it is not me, you, underlying agents (*des suppôts*), who flee, it is intensity which loses itself in its own movement of expansion. Imagine the universe in expansion: does it flee from terror or explode with joy? Undecidable. So it is for the emotions, these polyvalent labyrinths to which, only after the event, the semiologists and psychologists will try to attribute some sense.

—So you thereby challenge Spinozist or Nietzschean ethics, which separate movements of being-more from those of being-less, of action and reaction?—Yes, let us dread to see the reappearance of a whole morality or politics under the cover of these dichotomies, their sages, their militants, their tribunals and their prisons. Where there is intensity, there is a labyrinth, and to fix the meaning of the passage, of suffering or of joy, is the business of consciousnesses and their directors. It is enough for us that the bar turns in order that unpredictable spirals stream out, it is enough for us that it slows down and stops in order to engender representation and clear thought. Not good and bad intensities, then, but intensity or its decompression. And as has been said and will be said again, both dissimulated together, meaning [*sens*] hidden in emotion, vertigo in reason. Therefore no morality at all, rather a theatrics; no politics, rather a conspiracy.

We do not speak as the liberators of desire: idiots with their little fraternities, their Fourieresque fantasies, their policy-holder's expectations over the libido. We have nothing to do any more with regilding the heraldry of the *tragic*. The tragic still necessarily presupposes the great Zero, prison guard of destinies, mute allocutor, Jewish god, or enigmatic locutor, Greek oracle. What does the unfaithful one seek in his peregrinations? What he betrays, or what he encounters? He necessarily betrays what he encounters, and necessarily encounters what he betrays. Hence his joy and terror are intermixed, a vertigo which sweeps away the signposts and the directions of the movement, which destroys the landmarks, the egos. It is not the tragedy of a destiny, nor the comedy of a character (it can be presented in this way, of course); no longer the drama of totalization; rather the strangeness of fictive spaces, Escher's waterfalls whose point of impact is higher than their source.

Notes

1 St Augustine, *City of God*, tr. Henry Bettenson (Harmondsworth: Penguin, 1972), Bk VI, ch. 9, p.246.

2 ibid., p.244.

3 *Acéphalie*: the Acephallus, from a drawing by André Masson, was taken up by Georges Bataille, to some extent as an answer to the Nietzschean problematic of the Overman and the Death of God: 'The acephalic man mythologically expresses sovereignty committed to destruction and the death of God, and in this the identification with the headless man merges and melds with the identification of the superhuman, which IS entirely "the death of God".' See Georges Bataille, 'Propositions', in *Visions of Excess*, tr. Allan Stoekl, Carl R. Lovitt and Donald M. Leslie (Manchester: Manchester University Press, 1985), pp. 199–200.—*tn*

4 Sigmund Freud, *Jenseits des Lustprinzips*, tr. James Strachey as 'Beyond the Pleasure Principle', in the *Standard Edition*, ed. James Strachey (London. Hogarth Press, 1933–74; hereafter cited as *SE*), Vol. 18, pp. 49 ff.

5 Sigmund Freud, *Die Verneinung*, tr. James Strachey as 'Negation', in the *SE*, Vol. 19, pp. 235–9.

6 Sigmund Freud, 'New Introductory Lectures in Psychoanalysis', Lecture 32, in the *SE*, Vol. 22, p.110.

7 Jorge Luis Borgès, 'The Theologians', in *Labyrinths* (Harmondsworth: Penguin, 1970), pp. 154–5.

8 Jorge Luis Borgès, 'The Meeting', in *The Aleph* (London: Picador, 1973), pp. 103–13.

2
The Tensor

Semiotic Sign

Let's take up this business of signs once more, you have not understood, you have remained rationalists, semioticians, Westerners, let's emphasize it again, it is the road towards *libidinal currency* that must be opened up by force. What the semioticians maintain as a hypothesis beneath their discourse is that the *thing* of which they speak may always be treated as a sign; and this sign in its turn is indeed thought within the network of concepts belonging to the theory of communication, it is 'what replaces something for someone' says Peirce, repeats Lévi-Strauss, which means that the thing is posited as a message, that is, as a medium enriched with a sequence of coded elements, and that its addressee, himself in possession of this code, is capable, through decoding the message, of retrieving the *information* that the sender meant him to receive.

Immediately then, *ex hypothesi*, the thing is hollowed out, becomes a *substitute*: it replaces the 'information' for that someone who is the addressee. This replacement, of course, may be conceived in two ways, according to two very different lines of thought. One could say that the sign replaces what it signifies (the message replaces the information), this is, to put it as brutally as possible, the Platonism of the theory of Ideas, for example: the sign at the same time screens and calls up what it announces and conceals. This has all been said before by Port-Royal. Or we may think this substitution, no longer metaphorically, but according to the interminable metonymy that Saussure or whatever other political economist may conceive under the name of exchange; it is no longer signification (what is encoded), then, which the sign substitutes—this trick is invented: that signification itself is constituted by signs alone, that it carries on endlessly, that we never have anything but references, that signification is always deferred, meaning is never present in flesh and blood. We are filled with compassion for good old Husserl, we say: no, there are only differences, and if there is meaning it is because there is a sign, and if there is a sign it is because there is difference, not just any difference, one never passes haphazardly from one element to another, on the contrary, there is an organized voyage from one term to another, and extreme systematic or structural precision, and underneath it all, ultimately, if we have religious souls like Freud or Lacan, we produce the image of a great signifier, for ever completely absent, whose only presence is absentification, reserve and relief of the terms which make signs of it—substitutes for each other,—the image of a great zero which keeps these terms *disjunct*, and which we will translate into libidinal economy under the name, unpronounceable of course, of Kastrator.

See what you have done: the material is immediately annihilated. Where there is a message, there is no material. Adorno said this admirably of Schoenberg: the material, he explained, in serialism does not count as such, but only as a relation between terms. And in Boulez there will be nothing but relations, not only between pitches, but also between intensities, timbres, durations. Dematerialization. Here a long examination is necessary: is this dematerialization the equivalent of what capital does in matters of sensibility and affect? Is it also simply an abstraction of pieces of the pulsional band, its dissection [*découpage*] into comparable and countable parts? Or is it, under *cover*, and as a result, of this squaring off, indiscernibly, an opportunity for a refinement and an intensification of the passages of affects? And if this is the case, then is this 'dematerialization' not, in the same space and time, the cartography of a *material* voyage, of new regions of sonorous, but also chromatic, sculptural, political, erotic, linguistic space, being, as a result of the *mise en signes*, conquered and crossed by the trails of influxes, offering the libido new opportunities for intensification, the fabrication of signs through 'dematerialization' providing material for the extension of tensors?

We are sufficiently convinced that this latter hypothesis is the right one, but first let us pursue the description of some notable effects of the *mise en signe* in its own field.

Not only is the material commuted into a sign-term, but also the 'thing' which the sign replaces is itself another sign, there is nothing but signs. First consequence: the relation is therefore an infinite postponement, and thus sets up recurrence as a fundamental trait of the system, the reiteration of the *postponement of the signifier* guaranteeing that one will always need to work to determine the terms to which, in a given *corpus*, the term under examination can and must lead. The other consequence is that with the sign begins the *search*. This might have been the search for God, for signification, when the *metaphorical* organization of the signifier predominates. For we moderns, for whom the thought of this metaphor is absent, and who glory in substructural metonymic substitution, the object of the search is no longer God or truth, but the search *itself*, scientific research is not to be made a search for causes, we are well aware that this is not a good concept, but a search for 'effects' in the scientific sense, the search for a discourse that can produce locatable, predictable and controllable metamorphoses, a search, then, for discrimination. There is no sign or thought of the sign which is not about power and for power. The voyage of this search is not the drift of the mad and the plague-stricken, nor the transpatial exodus of the uncanny, it is the well-prepared flight of the explorer, foreshadowing that of the priest, then the soldier and the businessman, it is the avant-garde of capital, which is itself already simply capital insofar as it is the perpetual activity of pushing back its frontiers, the incorporation of yet more new pieces of the band into its system, but incorporation with a view to revenue, to yielding a return. The sign goes with this business trip, and the business trip creates the sign: what is an African for a British explorer, what is a Japanese for an eighteenth-century Jesuit? Organs and partial drives to be reabsorbed into the normal organic body of so-called Humanity or Creation. Materials to dematerialize and to *make signify*. Do you really believe, say the white thinkers, that the Nôh actor, moving forward with his feet together, sliding over the stage floor as though he were not moving at all, means nothing? It is a sign, it is in the place of something else, there is a code, and the addressees know it, or in any case, even if it is unconscious, it exists, and we semiologists, Jesuits, Stanleys, conquerors, we will only have triumphed when we are in possession of this code and are able to *remake* it, *simulate* it—the model of all semiology is not *The Purloined Letter*, it is *The Gold-Bug*. These Africans, these Orientals, being dead, leave messages of treasures, we simulate them in codes. Lévi-Strauss: I want to be the language spoken by myths.

And thus, with this voyage of conquest which could not but have been inspired by the *mise en signe* (unless it is the opposite, a certain sort of voyage inspiring the *mise en signe*, but we are hardly partial to these futile questions of priority, all that is a gross package of little assemblages bearing on that thing, that material, that person—it is a *dispositif* where everything works in pairs), thus along with this voyage of research and conquest, where the latter is always postponed, comes, indissociably, an intention, an intention to forge a relation, an intention to yield a revenue. To rediscover the code of signs, *for power*, power as cause, power as aim. Every risk is taken, going to cohabit with the cannibals, being stationed at a frontier post, the microbes, radiations, all the deaths incurred, all the sins like the Jesuit in the *Supplément au voyage de Bougainville*, but taken intentionally, and so divisively. Not the zone and the moment of the strained tensors, but the zone crossed, moment of a movement, therefore the tensions and their attendant risks and pains *paid for* in the hope of an ulterior gain, perceived and experienced as *loss*, as concessions necessary for health, progress, knowledge, enlightenment, socialism; the thorn-torn rags of wasted flesh are inessential, the important thing being the *final revenue*, what will be gained from it, as all those holiday-making wage earners will testify, as will their bosses, the rich and their masters: that is to bring back the images, photos, films, words, the prestige, tourism of the return, retourism, a series of explorations, and always the same itinerary. Here we encounter the question of interest, for tourism, or conquest, is interesting-interested insofar as the *expenditures*, not only those of equipment and maintenance, but also *affective expenditures* which are eventually very heavy, like Caesar at the Rubicon, are nothing more than *advances*, insofar, then, as desire is lost only the better to be recovered.

But we must emphasize that it will not be recovered, but will be recovered there, where is it? nowhere other than in the accounts-book, in the open, booklike, space-time as a result of the intention of the *mise en signe*. It will not be recovered since there is only postponement and difference, and since there is never any question of desire and its proper modality in the constitution of signs: semiology as the preamble to all the sciences ignoring, as they all do, the desire that it itself fulfils. Another consequence then: with the sign, if we have intention and postponement, we have also the opening up of diachrony, which is only a drawing-out of the tense of the compact immobile tensor into an *always past* and a *still to come*, an *even now* and a *not yet*, into the game of de-presence, the very game of semiotic nihilism. How does signification stand in relation to its signs?

Before them since they are but its by-products; always behind them since their decoding is endless. In this apparently senseless pursuit, the constitution of meaning, however, there will be some hermeneut or pessimist who will say to us: look, we never *have* meaning, it escapes us, it transcends us, it teaches us our finitude and our death,—so, while the edifying pastor tells us this, his soldiers and his businessmen collect organs, pulsions, pieces of the film, stock-pile, capitalize them. And the time we 'know so well', 'secondary' time according to Freud, the *a priori* form according to Kant, the Bergsonian–Husserlian–Augustinian conscious unfolding, is fabricated in the double game of this despair and this hoarding, despair of lost-postponed meaning, of the treasure of signs which are simply 'experiences' happened upon, run through, the Odyssey.

Already with Ulysses the *thing* which the sign replaces has itself become a sign; look at Ulysses with Nausicaa and see what sort of *love* the Westerner can manage in his pathetic *conqueror's* machismo; women to him are like Negroes and Chinese, a challenge, success guaranteed, one moment in the hoarding, an unexpendable exteriority in an endless process of the *mise en signe*, of the accumulation of things-become-signs in systems. We, we desired that Ulysses does not return, we cried with Nausicaa, we said to her: you have been too Greek, neither submission nor domination were necessary, but to be side by side, only then could he have gone *astray*, and have been rendered incapable of obtaining and registering his yield. But, she responded, is it even possible not to enter the masculine Greek capitalist game of domination? To be side by side, said the beautiful princess, is not to be alongside, but to be inside and nevertheless indissociably in the margins. Was it up to me to save this asshole anyway? In wanting me to save him, you are acting on my behalf, as he has done, you subordinate me to your plans, of course you no longer want his return and revenue, you want his 'perdition'—but in your eyes that would be his salvation, and so I would remain his slave, his moment, his springboard, and you would henceforth retain me within a dialectic. To desire that Nausicaa 'lose' Ulysses, she is correct, is to remain Western, it is the sign again, barely displaced; after all there are explorers who become Negroes, pagan priests, Polynesian Jesuits, mutineers on the *Bounty*—do you really believe that the salvation-intention is less urgent for these people than it is for their City masters, Rome and the Royal Navy? Less urgent with our friend Jaulin than with his master-enemy Lévi-Strauss? There remains something *saved* in these ruinous voyages, the intention in quests for intensity. You don't get rid of return and revenue through departure and export. Here, friends, let us be alert to duplicity and cultivate it.

One further consequence for the informational constitution of the sign: there is someone for whom the message *replaces* the thing signified, there is a subject (two subjects), that is to say an instance to which all the predicates, all the postponements of meaning, all the events experienced and toured, are related. This someone is something that will expand in proportion to the *experience* accumulated (experience, remember what Hegel said, where the subject will never stop saying that he is forever dying, oh hero, oh Ego!), to the extent that events, tensors, passages of intensity, find themselves split into signs—and then these signs, it is the 'receiver', the addressee who will assure their stock-piling and ownership, and he will say: look, I have been to Egypt, look, I have navigated between Charybdis and Scylla, look, I have heard the sirens, look, I left my dwelling for the wilderness, and he will say, all these, these emotions, are messages that I have heard, I must understand them, they speak to me, it has spoken, who is the sender? The I is constituted in this relation of the sign as both addressee (what Kant calls *Sinnlichkeit, Rezeptivität*) and the decoder and inventor of codes (intellect, *Selbsttätigkeit*, autonomy). Receptivity is here only the indispensable, constitutive moment of autoactivity. The I is first of all an ego, but it will become *itself* through *construing* what it or the other says (since it is not there). The same 'dialectic' of the intense and the intentional splits things experienced, it splits the ego constitutively, it is its constitution, receptive/active, sensible/intelligent, donee/donor—all this counting only, we repeat, in the configuration of the sign, part passivity, part activity, part message received, part decoding intelligence, part meaning, part understanding, part emotional opacity, part intentional capacity; and even Husserl with all his intentionality must inject passivity into his meditation, the passive synthesis. And, of course, it will be merely a moment in the construction of intentionality, oh the pretty movement of the jaw by which the head grasps meanings, takes them up, oh formation of capital, gracious game of sublation.

Two more things on semiotics. It thinks in concepts. This is because the sign is itself nothing but the concept. Not only in its stable static constitution of the term whose connotation and denotation are assignable only through being put into regulated relations with other terms, through groups of allegedly well-formed propositions in a clarified formal system; but also in its conceptual dynamism, it is the sign as conquest, for the concept *works*, like the sign, it is frenetic, it seeks borders, its frontiers, it advances on its exteriorities, it touches them and just as it touches them, they cease being exteriorities, it never attains them, and at the same time this allows it to marvel at the force of the negative, oh stupid imperialism dressed up as tragic labourism, oh the hilarious 'labour of the concept'! —Right, it is the same self-styled 'labour' with the sign: it is not so simple as you make out, you say to us, the metonymic relation between terms is not only endless, it is constantly breached, crossed, by other chains, Freud taught us this, and in the event each term is a crossroads of several routes, a vertigo, and their interlacing is a text or texture where not one but several meanings are woven together, each one pulling the term towards itself, and that is the labour of the sign. Oh exquisite polysemia, tiny rift of the well-informed, little, recalcitrant disorder, sugared deconstruction. Don't even hope to catch the libidinal in these nets.

One last point, which has already been made a thousand times: semiotics is nihilism. Religious science *par excellence*. Consult the Victorins of the twelfth century for a fine example of semiotics, the attempt at reading Creation in its details, at understanding the givens as messages in order to make a code of them; and already this refinement: Hugo and Richard de Saint-Victor know that they are not and will never be *in possession* of the code; thus with this refinement they already love that aspect of things which denies them the code, they love the negative of the code in the message, they value the labour of this negative, the text, the *dissimilitude* of things, and find beauty in it. It is a religious science because it is haunted by the hypothesis that someone speaks to us in these givens and, at the same time, that its language, its competence, or in any case its performative capacity transcends us: the very definition of the unconscious we find in the boldest semioticians, Lacan, Eco. Thus the sign is enmeshed in nihilism, nihilism proceeds by signs; to continue to remain in semiotic thought is to languish in religious melancholy and to subordinate every intense emotion to a lack and every force to a finitude.

Dissimulation

We know your objection, semioticians: whatever you do or think, you tell us, you make a sign of your action and reflection, you cannot do otherwise, due to the simple perspective it provides on the referential axis of your action-discourse, hollowed out into a two-faced thing, meaning-ful/meaningless, intelligible/sensible, manifest/hidden, in front/behind; whenever you speak, you tell us, you excavate a theatre in things.

Fair enough, we don't deny it, we've been through it and go through it all the time, it is in no way a matter of determining a new domain, another field, a *beyond representation* which would be immune to the effects of theatricality, not at all, we are well aware that you are just waiting for us to do this, to be so 'stupid' (but such an error does not warrant this name, we will soon reclaim stupidity) which amounts to saying: we quit signs, we enter the extra-semiotic order of tensors. We are well aware that were we to say this we would entirely fulfil your desire, for it would be so easy for the first semiotician to come along to recover our alleged exteriority with the little African imperialist labour of exploration, of ethnology, the mission, the trading post, the pacification of the colony. We are well aware that this is the fate you gleefully prepare for our libidinal economy, just like that which capital prepares for the workers' demands, Whites for *coloured people*, adults for children, the normal for the mad, 'men' for 'women'. Very intimidating. *Everything* at present is played out here, it is here we must fight, trace out our route, not the frontiers of our empire, but our lines of flight as Deleuze says.[1]

We must first grasp this: signs are not only terms, stages, set in relation and made explicit in a trail of conquest; they *can also* be, indissociably, singular and vain intensities in exodus.

Is it a question of another kind of sign? Not at all, *they are the same* as those turned into theory and textual practice by the semiotician. The first thing to avoid, comrades, is pretending that we are situated elsewhere. We evacuate nothing, we stay in the same place, we occupy the terrain of signs, we merely say: ritual death for the Guayaki, you interpret it as the compensation for an exchange between the living and the dead designed to keep world-wide equilibrium intact, which you then make into a sign referring to other signs in the general structure in Guayaki culture—we *understand it otherwise*. It speaks to you? It sets us in motion. Marcel's father climbs the stairs with his lamp: you see in his son's excitement the meaning-effect of the Oedipal structure, we seek to carry them on towards the construction of other things, texts, images, sounds, politics, caresses, and if possible, just *as productive of movement* as Proust's text. And when I say '*as* productive', it is badly put, for it is not a matter of quantity; it must be understood as the singular quality of this text giving rise to prolongations, ramifications, the invention of new libidinal fragments which no other object could have engendered. First, therefore, a different reaction, a different reception. We do not suppose, to begin with, that the signs, in this case Proust's text and that of Clastres, transport messages that are communicable in principle. We do not start off saying to ourselves: there is someone or something that *speaks* to us, I must understand them. To understand, to be intelligent, is not our overriding passion. We hope rather to be set in motion. Consequently our passion would sooner be the dance, as Nietzsche wanted and as Cage and Cunningham want. (And you must immediately understand that here, on this methodological point, there will be the worst difficulties, the greatest mistakes, we will have hoards of false dancers wanting to call themselves our friends, in the first place, and then there will be censors who will explain to us, as if we didn't already know, that in order to dance we must first hear; but we answer that by saying that it is not the same thing to dance by transit and to listen in order to understand; and finally at this very point we will have taxing analysts, who will say to us: oh yes, you extol the *transition to the act*, that is what they call dance, you perform *actings-out* in order to avoid *workings-in*; alas, these will be the most difficult to subvert.)

A dance, then, not composed and notated, but on the contrary, one in which the body's gesture would be, with the music, its timbre, its pitch, intensity and duration, and with the words (dancers are also singers), at each point in a unique relation, becoming at every moment an emotional event, as in Cage's *Theatre Piece*, as in the execution of a piece of Nôh theatre by an actor inspired by Zeami's *Flower of Interpretation*. One could remain still for a long time, inert, waiting for the moment of this flower, this encounter, this *tuchè* where something is set alight on what is called the body, and this waiting must also be loved, just as beautiful, this immobility, just as changing and motive as the fracturing-unfolding of the play of the graceful pale hands and their violence when they are beaten against the tambourine in the Korean courtly dance called *Yu Ch'o Shin*.

For there is also the something we seek in a face in a Montparnasse night, in a voice on the telephone, something about to happen, a wavering or a direct tone of voice, a silence, a fixedness, an eruption; but that doesn't come. And this, far from evoking resentment or disgust, this reserve is loved with the most demanding impatience.

A dance includes suspense, as music includes silence. And the important thing not being whether it is 'well composed' (it must, however, be well composed), but that in the event of this semiotic perfection there is tension. That the structure be merely something that 'covers' the affect, in the sense that it acts as a cover: that it is its secret and almost its dissimulation. This is why we must dearly love the semioticians, the structuralists, our enemies, they are our accomplices, in their light lies our obscurity. Here, were I composing, a eulogy to dissimulation would be grafted on.

Let us be content to recognize in dissimulation all that we have been seeking, difference within identity, the chance event within the foresight of composition, passion within reason—between each, so absolutely foreign to each other, the strictest unity: dissimulation. Thus the Antichrist preaching in the square painted by Signorelli in an Orvieto fresco is exactly like Christ, so it is true that Christ *dissimulates* the Antichrist in the sense that he conceals his fearsome mission from the latter in his speeches, and when he says 'Love one another', it would take very little for the most disastrous misunderstanding to ensue (and in fact it does); and the Antichrist too dissimulates Christ in so far as he simulates the latter, as close to him as makes no difference, this being the *'dis-'* of dissimulation, or dissimulation. Our reception of the sign dissimulates its semiotic reception, which also dissimulates ours, although not in the same way, without necessitating that one judge there to be an Antichrist, and which one he is.

But understand this, to change references, that the two principles, Eros and death, of Freud's final pulsional theory (*Jenseits*, 1920), are not two instances each endowed with a distinct functional principle allowing their identification from their respective effects or symptoms in the 'psyche' or on the body. It is not the case that Eros is the producer of wholes, systems, compositor or master-binder, and that the death drives *on the other hand* are the destroyers of systems, the deconstructors, the unbinders. When, on the hysteric's body, fragments of the great band are circumscribed and excluded from the regulated circulation of affects, placed outside normal intensity, 'anaesthetized', when the muscles contract and remain taut, the respiratory tracts are choked, provoking asthma, these are little pulsional *dispositifs* (a fragment of the organic respiratory system, a piece of the organic system of striated or smooth musculature) which form totally self-dependent wholes: will it be said that it is Eros, insofar as he is the maker of wholes, who is responsible for this? Or rather death, because these wholes are jammed? But jammed in relation to what, to which normality? Dora the organic's respiratory system is jammed, Dora the hysteric's respiratory system works wonderfully, and there is no need to seek a *secondary benefit* for her troubles. The benefit is immediate, there is no benefit, there is a pulsional machinery put in place, which functions *on its own account*, and this machinery does not work according to death or according to Eros, but according to both, erotic as a regulated machine (a machine upon which discourse will try to produce a reasonable simulacrum in Freud and Lacan's texts), lethal as a deregulatory machine (which the analyst wants to repair)—but also mortal as regulated (because it condemns Dora to a sterile repetition), and alive because of its deregulation (because it attests to the fact that the libido circulates and invests over the organic body, in its unpredictable displaceability).

There are two principles then, and these principles are not instances identifiable according to their respective functions, Eros being capable of unbinding and setting free, death binding to the point of being a strangler, and Freud himself, who didn't see this clearly, nevertheless recognized it at the end of *Jenseits* when he says in the space of a few lines first that the pleasure principle is subordinated to the death drives: it is then that he understands these latter as a system of compulsions to repeat which want to bring *everything* back, even the most painful things, like the dreams in traumatic neuroses, and that it is necessary to suppose a binding through repetition prior to all discharge if it is true that this requires channels of facilitation and specific actions in order to produce satisfaction;—and, a little later, that the Nirvana principle is subordinated to the pleasure principle, here understanding by 'Nirvana' this excess of force which forces the discharge beyond the metabolic rule to which the 'psychical apparatus' (or the body) is subjugated, and which threatens to make this latter explode. In each unique event the functions are undecidable; it is always a question of retaining the possibility that it may not be possible to assign an affect, that is, *simply a sign*, to one pulsional principle and one alone. And it is clear that it is not then a question of *polysemia*, not of overdetermination, this cannot be maintained by saying 'Death will add its effects to those of Eros', or vice versa; it is not a question of the fact that the sign, Dora's cough, is caught up in *several networks* or structures producing meaning.

It is quite clearly a question of the fact that the sign is on the one hand caught in these networks, thus localizable in metonymic systems (still, often with Freud himself, in metaphoric systems) each differing from the others, that it is heterosemic or heterological and consequently subject to semiotics—but *furthermore, Jenseits*, that it is not assignable to a specific function nor therefore to the play of its effects of meaning, nor to any other, that it is indissociably a sign of referral and through referral, but without an assignable referral. At the same time a sign which produces meaning through difference and opposition, and a sign producing intensity through force [*puissance*] and singularity. Libidinal intensity; we are almost tempted (but we will not do this, we have become sly old foxes, too often trapped) to give it a priority, and to say: in the last instance, if you, semiologists, have any cause to set up your nets of meaning, it is *primarily because* there is this positive incandescence, because first of all it is Dora's throat which seizes up, because there is, in short, a given, and this given is indeed the intensification of a particular region of the beautiful Dora's body, it is this region indeed which has become an intelligent-intelligible sign! But we are not even saying this, we are indifferent to priorities and causalities, these forms of guilt, as Freud and Nietzsche said. Order matters little, what is, however, of great importance is the fact that this same symptom has inevitably two simultaneously possible receptions.

Is there any need to mention the hilarious perspectives opened up by this idea of dissimulation in matters of theoretical discourse especially, and also in this business (blandly taken on these days under the label of Freudo-Marxism) of the dialectic of theory and practice?

Intensity, the Name

Were it necessary to give an example of the way in which the tensor can dissimilate itself in semantics and dissimulate this latter, we could take that of the proper name. It is primarily of this name that Frege and Russell speak, which poses the logician a problem since it refers in principle to a single reference and does not appear to be exchangeable against other terms in the logico-linguistic structure: there is no intra-systemic equivalent of the proper name, it points towards the outside like a deictic, it has no connotation, or it is interminable. A small difficulty which the logicians resolve with a concept (having no choice of means), that of the predicate of existence. Hegel already knew this: the *Meinen*, and the obstacle that the gift of existence, flesh and bones, as Husserl will say in turn, can oppose to any systematization of signs. So, to whomsoever asks, 'What about Flechsig?' we will reply:[2] there exists at least one individual such that he can be named Flechsig, he is Schreber's doctor—thereby keeping within the reference as if it were an anchoring. But the name of this same individual gives rise to a *dividuation* when it is gripped by Schreber's delirium. It will render compatible a multitude of incompossible propositions concerning the same 'subject' of the statement. Of the predicate 'Flechsig', it will be possible to say simultaneously that he is a cop, that he is God, that he is a lover seduced by Schreber's feminine charms, that he does everything he can to prevent the president from shitting, that he is a member of a noble family of long standing which was involved with Schreber's family. What makes this a delirium? Simply the fact that it is stated.

It is the same delirium that a writer, barely more prudent for having interposed a subject of the statement between himself and his text, called Marcel, the same delirium as over the proper name of Albertine.[3]

It is the same delirium as that of Octave over the proper name of Roberte,[4] the deputy-whore, the virtuous libertine, the undefinable offered-refused body, dissimulatory body *par excellence* because a dissimulation in two senses: on the one hand the Huguenot and reveller can take on the function of the sign in the equally thinkable networks of respectability and sensuality; but on the other, each of these assignations dissimulating something, not the other as such, insofar as it belongs for its part to a regulated, apparently regulated network of respectability, simply displaced, the MP being as thinkable as the whore each according to their own order—no, each assignation dissimulating the sign as tensor, and not the other sensible sign, and the tensor sign in that the proper name of Roberte covers an area where the two 'orders' (two orders at least, there must be more) are not two, but indiscernible, where the name of *Roberte* is like a disjunctive bar turning at high speed around some point or other—the gaze, the vulvar slit, the gloved thumb, an intonation—and displacing itself in an aleatory fashion on the segment which forms this bar. If Roberte is a tensor, it is not because she is both a slut and a thinker, but because she exceeds, *jenseits, both these assignations* in the vertigo of an intensity where, if the inside face of the thigh is exposed at the edge of the skirt, if the flesh of the thumb strains towards the seducer's mouth, if the nape twists under his teeth, it is certainly because of an authentic prudery and a sincere sensuality, but this is beyond reason's capacity to explain, because of a pulsional figure according to which influxes which do not belong to Roberte, or to anyone else, are disposed of and drain away. Roberte is not someone's name (predicate of existence), even if this were to be double, it is the name of this unnameable, the name of Yes and No, and of both the first and the second, and if the proper name is a good example of the tensorial sign, it is not because its singular designation creates difficulties when one thinks in concepts, but because it covers a region of libidinal space open to the undefinability of energetic influxes, a region in flames.

The same goes for Schreber. If we stick to the *Memoirs of My Nervous Illness* we can see the vertigo which is localized, as it were, on the name of

Flechsig. I must, Schreber thinks, become a woman so that God may impregnate me and so, by giving birth to new men, accomplish, through me, the salvation of humanity. This change of sex is a miracle; but every modification of the body is a miracle in Schreber's eyes and must be imputed to a unique force [*puissance*], or in any case to the remarkable decisiveness of a force [*puissance*] (this marking Schreber's religion out as being quite Roman, closely related to the penetration of divine instances into the most 'quotidian', the simplest, acts, of this secularization of the sacred or sacrilization of the secular). And so for defecation: it will provide matter for dissimulation, this will apply to Flechsig (dissimulated through God); and if we may describe these continual ambivalences of the fates of the pulsion, the important thing is that there remain no less indiscernibility of incompossibles at every instant, giving and retaining shit, Flechsig protector and executioner, God lover and prosecutor, my body man and woman, my divine and my human self; and still something *more* besides.

Defecation is not natural, but miraculous. In this case, in this *miracle of shitting*, which Freud cites in its entirety, we see what delirium can accumulate under only one name. If defecation requires the miraculous intervention of a 'One' who is both Flechsig and God at the same time, what is this the *sign* of? Of the love that *one* has for Schreber, of the assistance that one* lends him? No; or rather yes, but very indirectly. This compassionate love is only alluded to in the President's discourse, and it appears inverted. If Flechsig-God miraculates defecation, and denies Schreber's body the natural use of this function, it is strictly speaking in order to facilitate the *demiraculation in extremis* of the act of shitting, and thereby to persecute the President: they send people into the toilets before him to take up all the seats. In this way, they cut short the 'generation of an extremely intense feeling of *spiritual voluptuousness*' which accompanies successful defecation. And if they use him thus, it is because such *jouissance threatens* Flechsig-God, in that it enslaves them to the President's body, as is the case with every strong *jouissance*. An example: 'God would never take any steps towards effecting a withdrawal . . . , but would quietly and permanently yield to my powers of attraction, if it were possible for me always to be playing the part of a woman lying in my own amorous embraces, always to be casting my looks upon female forms, always to be gazing at pictures of women, and so on.'[5] It is not therefore through love

---

*Although clumsy, and apart from Lyotard's emphasis of it, I have retained the impersonal pronoun in accordance with Schreber's use.—*tn*

that one miraculates Schreberian defecation, but in order to defend oneself against the seduction it exerts. Flechsig lover, but on the defensive. But Flechsig persecutor, also false, who, asking Schreber 'Why don't you shit?', provokes him to answer: 'Because I am so stupid or something.'[6] Flechsig humiliating his victim. Then again, stupid Flechsig-God, incapable of understanding that a human creature has no need of the miraculating intervention of an All-Powerful in order to defecate: 'The pen almost shrinks from recording so monumental a piece of absurdity as that God, blinded by His ignorance of human nature, can positively go to such lengths as to suppose that there can exist a man too stupid to do what every animal can do—too stupid to be able to shit.'[7]

Don't all these contrary properties simply form a polysemia around the name of Flechsig? We shall see. But before that two remarks that announce what is to come. First: observe the immensity of this stupidity, which extends far beyond Bataille's bestiality, since the latter continues to know what he is doing, even if consciousness no longer knows, and this is the whole *acephallic* secret of minor eroticism, whereas with Schreber we must flounder about in the swamp of an uncertainty that fashions the instincts themselves, montages of the beast, that we are on this side of what animal acephalia knows, that the 'body' no longer knows how to shit when it 'needs' to, that the shit is unaware of its route towards the exit. Incredible stupidity of the mad body, into which Flechsig will plunge Schreber. As opposed to the organic body, montage of montages, functional assemblage, erotic enlightenment, this libidinal body appears to have no established channels for the circulation and discharge of impulsions. Not the profundity of stupidity, but immensity, absence of measure. *Libidinal stupidity* is something quite different from Bouvard and Pécuchet's stupidity, which consists in reciting, quoting once more by dipping into the *common fund* of statements, and this is very nearly the same thing, since, like it, it rests on the destruction of the subject capable of answering for its words and deeds, it rests on the loss of identity (signalled in Flaubert by the duo that constitutes the stupid hero).[8] Stupidity inseparable from the dissimulation of which we here speak.

Second remark: this stupidity turns up again in the strange notion of femininity implied by Schreber's text, quoted above; it is 'there is' woman rather than being a woman, this *'there is [y avoir]'* being indifferently translated by: behave like the woman in coitus and also *behave like this woman's man* ('playing the part of a woman lying in my own sexual embraces'), to see woman, to see the woman-image—and further doubt-lessly: be the woman seen, etc. Once again the stupid immensity of the libidinal band. To the proper name of Flechsig, tensor *par excellence*, corresponds the becoming anonymous of Schreber's body—a body without regulated organic functions, a sexless or multi-sexed body. Shall we now say that this name 'Flechsig' is only the predicate of several statements which imply that, under it, incompossible pulsions are activated together? *Flechsig loves me*, since he makes me shit-come; *Flechsig hates me* since he forbids me to shit-come; *I love it that Flechsig should hate me* because my own persecution is necessary in order that I may accomplish the salvation of future humanity; *I hate it that Flechsig loves me*, for I would like defecation to be as natural for me as it is for others . . .

Let us now interrupt the enumeration of these, already simplified, statements. Let's ignore the reading that Freud makes of Schreber's relation to Flechsig: it is an exemplary semiotic and conceptual reading, because it turns all these statements and several more besides, into terminal phrases resulting from transformations bearing on a single nucleus which would be: *I (a man) love him (him, a man)*[9]. Transformations due, as in the unfolding of the phantasy *A Child Is Being Beaten*,[10] to pulsional displacements through repression or regression, therefore implying a use, hardly generative, of course, but nevertheless perfectly regulated-regulatory, of negation.

Let us rather discuss the following point: do our statements (be they four or *n* in number, whatever; who would dare claim to exhaust their potential series?) really give rise to what we seek under the name of dissimulation? Do they not rather provide a polysemia; on the one hand, a homonymy, Flechsig the lover being the homonym of Flechsig the executioner; on the other hand, synonymy, Flechsig lover and executioner being the synonym for God (synonymous group to which Freud will not hesitate to add the Father)—so many relations which are well known and will be accepted by the semiologist, not at all as objections, but as encouragements for his method. Everything leads us to these transformations, it is true, through which we hardly get anywhere near libidinal economy. If Flechsig, like our previous example Roberte, is a tensor sign, and not merely 'meaningful', it is not through the polysemia of statements which are attached to her name, it is through the vertigo of anal eroticism which grips the libidinal Schreberian body of which the name of Flechsig is the extension. Vertigo because here once again, around the anus, the revolution of the disjunctive bar will become furious to the point that the President's arse will pass into solar incandescence, to the specific point where facilitating or forbidding the passage of matter (of the faeces or the divine member) will become henceforth undecidable, both movements being invested and triggered off together: 'It is brought about by my faeces being forced forwards (and sometimes backwards again) in my intestines; and if . . . enough material is not present . . . '[11] and that in this constant struggle between constipation and diarrhoea, between hetero- and homosexuality, between virility and femininity, it is the position of the sun, of the gods, of the doctors, of the men, which begins to turn around itself forbidding every stable distribution and all 'thought'. This incandescent vertigo bears the name of Flechsig, and it is in this way that it counts as a tensor sign.

It extends the spinning-top game beyond Schreber's organic body, into unexpected regions of the libidinal band; this name grasps them or rather brings them into existence at a stroke, like pieces of the vast *anonymous* erectile maniac labyrinth, ah, so you thought you were a doctor working on restoring my solar anus to the pathetic proportions of pre-genital Oedipal regression; by saying Flechsig, by building my metaphysical and historical novel on Flechsig, putting Flechsig at the beginning and at the end of my loves and hates, I make you, doctor, not into a piece in my paranoiacs' game, as you think, but into an unpredictable scrap of the immense band where anonymous influxes circulate. Your name is the guarantee of anonymity, the guarantee that these pulsions *belong to no one*, that no one, not even the 'doctor', is sheltered from their course and their investment. This is what you fear and why you lock me up. What is woven under the name of Flechsig is not then just the wise polysemia found in the most anodyne of statements, it is the incandescence of a piece of the body which can have no further assignations, for it invests both the for and against, and furthermore, it is the transmission of this unthinkable burning to other libidinal regions, notably here the languages of history and religion, their invention and capture in the anal vertigo, their sexualiza-tion, as we were saying, their plugging into the mad anus, the extension of the latter to the former. And so it is the alleged frontier of Schreber's body which finds itself violated by the name of Flechsig (just as much as the alleged frontier of the body of Flechsig). This limit itself is pulverized by the vertiginous rotation, the President's body is undone and its pieces are projected across libidinal space, mingling with other pieces in an inextrica-ble patchwork. The head is now simply any fragment at all of the skin. Flechsig my arse. Beyond synonymy and homonymy, anonymity.

'Use Me'

What if this proper name were the *pimp*? That is to say God. Let's read Schreber again: 'It was mentioned in previous chapters that those rays (God's nerves) which were attracted, followed only reluctantly, because it meant losing their own existence and therefore went against their instinct of self-preservation. Therefore one continually tried to stop the attraction, in other words to break free again from my nerves. . . . Always the main idea behind them was to 'forsake' me, that is to say to abandon me; at the time I am now discussing it was thought that this could be achieved by unmanning me and allowing my body to be prostituted, like that of a female harlot, sometimes also by killing me and, later, by destroying my reason (making me delirious).'[12] And Schreber adds, like a real 'whore': ' . . . with regard to the efforts to unman me it was soon found that the gradual filling of my body with nerves of voluptuousness (female nerves) had exactly the reverse effect, because the resulting so-called 'soul-voluptuousness' in my body had rather increased the force of attraction.'[13] Like a true whore, or rather swept along by the force [*puissance*] of dependence?

First, however, *who* wants this scandal, this feminization?

> It was, moreover, perfectly natural that from the human standpoint (which was the one by which at that time I was still chiefly governed) I should regard Professor Flechsig or his soul as my only true enemy—at a later date there was also the von W. soul, about which I shall have more to say presently—and that I should look upon God Almighty as my natural ally. I merely fancied that He was in great straits as regards Professor Flechsig, and consequently felt myself bound to support Him by every conceivable means, even to the length of sacrificing myself. It was not until very much later that the idea forced itself upon my mind that God Himself had played the part of accomplice, if not of instigator, in the plot whereby my soul was to be murdered and my body used like a strumpet.[14]

The prostitute accepts prostitution in the name of a superior interest. She wants it, and is thus very much the same as a martyr: she testifies through her humiliation, Magdalene as Jesus. She begins by testifying *against* her saviour. The dissociation of the two instances is still far too naïve: in terms of affects, it is God to whose eyes suffering is exposed and to whose heart it is offered; in terms of political economy, it is the pimp, here Flechsig, Herod, or Pilate, who makes money from this suffering, drawing a profit from it and thus ignoring it as such. Then in retrospect (while writing the

Memoirs: 'I may say, in fact, that this idea has in part become clearly conscious to me only in the course of writing the present work'),[15] the two names, Flechsig and God, are condensed, the court of appeal proves to be just as criminal, or even more so than the agent of the crime. Then the pimp-God-doctor takes on his full libidinal dimension: the terrestrial order, says Schreber, is truly violated by this project of my transformation into a woman (into a prostitute), there is no court of appeal, God is also my prosecutor, he is not the upright judge who receives my pain, he is the pimp who necessitates and profits from it, and consequently, he both reveals and exploits it in the duplicity of pain-*jouissance*.

Schreber is protesting here, and we must see in his struggle to leave the hospitals in which *they* confine him, the same fight that a whore may wage to escape the environment and the brothel or the crossroads where one confines her. But this protestation has its own ambivalence. For, as we have seen, Schreber desires to be God's prostitute, to come as a woman and to make him come, if not as his (male) lover, then at least as his master. This is why he wants to be *all women and all women all the time*, and the 'endlessly', the 'continually', which in his hands serve to define the condition which according to him is that of the Flechsig-God's *jouissance*, that *there was always woman*, this is the poor creature's effort to measure up to divine omnitemporality: 'Even when I lived alone in my studio', says Xavière Lafont, 'the telephone would ring day and night, checking on my whereabouts . . . They [the pimps] have all the time they need to search for you, even in America if they so wished.' And even when she had left her profession, 'I was often wakened by telephone calls in the middle of the night . . . No-one on the other end. Only the rasp of breath, and then he hung up.'[16]

In the formation of this ambivalence which confuses God and the pimp, God and Flechsig, 'punishment' is a decisive element; Schreber calls it persecution. It is nevertheless identical to what Xavière endures: being locked up, put into a state of dependency, the clinic as the law of the milieu. Here Xavière is exactly right:

> Punishment is still the means of making a human being accept the unaccept-able. But it is also the sado-masochistic bond which ends up making you suffer 'something' for your clients. This something has no name. It is beyond love and hate, beyond feelings, a savage joy, mixed with shame, the joy of submitting to and withstanding the blow, of belonging to someone, and feeling oneself freed from liberty. This must exist in all women, in all couples, to a lesser degree or unconsciously. I wouldn't really know how to explain it. It is a drug, it's like

having the impression that one is living one's life several times over all at once, with an incredible intensity. The pimps themselves, inflicting these punishments, experience this 'something', I am sure of it.

This something without a name, why then give it the name of sadomasochism as she suggests? We are right at the heart of dissimulation. If Flechsig is the name of *vertigo*, the pimp or the community of pimps is so too. What succumbs to punishment, with regard to this vertigo, is the illusion of the self: 'They have succeeded, since I now only existed through them.'

But of course, as in the dear old dialectic of the master and the slave, this extreme dependency may be manipulated by 'the woman' as a weapon against the dominator. In love, this may be manifest in the feminine orgasm which pulls the body towards blinding confusion; thus Schreber wants to be more of a woman and a prostitute, and consequently always more mad, more 'dead', in order the better to seduce Flechsig and God. Is this then intention rather than intensity? And right where we thought we found with Xavière the *force*, the force of *powerlessness* [*impouvoir*] ('I did not say that I regret this life. But you will always fail to understand this. It is like cocaine. Such intensity could never be found in normal life'), does this not provide a place of *power* and connive with every weakness? Assuredly. But this is no reason to erase the basic thing; intensity is dissimulated in signs and instances. If the proper name is pimp or God, it is also the occasion of this 'unnameable' something. If the self succumbs to dependency, it is not merely according to the petty comings and goings of the preoccupations of power.

In the dead of night, in the utter exhaustion of palms and expressions, penis and vulva in rags, the earth indiscriminately scorched, this order may yet issue from the depths of a woman's hoarsened throat: 'Use me', and this means: There is no me. Prostitution is the political aspect of dependency, but it also has a libidinal position besides. This is what Sade overlooked. The question of 'passivity' is not the question of slavery, the question of dependency not the plea to be dominated. There is no dialectic of the slave, neither Hegel's nor the dialectic of the hysteric according to Lacan, both presupposing the *permutation of roles on the inside of a space of domination*. This is all macho bullshit. 'Use me' tends towards the direction of the erect member above the loins, the illusion of power, of the relation of domination. But something else altogether happens in these loins, so much more important, the chance of the abolition of a *centre*, of a *head*.

When the man, Flechsig, the pimp, employs this manifest 'demand' to 'use' to become a head himself, to become power—he becomes defensive, he does not dare listen to the impact of the offer and follow it up. The passion of passivity which stimulates this offer is not *one single* force, a resource of force in a battle, it is force [*puissance*] itself, liquidating all stases which here and there block the passages of intensity. It would be wrong to think that the spread buttocks, the anus and the anal passage offered by the woman bent double, as though foraging, is some kind of challenge in the nature of a potlach—'Here's what I've got for you, let's see what you've got for me.' This offer is the opening of the libidinal band, and it is this opening, this instantaneous extension and invention that the power-broker, the pimp, and the politician refuse themselves. They are content to use every petty trick in order to capitalize on libidinal intensities in the interests of surplus-value: the over-exploitation of the force of *jouissance*, lapsing into slimy Chinese speculations. For this interest, this third party intercession, are doubtless also true of the erotic intelligence. Unless one is constrained to wonder, just as one must concerning the baroque machinery which connects Schreber's body to Flechsig's, whether the erotic consists in shutting down, hoarding, indeed capitalizing on force, as the abundant suggestions we come across in Chinese texts, or in *Les Liaisons dangereuses*, testify; or if, throwing intelligence into the stakes, incorporating 'ice' into the energetic pathways, that is to say the burning tension of calculation, having no other function than to *intensify* neglected regions and passages; and not intensification by means of the counterpoint of *secondarity*, calculation, the other space-time, the other body, contrasted or alternated with primacy, but through the heightening of intensities, through the *incorporation of the head* into the libidinal band, by setting the capital and capitalist machines to work for the benefit of pulsional circulations, through the eroticization of the understanding. Imagine the little businessman or the little accountant placing his base arts in the service of his glands.

So, Sade's stupidity which Klossowski, even in 'Le Philosophe scélérat',[17] is unable to shake off. At least the stupidity of a Sade. There is another Sade, who is Spinoza and Lucretius, the Sade of 'Français, encore un effort pour être républicains', a libidinal materialist, the one we here desire and desire to sustain.

'Use me' is an order and a supplication, imperious supplicant—but what she demands is the abolition of the I/You relation (which is, like the master/slave, reversible) and also the use-relation, of course. This supplicant would appear to be pure religiosity insofar as she demands dependence. Isn't this what Jesus Christ said on the cross? But Jesus can demand dependence *because* he offers his body in payment for the sinners: the exorbitance of his suffering, of his abandonment, the terrible Schreberian *demiraculation* that he endures, the relinquishment perpetrated and fulfilled by he who is loved and who is thus all-powerful—this exorbitance, Jesus sets it as the price for the redemption of sinners. Jesus is consequently a calculating prostitute. You have me die, this is wrongdoing, but through this the whole world will be saved: the perverts or cretins ('they know not what they do') will be redeemed in the gracious body of creation, that is to say, of capital. And God is a pimp, saying to Jesus, his woman, as he says to Schreber: do this for me, do it for them. Would you say he wins Jesus over? And I answer: he wins a prostitute, who sells the most unexpected parts of his body, his looks, his sartorial skills, his shoes, and does he win Schreber? This is not the question. The prostitute, like Jesus and Schreber, invents herself and poses as a subject through the calculation, even if it is pure phantasy which she imposes, and which suffices to *convert perversion* to concentrate it. And don't forget that, like Jesus and God as well, the prostitute is of course her client, but she is also his procurer. The mystery of the Trinity which is that of Similitude is the very machinery which produces the meaningful sign and dissimulates the tensor sign. Once again, don't let yourself be taken in.

'Use me': a statement of vertiginous simplicity, it is not mystical, but materialist. Let me be your surface and your tissues, you may be my orifices and my palms and my membranes, we could lose ourselves, leave the power and the squalid justification of the dialectic of redemption, we will be dead. And not: let me die by your hand, as Masoch said. Here lies the wreckage of the supreme ruse, voluntary or involuntary, so that this ultimate order, emanating from the body already exhausted by caresses and insomnia, resurges in the howl of unleashed partial drives, the subject-function. Hegelian gloss of the supplicant: be my master, your will be done. This is how Sade, Freud and Bataille understand it, introducing politics even here, and therefore order all over again, strategy, the rationality of war, Laclos and Clausewitz.

But what does she want, she who asks this, in the exasperation and aridity of every piece of her body, the woman-orchestra? Does she want to become her master's mistress and so forth, do you think? Come on! She wants you to die with her, she desires that the exclusive limits be pushed back, sweeping across all the tissues, the immense tactility, the tact of whatever closes up on itself without becoming a box, and of whatever ceaselessly extends beyond itself without becoming a conquest. In the face of this, the self-obsessed mediocrity of he-men(!) who snigger while thinking they are unmasking and exploiting the hysteric or the woman and her alleged lie, a mediocrity similar to the politicians, written in the note which Lenin sent by courier through the corridors of the Winter Palace to Trotsky (we are not exaggerating at all): 'What if the White Guards kill you and me? Will Svyerdlov and Bukharin be able to manage?',[18] the words of a middleman, best described by Xavière again: 'At first, you take them for 'bon vivants'. They are well dressed, often slightly effeminate. They are not necessarily homosexuals, but you feel that they could be. In any case they are not great lovers. They always go about in groups.' For they require an organization, those village perverts, as Deleuze and Guattari (themselves) say.

'What does a woman want?' asked Freud. She wants the man to become neither man nor woman, that he no longer age at all, that she and he, different people, be identical in the insane connections of every tissue. 'It would be more in keeping with the realization of desire, in the afterlife, that one be there finally delivered from sexual difference', writes Schreber, citing Mignon's song in *Wilhelm Meíster: 'Und jene himmlischen Gestalten/Sie fragen nicht nach Mann und Weib* [And these celestial figures, They no longer ask whether one is man or woman].' And so this will that everything flare up and catch fire is called the death drive by the thinkers, of course(!), those who think only, in the name of life, of collecting, uniting, capital-izing, conquering, extending, closing up and dominating. The Greeks Lenin and Trotsky, pederasts who go about in groups, prostituting the women-masses. But included in their infamous proper names as directors, the insane petition of the masses, which is not 'Long live the Social!' (and still less 'Long live the Organization!'), but 'Long live the libidinal!'

Simulacrum and Phantasm

With the proper name and its dissimulation, we approach one of the epicentres of the Klossowskian problematic, present in his reading of Nietzsche, of Fourier, of Sade, in his philosophy of writing, of narration, of politics; Klossowski himself draws attention to this epicentre in 'Protase et apodose':[19] 'We come then to the meaning of the simulacrum (in the interpretation which St Augustine gives to this term, according to Varro's *theologica theatrica*), taken up again by me in *Le Bain de Diane* and *Le Cercle vicieux*, in relation to the phantasm (*Wahnbild* and *Trugbild*).'

First of all, what is the simulacrum, in Augustine's polemic against Roman paganism? What is at stake under the name of simulacrum is the very position of the sign which we have just criticized, its theological stock. In *The City of God*, Augustine takes as his adversary and as the representative of Roman paganism, Varro the theologian, the grammarian, philologist, rhetorician, and will attempt to turn him into an accomplice. Varro distinguishes three theologies: one natural, discursive, philosophical, which Augustine means to recover and save; another mythic, theatrical, gestural, poetic (these are his words); and finally a civil or civic, political theology. Augustine's strategy consists in dissociating the two latter from the former, presenting the last two as infamous parodies of the first one, the only honest one, for these parodies sanction not only circus games, but the political game as a circus. And facing this parodic politics, he will set up a natural politics, a philosophical politics, a divine citizenship. Subsequently he must therefore extract politics from the theatrical, show that everything which rests on theatricality, representation, is to be rejected in imperial politics, with the motive that 'we cannot ask or hope for eternal life from the gods of poetry and the theatre, the gods of the games and the plays.'[20] (And why not? Why should the criterion of eternal life be pertinent to theological and political matters? And is there not an eternity in the intense instant of a circus game? Is death not included in *jouissance?*)

Thus Augustine sets up a theatre, he circumscribes an inside and an outside which in fact, in Roman public life, were not separate—at least we are going to phantasize them in this way—which are even non-existent as opposed terms, if, as Varro says, it is true that the theatrical is only the mirror of the political, as the political is for the natural, if there is a non-degenerating equivalence between the two and if it is ruled out that the transcendence of the 'natural divine' could be set up as such. Let's take our interpretative phantasy further: natural theology is philosophical; the principal site of investment here is language. What is natural theology? The libido inventing unheard-of statements, adding supplicative phrases to the pulsional band, prayers, apologias, reflexive metaphysics. Strange work in the flesh of words, where the term *nature*, since the Stoics, occupies a conspicuous place, an arbitrary term if it is a term at all, the idea of an autonomy, but enveloping and penetrating everything, not an outside over there to be regained by ridding oneself of a false immanence here, but on the contrary a force [*puissance*] immanent to all things and as such never dissociable. In consequence, both civil and theatrical theology turn out to be sanctioned by this natural theology: the first of these two signifies that the libido invests its energies of life and death on the space of the city, and that it first circumscribes this space, and still earlier that it *invents* additions to the labyrinthine band who would be 'politicians', a whole imagination of the *civitas* or the *politeía*, of the equality of men within it, the position of women, of slaves, children on its peripheries, and also the invention of new statements once again, rhetorical and not philosophical. It is not, however, a question of this invention being less noble, that is, discredited, with regard to the natural. The political and the natural for the Stoic and Sceptic religion of these Romans are not hierarchized, there is nothing less neo-Platonic than these warrior-erotician-banker-philosophers. It is the same for the theology of poetry and mythology, it is no longer a question of their being discredited, since this theology attests to the fact that other investments in language are still possible, those which produce statements which in Plato and Augustine are (down)classed as imaginary or fantastic, under the pretext that these propositions which create tales, epics, dramas, lyrics, novels, are not 'true'. (And the ghettoization of art and artists begins here, in *The Republic*, and not therefore only with the bourgeoisie.) And under its theatrical, gestural form (which Augustine particularly studies), this production of gods is an invention not only of new words and syntaxes, but also of spatial and sonorous arrangements, it is not exclusively inscribed in languages, but also in movements of the body, being provided with actions, costumes, masks, musical instruments, buildings, that is to say these elements are the most materially arbitrary, the most libidinally efficient.

In consequence this Roman theatre, this theatricality of the circus and the political assembly, far from implying the Platonic division of the cave, which is effectively the theatrical division between a real outside and an inside *simulating* this outside (to simplify), rests on the contrary on the conviction that *everything is a sign or a mark, but that nothing is marked or signified*, that in this sense, signs are signs of nothing, not in the sense that they refer to a zero which would be what causes them to signify, but in the precise sense in which we have spoken of tensor signs: each thing and part-thing being on the one hand a term in a network of significations which are unremitting metonymic referrals, and indiscernibly, on the other hand, a strained singularity, an instantaneous, ephemeral concentration of force.

It is this wise affirmative madness which Augustine wants to destroy in the interests of nihilist wisdom, the present intensity is not only devalued, but almost obliterated, where the concept of conscious time, ceaselessly referring the event from instance to instance in the to-ing and fro-ing of the future and past, will demand that the entire network of absences be hung on a Presence, on a Present omnitemporally real, but itself absent, where with this tissue of referrals the semiotic machine is henceforth in position ready to close every intensity up in a sign, as a value standing for something absent.

This is where the Augustinian thesis of the simulacrum takes up its position, the thesis of generalized Similitude, that is to say the basis of every semiotics, or at least every metaphorics: everything is what it is because each thing resembles another thing, and given this there must be a Resemblance, a *Similitudo*, by participation in which all similar things are similar. Augustine calls this *métochè* the Word: the son a perfect imitation of the father, representing what the latter engenders in such a complete and thorough manner that the son is what he imitates while remaining quite distinct from the father, the mystery of duality within unity which is the same as the enigma of the sign. The son or word is the *Simulacrum in itself* if it is true that the image or simulacrum relationship between the two terms has to be one not only of *similitudo*, but of engenderment: the son, exactly like the father is also what emanates from him. All things are therefore in a relation of resemblance if they are not all images of one another; and of course a hierarchy of things is established which depends on the contents of the *similitudo* (and correlatively those of the *dissimilitudo*) in their interrelations. And if the father-son relation gives the resemblance itself which the whole inferior hierarchy, to its lowest depths, will participate in, on the contrary, there must be the least resemblance, the most dissimilar, the dis-simulated and the dis-similated; and since nothing exists but through similitude, nothing which is not a simulacrum, the absolutely dissimilar would be nothingness.[21] The last being, if it is not nothingness, is at least an illusory simulacrum. This is the body: '*Vos quidem*', says Augustine,[22] *nisi aliqua unitas contineret (corpus), nihil essetis, sed rursus si vos essetis ipsa veritas, corpora non essetis.*' So if there is a corporeal unity, it is almost by paralogism: the unity of the body can only be infinitely precarious, and, as far as the general theory of the simulacrum is concerned, false. (Its precariousness pleases us, its 'falsity' has no other meaning for us than that it situates this thesis of simulacra as a pathetic theory of truth.)

In this hierarchy of similitude, the theatricality of nihilist representation is set up. The *truth* of a being, since we must speak in this way, taken as a sign, turns out to be situated *outside* the sign, and even, since Augustine conceives of the sign under the category of the metaphor, *above* it. This being *signifies something other* than what it is: it signifies that of which it is the simulacrum, but, because it is not what it signifies, it also signifies the distance which keeps them apart, dissimilitude, the lack of being (*manque d'être*) which separates them. (This is why the Victorins, and the whole hermetic tradition before them, can say that ugliness, which attests to this separation, is precisely what does most honour to the divine.) Nihilism in its entirety stands here: meaning deferred, and lack slips into this deferral. There is the same construction in Hegel: between one formation (*Gestaltung*) and another, an identity-alterity split, other names for resemblance-dissimilitude, and in the *Aufhebung*, consciousness of their indissociability. The trinitary theme is given straightaway in Graeco-Christian thought. Thereafter, there are only variations of the above. Look, for example, at Augustinian trinitarism as he makes it plain in the *De trinitate* (XI, 8, 14), where it states: '*Sensus accipit speciem ab eo corpore quod sentimus, et a sensu memoria, a memoria vero acies cogitantis*',[23], and compare it with the 'Young-Hegelian' reflection found in the 1803–4 manuscript, where the master dialectician writes: 'Colour in its three Potentialities: in sensation, as the determinacy of *blue* for example, and then as a concept, as it is related to the other [colours] as opposed to these colours, equal to them, [therefore, colour consists] in that colours are colours and thereby exist in a simple and universal manner as colour.'[24] Thus: 1st, *this blue*, as a singularity = the Augustinian *sensus*; 2nd, *blue as such*, as opposed to red as such, as oppositional reference to the other names = *memoria*; 3rd, *colour as such*, the meta-unity of the blue, the red, etc. = Augustine's *acies*.

The thing stands for something else, and it is *less* than what it represents. In order that it be what it is, there has been a lack of being. What is given to us, insofar as it is not similitude itself, is *deficient in force* [*puissance*]. The theatricality of representation implies this deficiency, this depression. It is in and through this deficiency that the figure of alienation comes about. E. dí Negri[25] retraces the genealogy of this term: Paul wrote of the incarnation that Christ 'was utterly crushed by taking on a servile image' (Philippians 2: 6–7); *ékénôsén*, says the Greek, rendered by the Vulgate as *exinanivit*, 'drained away, worn out'. It is through Luther, who translated: '*hat sich selbs geeussert*' ('Jesus was taken outside himself') that Hegel receives this nihilist tradition, and will transmit it to Marx and the politicians under the name of alienation.

It is just the same for whomever the metonymic sign is offered to. What is given to me *through* the sign is exactly what has been rejected, and it will be constituted as the collection of the memories of signs to be signified and of anticipations of the signification to be made manifest as signs. It will form its semiological being in the fusion of two nothings, past and future. This semiological being called consciousness will thereby produce what is called temporality, on the basis of the nihilism constitutive of the sign: 'The death which the soul must conquer is not so much the one death which puts an end to life, as the death which the soul ceaselessly experiences for as long as it is alive in time.'[26] Absent subject, dead life, signification lacking, signs marks of incompleteness, negative temporality, death as deliverance, the transfer of true life to an elsewhere: semiotic metaphysics with all its ins and outs; and nihilist theology. It is on and with this generalized lack that the great Signifier is constructed, the great God, also absent, but alleged principle of all presence and signification. Master of signs and their ek-sistence, amen. Do you see how love of linguistics, love of psychoanalysis, and their conjugation is able to register the least rupture by reference to this theology? Don't you see rather that they are rejections or resurgences of this theology? of the *same* theology, of the same disappearance of the pulsional body in a discourse of denial?

On the other hand, there is the phantasm in Klossowski's sense of the word. Not the little *mise en scène*, the *day-dream* or the *Traum*; not the little story one tells oneself, or which even tells itself (for example in the hysterical attack, the scenario); and neither is it the matrix that directs—as Freud understands them, both are, once again, substitutes for something else, there to replace the *satisfaction* of a forbidden desire, to be a vicarious stand-in for an impossible libidinal meaning, and like any semiological sign, are built from lack. What Klossowski understands by the name *phantasm* would indeed be better conceived, as Klossowski himself suggests, as an object *fabricated* out of pulsional force turned away from its 'normal' use, as a generator; unless it is a matter of the 'perverse' phantasm which is set up in Sade's work (and also in Klossowski's). Let's leave the question raised by this 'turning-away' for the moment, in which, it is plain, we will recognize the same nihilism we have just denounced in the theory of the simulacrum, and therefore the persistence in Klossowski, and doubtless also in Sade, under the idea of perversion, of a theology of dissimilitude belonging necessarily to the Augustinian theology of *Similitudo*. Let's leave this discussion for a moment, remarking beforehand that the suggested position of the phantasm, which makes of it something like a manufactured object, a product the 'consumption'[27] of which would be the voluptuous emotion itself, is, in this regard at least, fully affirmative: the pieces of the postured body which produce pulsional force and which are vainly consumed as intensities of *jouissance*, are then conceived as *substitutes for nothing*, they are those very things engendered by the impulsion by means of its intensification and circulation, are pieces 'invented' and added as a patchwork to the libidinal band. And just as it is then necessary, if we maintain the *analogy* suggested in *La Monnaie vivante* between the phantasmatic and production, to conceive the latter under the same category as perpetual metamorphosis, so we will conclude that there are no more *objects* or *subjects* in the perpetual transformation of libidinal energies than there are in that of all possible energies in the heart of the so-called production process in the wider sense. We certainly lay no claim to such an analysis, and Klossowski is far from being completely won over by it; but it has, at least, the advantage of making modern minds, convinced of the positivity of political economy, imagine what the positivity of libidinal economy might be. The phantasm here is not an unreality or a dereality, it is 'something' which grips the crazy turbulence of the libido, something it invents as an incandescent object, and which it instantaneously adds to the band traced by its trajectory. Just like a *product*, all things being equal. And under these conditions, there is no justification—still on condition that the Sadean-Klossowskian theme of the turning-away of forces is ignored—in searching for a truth of this 'object'-phantasm *outside* it, instantiating its signification on a great Signifier. Strictly speaking its signification is quite simply not in *question*. (But we know that one cannot sustain this, we know . . .)

Since there is no semiotic nor any intelligent sign without the most rudimentary memory, the 'semiotic' of intensities which Klossowski draws out at the end of *Nietzsche et le cercle vicieux* always involves an amnesia. (There again, of course, in the very word 'amnesia', it will not be difficult to spot, in what it includes of the negative, the recurrence of a secret reference to a body that remembers, to an organic body. Is it our fault if we are required, line after line, patiently (and uselessly), to dissociate what belongs to the understanding from what belongs to intensity?) Thus, says the *Baphomet*, 'memory is the domain (of the creator), mine is my self forgetting in those who are reborn in me'. And even this proper name of

Baphomet, 'one cannot remember it as long as one is still coming back to oneself'.[28] Proper name of the return, which is not coming back to oneself, but rather the aleatory and instantaneous trajectory, not even *over* a libidinal body pre-existing this trajectory, but forming pieces of this body, *lost* at the very moment it is formed. This is why the Baphomet can say: 'I am not a creator who enslaves being to what he creates, what he creates to a single self, and this self to a single body . . . I am not a master who reaps, as He does, what he has not sown.'[29]

That one is, with this strange 'semiotic', indeed closer to the evanescent labyrinthine band traced by intensities, Klossowski demonstrates by forging the phantasy of the interpenetration or immediate invasion of 'intentions' by one another in minds deprived of bodies, and it will not be hard to understand that this body of which the 'breaths' are deprived is precisely the dull, odious, inept organic body of the *habeas corpus*, of having and memory:

> As soon as one pointed out anything whatsoever, beginning with the fact of being able to do without the body, one changed oneself in changing each 'interlocutor': one changed oneself in the sense that he who expresses himself bodilessly immediately passes into the thing expressed; and at the same time one changed the one whom one was addressing, in the sense that he who receives the expression of a thing that he nevertheless already knows and sees inside himself, experiences in this very understanding the way of seeing of the one addressing it to him . . . For as their bodies no longer imposed any limits on their respective intentions, they mutually invaded each other.'[30]

The question of violence, then, is posed with a quite new simplicity, it is displaced into an indifferent and tender cruelty:

> Yet what can we say of the violence of one breath towards another? Can the latter condemn the first for having destroyed its fragile habitation, when it should be free of all need to remain the same? . . . Relieved of the need to remain the same, the victims' breaths merge with the victimizers once they see them coming. The latter seem not to know the shame of seeing themselves thus welcomed by the others. No accusations or regrets on either side, and no forgiveness . . . There is no moral atonement here, and such could hardly be required. A violence of another order is born of our condition: it is effected by means of a total indifference. It is this indifference itself: and it leaves no trace, which is the worst form of violence![31]

The suppression of memorable and mnesiac bodies permits the interpenetration of intentions, that is to say their abolition for the benefit of anonymous intensities, for which there remains no instance to *answer* and to *limit*.

This indifference, which has nothing to do with being cold, is that of the fire which burns everything inflammable. Like the bar turning on itself, it leaves no trace, if it is true that the great skin is never given in its entirety and that in this sense there is no world, no body, no *inscription* because there is no assignable site of inscription. Only punctual incandescences, without instantiation. This is what we see: the same palm which an instant ago was gliding over the material covering the breasts and brushing the pale surfaces of the pronators, now so tense it might burst, sweeps down in several brusque slaps between the legs, onto the vulva. This is what we see: the person doing the beating is the first surprise. This is what we see: the thrashed surfaces curl up, the fingers previously in abandon between the legs, still moist from the juices of the slit, forming a lattice before the eyes to protect them so that they may continue to see. We see fear everywhere, before the absurdity of this event, we will come to comprehend that between this phantasy of a supreme indifference by excess of interpenetration on the one hand, and the rather Sadean theory of the phantasm on the other, there must exist a kind of hesitation, and perhaps incompatibility. There is as much indifferent invasion of intensities inscribed necessarily in an eternal turn where identities, and previously therefore proper corporeal volumes, are lost, as there are on the contrary required by the phantasm, just like an industrial product in the universe of appropriation and reserve. The emotion capable of arousing the phantasm and in which it is consumed does not in any way issue from the immediate, violent and anonymous, ephemeral interpenetration of breaths, that is to say from libidinal impulsions; on the contrary, it results and grows from the existence of *a body*, that of the 'victim', on the surface of which the irritating manoeuvres of the perversion will set up affluxes of disorder and whose disarray and relinquishment will return, in the form of a voluptuous flux, to assail the surfaces of the body of the 'executioner'.

If, as has been divined, the phantasm retains its force of the turning-away of energies far from reputedly natural ends, if it does so only insofar as it presupposes and maintains a reference to a unity, this is what intensifies voluptuousness, not through the loss of identities, but only through their transgression. Perversion, says Klossowski commenting on Sade, is what is 'proper to the decomposition of what the term of sexuality embraces in a generic manner, that is on the one hand, as the voluptuous emotion prior to the specific act of procreation, and on the other hand as the specific instinct of procreation, two propensities whose confusion founds the unity of the individual proper to his reproduction'.[32] Here we clearly see everything that may remain of the Christian and the nihilist in a solely criminal philosophy: that intensity issues from the decomposition of sexuality held to be naturally or divinely propagative, we must conclude that it is only in regard to this natural or this divine, in short to the absent body of the signifier, that it exists. Almost all of Sade, once again, is to be added to a file, beginning with the use of blasphemy that he recommends to intensify *jouissance* and which clearly shows the role that God continues to play in its formation. The Klossowskian phantasm, on the other hand, wants, *somewhere, at least one body* to transgress: for it consists precisely in a *fragmentary* use of the body of the victim, where the act of exceeding its reproductive finality will be an occasion for voluptuousness, when a particular fragment of its surface will be, so to speak, removed from the total volume. There would be no belief in God; that would already have to be called sacrilege. Every treatment of a spherical volume as if it were a finite surface is blasphemous. When, instead of helping the male member to engage with its vaginal refuge, the palm constrains it to circumscribe and to stroke an armpit, a buttock, an ear—blasphemy. But such indeed is the phantasm for Klossowski: not, of course, a substitute for an impossible 'reality', as Freud understands it, but the cutting-out from the other's body of a fraction of its surfaces, and the annexation of this to the body of the phantasizing subject.

Syntax as Skin

It is not easy, as we can see, to follow the fault-line between the intelligent sign and the intense sign. At the heart of the Klossowskian phantasm, however strongly affirmative, we again find the instantiation, the referral of the emotion to a total body, which will moderate it. In other words, in the lexis of pagan theatrics, the divine names which Augustine derides are already functional names, names of functions, and do not therefore count as this anonymous proper name which we have attempted to get at through the name of *Flechsig*, for example, but rather count as kinds of *agents* [*actants*] in a narrative structure. What is made apparent by this agent-function of the fragment of the body in play in the Klossowskian phantasm, is even something like libidinal currency, or rather like the *libido in so far as it can be exchanged for money*, if it is true that the phantasm of desire, *inexchangeable* in itself, finds, however, in its constitutive reference to the alleged Body, which is a 'universal' (like 'colour' for Hegel), its capacity as a *negotiable* thing. Incipient prostitution; la Tosca before long (did you really believe she made genital love with Cavaradossi?).

Augustine, ears pricked, does well out of our retreat: to admit that Pertunda and the others are already communicable and exchangeable abstractions does not tell the whole story, he will say, you ought still to recognize that my God became flesh, that the engendering of his son, through the good theory of *Similitudo*, is a movement towards singularity and dissemblance, towards the intensity of pain and pleasure. Do we not also discover here the principle of indiscernibles reversed, to which Freud has already led us when Eros and the death drives are in question?

Don't let's go too fast, let's distinguish, become more refined. There is in Klossowski a theory of the *simulacrum*; it is different from Augustine's. It does not say: everything is simulacrum, a substitute lacking, what's more, an infinite wealth, the rejected residue of a divine Body; it is not Platonic; it says: apart from, and no less real than, phantasms (Klossowski never doubts the real) there are verbal, plastic or written transcriptions of these phantasms, there are artefacts which *count as* inexchangeable phantasms. Here then is the *exclusive* relation that Klossowski admits between the voluptuousness object and its simulacrum: 'If the phantasm is in each in fact a singular case—to defend it against *institutional* signification given it by the gregarious group, the singular case cannot but have recourse to the simulacrum: that is a *counting-as* its phantasm—so it is for a fraudulent exchange between the *singular* case and the *gregarious* generality . . . The singular case *disappears* as such from the moment it *signifies* what it *is for itself*; in the individual it is only his *species case* which assures his intelligibility. Not only does it disappear as such as soon as it formulates its own phantasm: for it cannot do so save through *instituted signs*—but it cannot be reconstituted by these signs without thereby excluding from itself all that becomes *intelligible* in it, exchangeable.'[33]

The simulacrum, because it is communicable (perhaps even destined to communicate the intransmittability of the phantasm), introduces exchangeability: therefore it is money, a sign, it *counts as something other* than its own material and arrangement, and it is devoted to circulation. Let us now examine the union of the phantasm and the simulacrum: it supposes both an 'adulterous coherence' and a 'fraudulent exchange', these are Klossowski's words: an adulterous coherence because, in order that the intellect can transcribe the phantasm in communicable signs, it must take the side of intensity against the unified body of the subject and society, without which the simulacrum it forges would not be a simulacrum of anything at

all. Sade's intelligence 'fools' the institution with intransmittable passionate singularity. The fraudulent exchange, however, in the signs
employed to forge the simulacrum, to recount stories, to paint *tableaux
vivants*, cannot but betray and disguise the inane intensity, which, moreover, is already lost when it is declared. Hardly any divergence between
libidinal economy, by the coherence it demands of the intellect, and
political economy in the necessarily fraudulent exchange that it sanctions
with instituted signs, the simulacrum repeats in its duplicity that which we
never cease to find in signs: it is at once a vain passionate sign and an
exchangeable rational sign; at once *vouloir* in the sense of *Wille*, and *vouloir
dire* in the sense of meaning.

Yet this comforting agreement deserves to be broken. Let's play the
disciple, much more diligent, of the master of *tableaux vivants*; with him, we
must push the principle of duplicity much further. Language, so far as
linguistic simulacra are concerned, is not only the exchange, even the
fraudulent exchange, of the phantasm, it is also *itself* inexchangeability and
intense singularity: 'For if we have recourse to language, it is because,
through the fixity of signs, it also offers the equivalent of our obstinate
singularity.'[34] The relation of the linguistic simulacrum to the phantasm is
not only one of substitution, of counting-as, of the intelligent sign—it is
also that of a recovery, of a trespass; both are of the same ilk, one does not
hide the other, its value is not only that of its capacity as a mediator of
exchange (of purchase), of a postponement, but also of an *actual moving
force* [*puissance*]. The book, through its text, is like the skin of a body. At the
beginning of *Les Lois de l'hospitalité*, Klossowski writes: 'My syntax constitutes the tissues of Roberte's skin.' If the text is a phantasm, it is indeed,
in Klossowski's eyes, because of its proper inflexibility. The exclusions of
possible syntaxes and semantics that constitute style produce on the skin of
language the same effects of intensification, of charge and drainage as can
be obtained from certain fleshy surfaces through the austere rigour of an
erotic *dispositif*.

Do we then rediscover the condition proper to the Klossowskian
phantasm, counting only as an affect insofar as it is referred to a unitary
instance? No, it is something else altogether, quite a different understanding of the term, quite different, and fully bound up with what we
have just said concerning the 'fraudulent exchange', which we have come
to understand as betrayal of intensity by the intellect, and which we must
now understand as investment in intelligent commerce itself by emotional
affluxes. The fraud here is that under the pretext of rendering the

phantasm communicable, and translating it into signs and syntax, these are the figures of language which will in their turn receive their libidinal charge. The nihilist capacity for postponement and regulated oppositions, is what is invested now by desire in the simulacrum, and which will give to this latter the consistency of the phantasm: for indeed, the figure of language, 'syntax', does not count only as the substitute for surfaces of flesh invaded and annexed in the consumption of the phantasm, rather it is such a surface. The signs which the pen traces on the paper are not simply means of communicating an emotion which is outside them, and which would be, so to speak, lost due to the fact that it was written (writing being thus understood in a properly nihilist way, as Blanchot does, 'to write is to kill, that's all'), but these written signs being simultaneously, by themselves, not in spite of but by dint of and in proportion to their rigidity and invariance, products of phantasmatic consumption.

We here perceive in outline what, for us, is the most important thing of all, the possibility of imagining syntax, the law of value, and finally trade, and hence this meta-trade which is capital, as *intensive* regions, not merely deintensifying, like rags of the patchwork added by the mad rotation of the disjunctive bar. We perceive this monstrosity: this bar which disjoins, and which thereby delimits properties (body, goods, Self), and regulates transfers from one to the other, which is therefore the basis of the law of exchange, called the law of value or the cost of production itself—if it itself is 'invested', if it itself is what serves as the object of attraction for the pulsions, it is necessary that *at the same time* it separates and distinguishes, and in doing this, it burns and mixes the reserves that it regulates in its insane rotation, its syntatic 'ice' must be its incandescence. This is so, of course, at the price of allowing this imagination, and of grasping its range as the possibility that one will be able to understand how writing and negotiating and capitalizing can produce ecstasy. *La Monnaie vivante* [Living Currency] means: intense intellect, priceless trade, impassioned reason.

Once again then, the duplicity of the sign, the question of which may now be formulated in these terms: when the emotion (phantasm) speaks (simulacrum), is it not necessary that there be *adultery or prostitution*? Adultery of words with intensities to the detriment of the concept, prostitution of intensity in the interests of exchanges. If for Klossowski the art of making simulacra is to be classed under the rubric of adultery because it is the law of syntax in all its rigour, the disjunctive bar, which finds itself invested as an opportunity for *jouissance* and vertigo—for Baudelaire, it is with prostitution that the artistic action of translating phantasms into simulacra must be identified. We remember: 'What is love?—the need to escape oneself . . . All love is also prostitution.' And: 'What is art? Prostitution.' 'The day the young writer corrects his first proofs, he is as proud as a scholar who has just caught his first pox.'[35] In dandyism, *jouissance* is instantiated on the universalization of trade and the concomitant destruction of every *eloquent* emotion, as Bataille says on the subject of Manet; this is the system's ice incarnated in new sluts, completely stripped of all romanticism, of all nostalgia for an elsewhere, 'pitiless Sages', machines for calculating as accurately as possible the price of every demand issuing from the client which aims for an erotic manoeuvre not programmed in current consumption, cold machines whose calculable automatism, far from deceiving the dandy, rushes him towards the zenith of his *jouissance*.

The theme of adultery in Klossowski's work, for example, in *Les Lois de l'hospitalité*, brings the theme of prostitution with it. If the husband becomes his wife's pimp, if he pushes her into his nephew's arms, it is not so that on this occasion libidinal energy may be converted into money that he will collect, it is not so that the tensor signs of the perverse emotion give way to the intelligent signs of the trade of pimps, it is in order to assess the impossible price he accords to Roberte, and therefore to introduce measure, weight and thought into the unthinkable excess of what binds him to the pieces of the body-his wife. In Baudelairian prostitution, the intelligent sign (dead currency) relays intensity and *displaces* it on *itself*; in Klossowskian adultery, intensity remains instantiated 'eloquently' on a *phantasm*, that is, an assemblage of fragments (the gaping of a knicker-hem, semi-extension of a fore-arm, the nipple swelling from an unlaced corset) subtracted from an impossible body which bears a proper name. And what Octave hopes to gain by provoking his wife's adultery, is amongst other things a sort of global view over this body (quite a different passion from voyeurism), that is to make a single name correspond to a single unified body supposed to correspond to it. Octave is not therefore so much a pimp as a *politician*, if it is true that all true politics is haunted by the phantasm of the unitary body, but only insofar as this body simply escapes the grip of the institutions of unification; beyond bourgeois society, through the class-body.

Machiavelli wrote: 'You must know that there are two ways of contesting, the one by the law, the other by force; the first is the method proper to men, the second to beasts; but because the first is frequently not sufficient, it is necessary to have recourse to the second. Therefore it is necessary for a prince to understand how to avail himself of the beast and the man.' And he adds this: 'This has been figuratively taught to princes by ancient writers, who describe how Achilles and many other princes of old were given to the Centaur Chiron to nurse, who brought them up in his discipline; which means solely that, as they had for a teacher one who was half beast and half man, so it is necessary for a prince to know how to make use of both natures, and that one without the other is not durable.'[36] At the centre of the labyrinth which serves as a tailpiece in *Nietzsche et le Cercle vicieux*, we will find, not a Minotaur, stupid beast with his monotonous appetite, but a Centaur, a monster more intelligent than the most intelligent of men, the image of the marvellous dissimulation of signs into one another, supreme wisdom which includes the stupidity of bestiality. Octave is equally a centaur, adultery is a centaur, desiring not simply the country which his hands, his lips and his penis are legally authorized to cross, but insofar as this country is 'real', it escapes him; and this is why Octave redoubles his efforts to prolong Antoine's stay at his bestial hindquarters, because, as a receiver of force, the Prince of the law knows how to metamorphose himself. And if Caesar must be removed from his mother's womb by opening it up by force, against nature, it is because Caesar, political master, is a monster made of man and beast.

In prostitution, one goes from intensity to order; in adultery, from order to intensity. But it is the same route, immobile dissimulation, the voyage on the spot which crosses the extremes of pulsional stupidity and notional clarity. This is the same indiscernibility of signs, which removes from us, we libidinal economists, all appetite for vulgar romanticism and for equally tedious formalism, for a politics of spontaneous passions, and just as much for a politics of understanding. We work at a refinement of dissimulation, structure is stupid and pathos sterile.

We must equip ourselves in particular with *economic* signs, to which we have of course already been led by adultery—but especially by prostitution, which could not fail to do so—signs of this same coefficient of dissimulation that we find in other spheres, and of which they are nevertheless also events themselves. We must grasp that currency (more generally every object in the system of capital, since they are commodities and therefore currency), actual or potential, is not merely a convertible value in a universal process of production, but *indiscernibly* (and not oppositionally, dialectically) a charge of libidinal intensity. We must grasp the fact that the system of capital is not the site of the occultation of an alleged use-value which would be 'anterior' to it—this is the romanticism of alienation. Christianity—but primarily that it is in a sense *more than* capital, more ancient, more extended; and then that these so-called abstract signs, susceptible to provisional measurement and calculation, are in themselves libidinal. Economic theory or even structural anthropology conceives these signs exclusively as terms in play in a system of communication which regulates their circulation, the need for them itself produced by the partners of the exchange, their exchange-values and use-values. If we also approach them as proper names now, as signs of intensity, as libidinal values (which are neither useful nor exchangeable), as pulsations of desire, as moments of Eros and death—then, then . . .

Prostitution exchanges the phantasm (which *is* the client) against the signs of the economic system (currency); but it also introduces the intelligent sign, communicable currency, into the singular and vain 'monstrosity' of the phantasm, and in this way it dedicates the 'adulterous coherence' of the thinkable to the unthinkable. Price is combined and mixed in with the *exorbitant*; that which has no comparison, is paid for, and is therefore evaluated. This confusion, more monstrous than the phantasm by itself could be, is at once impossible and inevitable. We have understood why 'impossible'; but inevitable because the singularity forces itself to be communicated, because extreme pathos extends its empire to the skin of language, because the most purple sexual arousal, almost blinding, also offers words, not necessarily obscene, but always intelligent signs invested and relinquished, because the arse being buggered is also a face which talks to us. Confusion is inevitable simply because language is not a separate sphere, because it belongs, in rags, to the same band as these grey-gold loins which start to move under your hands, and as these buttocks, rocking your scrotum and easing your purse. The communication of the cry is its affirmation, the extension of the gyratory madness into the domain of meaning and order, Logos, which the West, and the philosopher especially, has always wanted to keep sheltered from the monstrosity of lovers and impious politicians.

Exorbitant

In Sade the group of relations surrounding the *value* of the monetary sign and its *intensity* are quite different from those one finds in prostitution. From the very beginning the client's body is the same as the procurer's, Antoine and Octave together are as one (and perhaps thereby share Sade's republicanism). The Society of the Friends of Crime is not the society of procurers. The *Milieu* embodies the duplicity of signs: adultery of money with *jouissance*, fraud of *jouissance* when it is converted into currency. The sign of these exchanges becomes the accomplice of untransmittable phantasms, the consumption of the pulsional singularity is bought at the price of universally estimable sums in the form of money. Like Hegel's *Mitte*,[37] the *Milieu* assures the institution's permeability by desire; in this little different to the Police. 'Perverse' pulsions are channelled by it towards the social body, the body of exchanges, towards the circuit of the communication of exchanges and goods. *Milieu* of duplicity and dissimulation *par excellence*, even if it has no need to hide itself, just like the Police, since it too is concerned with the detection and regulation of allegedly socially perverse partial drives. We would dearly love to write the *parole* of the *policeman*, the dissimulated-dissimulating speech *par excellence*, not because its real aim is other than its declared aim, which is not its own, but by virtue of its *interest* for the *passions* of the interrogated: the comprehensive desire of the commissioner, always more comprehensive, more embracing, moulding itself into, connecting onto the most intense regions of the interrogated's desire, his most unknown desires (for example, passivity, submitting to beatings), thus inscribing itself in an arousing, erotic, perverse, infantile relation—to the end, however, of *concentrating* all these partial drives in the circle of trade and in the total body, one of the producers of which is the policeman. 'Making someone talk' here being nothing other than the reestablishment of *jouissance* in the place assigned it by order.

The pimp is an element of the same figure, working more on the side of the passions than on the side of interest, thus complementing the preceding case. His function still remains to refine the libido from the fragments of the negotiable body of prostitutes, to heighten its quality by a continual exercise of relinquishment rendering them available at every moment to the strongest energetic passages. *This availability at every moment* is what produces vertigo in great prostitution: it is, like the creations of the pimp on the woman's body, at once the mark of her *signification* as a communicable and negotiable sign, the remarkable madness of her disappearance as a person and of her abolition in the anonymity of impulsions. Within the *power* relation, such availability is called slavery or at least *Knechtschaft*; but it is at the same time within the order of *forces*, force and anonymity surpassing every domination. Without there being any dialectic between the two positions, since there is no interval: for example the same *arrogance* of *Jacques le Fataliste* counts both as an outburst against the position of the master and therefore an attempt to reverse it on the one hand, and on the other as the anonymous production of a libidinal 'knowledge' [*savoir*] passing beyond every hierarchy; this arrogance being that of the inflexible partial pulsion, and in this sense, never aggressive, never receptive to social reasons for struggle. In the story of *F.B.* or *O*, everything marks the vertigo of the pimp in a similar manner, the master of bodies reduced to registered initials, a region of routes for nameless intensities. The woman's initial and the prisoner's registration number result from a supplementary labour on the proper name, by which it is almost effaced, as every corporeality closed up on itself, and as every subjective reserve, must be; but also maintained in its effacement, since it is by the anonymity lodged in the name that the aberration makes itself noticeable.

There is none of this in the Society of the Friends of Crime, however. A society cut off from the social body, neither catching the perverse passions nor concentrating them in it. Compared to the pimp and the cop, the criminal is a very rich man, £25,000 annual income, 10,000 francs in expenses per victim for the furthering of *jouissance*. And his function is not at all the concentration of the partial pulsions: these, expended in profusion on the bodies of subjects, will never be inscribed on the social body, as money, thanks to the criminal's intervention. Conversely, this leads its revenues away from the circulation of goods and devotes them to pure voluptuous consumption. If there is venality of *jouissance*, it is certainly not through poverty, but thanks to the greatest luxury and in order to increase that luxury. 'The phantasm's equivalent (the sum paid)', writes Klossowski,[38] 'represents not only the emotion in itself, but also the exclusion of thousands of human lives. Value is even augmented by this scandal, from the gregarious point of view.' And he establishes criminal equations, which cannot be those of the procurer, in the following way: '*Exclusive voluptuousness = famine = annihilation = the supreme value of the phantasm . . . A phantasm = an entire population.*'[39]

It will be said that this is still to conceive of Sade in a nihilist fashion, subordinating the libidinal force (*puissance*) of the arrangements of the Château de la Forêt-Noire to the fact that they cost the price of the lives of thousands of mouths to feed. Is it not enough that the victims bought would be destroyed inside the château in order that we may begin to understand the deadly inanity of the libido, without any need, above the market, to calculate what it costs for those outside? But the function of this infamy is not 'supplementary'.

It must be related to the peculiar status of the criminal; he is at the same time both pimp and client, or rather, neither one nor the other. The pimp brings the partial pulsion of the client back into the bosom of the ghost-body of society, under the form of the monetary equivalent; the client, in consuming his pulsional energy in the production of his phantasms with the help of the prostitute, produces a *libidinal equivalent of currency*. But it is essential that the criminal leave the system of equivalence between the pulsion and the money; if money remains present in its libidinal 'account-ancy', it is no longer as the substitute or the simulacrum, it comes under the heading of a *region of the body* (which can no longer be, then, the alleged social body, but necessarily the great libidinal skin) which like any other can and must be grasped by the libido and be submitted to its consummatory irradiation. Currency, language itself become the object of the libertines' manoeuvres in the same way as is the body. We know that from *Journée* to *Journée* Duclos 'tells the story' of her monstrous life, which is simply the diachronic development of the combinations of infamies; this criminal's 'narrative' is to language as the money spent on crime perpe-trated by the four master libertines is to political economy: not the substitute in words for 'real' arrangements—we know that they practise this in abundance—but *reality* extended well beyond the supposedly 'practical' (unduly endowed by a nihilist tradition with the exclusive privilege to determine reality) right into those regions occupied, according to this same tradition, by substitutes for things and persons, i.e. the regions of money and language. The criminal perpetrates, on *the skin of currency* as on that of beings and words, the same plan of intensification to excess, the execution of which can only be followed by the calcination of the excited surfaces, and this is why signs of exchange here, as opposed to what happens in prostitution, are not only taken out of the circuit of commu-nication, but devoted to destruction; at this point one wonders if the Society of the Friends of Crime is economically viable. In any case, it is not capitalistic, what it accumulates is a wealth of ruins.

Nevertheless, Klossowski understands this ruinous use of monetary signs in a very different way, more 'progressively': it constitutes, he says, a protest against the prostitutive function of cash in society. It is precisely when the pimp establishes a relation between perversion and the social body, between the tensor sign and the intelligent sign, and when he thus proves to be the only really institutive connection of the negotiating body itself, that the criminal is used as a *disconnection*: the withdrawal of his fortune and its squandering to the ends of untransmittable pleasure are provocations destined to give rise to the alternative, before which *dissimulation* or duplicity of signs necessarily invests a politics of the libido: either recognize that 'the repudiation of complete monstrosity by *institutions is reversed into de facto prostitution, material and moral*',[40] admitting therefore that the generalized system of commodities is the system of prostitution under the cover of the trade of objects and services, and nothing else besides—or 'affirm that there is only one authentically universal communication: *the exchange of bodies by the secret language of bodily signs*',[41] of which Sade's woman criminal provides the principle and illustrates one effect, the effect of insurrection or perpetual shaking of the circle of exchanges by the passions, to speak in the manner of Blanchot.[42]

It is from posing the libidinal political problem under this alternative: either the communication of beings through the exchange of their bodies, called 'perversion', or prostitution under the sign of dead currency, which is capital, in any case mercantilism, that Klossowski forges his impossible fiction of a living currency. 'One should imagine for an instant', he writes,

> an apparently impossible regression: that is an industrial phase where the producers have the means to demand, in the name of payment, objects of sensation on the part of consumers. These objects are living beings. According to this example of barter, producers and consumers thereby constitute collections of 'persons' allegedly destined for pleasure, emotion, sensation. How can the human 'person' fulfil the function of currency? How could the producers, instead of being paid by women, ever come to be paid 'in women'? How would the entrepreneurs, the industrialists, pay their engineers, their workers? 'In women.' Who will keep this living currency alive? Other women. Which presupposes the reverse: women pursuing a career will be paid 'in boys'. Who will keep alive, that is to say, who will sustain this virile currency? Those who have feminine currency at their disposal. What we are saying here in fact exists. For, without literally returning to barter, all of modern industry rests on an exchange mediated by the sign of inert currency, neutralizing the nature of the objects exchanged; rests, that is, on a simulacrum of exchange—a simulacrum which lies in the form of manpower resources, thus a living currency, not affirmed as such, already extant.[43]

Before we marvel at this phantasy, let's measure the exact range its author attributes to it:

> Living currency, the industrial slave at once stands for a sign guaranteeing wealth and this wealth itself. As a sign, it stands for all kinds of other material riches; as wealth, it meanwhile excludes every other demand that is not the

> demand of which it is the satisfaction. But satisfaction, strictly speaking, is
> equally excluded by its quality as a sign. This is how living currency essentially
> differs from the condition of the industrial slave (personalities, stars, publicity
> puppets, hostesses, etc.). The industrial slave could not lay claim to the category
> of the sign, since she differentiates between what she is prepared to receive as
> inert currency, and what she is worth in her own eyes.[44]

The creature become living currency occupies a quite different position from that held by the woman that Klossowski calls the 'industrial slave'. This latter offers, on the whole, nothing really new if one compares it with the status of the labour-force-commodity as it is waged in the production industries in the large sense. The puppet whose bodily image accompanies the offer of commodities, tights, refrigerators, choc-ices, is simply one component element of the commodity constituting the publicity-object (poster, 'blurb', commercial). The same goes for the air-hostess, etc., all things being equal. Of course, the interest which this economic power shows in this body and this face appears to be indissociable from a consideration of their libidinal force [*puissance*]. But *de facto*, this last fact is basically ignored; the images offered to the potential consumer do not have as their function the stimulation of his phantasmatic forces [*puissances*], but the stimulation of his propensity to buy the choc-ice or the refrigerator; they do not claim to make him spend his libido, but his money. It is not a question of intensive force [*puissance*] here, it is only a matter of psycho-economic power: but the libido is not a psycho-economic 'motivation'. The industrial slave therefore, by her position as a meta-commodity, is subject to the libidinal neutralization which is standard practice in the constitution of all objects in play in industrial production and exchange. The consummation it suggests is not consumption. This remains ignored by the financial system which employs the woman for the purposes of publicity; the *price* that may be accorded to the intense *jouissance* of her body in its unexchangeable singularity is not realized in the financial system, it remains 'exorbitant', it has to be said, 'valueless'. The industrial slave is therefore committed to the most classical split between the merchant's possessions and the lover's concerns.

In a woman-living currency, it would be, by contrast, the emotional force [*puissance*] of her body that would directly determine her libidinal *price*; Klossowski says: 'immediately' (but we will see that this immediacy is impossible). In this way she will be 'wealth': for all that she 'excludes every other demand', and cannot count as the substitute for something else: extinguish the transfer and the destruction of the rest follows. Here

Klossowski suggests an analogy with gold, in which he sees a political-economic metaphor of libidinal *price*: for like this latter, gold is useless, and it is precisely because of this that it is precious, being opposed to all instrumentality; its uselessness may recall the inanity of the passional material in the sphere of use. This useless referent nevertheless serves as a standard for the value of currencies, according to Klossowski, and does this in the most arbitrary way: it is according to the same unpredictable conjunction that the libidinal *price* of the currency-body ('concrete currency') will determine the negotiable value of commodities, from 'price' to 'value' the consequence remaining undecidable and the incommensurability impenetrable.

We here discover the two traits which reunite and confound the tensor sign and the intelligent sign in one and the same 'thing': indissociability and non-deductibility. The woman-currency would be dissimulation itself; she is not only the point of intersection of more or less divergent signifying chains, a degree of polysemic density and overdetermination, she is *in excess* of the infinity of the deathly tension which the libertine tracks like a beast over the plains and valleys of her body. Between its value-function and its tensorial force [*puissance*], the currency of the body offers the duplicitous relation, already encountered, of incompossibility and indissociability. It is because the order of intensities is not translatable or *convertible* into that of values, that currency, be it the singular body prepared to provide the material for 'perverse' phantasms, cannot but remain abstract or dead, and that Klossowski must indeed, *contradicting* his whole project in these few words, add to the recognition of its libidinal singularity ('it excludes every other demand if it is not the demand of which it is the satisfaction') the admission of its neutralization in the intelligible sign: 'Strictly speaking, satisfaction is equally excluded by its quality as a sign.' The question of *jouissance* is, however, exposed by currency come alive, according to a fully aporetic nature: a body of intensities, this currency seems to lend itself to *jouissance*; but as cash devoted to payment, it cannot but defer it, just as, since it is excluded, the prostitute's skin can become excited under the caress of a client.

How does the Klossowskian system differ from prostitution? In that the use of the woman is not to be bought by money, since this use is on the contrary authorized by a certain claim of which the 'client' is the beneficiary, rather than the woman's 'master'. The prostitute's body is entirely maintained within the network of venal values, even if it happens that the *jouissance* that it obtains from the client fraudulently 'escapes' her in order to be consumed as intensity; but the body of living money does not *refer* to dead money, and in this sense, it is not a commodity, but rather money, since, if not its acquisition, then at least its enjoyment [*jouissance*] earns the acquittal of debts and the extinction of claims.

Is there now a split between the organization imagined by Klossowski and the houses Sade dedicates to the debauchery of men and women in the pamphlet 'Français, encore un effort . . . '? The split lies in an important point, republicanism. In Sade's houses, which are public property, every citizen, whatever their sex, has the power to convene there, to enjoy, however they please, every citizen, male or female. The 'motive' of the convocation is not, for Sade, in any way economic, and the *jouissance* gained from the object which Klossowski called phantasmatic never comes to be the extinction of a debt. The sole debt Sade recognized and counted in his houses is a debt of *jouissance*, which is political, and by which every citizen is potentially and continually burdened with regard to all other citizens. This independence, forcefully maintained by the marquis, of the libidinal with regard to the economic, is the split within Klossowski's phantasy: the Sadean theme is a political theme; the production and exchange of commodities plays no part in this. The houses of debauchery are civic institutions, and as such have as an indirect but essential function, concentrating the libido on the circle of the *political* body. Here are two versions: 'If . . . one passion has no more need of the whole range of the liberty of another one, none without doubt is as despotic . . . every time that you deny a man the secret means of the expression of his heart, he will throw himself into venting it on the objects around him, he will trouble the government. If you wish to avoid this danger, allow a free development to his tyrannical desires which, in spite of him, ceaselessly torment him . . . '[45] Thus one gives vent to the perversion within peripheral institutions, in this, utterly true to the Greek model.[46]

But Sade also says exactly the opposite: that a republican government always menaced by the despots surrounding it must have as its sole morality its maintenance by any means, that it is ruled out that the means are all moral, that on the contrary it must be *immoral* men who by their movement of perpetual *insurrection* keep the republican government on the alert. Thus the houses of which he spoke, far from having the function of the appeasement of the excitations provoked by the pulsions in the citizens, replenish, rather, what sustains them. Functional duplicity of the sites of luxury as regards the political sphere itself, at once the charge and discharge of energies: criminality, this perpetual mobility of those which

Plato, in *The Republic*, named *hornets*, and which he wanted to eliminate, provides the government with a twofold service, in the danger presented to it from the excesses of its insatiability, by requiring the institution of criminal spaces which are discharge points for them and for it. Here Sade revives the great Machiavellian tradition of the connivance of the politician and the beast, the tradition of Chiron the Centaur, instructor to Princes, duplicitous politician *par excellence*.

In Klossowski, who is a modern man, there is neither city nor government, the republic no longer exists, the only body with a totalizing pretension is the body of capital, it is an open secret that today's politicians are only the executors of the impulsional imperatives of capital, and that they have no need to receive the great excess of stupidity or bestiality from a Chiron as the endowment of political genius; they are rich enough if they are endorsed by a civil service college. It is in economics that the post-Marxist Klossowski seeks the conspiracy of the pulsions on the 'social body'. But he is not content to protest as Marx does against the indirect extension of prostitution into all activities through the intervention of commodities. He also draws out the implication suggested by this fact, he sees in capitalism the return, but unaffirmed and unrecognized as such, of what it rejects, that is, libidinal intensity, in the very heart of the most apparently neutralized exchanges. (An analysis which, at first sight, does not appear to be unrelated to that of Baudrillard, for whom commodity fetishism, denounced and largely ignored by Marx himself, is the transcription, in the order of political economy, of the *foreclosure* underlying this order, at the same time as it institutes it.) Klossowski consequently says: there is *little to be done* ('what we are speaking of in fact exists') in order that what today passes into the oblivion issuing from the production and exchange of goods, violates, under the screen of dead money, the exchange and consumption of phantasms—in order that this be fully emphasized, and that this production and exchange immediately become the circulation of *jouissances*: the imaginary *living currency* has no other function than to claim to reestablish intensity *on* the circle of trade itself and thus to stop treating desire as banned from it, and to help oneself to the body of capital as a convenient expedient to attain the unspeakable aims of the species ('to be paid in women'). But in the same way as the Klossowskian idea of intensity is not affirmative (at least in *La Monnaie vivante*, it is not the same in *Le Cercle vicieux*), in the same way as it persists (this can be clearly seen in what he nevertheless judges to be an important corrective in this regard, in 'Le Philosophe scélérat') in remaining within the nihilist tradition of transgression (of propagation), of perversion (of the medium), of turning-away (of energies), and concurrently, if not in the phantasm as substitute, then at least in the simulacrum as the reduplication of the phantasm—so the establishment of *jouissance* in the midst of the circuit of trade can, in his eyes, only take on the form of a *currency*, even if this is living: heavy then with the millennial heritage of prostitution and substitution, that is to say of the dualism which we, libidinal economists, will terminate.

As soon as one admits the inexchangeability of phantasms, one must accept decisively the necessity of the conservation of political economy and capital. Since it results from this inexchangeability that they are inevitably substituted by doubles or simulacra, and therefore that libidinal 'riches' are misrepresented in the economic signs of this wealth which they represent but which, also, will for ever differ from them in terms of consumption. That currency is living does not suppress the fact that it is currency, on the contrary. By extending to the erotic bodies themselves, the new political economy makes *these too* into simulacra, appearances, and composes, with these fragments of assembled flesh, tableaux, also said to be *'vivants'*, for which Klossowski has such affection, a kind of *terrestrial city* which is only the duplicatum of another city, always out of reach. In this sense, *La Monnaie vivante* continues the Augustinian religion of *The City of God*, and the 'life' which excites this currency and these tableaux is a kind of death, in conformity with the tradition of the Fathers.

We must nevertheless pay homage to this fiction at the very moment that we distance ourselves from it. For what is sought in the phantasy of these *golden bodies* is also totally opposed to the lessons of Augustine. The exchange of pulsional zones in excessive arrangements (exorbitant 'phantasms') can and must be understood, in the work of Klossowski himself —and this is explicitly the case in *Le Cercle vicieux*—not as an exchange in the sense of two contracting parties each intending to swap two objects of equivalent (marginal) utility, but as a metamorphosis in which the invested regions (and we have seen that, according to Sade, whom Klossowski follows here, this might be language *or even money*) exist only to the extent that they are crossed by energy, by the greatest or the most delicate or the most gentle tension and pain, unpredictably and ceaselessly. This 'exchange' is the passage of intensities running from one proper name to another, from one initial to another, from one reference number to another, without a return to the same and therefore without capitalization, without which there can be no instance, structure, great Zero of input/output matrices, no Memory, to register the energies expended here and amassed there. Understood in this way, it is 'life' which is in fact currency in the sense that there is nothing but simulacra, signs of course, but without reference to *another order*, to a signified; a political economy assuredly, but one which, far from being the betrayal and travesty of libidinal economy, is this libidinal economy; a political economy without a betrayed or alienated 'origin', without a theory of value. A currency therefore in the sense of Roman paganism and theatrical theology admitting only tensor signs, only masks hiding no face, only surfaces without a back stage, only *prices without values*.

It is undoubtedly because he has not broken with the problematic of *alienation*, which is Augustinian just as much as it is Marxian, that Klossowski hesitates in his evaluation of capitalism and therefore over the exact range to give to a libidinal use of signs. He may indeed insist on the strict analogy which reigns between the useful product ('instrumental') and the phantasm, between the consumption of the product and the voluptuous emotion, between the 'industrial world' and the perverse society—but it is just as much in order to declare that it must be suspected: 'Strictly speaking there exists no economy of voluptuousness which would benefit from industrial means'; and even to superimpose an overtly 'perverse' relation onto this analogy: 'a purely analogical relation leads to nothing, if one does not start from the point of view of *objects* and *needs* in order to detect the struggle of affects against their *inadequate formulation, materially* reconverted *to the state of a demand for goods* which only corresponds to them in a perverse way.'[47] Now, is it not obvious that this perverse relation proceeds from a return of the thought of alienation to the heart of the erotic? Elsewhere, Klossowski says that the pulsions are always in combat against themselves: it therefore has no need of capitalism in order to be 'inadequately' formulated. It remains that this inadequacy, wherever it comes from, exists only with regard to a manner of thinking concerned *with* and determined *by truth*. Between the intelligent sign and the tensor sign, between the currency and the pulsion, we say that the relation is not of formulation, expression, or translation, of betrayal, but of coexistence and dissimulation. And because the problem of capital, and that of currency, cannot be that of *enfranchising* the desire of its grotesque masks, those of capital being neither better nor worse, more or less 'authentic' than the others. It is of decisive importance to recognize that over a period, new 'signs' appear, new statements—amongst the number of which Klossowski's are first—new 'practices', new 'works', which libidinally, *just as much as* economically announce the ruin of the distinction between the sentiments and business, between the affect and labour. *Like those of capital,* these signs are duplicitous, and there is no question of declaring *urbi et orbi* that with their appearance semiotics and political economics are ruined, and desire emancipated from the stocks of the system of values. Their intensity is new, in the manner in which they are inscribed into established regions, by the distances which they force back and evoke. Their relation to sign-values, to intelligent signs, is wrapped in a new duplicity. Rather than greeting a dawn, we should honour the new dissimulation in them. There, where there are only surfaces, conspiracy and secrecy reign.

Notes

1 See Gilles Deleuze and Félix Guattari, *Anti-Oedipus*, tr. by Robert Hurley, Mark Seem and Helen Lane (London: Athlone, 1984).

2 The name Flechsig refers to Schreber's former physician in Daniel Paul Schreber's *Memoirs of my Nervous Illness*, tr. Ida MacAlpine and Richard A. Hunter (Cambridge, Mass.: Harvard University Press, 1988; hereafter cited as *Memoirs*). The work was, of course, analysed by Freud in his 'Psychoanalytical Notes on an Autobiographical Account of a Case of Paranoia (Dementia Paranoides)', in the *Standard Edition*, ed. and tr. James Strachey (London: Hogarth Press, 1953–74; hereafter cited as *SE*), Vol. 12. In the following section, Lyotard will wish, beyond Freud's interpretation, to analyse the name of Flechsig as a tensor sign.

3 See Marcel Proust, *A la Recherche du Temps Perdu*.

4 See Pierre Klossowski, *Les Lois de l'Hospitalité* (Paris: Gallimard, 1965).

5 Freud, 'Psychological Notes . . . ', *SE*, Vol. 12, p.34.

6 ibid., p.26.

7 ibid., p.27.

8 As Suzanne Lafont, in an unpublished work on [Flaubert's] *Bouvard et Pécuchet*, shows.

9 Freud, 'Psychological Notes . . . ', p.63.

10 Freud, 'A Child Is Being Beaten', in *SE*, Vol. 19, pp. 179–204.

11 Freud, 'Psychological Notes . . . ', p.26.

12 Schreber, *Memoirs*, p.98.

13 ibid.

14 Freud, 'Psychological Notes . . . ', p.19.

15 ibid.

16 Xavière Lafont, 'Justine "73', *Le Nouvel Observateur*, 19 March 1973

17 Pierre Klossowski, 'Le Philosophe scélérat', tr. Alphonso Lingis, as 'Sade, or the Philosopher-Villain', in *Sub-Stance*, no. 50 (1985), pp. 5–25.—*tn*.

18 Leon Trotsky, *My Life* (Harmondsworth: Penguin, 1972), p.352.

19 Pierre Klossowski, 'Protase et apodose', *L'Arc*, 43 (1970).

20 St Augustine, *City of God*, tr. Henry Bettenson (Harmondsworth: Penguin, 1972), Book VI, ch. 6, p.237.

21 Etienne Gilson, *Introduction à l'étude de saint-Augustin* (Paris: Vrin, 1929), p.268.

22 St Augustine, *De vera religione*, XXXII, 60: 'In fact, unless one is in some way enclosed in one (body), one is nothing; but if, on the other hand, one is perfectly truthful, bodies do not exist.'—*tn*

23 St Augustine, *De trinitate*, tr. Stephen McKenna (Catholic University of America Press, 1963), Book XI, ch. 8, 14: 'For the sense receives the species from the body which we perceive, the memory receives it from the sense, but the power (acies) of thought receives it from the memory.' Translation modified—*tn*

24 G. W. F. Hegel, *The First Philosophy of Mind* (1803–4).

25 E. dí Negri, 'L'elaborazione hegeliana di temi agostiniani', *Revue internationale de philosophie*, VI (1952), I, 19, pp. 62–78.

26 St Augustine, *De immortalitate animae*, quoted by P. Landsberg, 'Du concept du vérité chez saint Augustin', *Deucalion*, 3 (October 1970).

27 *Consommation*: the French word is used both in the context of the 'consumption of a good' and of the 'consummation of a marriage'. Lyotard here draws explicit attention to this inextricability of political and libidinal economy, and uses both senses throughout this work.—*tn*

28 Pierre Klossowski, *The Baphomet*, tr. by Sophie Hawkes (New York: Eridanos, 1988), p.100 and p.99, respectively.

29 ibid., pp. 98 and 97.

30 ibid., pp. 86 and 87.

31 ibid., p.150.

32 Pierre Klossowski, *La Monnaie vivante* (Paris: Losfeld, 1970), non-paginated (pp. 19–20).

33 Pierre Klossowski, *Nietzsche et le Cercle vicieux* (Paris: Mercure de France, 1969), p.367.

34 ibid.

35 Respectively: 'Mon coeur mis à nu', 'Fusées' and 'Mon coeur mis à nu', Charles Baudelaire, *Journaux Intimes*, (Paris: Librairic José Corti, 1949).

36 Niccolò Machiavelli, *The Prince*, tr. W. K. Marriot (London: Dent, 1911), ch. 18, p.141–2.

37 G. W. F. Hegel, *Realphilosophie 1* (Jena, 1803–4), ed. J. Hoffmeister (Hamburg: 1967).

38 Klossowski, *La Monnaie vivante*, n.p. (p. 84).

39 ibid.

40 ibid. (p. 79).

41 ibid.

42 Blanchot, *L'Inconvenance majeure* (Paris: Pauvert, 1965). Blanchot, however, like Sade, sees here a principle instead.

43 Klossowski, *La Monnaie vivante*, n.p. (p. 89).

44 ibid. (p. 92).

45 Marquis de Sade, 'Français, encore un effort pour être républicains', in *Philosophie dans le boudoir* (Paris: J-J. Pauvert, 1972), p.211.

46 See below, Trade, p.156 ff.

47 Klossowski, *La Monnaie vivante*, n.p. (pp. 26–9).

3
The Desire Named Marx

Libidinal Marx

We must come to take Marx as if he were a writer, an author full of affects, take his text as a madness and not as a theory, we must succeed in pushing aside his theoretical barrier and stroking his beard without contempt and without devotion, no longer the false neutrality which Merleau-Ponty advised in the past for someone who, he said, has now become a classic and must be treated no differently than Hegel or Aristotle—no, stroke his beard as a complex libidinal volume, reawakening his hidden desire and ours along with it. There is no need to criticize Marx, and even if we do criticize him, it must be understood that it is in no way a critique: we have already said and repeated that we laugh at critique, since it is to maintain oneself in the field of the criticized thing and in the dogmatic, indeed paranoiac, relation of knowledge. Marx's desire interests us, not for itself, but inasmuch as it informs the themes of writings which metamorphose into themes of social and political 'practices'. Marx must be introduced, the big fat Marx, and also the little Marx of the Epicurean and Lutheran studies, this entire continent, into the atlas of libidinal cartography—or rather the reverse: to start crossing this strange country with our affections and disaffections, letting our attachments and our deceptions circulate, refining our analysis here, neglecting it there, because we have neither the hope nor the intention of setting up a portrait of the work, of giving an 'interpretation' of it. We do not interpret, we read, and we effect by writings. We have, for a long time, having read Marx, operated by means of practices (since this is the word left us by the Greeks as a disastrous heritage). We say this not to render the libidinal use we make of the Old Man more justifiable or less shameful; rather to situate these 'practices' in the sphere of what rightly belongs to interpretation. A Marxist political practice is an interpretation of a text, just as a social or Christian spiritual practice is the interpretation of a text. So much so that practices are themselves texts, insofar as they are interpretations. And this is precisely what we desire not to do here. We no longer want to correct Marx, to reread him or to read him in the sense that the little Althusserians would like to 'read *Capital*': to interpret it according to 'its truth'. We have no plan to be true, to give the truth of Marx, we wonder what there is of the libido in Marx, and 'in Marx' means in his text or in his interpretations, mainly in practices. We will rather treat him as a 'work of art'. We will take some incontestable detail, considered minor, and which in fact it is in regard to the manifest themes of the work; quite certain, however, that it is not so for the libidinal geography of the continent.

We note even this, libidinal economist friends: we feel almost obliged, as you've just heard, to make some sort of a declaration of intentions, a little solemn, vaguely epistemological (as little as possible, nevertheless, take note), at the shores of this continent. No other continent would extract such declarations from us—although they remain somewhat stupid and certainly useless. We could say that it is through suspicion and intimidation, warned as we are by a militant past of, when laying a hand on Marx, even and indeed especially if it were to screw with him, we are closely watched by the paranoiacs calling themselves Marxist politicians and in general all the Whites of the left. We would therefore prudently warn: it is in this state of mind, this state of heart, this state of body that we approach the Old Man.

But the libidinal 'truth' of our preamble lies elsewhere. It already states the essential which is this: the Old Man is also a young woman to us, a strange bisexual assemblage. The *dispositifs* which channel their impulsions into theoretical discourses, and will give rise to organisms of power, the very ones which will harden into the German Party, the Bolshevik Party, these *dispositifs* are of course 'compromise-formations', they are so many attempts to stabilize the forces on the libidinal front, mediations—oh how 'alienated', as he loved to say—interposed between the fluxes of desire and the regions into which they travel. This happens not only in certain themes, or at least in certain 'minor' motifs, some of which we will pick out, its position is established first of all in something quite astonishing: the perpetual *postponement* of finishing work on *Capital*, a chapter becoming a book, a section a chapter, a paragraph a section, by a process of cancerization of theoretical discourse, by a totally pulsional proliferation of a network of concepts hitherto destined on the contrary to 'finalize', to 'define' and to justify a proletarian politics, hence by the racing of a discursive machinery explicitly, however, laying claim to rationality (theoretical-practical). Is the *non-finito* a characteristic of rational theory? We are able to support this, in these post-relative days; but for Marx (and therefore for Engels the impatient!), it must rather have been a bizarre, worrying fact.

We say that this postponement, which results in the 'Economy' never being completed,[1] and in the calculations of *Capital*, Book 3 being false,[2] already demonstrates a whole *dispositif*, a libidinal monster with the huge fat head of a man full of warrior's thoughts and petty quarrels, and with the soft body of young amorous Rhénane—a monster which never achieves the realization of its unity, because of this very incapacity, and it is this 'failure' which is marked in the interminable theoretical suspense. What we have here is not exactly the centaur, the master of politicians as Chiron was the master of Achilles; rather, it would be the hermaphrodite, another monster in which femininity and masculinity are indiscernibly exchanged, thereby thwarting the reassurance of *sexual difference*. But it is exactly this which is in question in the 'Economy', and we maintain, dear comrades, the following thesis: the little girl Marx, offended by the perversity of the polymorphous body of capital, requires a great love; the great prosecutor Karl Marx, assigned the task of the prosecution of the perverts and the 'invention' of a suitable lover (the proletariat), sets himself to study the file of the accused capitalist.

What happens when the person assigned to the prosecution is as fascinated by the accused as he is scandalized by him? It comes about that the prosecutor sets himself to finding a hundred thousand good reasons to prolong the study of the file, that the enquiry becomes meticulous, always more meticulous, that the lawyer submerged in the British Museum in the microscopic analysis of the aberrations of capital is no longer able to detach himself from it, that the organic unity, that this swarming of perverse fluxes that is supposed to have to produce (dialectically), never stops moving away, escaping him, being put off, and that the submission of petitions is kept waiting interminably. What was happening then throughout the thousands of manuscript pages? The unification of Marx's body, which requires that the polymorphous perversity of capital be put to death for the benefit of the fulfilment of the desire for genital love, is not possible. The prosecutor is unable to *deduce* the birth of a new and beautiful *(in)organic body* (similar to that of precapitalist forms) which would be child-socialism, from the pornography of capitalism. If there is a body of capital, this body *is sterile*, it engenders nothing: it exceeds the capacity of theoretical discourse as unification.

'I do not want to be resigned to sending just anything', Marx wrote to Engels who presses him (31 July 1865), prior to having the whole work in his sight. 'Whatever defect they may have, it is to the advantage of my writings that they constitute an artistic whole, and I can only achieve this result in my own way and by never having them printed until I have them before me *in their entirety*.' These writings on their own, however, never constitute this *visible artistic whole* whose model is an (in)organic body, organic insofar as it is a complete and fecund totality, inorganic insofar as it is not biological, but theoretical here (the same unitary model which will be desired and 'recognized' in precapitalist forms or in socialism, this time on the socio-economic plane).

The young innocent Little Girl Marx says: you see, I am in love with love, this must stop, this industrial and industrious crap, this is what makes me anxious, I want the return to the (in)organic body; and it has been taken over by the great bearded scholar so that he may establish the thesis that *it cannot stop*, and so that he may testify, as the counsel to the poor (amongst which is the Little Girl Marx), to his revolutionary conclusions; so that he may perform the obstetrics of capital; and so that he may give, *to her*, this *total body* he requires, this child, at least this child of words which would be the anticipated double (the younger child born first) of the child of flesh: of the proletariat, of socialism. But alas, he does not give her this child. She will never have this 'artistic whole' before her, these writings 'in their entirety'. She will have suffering growing before her and in her, because her prosecutor will discover in the course of his research, insofar as it is endless, a strange *jouissance*: the same *jouissance* that results from the instantiation of the pulsions and their discharge in *postponement*. The *jouissance* of infinity. This 'perversity' of knowledge is rightly called (scientific) research, and intensity there is not, as it is in orgasm, 'normal', the intensity of discharge instantiated in a genital couple, but is the intensity of an inhibition, of a putting into reserve, of a postponement and of an investment in means. So much so that the prosecutor charged with obtaining proof of the pornographic ignominy of capital repeats, in his enquiry and even in his preparation and pleading, this same 'Don't come yet'—so to speak—which is simply another modality of *jouissance*, which is found in the libidinal *dispositif* of capital. While, as concerns the content, it is always in search of the lovable body which he-she desires, the form of this research already contains its denial and its impossibility.

This is why the attention which this body is able to command, and to which it must have the right, provokes the *bad temper* of the paradoxical defender of the poor. When the refugees from the Commune fled to London and the International was fully preoccupied with them, while in short something like the subversive 'reality' of this proletarian-socialist body, supposedly much sought after, comes to explode in the eyes of the world (and, it seems, in the eyes of the author of the 'Address to the Committee of the International' dated 30 May 1871), what does Marx find to write, on 9 November of that same year, to Danielson, his Russian translator, who is awaiting the corrections to the text of the first chapter? 'It is, without any doubt, quite useless to *await* a revision of the first chapter, for my time has for some months been so taken up (and on this point there is little hope of improvement in the near future) that I am unable to pursue my theoretical labours any more. It is certain that one fine morning I will put an end to all this, but there are circumstances where one is morally bound to busy oneself with *things much less attractive* than study and theoretical research.' Not very attractive, says the equivocal prosecutor, your fine proletarian body, again we catch a glimpse of the infamous prostitution of capital . . .

But, you say, this suspension of theoretical labour on capital, this is not for one second a pleasure in the sense of a security, an irresponsibility, it is on the contrary the result of a libidinal transaction, it is the price that the young amorous Girl-Marx's desire for the reconciled body is made to pay by the fat-headed Accuser-Marx with the shattered social body: ah, you dream of the relation of non-domination between men and things, and between men themselves, and between men and women! All right then, show the consistency of the dream, demonstrate that reality too, dreams this dream. That is to say: *you also pay*, pay in word-products, in articulations, in structured arguments, endlessly. Wasn't this said, in substance, in the peripheries of the work, in 1844: the proletariat is Christ, and his real suffering is the price of his redemption, and this is why it is not enough that a particular wrong is done him, a shopkeeper's wrong, a pathetic limitation of his profit-margin, for example, no, his redemption requires a total suffering, therefore a total wrong, as the proletariat will be for Marx, once and for all, and as Marx will be once and for all for the proletariat required by the desire named Marx: Christ the proletariat, Marx his witness-martyr? *Theoretical* discourse being his cross, his torture?

Certainly, we may put it this way, in terms of a religious metaphor. But it misses the essential, because it presupposes exactly what turns out to be in question in Marx's desire, it presupposes this *body of reference* as a sacrifice, body of capital for the martyr of the proletariat, body of the proletariat for Marx's martyr, without which sacrifice and martyr go up in smoke, and are no more than phantasms of guilt. In other words, the sacrificial metaphor is not libidinally neutral, it is not economically correct, it is topically 'correct', it requires a principle (be it imaginary, which none the less requires a 'symbolic' medium) of unification and inscription in comparison to which pain and pleasure, here those of Marx's research, may be counted, registered. And what if it was precisely this referential instance which Marx's inspection turned out to lack, this body of *Ratio*, of the account? What if what would prolong the research interminably were not, as 'psychoanalytic' or 'Nietzschean' crassness wouldn't fail to say, Karl Marx's 'masochist' desire or 'bad conscience', but the vertigo of a terrible discovery (always hidden): that *there is no-one* to keep the accounts of suffering and *jouissance*, and that this, too, is the domination of money-capital?

If we restrict ourselves to a 'critique' (which means, of course, *non-critique*) of whatever *guilt* or ressentiment there is in the assemblage of the desire named Marx and generally named *militant*,[3] we will *de facto* remain in the *religious metaphor*, we will replace the religious metaphor with an *irreligious* metaphor, still religious then, in which judgements will be discovered at work according to good and evil in reference to a 'new' god, which will be desire: movement will be good, investment evil; action as innovation and the force of the event will be good, reaction reiterating identity, evil. And how will we then describe the 'Marx' or 'militant' libidinal *dispositif*? We turn to the passion for expiation and ressentiment. Every reversal (of the 'first' into the 'last', but just as much of the dominant into the equal) which forms the figure of the revolution implies, we say, the intention of a price to (be) charged. If Marx authorized himself to set himself up as the proletariat's advocate, and petition against their exploiters, if he can declare to them: this is why it is you who will pay the price, it is, we say again, on condition that he had marked down the suffering, the expiation and the ressentiment on his own body and that he himself suffers and pays. Is this not the law which gives *the right to the desire for revolution*, in the sphere of ressentiment: that the militant had formed his own body into a monstrous composition, so that the woman-proletariat would obtain the most durable man-prosecutor and the greatest total pain, that all revolutionary ressentiment will be played out between Little Girl Marx and Old Man Marx on its body?

Far from emancipating ourselves through such a critique of what we detest, religion, ressentiment, guilt, morality, we will only invert its signs; Marx wants an (in)organic body, does his desire enslave it to a genital model? We want a schizophrenic model and an unstable body. Marx wants to charge? We want generalized gratuity. Marx accuses? We exonerate. Marx-the-proletariat suffers and redeems? We joyfully love all that appears. Etc. A new morality, a new religion, is in fact merely a very ancient ethics, itself strongly 'reactive', since the party of movement and existence has always existed *at the core* of religions, at least of those taking authority from a revelation, to act as a counter-poison in belief and in the *systems* of belief, every time that its adversary, the party of order and structure, has ended up wearying the faithful and even the priests. Do we want to be merely the saviours of a fallen world, then, the hearts of a heartless world, prophets (cruel, very cruel, as the programme goes) for a humanity without words? Do we bring new values then? In denouncing militant ressentiment, we are doing nothing other than *valorizing a certain sort of libidinal dispositif*, in fact the admirable viscosity of the fluxes ceaselessly setting up and wiping out on the great libidinal film; we affirm its *exclusive value*: but the exclusive value is called truth. Therefore we affirm: schizo-desire, there's truth! How then does the *dispositif of our affirmation* differ from that by which the ancient statements (love is the truth; renunciation is the truth; knowledge is the truth; socialism is the truth) were affirmed? Doesn't their reactive element lie in their *power of exclusion*? Are we too not going to exclude? How pitiful!

This, then, is not how the libidinal *dispositif* named Marx should be described, merely *described*; not as the effect of ressentiment. Our rule should be never to describe anything as effect; we should describe everything as *capable of effects*. Now there is, in the interminable postponement of the prosecution's revolutionary summation in Marx, a certain effective force; theoretical discourse ceases to be presented according to its closure even though this is what it *seeks*. What Marx perceives as failure, suffering (and maybe even lives through as ressentiment) is the mark on his work of a situation which is precisely the same as that of capital, and which gives rise to a strange success as much as to an awful misery: the work cannot *form a body*, just as capital cannot form a body. And this absence of organic, 'artistic' unity gives rise to two divergent movements always associated in a single vertigo: a movement of flight, of plunging into the bodiless, and thus of continual invention, of expansive additions or affirmations of new pieces (statements, but elsewhere musics, techniques, ethics) to the insane patchwork—a movement of *tension*. And a movement of institution of an organism, of an organization and of organs of totalization and unification—a movement of reason. Both kinds of movement are there, effects as force in the *non-finito* of the work just as in that of capitalism.[4]

Marx's inability to catch up with his book (a delay which is equally an 'advance' upon it, a form of temporal dislocation in any case), rather than being considered as an effect of masochism or guilt, should be compared with the way in which Sterne makes a theme of this delay in *Tristram Shandy*. In each case, the following configuration is involved: to fabricate a discourse, whether narrative or theoretical, implying a new, unprecedented organization of space and time, the writer (narrator, theoretician) uses space and time. With Sterne, this use (or this usury) is inscribed in the narrative itself, and devours it: the place and the duration occupied by the 'narrative act' little by little invade those which should be given over to the narration of the story and render this latter impossible, or at least transform it into the narrative of this invasion and this impossibility. With Marx, the effect that the 'act of elaboration' has on the space-time of theoretical discourse is not explicitly marked in this latter, and the final impossibility of the domination of the duration and location in a discourse (which is here theoretical and no longer narrative, but which nevertheless refers to a supposed 'story' taken as a reference) does not give rise to Sterne's desperate humour, to a style. With Marx, the expression of this despair remains repressed, caught and hidden between his activity of fabricating apodictic final statements and the statements, not even assertive, which he publishes in another text, those of confessions, letters, abandoned or withdrawn manuscripts, lecture notes, plans. But this despair gives rise, in whatever way, to theoretical suspense, it opens the void of: Wait until I have finished.

This void is that of the mediator alienating the subject (Marx, Sterne) and the object (the book), to speak in Marx's language; it is that of inhibition, which leads desire from its primary object towards the *means* of its realization; it is that of capital, which loves production rather than the product, and for which the product is only the means of producing; it is that of the 'communist' party, which loves not the revolution, but the means by which they are *able* to make it happen, which in their hands is only a pretext to the machinery for capitalizing the desire for revolution. Therefore, this void is that in which the mechanisms of power are constructed; but it is also the *supple* viscosity of capitalism as fragments of the body, as connected-disconnected singularities, as amnesia, decentred and anarchic, as harlequinade, as metamorphoses without inscription, as the undoing of totalities and totalizations, as ephemeral groupings of unforeseen affirmations.

There Is No Subversive Region

Let's repeat it over and again, we are not going to do a critique of Marx, we are not, that is to say, going to produce the theory of his theory: which is just to remain within the theoretical. No, one must show what intensities are lodged in theoretical signs, what affects within serious discourse; we must steal his affects from him. Its force is not at all in the power of its discourse, not even in inverse proportion to it, this would still be a little too dialectical an arrangement; no, its force erupts here and there, independently of the consistency of the discourse, sometimes in a forgotten detail, sometimes in the very midst of a solid conceptual mechanism, well articulated and rooted—but of course always in intelligent signs. What would a critique of Marx be (apart from the fact that there are already a hundred thousand such critiques)? We must inevitably say of him: oh he remained alienated, oh he brought out the symbolic system (this is Baudrillard), oh he is still religious (this would rather be us), oh he remained an economist (this was Castoriadis). Quite obviously he *remained* this, *forgot* that, is *still* such and such a thing—something which the critic is supposed to *no longer* be, to have *superseded*. Well, we have superseded nothing and we have nothing to supersede, we do not climb onto Marx's back here, 'armed with double spectacles, some Lilliputian stands on the extremity of the giant's posterior [it was Aristotle actually], announces amazedly to the world what an astoundingly new view is offered from his *punctum visus*, and ridiculously endeavours to demonstrate that the Archimedian point . . . on which the world hinges, can be found, not in the pulsating heart but in the firm and solid area on which he stands'—so the Little Girl Marx, Alice, wrote in the annotations to her doctoral thesis.[5]

Of course he remained *religious*. But what do we want-desire? A true atheism? Certainly not! A beyond of both religion and atheism, something like Roman parody, and consequently, we would not at all be content to have 'demonstrated' that Marx's politics and political economics are full of religiosity, reconciliation and hope—although we are constrained to do so and it is impossible to avoid this sort of knowledgeable discourse. We are, however, aware that this is set out in such a way that there is no trace of the emotions which induce it, and that, in consequence, its very position is reassuring, perhaps allowing only a certain anguish, apparently the only noble affect, to filter through, but not love, not anger, not some disconcerting surprise. It would make us happy to be able to retranscribe, into a libidinal discourse, those intensities which haunt Marx's thought and which, in general, are dissimulated in the brass-tacks solemnity of the discourses of economy and politics. We will show, therefore, how in Marx's own terms, political economy is a libidinal economy.

We are very close and very far then from what Baudrillard is doing,[6] and this is an excellent opportunity for us to try to explain why, since there is a *movement* in Baudrillard with which we feel synchronized and co-polarized. We are very close, read him and see; but also very distant, since what governs our brother's approach remains burdened in our eyes with hypothesis, theory and critique. This is not for want of denouncing critique as imperialism and theory as racism, in formulas we joyfully endorse. But as holy and beautiful as it is, his anger aims ultimately at the *true* once again, it reproaches political economy, even and especially if this was Marxist (because we were hoping for precisely the opposite from it), of remaining within the sphere of production, of value, of labour, and thus of *forgetting* something, repressing or rather foreclosing, in a sort of perversion, which Baudrillard previously qualified as fetishist, a relation between persons which would not be subordinated to the consideration of the product, but would be entirely governed by symbolic exchange, entirely centred on the *exhaustion* of the libidinal resources of love and death in a give-and-take heedless of the conservation of goods, heedless of power, bound up with rekindling *force* [*puissance*] at all costs. Political economy, therefore, would be something which begins somewhere in the history of humanity, in any case with a certain sort of social *dispositif*, far then from being the universal truth of every society, presenting itself veiled, in embryo, in archaic societies from which it would be absent; it would be the retroactive projection of the capitalist assemblage onto symbolic exchanges that would ignore all interest in order to count only as passion, and all equivalence in order to exhibit nothing but ambivalence.

One should sweep aside the little ploys of the 'determinant' and the 'dominant'[7] with the back of one's hand, the profoundly logocentric view according to which, of course, the Greeks were ignorant of labour, but would finally work without knowing it, and would, indeed, have to end up learning it although no longer under the name of the Greeks, but that of the Romans and the English—we say this is all very well, and we will march on in the same direction, certain that we must everywhere destroy the bastions of alleged economic rationality, as we must those of semiology. But, just as for this latter, we do not want to fall into the trap set by this rationality at the same moment that it is vanquished. This trap consists quite simply in *responding to the demand of the vanquished theory*, and this demand is: put something in my place. The important thing is this place, however, not the contents of the theory. It is the place of theory that must be vanquished. And this can come about only through displacement and flight. It matters little if we say: there is no history, if it is *replaced* with the linear history of stages of humanity's development, such as historical materialism imagines it, replaced by a history or even a simultaneity of discontinuous forms registering social formations in their internal and external differences. It makes little difference to say: there is no universal political economy, if we add: the *truth* of the social relation is the ambivalence of symbolic exchange, this alone gives rights to the erotic and lethal force of desire. All the more so because we are subtle enough, and this was formerly Baudrillard's very beautiful introduction to the article on fetishism, to recognize that *desire underlies capitalism too*, so that in some sense the former gives the right to the latter, that it is not a libidinal nothing, including in its investment a proper effect of nihilation (that of ambivalence). No sooner is this accord of capital with the order of desire accepted, no sooner is the 'perversion' marking it specified, than we find ourselves once more within theory and evaluation: 'And following the same revolutionary movement as Marx did, we must move to a radically different level that, beyond its critique, permits the definitive resolution of political economy. This level is that of symbolic exchange and its theory.'[8]

Are you saying that political economy rests on the ignorance of desire? No, but on the foreclosure of castration, answers Baudrillard. But what is this castration, what is foreclosure? Is desire marked by castration, and is it organized just as Saussure's *negative* underlies *la langue*? Strange game of hide-and-seek with ourselves: this castration, this negative, which here we name the great Zero, far from seeing in it the order of desire, which is the movement of energy, it is for us the order of capital in the broadest sense, that of the theology which capitalizes affects on the instance of the Other, *one* figure of desire. And it is of our libidinal economy that Baudrillard would be correct to say that it forecloses castration, and therefore desire. Do we maintain the opposite? Hardly. Let us take a precise case. When Baudrillard says: '*There is neither a mode of production nor production* in primitive societies. *There is no dialectic and no unconscious* in primitive societies,'[9] we say: there are no primitive societies.

First of all, methodologically (I'm afraid so . . .), this society of the gift and counter-gift plays, in Baudrillard's thought, the role of a reference (lost, of course), of an alibi (which cannot be found), in his critique of capital. Baudrillard does not mean to speak of nature and naturality.[10] How is it that he does not see that the whole problematic of the gift, of symbolic exchange, such as he receives it from Mauss, with or without the additions and diversions of Bataille, Caillois, Lacan, belongs in its entirety to Western racism and imperialism—that it is still ethnology's good savage, slightly libidinalized, which he inherits with the concept? It will be necessary to take a detour here, to examine Baudrillard's critique of the idea of nature, to refute the dichotomy he proposes between the 'good nature' which would be what lets itself be 'civilized', that is to say, dominated and exploited, and a 'bad nature' which would be rebellious. Carried away as he is against the materialism of forces and relations of production, which in fact demands this separation, he forgets that there is constantly, within Western political, that is, also sociological and ethnological, thought, since at least Plato in the *Timaeus* who will seek the guardians of his utopian Atlantis amongst the very ancient Egyptian 'savages', and certainly in Marx's socio-economic thought, there is the wholly inverted reference of a *good rebel nature*, of a nature good insofar as it is rebellious, insofar therefore as it is left outside, *forgotten*, foreclosed. Ethnology in its entirety, Lévi-Strauss's as much as Jaulin's, emanates from this phantasy (which is in its turn only one case amongst many of the *representationalization* [*mise-en représentation*] proper to the West, proceeding from its logophilia). We will show this in Marx, not in order to convince that this is the case, rather through a species of pleasure, through affection for the young girl that he is, dreaming of reconciliation and believing that this had taken place in the past, somewhere else, and that she and her lover, the proletariat, had been deprived of it. We will show that, speaking of the archaic labourer, this feminine Marx has some resonances not unrelated in general to those of Baudrillard forging his myth of symbolic exchange.

For what happens to whomever does not want to recognize that political economy is libidinal, is that he reproduces in other terms the same phantasy of an externalized region where desire would be sheltered from every treacherous transcription into production, labour and the law of value. The phantasy of a non-alienated region. Methodologically, to retrace Marx's movement, even extending it to the position of desire, begins religion all over again; so much so that there is something almost tragic when Baudrillard parodies the famous statement of 1843: 'For Germany, the critique of religion is substantially over', by writing: 'The critique of political economy is substantially over.' For, in this text of 1843, which intends to *start something else*, a politics which would be non-philosophical, that is to say, religious, Marx allows his thoroughly religious love for a lost consubstantiality of men amongst themselves and with nature to show through: it is there in particular that his desire for return, so similar to that of Rousseau, gives itself free rein, weaving the absolutely Christian scenario of the martyr of the proletariat as the sacrificial episode necessary to the final salvation: 'A class must be formed which has radical chains, a class in civil society which is not a class of civil society, a class which is the dissolution of all classes . . . a sphere which is . . . a total loss of humanity and which can only redeem itself by a total redemption of humanity,'[11] etc.

I am not saying that this scenario exists in Baudrillard, far from it; but there is, inevitably, the reproduction of that same thing which underlies it and which Marx's desire required ('it is necessary . . . '), a region which would not be in society and which would be: 'Generations placed or left out of circulation, *off limits*, by the very development of productive forces'; and of this production of marginals, it will be said, just as, in the past, Marx said of the production of the proletariat: 'New contradictions emanate from this.'[12] Once again, our intention is not to reduce that to this, and not for a moment do we stop loving and stoking the anger of the anti-economist. Moreover, he takes a great deal of care to show that these contradictions are in no way 'dialectical', and to oppose subversion (which does not itself enter the order of political economy) to the claims and counter-claims which are just the basic constituents of the game which capital plays with itself. There is no dialectic in Baudrillard, and this is because the *subversive reference*, that of the good savage and the good hippy, is in his eyes *positively* present in modern society, not *negatively*, as Marx imagines the proletariat to be. The marginals are libidinal affirmations, the proletarians were negations of negation in a journey and a sublation [*relève*]. We fear only the consequences of this small detail, of this 'methodological' nuance: that the affirmative should be delimited *as a region*. Since every region gives rise to regime and reign, to sign and mechanism, and if therefore all one's hopes were placed in it, one is certain to despair. Perhaps, as politicians, *we still and always desire to be in despair . . . ?*

Every Political Economy Is Libidinal

There is one thing, then, which makes us say: there is no primitive society, that is to say: there is no external reference, even if immanent, from which the separation of what belongs to capital (or political economy) and what belongs to subversion (or libidinal economy), can always be made, and cleanly; where desire would be clearly legible, where its *proper economy* would not be scrambled. And this should be clearly understood: 'scrambled' does not mean 'thwarted', tainted, by a foreign, evil instance. This is simply the problematic of alienation, it is, to invoke another brother, what still belongs in *Anti-Oedipus* to the thought of an error or of a criminal act. 'Scrambled' means that the economy of desire cannot be attributed, just like ambivalence, not only because it is Eros and the death drive, but because the effects of each instance are inascribable, as we have said. Scrambled then, by itself and in itself, not crossed and alienated by another political economic order. *There is no alienation* from the instant one escapes the critical relation. *There is as much libidinal intensity in capitalist exchange as in the alleged 'symbolic' exchange.* And this is the second thing to be said in a more provocative or affirmative way, concerning our gloss of 'there is no primitive society'.

Not merely: there is no other 'regional' reference, but: capitalism *is also* a primitive society, or: the primitive society *is also* a capitalism. This latter statement first: of course, savages do not capitalize goods; but who considers that it is only the fully mercantile instance of the great Zero that sanctions and indeed demands the *scrupulous balancing of the inflows and outflows of affects* (in the form of relatives, words, beasts, lives, sexes), hanging over and maintaining these societies? Take the ethnological descriptions that you might set against us as embarrassing counter-examples, the most embarrassing; at random, the mad witches that Michel Leiris frequents in *Gondar*,[13] the terrifying murder, the Jakugi's wooden arch hung for three nights over the neck of the young girl who must perish, a murder announced, honoured in an insomniac chant, so admirably described by Pierre Clastres.[14] Of course there are extreme intensities here and there, and ambivalence, this is the least one can say. But even this possibility of the Indian hunter's criminal love and hate with regard to his fellow countrywoman is not important, nor is the orgasmic and mortiferous exaltation of women stained with the blood of sacrificed beasts; what is important is that these indisputable intensities *are also read* in terms of order, and even of the return to order, that the tensions which all at once inscribe themselves at the extremities or at the centre of the social surface fully participate in the sense that they do not in any way subvert it, but literally compose it, and thus circulate in it as exchangeable, intelligible, semiotic signs. Good, Baudrillard would doubtlessly put up with us speaking in this way: societies of the gift and counter-gift, he would say. But, if so, he would then have to admit this: that 'symbolic exchange' is also an exchange in the sense of political economy.

However, let us now try this other proposition, and see what comes of it: this *dissimulation* of intensities into values and values into intensities is no less active in capitalist society. Just as there is a capitalist order of savages (which *sanctions* Lévi-Strauss's imperialism, but what imperialism is not sanctioned by a guarantor of order, by a desire for balancing out, active in the dominated society itself?), so there are errant forces *in* the signs of capital. Not in its margins as its *marginals*, but dissimulated in its most 'nuclear', the most essential exchanges, the most 'alienated' or 'fetishized' exchanges in Baudrillard's eyes. If we do not recognize this, then in ten years' time we will start up another new critique, the critique of the 'critique of the political economy of the sign'. But it is extraordinarily difficult to recognize the *desire of capital* such as it is instantiated here and there; as, for example, in labour, in the awful mundane sense of the *grind* for which not even the worker today has enough words of contempt and disrepute; or as in the *object*, the same object whose *force* [*puissance*] Baudrillard's fascination has for its part, justifiably, so helped us to recapture through its power: isn't fetishism an opportunity for intensities? Doesn't it attest to an admirable force of invention, adding events which could not be more improbable to the libidinal band? From where would you *criticize* fetishism, when you know that one cannot criticize homosexuality or masochism without becoming a crude bastard of the moral order? Or again indeed, investment in the *time* of capital, this strange simultaneous placing-in-reserve and anticipated expenditure of libidinal intensities, which is implied in the system of banking and currency; an analysis of this might be attempted later. Or more simply, investment in the system as such, in general, a characteristic by which one Gell-Man, a great physician, finds himself a collaborator with a Westmoreland, a pathetic scientific 'criminal' from the Vietnam war, one characteristic of the decisive congruence, and doubtlessly not exclusive of others, between science and capital. And yet the investment in the system, in value, in the constitution of pieces of the libidinal band in terms which only have value through 'difference' or reference, and in the establishment of the *laws* of these cross-references—that is to say the deranged investment in the bond and its accomplice, lack ('Like a drug whose supply one doesn't even ask for again—for the lack of it is as much a having as any other.'[15])—in the sense of Freudian libidinal economy, in the *Metapsychology* or *The Ego and the Id*, can't this investment give rise to vertiginous intensities? Were not Einstein's most artistic inventions also driven by this desire, by the conviction that God, as he said, certainly does not play at dice? And what is *lost* in this? Nothing at all.

But, you will say, it gives rise to power and domination, to exploitation and even extermination. Quite true; but also to masochism; but the strange bodily arrangement of the skilled worker with his job and his machine, which is so often reminiscent of the *dispositif* of hysteria, can also produce the extermination of a population: look at the English proletariat, at what capital, that is to say *their labour*, has done to their body. You will tell me, however, that it was that or die. *But it is always that or die*, this is the law of libidinal economy, no, not the law: this is its provisional, very provisional, definition in the form of the cry, of intensities of desire; 'that or die', i.e. that and dying from it, death always in it, as its internal bark, its thin nut's skin, not yet as its *price*, on the contrary as that which renders it unpayable. And perhaps you believe that 'that or die' is an *alternative*?! And that if they choose that, if they become the slave of the machine, the machine of the machine, fucker fucked by it, eight hours, twelve hours, a day, year after year, it is because they are forced into it, constrained, because they cling to life? Death is not an alternative to it, it is a part of it, it attests to the fact that there is *jouissance* in it, the English unemployed did not become workers to survive, they—hang on tight and spit on me—*enjoyed* [*ils ont joui de*] the hysterical, masochistic, whatever exhaustion it was of *hanging on* in the mines, in the foundries, in the factories, in hell, they enjoyed it, enjoyed the mad destruction of their organic body which was indeed imposed upon them, they enjoyed the decomposition of their personal identity, the identity that the peasant tradition had constructed for them, enjoyed the dissolution of their families and villages, and enjoyed the new monstrous *anonymity* of the suburbs and the pubs in the morning and evening.

And let's finally acknowledge this *jouissance*, which is similar, Little Girl Marx was clear on this point, in every way to that of prostitution, the *jouissance* of anonymity, the *jouissance* of the *repetition of the same* in work, the same gesture, the same comings and goings in the factory, how many penises per hour, how many tonnes of coal, how many cast-iron bars, how many barrels of shit, not 'produced', of course, but *endured*, the *same parts of the body* used, made use of, to the total exclusion of others, and just as the prostitutes' vagina or mouth are hysterically *anaesthetized*, through use, through being used, so the worker's ear as described and analysed by Tomatis, who, next to an alternator functioning at 20,000 Hz, peacefully writes his letters and hears the finest noises; and when Tomatis makes his audiogramme study, he notices that the resonant range corresponding to the alternator functioning at 20,000 Hz, is neutralized, *mute*. Hence a hysterical treatment of a fraction of the auditory body, whore assemblage, the libidinal use demanded, of course, by the 'conditions of labour', which are also, however, those of prostitution. It goes without saying, of course, that we say this without any condemnation, without any regret, on the contrary by discovering that there has been, and perhaps still is, the extraordinary dissimulated-dissimulating force of the worker, force of resistance, force of *jouissance* in the hysterical madness of the conditions of labour which the sociologists would call *fragmented* without seeing what libidinal intensities these fragments can convey *as fragments*.

How can we continue to speak of alienation when it is clear that for everybody, in the experiences he *has* (and that more often than not he cannot properly *have*, since these experiences are allegedly shameful, and especially since instead of having them, he is these experiences) of even the most stupid capitalist labourer, that he can find *jouissance* and a strange, perverse intensity, what do we know about it?—when it is clear that not one 'productive' or 'artistic' or 'poetic' metamorphosis has ever been accomplished, nor will be, by a unitary and totalized organic body, but that it is always at the price of its alleged dissolution and therefore of an inevitable stupidity that this has been possible; when it is clear that there has never been, nor ever will be such a *dissolution* for the good reason that there has never been nor ever will be such a body bound up in its unity and identity, that this body is a phantasy, itself fairly libidinal, erotic and hygienic = Greek, or erotic and supernatural = Christian, and that it is by contrast with this phantasy that all alienation is thought and *resented* in the sense of ressentiment which is the feeling aroused by the great Zero as the desire for return. But the body of primitive savages is no more a whole body than that of the Scottish miners of a century ago, there is no whole body.

Finally, you must also realize that such *jouissance*, I am thinking of that of the proletariat, is not at all exclusive of the hardest and most intense *revolts. Jouissance* is *unbearable*. It is not in order to regain their dignity that the workers will revolt, break the machines, lock up the bosses, kick out the deputies, that the victims of colonization will set the governors' palaces on fire and cut the sentries' throats, no, it is something else altogether, there is no dignity; Guyotat has so admirably put this into writing with regard to Algeria.[16] There are libidinal positions, tenable or not, there are positions invested which are immediately disinvested, the energies passing onto other pieces of the great puzzle, inventing new fragments and new modalities of *jouissance*, that is to say of intensification. There is no libidinal dignity, nor libidinal fraternity, there are libidinal contacts without communication (for want of a 'message'). This is why, amongst individuals participating in the same struggle, there may exist the most profound miscomprehension, even if they are situated in the same social and economic bracket. If some Algerian fights for four years out in the brush or for a few months in the urban networks, it is because his desire has become the desire to kill, not to kill in general, but to kill an invested part, still invested, there's no doubt about it, of his sensitive regions. Would he kill his French master? More than that: he would be killed as the obliging servant of this master, to disengage the region of his prostitute's consent, to seek other *jouissances* than prostitution as a model, that is to say as the predominant modality of investment. Nevertheless, instantiating itself in murder, perhaps his desire remained still in the grip of the punitive relation that he meant to abandon, perhaps this murder was still a suicide, a punishment, the price due to the pimp, and still servitude. But during this same struggle for independence, some other 'moderate', even centrist, Algerian, decided on compromise and negotiation, he sought quite another disposition of *jouissance*, his intelligence dismissing such a death and swearing in calculation, already nourishing contempt for the body and exalting words as negotiation demands, hence also his own death as the death of flesh in general, not as the prostitute body, a very acceptable death to the Western talker. Etc.

Now these disparities, which are heterogeneities of investment in the erotic and deadly fluxes, are of course also found within any social 'movement' whatsoever, whether minute, on the scale of a factory, or immense, when it spreads to a whole country or continent. But apart from the movements of open revolt, notice that these singular 'hysterical' *jouissances*, for example, or those we might call 'potential', so akin to modern scientificity, or again those by which a 'body' is installed within the increased reproduction of capital, where it is entirely subordinated to the measurement of time saved and time advanced—and indeed all these instantiations (brutally sketched here), even when the capitalist machine is humming in the apparent general boredom and when everybody seems to do their job without moaning, all these libidinal instantiations, these little *dispositifs* of the retention and flow of the influxes of desire are *never unequivocal* and cannot give rise to a sociological reading or an unequivocal politics, to a decoding into a definable lexis and syntax; punishment incites both submission and revolt, power, the fascination of pride and autodepreciative depression, every 'discipline' demands passion and hate, even if these are only the *indifference* in Marx's sense, of whomever performs it. Hence ambivalence, said Baudrillard. And we say: much more than that, something else besides this condensed house of love and disgust or fear, which in general will be vulnerable to the attack of a semiotic or hermeneutic analysis of affects; no interpreter is afraid of polysemia; but at the same time and indiscernibly something which is a functioning or *dysfunctioning* term in a system, and something which is abruptly implacable joy and suffering; at once ambivalent signification and tension, dissimulated into one another. Not only the *and/or*, but the silent comma: ','.

Every Political Economy Is Libidinal (contd)

How many iron bars, tonnes of sperm, decibels of carnal shrieks and factory noises, more and still more: this *more* may be invested as such, it is in capital, and it must be recognized that not only is it completely inane, we fully accept this, it is no more nor less vain than either political discussion on the *agora* or the Peloponnesian war, but it is especially necessary to recognize that this is not even a matter of production. These 'products' are not products, what counts here, in capital, is that they are endured and endured *in quantity*, it is the quantity, the imposed number that is itself already a motive for intensity, not the qualitative mutation of quantity, not at all, but as in Sade the frightening number of blows received, the number of postures and manoeuvres required, the necessary number of victims, as in Mina Boumedine, the abominable quantity of penises which penetrate through many entrances into the woman who works lying on the oilcloth on a table in the back room of a bar:

> She sucks and shakes in a sweaty haze / she sucks the knobs waved in her face / she shudders as the trouser flies wound her / her vision reels / entrances and sham exits / awakening in hospital / the bar door grinds / Mina is this door / diastole and systole / her heart is going to burst / she attempts to count the openings of the door / she says to herself that she will become so many dicks / she loses count and retains the grinding / she is made to drink coca / she has a funny taste at the bottom of her throat / she is a wounded bird / a shivering bruised bird / she lies at the roadside / she has had an accident . . . You have counted well / not all the time / you rested against me yes all the time / I didn't leave you for a moment / the fortieth in the cunt alone / Mina in quarantine / I disgust you / tell me that I disgust you / I will play the whore for you / I will do my hundred a day on the oilcloth with the little blue squares / the smell of the acetylene torch / the whistling of the torch / the whistling of its suffering / she is dead assassinated / in the light of the wretches / she was dead here for months / for years / the hundred a day on the oilcloth in the back shop and the bucket of water / when she was finished to reawaken her / the frozen bucket of water / and all at once all over again the whistling of the lamp / then she was not dead / she was not dead enough / she had to start again . . . [17]

Use erogenous zone numbers,[18] more and still more, isn't this a decisive instantiation of intensity in capitalism? Are we, intellectual sirs, not actively or passively [*passivons*] 'producing' more and more words, more books, more articles, ceaselessly refilling the pot-boiler of speech, gorging ourselves on it rather, seizing books and 'experiences', to metamorphose them as quickly as possible into other words, plugging us in here, being plugged in there, just like Mina on her blue squared oilcloth, extending the market and the trade in words of course, but also multiplying the chances of *jouissance*, scraping up intensities wherever possible, and never being sufficiently dead, for we too are required to go from the forty to the hundred a day, and we will never play the whore enough, we will never be dead enough.

And here is the question: Why, political intellectuals, do you *incline towards* the proletariat? In commiseration for what? I realize that a proletarian would hate you, you have no hatred because you are bourgeois, privileged smooth-skinned types, but also because you dare not say the only important thing there is to say, that one can enjoy swallowing the shit of capital, its materials, its metal bars, its polystyrene, its books, its sausage pâtés, swallowing tonnes of it till you burst—and because instead of saying this, which is *also* what happens in the desire of those who work with their hands, arses and heads, ah, you become a leader of *men*, what a leader of *pimps*, you lean forward and divulge: ah, but that's alienation, it isn't pretty, hang on, we'll save you from it, we will work to liberate you from this wicked affection for servitude, we will give you dignity. And in this way you situate yourselves on the most despicable side, the moralistic side where you desire that our capitalized's desire be totally ignored, forbidden, brought to a standstill, you are like priests with sinners, our servile intensities frighten you, you have to tell yourselves: how they must suffer to endure that! And of course we suffer, we the capitalized, but this does not mean that we do not enjoy, nor that what you think you can offer us as a remedy—for what?—does not disgust us, even more. We abhor therapeutics and its vaseline, we prefer to burst under the quantitative excesses that you judge the most stupid. And don't wait for our spontaneity to rise up in revolt either.

Let me open a parenthesis of hatred, here, a word will suffice against the great cesspool of consolations called *spontaneity* and *creativity*, that some dare to connect onto the courses, wayward certainly, but never vulgar until then, traced by the impulsions of *Socialisme ou barbarie* in the field of political practice and theory. In 1964, apparently over questions of theory and orientation, we broke with Castoriadis who, rightly bored with reassessing historical, dialectic and diarrhoetic materialism, nevertheless proposed to put in its place the abominable super-male thing of generalized creativity: in modern capitalism, he explained (but read it yourselves, he is publishing his complete works[19]), the central problem is no longer exploitation, but the destruction of any real human communication, the annihilation of men's capacity to ceaselessly create, by themselves, *sponte sua*, new forms of relations with the world and with others. Against privatization, he brings back active socialization; against alienation, this always active creativity. Everywhere and always, creativity. From what do men (women, children, let's not leave anyone out) suffer in 'affluent' society? From their solitude and from becoming passive; and why? Because their power to communicate and to love, their capacity to invent new responses, and to try them out on the most radical problems, is annihilated, he says, by the bureaucratic organization not only of their working lives, but of every aspect of their lives. A bureaucracy which is not some small defect in the otherwise complete social body, for example, in the sense in which the Poujadists speak of administrative bureaucracy, Crozier genially seeing in it the relinquishment of the old royal, Jacobin centralism, in administrations (*sic*), Trotsky denouncing it as a cancer devouring a state which is otherwise proletarian. No: global bureaucratization, as Bruno Rizzi said.[20]

But of course, under the name (although it is very clumsily inherited from Trotskyism) of bureaucracy, we were quite in agreement that this had to be understood: not a new political phenomenon, not only an extension of the apparatus to new sectors of social life, not only the simple consolidation of a new dominant social class, but moreover the production of another humanity for which the revolutionary thought *of making* that we inherited after a fashion from Marx, even if this was through the entire leftist opposition, was no longer appropriate. And we were quite in agreement that it was necessary, in a sense, 'to restart the revolution',[21] as the introductory text presented by Castoriadis and his group was entitled. Nevertheless, we went over to the adverse camp which continued *Pouvoir Ouvrier* for some time, a camp classed as traditionalist in questions of diamat and histmat,[22] and which on the contrary should have been called a camp for refugees or homeless persons, so diverse were the preoccupations of those who found themselves in it, as the discords which erupted after the first attempts at theoretical or practical research and the resignations show.

If I mention a word on this subject, and on purpose a thoughtless word at that, it is: (1) because it serves nothing to shroud the affair in the solemn dress which tends to envelop 'Politics on the grand scale' and which is so inclined to maintain the already established myth of *Socialisme ou barbarie*, a myth that should be damned more than any other; (2) so that our readers are warned that our weighty predecessors are as light as our successors; (3) so that they consider our flight into libidinal economy for what it is, the solution to a long pain and the breach out of a difficult impasse; (4) and so that they understand these few lines of hatred as the expression of our laughter, behind our anger, at the hole that Castoriadis believed he had made, and made others believe he had made, in the wall which was obstructing everything we did as 'militants', our thoughts, our lives, our acts (and this was no small matter, it wasn't a question of having the party card, or selling political rags on a Sunday morning in the market), our laughter at, and against, this hole which connected us onto nothing which we already did not know, which did not make our bodies and heads flee towards unheard-of dispositions at all, but which wisely channelled them towards a 'new' *vision of the world*, towards a 'new' *thinking*, towards a humanism of creators at heart similar to that of some big, philanthropic American *boss*, towards a *theory*, yet again, a theory of generalized alienation which necessarily implied as its double a theory of generalized creativity—the only means known, since Hegel and undoubtedly Jesus as well, of not being alienated without being god. Therefore a 'new' religion, then, man made god, a Faustian religion which betrayed as ever and continued to betray its antiquatedness, as an innocent friend remarked to us one day, in the incoherence of the very expression 'worker's power' [*pouvoir ouvrier*].

For 'worker', that ought to have been the taking into consideration of the very *force* [*puissance*] of what is dominated, and it is not then a matter of revealing the scandal of power as what could console or cure him: not just because *no-one* has to judge it (and I am not even saying: if not the interested parties themselves—since it is no more them than any others, without doubt); but again because this force belonged to us as politicians, it was for us to lower the flag before it, to take it into full consideration, and then the perspective of power would be abandoned, it should not have begun, as soon as it was perceived, and perceived in its extension, to be understood negatively, by nihilists refusing to call it *force* [*puissance*], the force of holding the untenable, *and also* the force of not holding it and making everything shake, the self included—hurrying, on the contrary, to call it privatization, passivation, alienation, loss of creativity, that is to say, hurrying to set it up as lack and present the maximum as the thing to bring about or bring back. Finally we need not have said: restart the revolution, instead, and this would have been the hole, we had to say: let's also eliminate the idea of revolution which became and which perhaps had always been a little nothing of an idea, the idea of a reversal of position in the sphere of political economic power and therefore the idea of maintaining this sphere, or even, to be fairer to Castoriadis, the idea of a reversal of position in *all* spheres; even this thought of a generalized reversal had to be broken in its turn, for it was once again a wall, the same wall of the same impasse, since where there is thought of reversal, there is the theory of alienation, nihilism and theoretician-saviours, heads, depositories of knowledge. 'Thinking heads are always connected by invisible threads to the *body* of the people', a delighted Marx wrote to Meyer (21 January 1871).

This is where my hatred lies: knowledge carried on, we thought we had correct knowledge—how very sophisticated to know, knowing that one does not know, to know, presenting oneself sincerely as not knowing, to know how to construct in an open, decided, instigating way, the knowledge ultimately of an analyst—; and so, thanks to this piece of sophistication, we hoped to avoid adultery—not the thoroughly legal and well-sanctioned nuptials—of this knowledge with power, we said: we are militants who are no longer militants, we are no longer the bearers of good news, we put ourselves at the service of people when they desire to do something, a strike, a boycott, an occupation, etc., whose *form* is not established, we will be their agents, their *go-between*, we will draw up their tracts, circulate them, we will be almost non-existent—and I have to say that this was all well and good, this desire for a servant's position in the homes of these men who were born masters, this search for hysteria, Lacan said, for these inevitably paranoid militants. But we kept going with knowledge, since absolute mind may indeed make itself the servant, it *must* become the dialectical servant of all the regions it traverses, the words it utters do not say what they mean, they are equivocal, not at all in the sense of dissimulation, equivocal on the contrary because interchangeable, the dirty little ambivalence, the master becoming the servant and thereby becoming or rebecoming the true master, the militant doing away with himself as the boss (or even as the little soldier of the revolution) and thereby remaining the true boss, the words from the mouth turned humbly towards the sun were already the words of the power to come, sent out from the tribunal, because they belong to knowledge, the new revolution began again before turning sour like its predecessors, should its new servants play its spokesmen.

Hatred for the fac-simile. What does it matter what you say if the position of discourse remains the same? (Within the group, only Philippe Guillaume understood that early on.) To restart the revolution is not to rebegin it, it is to cease to see the world alienated, men to be saved or helped, or even to be *served*, it is to abandon the masculine position, to listen to femininity, stupidity and madness without regarding them as evils. Hatred for the pimp who *disguises* himself as a girl without having the desire to be one, sinister masculine caricature of the nobleman in drag.

End of the outburst. Renouncing therefore critique and consolation. Quantity can be invested as such, and this *is not* an alienation (and, furthermore, it existed in the 'prestigious' consumption of so-called precapitalist societies—but Baudrillard knows this better than we do).

Fragmentation can be invested as such, and this *is not* an alienation. It is a phantasy, not simply reactionary, but constitutive of Western theatricality, to believe that there were societies where the body was not fragmented. There is no organic body for libidinal economy; and no more is there a *libidinal body*, a strange compromise of a concept from Western medicine and physiology with the idea of the libido as energy subject to the indiscernible regimes of Eros and death. François Guéry, in his commentary on the fourth section of Book 1 of *Capital*,[23] shows that the humanist protests, such as those of Friedman or Marcuse, against part time work rest on an error in the localization of the *scission of the body*: of course, he says, the body of capital, in taking possession of the productive body in the factories as Marx described it, and *a fortiori* in large semi-automated industry, breaks the organic body into independent parts, requiring 'an almost superhuman subtlety' of some of them which 'will go hand in hand with a more and more extensive mechanization of skilled actions'; but, he adds, this is 'only an anachronistic phenomenon affecting the antique mixture of the biological and the productive body. The really great scission of the body is not there.' It 'relies on another scission, practised in the very heart of the biological body: the one between the body, *then* reduced to a machinery, and the intellectual forces of production, the head, the brain, whose present state is the *software* of the information scientists.'[24] How are we to understand that the really pertinent cutting line is, for Guéry, this one rather than the first? This is because he admits a certain image of the medieval corporation, or rather the eternal corporation, operative '*throughout antiquity*', until the Middle Ages, an image which is that forged by Marx and which is that of a 'body machining forces', 'the organic forces of the human body, *including the head*'. And Guéry insists: 'This has its importance: the man's head is machined by the corporation, but as an organic part of the body. There is no question, then, of an internal hierarchy where the head would be spacially and qualitatively situated at the summit, higher than the manual forces, the lungs, the arms, fingers, legs and feet.'[25]

Let us admit that, in the field of productive labour, the corporation is indeed this non-hierarchical body; it remains the case that such a characterization stands only on condition that this field is isolated, separated from the political organization from which it is taken, whether this be Oriental despotism, the free town, the city, or the empire, and—to stay with Greece—on condition that the appearance of speech as *political technè* is not taken into account, which is equivalent, all things being equal, to a process of cephalization and even of capitalization reducing each manual task to a fragmentation subordinated to the political body. In other words, the *head* did indeed exist in the age of the corporation, not in the corporation perhaps, but certainly in the 'social body'. The social body may not be the body of political economy in our age, and the productive body does not perhaps take on the form of the concentration of the partial drives (for it is a question of these), it is the political body which effects this concentration, but it is no less extant here, and the folding down onto the central Zero, which is not necessarily currency (in Sparta, for example), but always the centre of speech and the sword, sets up no less of a hierarchization of these pulsions and social entities where they give way to free play in a privileged way.

This much will be said of a non-political, therefore a 'primitive' or a savage society, given that concentration does not take place in war and discourse, at least not systematically. What we must take a look at here, beyond an 'error' which appeared to be an error of detail, is the phantasy, so powerful and constant in the best Marxist heritage, of a happy state of the working body, this happiness being (in the pure tradition of the West) thought as the self-unity of all its parts. But under examination, this phantasy will be seen to be nothing other than Baudrillard's primitive society in another guise. 'Symbolic exchange' is also a political economic exchange, just as the law of civic speaking in Athens, and the tetralogos[26] is also a law of the mercantilization of discourse, and, complementarily, just as the scrupulous fragmentation of tasks in the regulated disciplines implies their subordination to a central Zero which, while not being professional (perhaps), is no less the *caput* of the alleged social body.

There Are No Primitive Societies

One more word on symbolic exchange. In violation of our principles, let's devote a few pages to *criticizing* it. It is an idea in which two concepts of the symbolic come to be confounded: the Maussian concept of the gift charged with ambivalent affects, the Lacanian concept of an order, as a marker of discontinuity, which *makes* the materials (for example, the day's residues in the dream-work) *signify* by their simple and arbitrary insertion into chains. But let's leave this slightly academic critique by way of the confusion of concepts, to release its intensity in that form in which it appeared to us, one evening when between a piece of music by Kagel and a piece by Boulez we were pissing in the deserted urinals in the Donaueschingen

Konzerthalle. Where does it go? we wondered. And the idea formed that the fear of impotence [*impuissance*] is this question: what if it went nowhere? That is to say: unconnected pieces of the body, not entering into the circuit of metamorphoses. It is going to be lost? No, rather the opposite: *it is going to remain*. Impotence (which is not powerlessness, which *may on the contrary be power*) would therefore be: it remains, it no longer metamorphoses. It is not at all a question of castration, but of keeping the metamorphic currents separate, non-connection in relation to the passages of intensity, depression.

Now, here comes the question of symbolic exchange: this fear is not, as we have thought, the fear of no longer being able to *give*. The category of the gift is a theatrical idea, it belongs to semiology, it presupposes a subject, a limit of his proper body and his property, and the generous transgression of this property. When Lacan says: to love is to give what one has not, he means: to forget that one is castrated. It should mean: one never has anything, there is no subject, and so there is nothing but love; not only is there never anything to give because one has nothing, but there is no-one to give, or to receive. It is in the theory of *signs* that donatory exchange (or the gift as the *primitive form* of exchange) may be represented as the attribution or devolution of an object charged with affects to someone who at the beginning of the cycle *didn't have* it: for the sign is just something which replaces something else, hides and manifests something else, for someone, *for the addressee* (and also for the sender). This problematic, coming from Jakobson to Lacan, that is to say the theory of communication, carries with it the entire philosophy of the subject, the philosophy of a body haunted by self-appropriation and property since the theory of communication is obviously just as much a piece of economic theory. Mauss must not be read as the discovery of a 'precapitalist', or at least a mercantilist, economy, but as the invention and the perfecting, in the heart of this economy, of its indispensable complement of anteriority-exteriority. Replace the gift with symbolic exchange and you remain in the same sphere, for exchange also takes place amongst unitary bodies or those destined to be unitary, even if they are prevented for ever (by the 'bar of the signifier') from bringing this unity about, and even if they are always driven by their splitting in two, by the *Entzweiung*, as Hegel used to say, to exchange something, even if only pieces of themselves; the exchangists remain perforated, like poles or ideas of (mercantilist) reason rather than as existants, it remains that exchange requires this polarization, this encephalization, and an in-and-out movement, a cycle of flows, the circle of a market and its central balance. Whether or not one exchanges affects does not modify this configuration, it simply dramatizes it.

And so we see that we will not manage to adjust new 'it is necessary' statements to the great skin by swapping mercantilist exchange for symbolic exchange. To criticize production is necessarily also to criticize exchange, *all* exchange, its concept. Exchange is no less 'humanist' than production. If we must get away from production, and we must, let's also give exchange the slip, the instantiation of fluxes and affects on these exchangist-entities. Circulation is no less suspect than production, it is only, as Marx well knew, a particular case of *production taken in the broad sense*. Let's rather place ourselves in the sense of this production in the broad sense, which is the general metamorphosis of everything which takes place on bodies and inscribes itself into the social body, haunted by the idea of a ceaseless general metamorphosis, or of a general production without inscription, which is nothing other than the great skin; we wonder instead what are the characteristics of the figure which makes the passage from this latter to inscribed production, the characteristics of the *dispositif* of inscription which constitutes social voluminosity.

The moral of the Donaueschingen urinal was experienced before its time in a similar environment: in the men's toilets of the Department of Mathematics and Information Science in the University of Aarhus, a small photo-electric device set off a flushing in the pan as soon as, your flies unzipped, you got your penis near it. There you have a 'new statement' and the certainty that there is no impotence; except through depression.

We can now pursue this 'critique' of symbolic exchange, still for pleasure, and it may even happen that we make some important discoveries here. There is a *condensation* in the idea of this exchange, it is therefore a very libidinal idea (and we love it as much as Baudrillard can love it, but there is a desire even greater than ours, a desire latent in capitalist society, which does not love this condensation, and which must be understood): a condensation, as we said, between Mauss's idea, which is a phenomenological description of interhuman relations, and Lacan's, which is a structuralist theory of the cutting up of elements of 'reality' and the production of meaning. In symbolic exchange there is implied, therefore, the relation of one subject to others, mediated by objects counting only as symbols of ambivalent affects, love and death (potlach passes for a model in this regard), and, at the same time, a *structural* relation which determines (arbitrarily and according to each culture) the qualities and quantities of the objects likely to become such symbols. When Baudrillard says:

there is no savage unconscious, is he doing anything other than expressing, in a provocative fashion, the aforementioned condensation: that is,
affirming that consciousness in its entirety (exchange between persons)
receives and assumes in primitive societies the unconscious in its entirety
(the organization cutting up the symbols and their exchange), and that
there is no impenetrable remainder?

This condensation is very interesting by itself: supported by the Lacanian
reading of Freud, it refers to the common 'source' of Lacan and Mauss,
which is chapter 4 of *The Phenomenology of Mind*. The struggle for recognition, which is of course the model, spontaneous or controlled, allowing
Mauss to decipher potlach and extend its range, is also what haunts the
image that Lacan has formed for himself of the unconscious. But there is
already in this image a primary condensation between death in the
Hegelian dialectic and castration in Freudian dramatics. If consciousness
intends to leave the simple certainty of the self, it must *leap outside* the
particularity of its 'natural life', explains Hegel, and this leap can only take
place on condition that this particularity is in effect renounced. Since it is
'my life', its negation is my death, and consciousness can only attain
universality on condition that it accepts the risk of this *irreversible expenditure*, i.e. that it gives up its life. So what is this but the Other? asks Lacan—if
not the master who makes 'consciousness' tremble sufficiently for it to
abandon its concern to be 'recognized' and withdraws into the equivocality
of its risked-maintained particularity or of its hoped for-lacking universality. The splitting of the subject which gives rise to the unconscious requires
this suspended death, terror in the face of 'castration', the menace of the
law, that is to say of the sword of justice. Therefore relinquishment is
constitutive of the subject.

That ultimately in Hegel there is *Vergebung, Versöhnung*, remission,
reconciliation, in the theme of absolute knowledge or of the subject-
substance, is apparent even though it is without doubt not illegitimate to
show that the very category of the *Aufhebung*, of this annihilation full of
reserve, is less well oiled than it might appear, and can conceal the extreme
risk of madness in the void.[27] Conversely, one might suspect that with
Lacan, the reader of Freud, the non-reconciliation, the impossibility for the
Ego to come to 'where It [*Ça*] was', is insurmountable. Far from it,
however; even at the privileged thematic level of the efficacity of the
cure,[28] entirely thought in terms of dialectics; but, more seriously still, the
Vergebung is present in thought as the quality of the schema; that the
unconscious is conceived (and practised) not as the other of discourse, but

as the *discourse of the Other*, results from a simple reversal which assures the subject, split in two all the same, of a second-level unity, a meta-unity which is not, of course, that of consciousness itself, but rather of language (that is, the language of philosophers or thinkers). For if the unconscious is structured like a language, even though consciousness cannot say everything because of its perpetual splitting in search of death-castration, the unsayable, the 'part' of the subject which is submerged in this primitive fear is still talking; the unconscious of course says something other than what consciousness says, and it doesn't know what it is saying; a dialogue or a dialectic of both halves is nevertheless practicable: Lacan calls it the cure. Remission of the principle is thus constituted by the silence of the master; although he refuses recognition, and one does not enter into dialogue with him, although he does not respond, but kills or threatens, whereas he is content, as Job did to his irascible father, to remind his *Knecht* that without him, he would be nothing, the Unnameable—well, despite everything, there is the hope, in Lacan, that silence will be given up, simply because death is assimilated to the life of the mind, to speech.[29]

By saying the unconscious is the discourse of the Other, Freud is reincorporated into Hegel, Judaism, for which the latter nevertheless demonstrates such an aversion, is recovered in Hellenic or Christian mediacy. One should remind oneself a little: the Jews, for Hegel, are the failure of the dialectic, that is, the failure of love; they are the rupture, incarnated in the story of Abraham, of all links with a homeland, with kinship, solitude in the face of a hostile nature, and impotence as regards being reconciled with it as Nimrod, Deucalion and Pyrrha were. 'The Jews could not, as the fanatics did later, abandon themselves to disintegration or death caused by hunger, because they were attached not to an Idea, but an animal existence; and they believed in their god because, completely separate from nature, they found reunion with this latter in him by virtue of a domination.'[30]

The Jews are not attached to an Idea, but to an animal existence; and they are therefore bestiality, a species of sick bestiality, against nature or unnatural, which can subsist only by recourse to the infinite, immense domination of a Master; and he will promise animal survival, the satisfaction of needs, but on condition that his domination is accepted and accepted ceaselessly, without dialogue, without the love of words and without the love of acts, *without symbolic exchange*, simply, in Hegel's sense, but solely through the gift without counter-gift which is, it appears, prayer and barbaric sacrifice. Consequently Abraham and his people are not real servants nor Yahveh a real master, since this master does not put his slave to work, and so the latter cannot tear himself from the terror of the rupture with nature, from the terror of death, by means of work. Abraham's existence 'is the impotence of the dialectic of the master and the slave, or rather the impotence of being [*l'impuissance d'être*], the absence of this dialectic, the reflexive fixation in this natural life from which this dialectic must leave'.[31] In this unnatural nature, in this bestiality which has lost the means to the satisfaction of its needs, in this dominated animality which sustains itself through servitude, do we see in this anything other than the outlines of one of the principal figures of the unconscious, or the Id according to Freud, the figure of the *impenetrability of the body*? To dialecticize the unconscious, as Lacan does, is to convert the Jews to the cult of the Son, to dissolve their body, furrowed with the ritualistic, absurd marks of belonging, into the diaphane of the insipid host, to ban dark bestiality and stupidity, to put the mind where there are pulsions. So, to posit the primitives as creatures without an unconscious, is to perform again on the Melanesians and the Indians the same truly classical-romantic operation that Hölderlin and the young Hegel performed on the Greeks, who were also not supposed to have an unconscious and to live in reconciliation and limpidity.

To sum up, the genealogy of the 'critique' of Baudrillard's symbolism: to derive the position of the unconscious from the phenomenology of consciousness, is to say that what the subject lacks at the same time as constituting it, is nothing other than what constitutes discourse-dialogue while never ceasing to escape it, that is, *death*, which, for Hegel, is the element in which the life of the mind swims, the same thing indeed to which Freud will dedicate what is without doubt his most frenzied, emotional text, *Beyond the Pleasure Principle*, where, however, he seeks to thematize it under the name of the death drives as what, far from entering into a dialectical relation with Eros-Logos, compels the repetition of the disorder until the body is destroyed, until the analysis is rendered 'interminable'. To say that savages have no unconscious, is once again to extend over every silence the imperialism of the tumult made by Eros, which, as everyone knows today, is quite simply the language of structure. No, undoubtedly, it must be clearly said: *there are no* primitive societies or savages *at all*, we are all savages, all savages are capitalized-capitalists.

Now this problematic of symbolic exchange, don't go thinking that it is a phantasy foreign to the desire named Marx, it is one of its principal formations.

Inorganic Body

Since it is the deafening clamour of Eros-Logos which is in question, let's draw out for a moment the thread, in Marx young and old, but a woman at every age, of the minor theme of *language*. The model for this thematic comes of course from Feuerbach, as can be seen in the text of his youth: 'The only comprehensible language that we may speak to each other', wrote Marx,[32] 'are our objects in relation to one another. We would not understand a human language, and it would remain ineffective; it would be on the one hand known and experienced as a prayer, as an imploring, and therefore as *humiliation*; it would thus be uttered in shame and the feeling of being scorned (*Wegwerfung*); and it would be, on the other hand, received and rejected as a shameless and delirious thing (*als Unverschäm- theit oder Wahnwitz*). We are mutually alienated (*entfremdet*) at this point from the human being, the immediate language of this being would seem to us like a violation of human dignity, while the alienated language of values makes things appear to us to be human dignity itself in its full legitimacy, in confidence and self-recognition.'

What is lacking in the language of *thing-values* (*sachliche Werte*), of values become things? The affect, what Rousseau called the accent. In this language, that of venal exchange and, let us add, that of the *concept*, which is also the exchange of the commodity of information, every passion appears delirious; incongruity, the immediacy of the demand (prayer, supplication) seems to be an obscenity. A Feuerbachian problematic, half Lutheran, half Rousseauist. Marx noticed this in spring 1844, while he was beginning his readings of political economy, and we can see according to what inevitably religious problematic. It is at about the same date that he published, in the *Deutsche-Französische Jahrbücher*, extracts from a peculiar text of Feuerbach's, *On the Essence of Faith in Luther's Sense*, where one should have no trouble discovering this same theme of *immediacy* carried to its conclusions: let us complete Luther's work, in destroying papism, he eliminated mediated alienation; in showing that God himself is nothing but the fulfilment of my desire, one will keep the supreme being from the fate of *Entfremdung*; let us say then that God is my god, that is to say me, insofar as he is my *jouissance*, and that 'the essence of faith is the essence of self-love'.[33]

Immediacy as the suppression of the *Mitte*, of what is interposed, belongs to the tradition of the Reformation, which passes as it is, through Feuerbach, into the Hegelian left and into Marx, including his analysis of economics: compare what you have just read concerning language with what Marx writes, at the same moment, concerning money: 'Money is the pimp [*der Kuppler*] between man's need and the object, between his life and his means of life. But that which mediates my life for me, also mediates the existence of other people for me.'[34] We see then that money for him is the language spoken by exchange-values. And he assigns this money a very similar characteristic to *equivalence* according to Baudrillard: *indifference*.

> In money, in total indifference as much with regard to the nature of the material and the specific nature of private property, as with regard to the personality of the private proprietor, this is the complete domination of the alienated thing over the man who strives for appearance. What used to be the domination of one person over another, is now the universal domination of the *thing* over the *person*, of the product over the producer. Just as the equivalent, value, establishes the alienation of private property, so money is the sensible, autonomous, objective existence, of this alienation.[35]

We see that it is Feuerbachian and Christian when *equivalence* is opposed, not exactly to *ambivalence* (although prayer, supplication, humiliation, shame, domination, are, let's be careful here, samples of reasonably 'ambivalent' affects), but rather to the person, and to the person *as producer*. There is an inextricable combination in these texts of Feuerbachism, i.e. secular Lutheranism, with political economy. The splitting of object and subject according to the opposition use-value/exchange-value or labour-force/labour-time, a splitting still thematized in the *Contribution*, in the *Grundrisse*, in *Capital*, finds its principle in a rupture or a bifurcation of immediacy, itself phantasized as the language of the heart. This impassioned language is lost, and neither the papist god in his 'candour', as Engels said at the time, nor even the reformed hypocrite god,[36] will be able to reinstate it. And political economy, that is to say capital, no longer works except to continue this cleavage, making it pass from hearts to things, and thus faking it. For the commodity-thing is always marked by the bar, while this latter is effaced. Such is the 'hypocrisy' of political economy, which Marx calls its fetishism, and which clearly corresponds to what Baudrillard interprets as the occultation of castration or ambivalence in the 'capitalist' object. Lost immediacy can only *simulate* its return in the apparent simplicity of the thing: it has the status of the *fetish*.

The analysis of the object as concealing the cleavage proper to desire is to some extent in continuity with Marx's nostalgia: where the latter opposes immediacy to mediated alienation, the thought of the signifier castrator opposes the recognition of this cleavage and ambivalence to their fetishist foreclosure. The same thing is not, of course, said in both cases, and this is not simply to open a field where only the philosopher's and the economist's discourses reign in questions of desire, which implies at least that one is going to stop thinking of activity alone as productive and reproductive and that one will accept in principle that it be granted its *non-productive force* [*puissance improductive*]. What cannot be believed is that to maintain such an opposition, whether it is given the name of immediacy/ alienation or of cleavage/foreclosure, one settles in the field of truth, one compares a capitalist state of things and desire, eventually judged false or at least deceitful, with an authentic state, one annihilates what one has, which is effectively capitalism and the libidinal formations which are found at work there, in favour of what one has not, i.e. beautiful savagery.

So once again the connivance appears between a philosophy of alienation and a psychoanalysis of the signifier, both nihilist religions; apart from Baudrillard's use of this latter, making it slip into optimism, towards the hope of a restitution of the true state of desire, whereas the strictly Lacanian version, if indeed it implies a dialectic of the cure, nevertheless rules out that the illusory *objet petit a*, in its function of the fixation of ambivalence and the occlusion of the 'want-to-signify' [*manque à signifier*], might never be dissipated: interminable analysis, permanent revolution. But these are nuances from within one and the same theology, a nihilism of loss: the Jews no longer await reconciliation and install their libidinal *dispositif* in the election, the resignation and the humour of the suppressed, whereas the Christians hope, dialectically, for forgiveness; nevertheless they surrender points to one another as concerns nihilism. In Marx, the alienation of the mediator, contrary to what he thinks, is still a Christian schema: the mediator must be destroyed, sacrificed in order that the alienation he fights, *and of which he is composed*, be removed, nowhere better said than in the narrative of Jesus's Incarnation and Passion.

You will now tell me that perhaps the young Marx was like this, but that as he aged, the concern with immediacy and the reference to a signifying coexistence without alienation disappear. Nothing of the sort, they are only displaced. The Feuerbachian aspect disappears, the Rousseauist aspect predominates. A paradise remains as secure ground for a critical perspective and a revolutionary project. This is the paradise of the 'inorganic body', at present: this same paradise which F. Guéry fantasizes under the type of corporate production 'of all antiquity', which Baudrillard imagines as a body impassioned with intense ambivalences, anterior to all political economy, and which Marx—although he comes round to this from the other perspective, precisely that of political economy—still suffers from because he needs it, in his critical perspective, as the quasi-exteriority on which all critique relies in order to criticize its object; the inorganic body thematized by Marx explicitly in a text as 'late' as the *Grundrisse*, in these terms:

> What M. Proudhon calls the extra-economic origin of property, by which he understands just landed property, is the pre-bourgeois relation of the individual to the objective conditions of labour, and initially to the natural objective conditions of labour—for, just as the working subject appears naturally as an individual, as natural being—so does the first objective condition of his labour appear as nature, earth, as his inorganic body; he himself is not only the organic body, but also the subject of this inorganic nature. This condition is not his product but something he finds to hand—presupposed to him as a natural being apart from him.[37]

If now we have not grasped that the expression 'He is the subject of this inorganic nature' is what explains the *function of satisfaction* fulfilled by the inorganic body in Marx's imagination: in all precapitalist forms of production, i.e. of the *commune*, 'the earth (is) the original instrument of labour as well as its workshop and repository of raw materials. The individual relates simply to the objective conditions of labour as being his; [the individual relates] to them as the inorganic nature of his subjectivity, in which the latter realizes itself (as subject).'[38] Are we in immediacy? Yes, but this immediacy includes communal collectivity (communist), which is also therefore a part of nature: 'This relation to land and soil, to the earth, as the property of the labouring individual . . . is instantly mediated by the naturally arisen, spontaneous, more or less historically developed and modified presence of the individual as member of a commune—his naturally arisen presence as member of a tribe, etc.' And in a note at this point, this remark: '[The labouring individual] thus appears from the outset not merely as labouring individual, in this abstraction, but has an objective mode of existence in his ownership of the land, an existence presupposed by this activity, and not merely as a result of it, a presupposition of his activity just like his skin, his sense organs, which of course he also reproduces and develops, etc., in the life process, but which are nevertheless presuppositions of this process of his reproduction.'[39]

Therefore: (1) the body of the earth is called *inorganic* only so as to be distinguished from the organic body of the worker himself; in fact it is a body organically bound up with the organic body and identical to it in every way in that, like it, it is *given* and not produced; (2) the commune itself is also a part of this great (in)organic body, for it is as a member of this commune that the 'labouring' body (which does not in fact appear as such) can enter into a productive relation with the earth. And belonging to the commune is itself also given and not produced. The three instances, proper body, social body, the body of the earth, are articulated together as so many pieces of the same machinery, which is *nature*. It is within this nature that 'production' is carried out, or rather, this 'production' is nature reproducing itself.

This image is constant. Open *The German Ideology* and you will find this long text quite explicit:

> Here, therefore, arises the difference between natural instruments of production and those created by civilization. The field (water, etc.) can be regarded as a natural instrument of production. In the first case, that of the natural instrument of production, individuals are subservient to nature; in the second, to a product of labour. In the first case therefore, property (landed property) appears as direct natural domination, in the second, as domination of labour, particularly of accumulated labour, capital. The first case presupposes that the individuals are united by some bond: family, tribe, the land itself, etc.; the second, that they are independent of one another and are only held together by exchange. In the first case, what is involved is chiefly an exchange between men and nature in which the labour of the former is exchanged for the products of the latter; in the second, it is predominantly an exchange of men amongst themselves. In the first case, average, human common sense is adequate —physical activity is as yet not separated from mental activity; in the second, the division between physical and mental labour must already be practically completed. In the first case, the domination of the proprietor over the propertyless may be based on a personal relationship, on a kind of community; in the second, it must have taken a material shape in the form of a third party—money. In the first case, small industry exists, but determined by the utilization of the natural instrument of production and therefore without the distribution of labour among various individuals; in the second, industry exists only in and through the division of labour.[40]

Hardly any difference between the two texts, twelve years apart; and if there were one, it would be to the detriment of the earlier text, which speaks of precapitalist property as a 'domination', whereas in 1857 the great figure of the (in)organic Body governs the whole text, precluding every relation of domination within itself, knowing only the effects of the immediate fulfilment of a partial function through other parts.

And one cannot dispose of this theme of lost naturality by saying that Marx merely *made use* of precapitalist forms of production in order to facilitate the concretion of their opposition to the capitalist form and to make this latter manifest in its full particularity, even if this were at the price of sheer mythologization of the former.[41] The alleged opposition does not exist; there is for Marx a mutation, a revolution, as the *Manifesto* says, between all these precapitalist forms and capitalism, a *difference* in the sense that in the latter alone an opacity exists, only in the latter does society misjudge itself, only in the latter can labour, which appears precisely like everyday reality, appear only on condition that it has become a completely denatured abstraction, finally, in the sense that in capitalism this abstraction alone requires a *Spaltung*, a scission not only of objects (into commodities and use-goods; into values and needs) but also of subjects into concrete bodies and registered labour forces. On the other side of 'precapitalist' immediacy, this scission is, for Marx, *what must be explained*: 'It is not the unity of living and active humanity with the natural, inorganic conditions of their metabolic exchange with nature, and hence their appropriation of nature, which requires explanation or is the result of a historic process, but rather the separation between these inorganic conditions of human existence and this active existence, a separation which is completely posited only in the relation of wage-labour and capital.'[42] There is more: this scission is not only to be explained, it causes there to be something to be explained, for the discourse of political economy is engendered from the vacuum or void which it opens in the social subject: what Marx (this time, the prosecutor, however) would have us understand in the Introduction (of 1857) to the *Critique of Political Economy*, saying that of course there was labour *before* there were wage earners and money before capital, but that the practice of 'labour in general', of 'labour *sans phrase*', is necessary, a practice, Marx says, which is that of the American worker, that of an indifference to the 'job' one does, which 'became a means to create wealth in general, and has ceased to be tied as an attribute to a particular individual'[43]—that this practice of the *scission* proper to capitalism is necessary in order that these practices come into their own as categories of political economy, practices indeed 'prior' to this scission. It is the scission which must be explained at the same time as it is in and from the scission that this need for explanation originates. One can only say that to invoke the extreme opposite of an undivided society would be only an explanatory facility for Marx, it governs his methodology (which is impossible, but that's another matter), and it governs his politics, which is quite explicitly, and constantly, to *do away with the scission* and to establish the great full common body of natural reproduction, communism.

This could not be put more clearly than in Book 1 of *Capital*, even though it is introduced under a somewhat shameful guise: 'Since Robinson Crusoe's experiences are a favourite theme with political economists, let's take a look at him on his island.'[44] There follow four illustrations of transparency, naturality, or immediacy, four forms from which 'the whole mystery of labour that surrounds the products of labour . . . ' is absent: let's miss out the lucidity of Robinson's political economy; there is no less clarity, however, in the obscure Middle Ages: 'But for the very reason that personal dependence forms the ground-work of society, there is no necessity for labour and its products to assume a fantastic form different from their reality. They take the shape, in the transactions of society, of services in kind and payments in kind.'[45] Does this mean that the *reality of desire* (supposing that this consists in its ambivalence . . .) is exhibited here? Why not? Marx doesn't say this, but ultimately the 'relations between persons' are, in Marx's eyes, as in anyone else's, fully transferential relations, and form a truly passionate human language. Baudrillard will object that Marx is not concerned with transparency at all; instead he is concerned with the unpretentious exhibition of the *law of value*: 'Every serf knows that what he expends in the service of his lord, is a definite quantity of his own personal labour power.'[46] A correction pertinent also to the two last examples of society whose political economy is thought to be crystal clear: the present reality of the rustic and patriarchal industry of a family of peasants; and finally the image of a 'community of free individuals, carrying on their work with the means of production in common, in which the labour power of all the different individuals is consciously applied as the combined labour power of the community'.[47] A collective Crusoe-ism, Marx says; is it communism nevertheless? There is no doubt that this latter is the (re)constitution of the great organic or inorganic, transorganic or transitive body. But the objection comes back: this transitivity is already placed *inside* political economy since it only concerns relations of labour, production and distribution. But Baudrillard's society without an unconscious is not only a pre-bourgeois political economy, it is a pre-political, libidinal economy, or even a pre-economy. Perhaps because in fact the frontier is moved *further forward* in the fantastic archaeology, 'before' production and not only, as it seems with Marx, before the occultation of labour power in capitalist relations; the re-placing of the critical line which then accepts as a criterion not only the foreclosure of desire in capitalist-capitalized practice, but also its denial through the very circumscription of a field of the economy. However, re-placing a frontier allows changes in the designations of the countries situated on either side; hence it will no longer be: capitalist economy *versus* pre-capitalist economy, it will be: political economy or equivalence *versus* symbolic exchange or ambivalence; but the system of oppositions remains the same, the formation of distinct *regions*, the constitution of a theatricality through exteriorization (of the peasant, of Robinson, of the socialist worker, of the marginal), critique made possible by the position of an uncritiqued ('what requires an explanation, is not the unity of active individuals and the non-organic conditions . . . ') set up as the site from which the critic speaks, and therefore nihilism. All of Marx rests on this nihilism.

Edwarda and Little Girl Marx

Marx *in toto*: the young woman and the theoretician; the young woman who dreams of reconciliation, the end of poverty and scission, therefore distances herself from (capitalist) 'reality' in order to oppose it to the (in)organic and transparent body, the young woman who performs this movement of the disengagement and annihilation of the given, who refuses the given and buys herself another, a simply refused given, the given of lost transparency. What does she refuse in the given? *Prostitution*. Recall the *Manifesto*: the bourgeois family rests on capital, it exists only for the bourgeoisie, 'but this state of things finds its complement in the practical absence of the family among the proletarians, and in public prostitution'; this is why, if the communist programme was to institute the community of women, it would not have a lot to do, it is already the institution of the bourgeoisie: not only does it dispose of proletarian women and girls, but 'bourgeois marriage is in reality a system of wives in common'. Women's communism merely displayed and made explicit their actual clandestine status as common property. But, say the authors, 'it is self-evident that the abolition of the present system of production must bring with it the abolition of the community of women springing from that system, i.e. of prostitution both public and private'.[48]

Already in 1844, Marx lays into crude communism which is only, he says, a generalization of *private property*, the institution of a species of *private or privative community*, for women in particular. The same position as in 1848: the placing in common of women is prostitution. But this reveals the secret of capitalism: 'Just as woman passes from marriage (according to the hypothesis of this crude communism) to general prostitution, so the entire world of wealth (that is, of man's objective substance), passes from the relationship of exclusive marriage with the owner of private property to that of universal prostitution with the community.'[49] This is clarified in a footnote: 'Prostitution is only the specific expression of the general prostitution of the labourer, and since it is a relationship in which falls not the prostitute alone, but also the one who prostitutes—and the latter's abomination is still greater—the capitalist, etc., also comes under this head.'

What the dreaming young girl rejects in capitalism is prostitution under the name of alienated mediation. 'This is the habitual vicious circle of political economy: the goal is freedom of thought; therefore for the majority it is mindless servitude. Physical needs are not the only goal; therefore for the majority, they are the only goal. Or conversely: marriage is the goal; for the majority then, there is prostitution. Property is the goal; for the majority then, no property at all.'[50] The central and persistent theme, whose range even extends when the opposition, marked from the start between marriage and prostitution, becomes a blur. For example in 1857, in the *Grundrisse*, again in a footnote (of course): 'The exchangeability of all products, activities, and relations with a third, objective entity which can be reexchanged for everything at all—that is, the development of exchange-values (and of money relations) is identical with universal venality, corruption. Universal prostitution, or, more politely expressed, the universal relation of utility and use, appears as a necessary phase . . . '[51]

What does the little girl recoil from, whatever her age? *From Madame Edwarda*. Bataille said: 'No use laying it all up to irony when I say of Madame Edwarda that she is GOD. But GOD figured as a public whore and gone crazy, that makes no sense at all.'[52] Marx overlooks nothing of this fatal conjunction, he cites Shakespeare, he comments on the two properties that the author of *Timon of Athens* recognizes in money: '(1) It is the visible divinity—the transformation of all human and natural qualities into their contraries, the universal confounding and overturning of things . . . ; (2) It is the common whore, the common pimp of peoples and nations',[53] and he will quote this once again in *Capital*, in the chapter on money. In the indifference or 'the equalization of differences' which results from mercantilism but even more from capitalism, and which the crude communism which Marx despises, dreads and rejects (and which therefore he desires) will simply generalize; he says that this is the destruction of the 'direct, natural and necessary relation of person to person' which is primarily 'the relation of man and woman',[54] he says that it is the denaturation of woman, therefore the denaturation of man and nature itself. And we say that this horror of money, of the world of money which sells to buy and buys to sell, of the world of capital as the *Milieu* of universal prostitution, we say it is the *horror* of (and therefore the lust for) the *'perversion' of the partial pulsions*.

What then does the system of capital present to the innocent Little Girl Marx? No longer a *body* indeed, but an abstraction, no longer the carnal 'artistic' unity, of an inside and an outside, of a hand and its tool, of a palm and a stretch of caressed skin, of a house and the surrounding countryside, of fatigue and its complementary rest, but the 'body of capital', which *is not an organic body*, which seems to her to be a body stricken with repugnant diseases, whose organs are separated by what should assemble them, whose 'mediatory' unity is not totalizing-immanent, but transcendent-detotalizing. The money of capital groups incompossibles together. It is not constituted by a slow process of birth and growth like a living being, but by intermittent acts of vampirization: it merely seizes hold of what was already there, racked by dissolution, labour-force on one side, masses of currency on another, means of labour on a third, and reorganizes it in another way,[55] it cannot exist as an 'organic' unity, its unity is extrinsic, like that which forms the impatient perversion of a client, the indifference of a prostitute and the neutrality of a procurer. Were capital to make every activity enter into its cycle of indifferent transformations, rendering their uses indiscernible, for Marx it would be just as though sexuality, having lost its anchoring, its finality and its justification in genitality and reproduction, were to disconnect itself from the infamy of the partial pulsions. Instead of amorous sensibility, sensuality in senselessness [*non-sens*]. Instead of the natural and immediate order, perhaps madness. 'She was seated, she held one leg up in the air, to open the crack yet wider she used fingers to draw the folds of her skin apart. And so Madame Edwarda's "old rag and ruin" loured at me, hairy and pink, just as full of life as some loathsome squid. "Why", I stammered quietly, "why are you doing that?"

"You can see for yourself", she said, "I am GOD . . . ", "I'm going crazy--", "Oh no you don't, you've got to see, look . . . "[56]

Edwarda's exposed vulva, her fainting fit in the street (for, as a brothel woman, she *can* nevertheless '*leave*', just like the wage earner, who is not a slave), her hatred for her client (' "I can't stand it any more", she shrilled, "but you, you fake priest. I shit on you!" '), her return in a taxi, copulating with some driver culminating in a gushing, bruising orgasm—this is what capital promises male and female lovers of organic bodies and affective harmonies. Capital is not the denaturation of relations between man and man, nor between man and woman, it is the wavering of the (imaginary?) primacy of genitality, of reproduction and sexual difference, it is the displacement of what was in place, it is the unbinding of the most insane pulsions, since money is the sole justification or bond, and money being able to justify anything, it deresponsibilizes and *raves* absolutely, it is the sophistics of the passions and at the same time, their energetic prosthetics; and if the 'unity' which it wants to apply to the social body so frightens Marx, it is because it has certain *anti-unitary* and *anti-totalizing* traits, amongst which the great libidinal skin may be discerned.

It is the discovery of this latter, at least the beginnings of its emergence in the cold waters of capital, which makes the young lover recoil. What is there left to love in this society, with what can one strike up a natural, immediate, impassioned relationship so dear to pure hearts? The task set Marx the Advocate by Little Girl Marx is to discover an object of love, a hidden priceless thing, forgotten in the subversion of prices, a beyond-value in the trade fair of values, something like a nature in denaturation. To rediscover a natural *dependence*, a We, a dialectic of the You and the I, in the sordid solitude of pornographic independence to which the capitalist function of money and labour condemns all affective expenditure.

If it is true that prostitution is the model of the relationship in capitalist society, then two things follow: the first is well known, all relations are mediated and folded back onto the *Milieu* of the pimp-capitalists; but the second, concealed in the first, is, *from the point of view of the consideration of an organic body*, the disappearance of this latter, its replacement by series of singular, anonymous and indifferent relations (but only from this point of view), between clients and prostitutes. The group of client bodies does not form an organic body, and neither do the prostitute bodies. It is only the collectivity of capitalist procurers that forms a body, a clandestine body, a major state, and it is only in the instantiation of the pulsions, of all the pulsions, on their centre of power, that there must be a sort of collective existence of clients and prostitutes, consumers and producers. The 'disappearance' of the organic body is the accusation, in sum, made by Marx and Baudrillard (but this goes further, in both senses), by which the *dispositif* of capital stands condemned.

But, far from this rejection setting us clear on the libidinal function, or the libidinal functions, relative to each economic 'post' of capital, it maintains on the contrary, in the form of a *denial* prior to all analysis, the idea that capitalism deprives us of intensities as affects. This denial is indeed what introduces political economy and semiotics as separate 'sciences', that is to say absurd and blind to their presuppositions, but it is also what continues to underlie the *critique* of these 'sciences'; and if Marx, who wanted to do this critique, couldn't avoid the nihilism of this denial, it is not by way of an error, it is because his whole critique draws its impetus from the following denial: *no, you cannot make me come*. Baudrillard remains no less in this line when he adds: you can only make me enjoy *perversely*, by placing me beyond ambivalence, by denying bisexuality and castration. For we do not see why this limitation would be proper to capital. We can clearly see, for example, what modes of *jouissance* are excluded from the circumference of Hellenic homosexuality, or from the hierarchical organization of medieval guilds. On the other hand, in the immense and vicious circuit of capitalist exchanges, whether of commodities or 'services', it appears that *all the modalities* of *jouissance* are possible and that none is ostracized. On these circuits, it is just as much a piece of the libidinal band which becomes clear in its ephemeral and anonymous polymorphism.

Now, therefore, we must completely abandon critique, in the sense that we must put a stop to the critique of capital, stop accusing it of libidinal coldness or pulsional monovalence, stop accusing it of not being an organic body, of not being a natural immediate relation of the terms that it brings into play, we must take note of, examine, exalt the incredible, unspeakable pulsional possibilities that it sets rolling, and so understand that *there has never been* an organic body, an immediate relation, nor a nature in the sense of an *established site of affects*, and that the (in)organic body is a representation on the stage of the theatre of capital itself. Let's replace the term critique by an attitude closer to what we effectively experience in our current relations with capital, in the office, in the street, in the cinema, on the roads, on holiday, in the museums, hospitals and libraries, that is to say a horrified fascination for the entire range of the *dispositifs* of *jouissance*. It must be said: the Little Girl Marx invents critique (with her fat bearded prosecutor) *in order to defend herself* from this horrified fascination, which the disorder of the pulsions also provokes in us.

Of course, prostitution is still an order, a separation and a distribution of pulsional movements onto distinct poles, each of which fulfils a definite function in the circulation of goods and *jouissances*. But intensities are lodged here no less than in every possible network. Madame Edwarda is not only a prostitute in this sense of order, which authorizes a semiotics and a sociology of prostitution; she is also a *madwoman*. What does her madness stem from? From excessively enjoying her profession. The rule of coldness is not respected: it is on the contrary the deregulation from frenzy and orgasm that she dares to obtain under cover of her job. Not the disjunction between what belongs to the (hypothetical) lover and what belongs to the client; *but the disjunctive bar turning on the disjunctive function itself*, intensity being produced without any reference to an outside, but by heating to white-hot *the operator of this exteriorization*. The taxi driver will have shot his load as if it had been just another lay; but he will have paid nothing, his vehicle will have served as a hotel bedroom, he had asked for nothing, and finally it is insanity he held and penetrated, and not neutral venal flesh. Edwarda the prostitute journeys beyond every pimp's organization, but in the same place, on the same terrain as this organization, by the very fact of her venal position as a body-commodity.

It is certain that her frenzy, snatched from the disjunctive bar, from what demarcates all passion between clients and courtesans, goes hand in hand with another characteristic sketched by Bataille, her autonomy within the prostitutive organization. If the prostitute is her own mistress, if she offers herself without even the excuse of the procurers' wickedness, if Jesus climbs onto the cross without having been invited there by his father, if then there is no-one to *collect* the price of *jouissance*-suffering, I am not saying that all would become clear, but that ultimately the veil of intentions whose intensities are dissimulated by the organization would clear a little, whether this organization is the trade in women or the organization of labour and its market, and reveal that it takes very little, even within the order of prostitutes and wage earners, to arouse Edwarda's lunacy anywhere (as Chaplin had shown in *Modern Times*: the skilled worker becomes a kind of mad god when his body lets go of the *jouissance* that he receives from machines, and which he transfers onto them): this minor requirement is the destruction of the circle of reference, of the *Milieu*, and of the divine triangle, that is, of capital as the site of the accounts. This does not mean that the law, the disjunction *separating* the woman from her client would disappear, on the contrary it remains an impassable bar (which will always be able to give rise to the return of power, to the return of the accountable, to the semiologist), but it is *on this bar* and *from this bar* that extreme *jouissance* will result, and this extreme *jouissance* is indeed an intensity in that it embraces not only the clientele, but also the staff, not only the client, but also the woman—so that outlined here, in *madness*, is the suppression of religion (whether gentle Jesus, the strict pimp or whatever capitalism).

Wasn't this what Sade planned in his profoundly *egalitarian* institutions of pleasure, and this equality is quite different to that which capital takes into account and devours in the petty fear of its equations, an equality of the availability to enjoy, not through property (this is capital), but through *jouissance* or even the 'right of possession over *jouissance*', as Sade says? In these Republican houses of debauchery, not only do 'all men have an equal right to *jouissance* over all women', but, 'under the special clause of abandoning oneself equally to all those who desire to do so, women must equally have the liberty to enjoy all those they deem worthy to satisfy them'.[57] Madame Edwarda is in the process of transforming the brothel where the group earns its living into one of these democratic houses of pleasure, a place where intensities emerge within political isonomy. And Marx, both the little girl and the old man, horrified, discerns how one inequality dissimulates the other, how venal equivalence encourages, while concealing it, the exchange of pleasures, and soon equal rights to *jouissance*, which is its limitless wandering. One equality is order; and the other, which is the same, but without the pimp and money, is the subversion of this order. Subversion by condensation: the girl is her own procurer, the worker his own boss. But above all the *jouissance* of fucking or labouring is not instantiated on an absence, the *Milieu*, Capital. The end of alienation?

It is perhaps nothing of the sort, Sade also sees in his strange institution of debauchery a factor of order, which is *political*. The circle of instantiations and accountancy is reconstituted, alongside the economic circuits, on the political circle. They will say: recuperation; certainly not; intensities never circulate as such, only as dissimulated; for want of doing this in venal equivalence they will therefore be dissimulated in Republican equality. This displacement, if it spread as Sade hoped, would indeed be a displacement, in no way a defeat of liberties, or rather of libidinalities, and Marx was not fooled by this. In capitalist prostitution, *he* denounces depravity; but *what* is exposed *here*, is polymorphous perversion without a master, the madness of Edwarda's 'flaps' opened by her own hands; madness and hazard and anonymity, since, as in masturbation, hands feeling for the nipples, the clitoris, the thin line on the glans, belonging neither to me nor anyone else, and since the erection and detumescence they produce is due to neither women's nor men's hands, is not their product, they are inassignable tensions.

Or as in this image of coupling: squatting on haunches, sodomized so that hairs mingle, left breast lodged in the bend of the left arm, the right in the hollow of the left palm, right nipple stiff and erect between the left thumb and index finger, head fallen back onto the left shoulder, mouth wide open, the gaping refuge probed by three bent middle fingers, the tongue and palate moistened by the liquids drawn from them. There remain two hands, four feet, breaths, the interface of sweat covering the back to torso contact. What belongs to whom?

Or in this image of separation: under their nails, they carry particles of skin gathered from tracks scratched onto the ridge of the hips, the spreadeagled arms, the base of the neck and the small of the back. This is not two identities disjoining from each other in the separation, two bodies each owned by a separate identity. The bar of division unpredictably crosses the fields of sight, touch, smell and hearing; the skin's texture 'belongs' just as much to the tongues that have loved it or hated it, not only to the alleged body which it envelops. Parts get inextricably tangled up with regard to the order of 'this is yours, that is mine'.

This order is the order of capital, but this disorder is the disorder of capital. Order counts and produces its writings, disorder is multiplied in these accounts, sending shock-waves through it. The figure of Madame Edwarda is repeated in that of the masturbator-writer, a superbly capitalist *dispositif*: 'On reflection', says Guyotat, 'what spectacle is more brutally exciting than that of a child wanking with his left hand, in this system, and writing with his right. In the resultant disarray, there must be seen one of the terms of this contradictory pulsional will, being at the same time seen and voyeur ("seeing"), pimp and whore, buyer and bought, fucker and fucked.'[58] Now, what did Marx the prosecutor's left hand do while he was writing *Capital*?

Force

The *critique* of political economy is therefore instantiated on the (in)organic body; it is this beautiful body of reconciled genitality that allows the characterization and rejection of capitalism and wage earners as arising out of prostitution. The whole 'critique' is articulated in the following simple statements: profit hides surplus-value, surplus-value issues from the occultation of the use-value of the force of labour by its exchange-value; that is: from the occultation of its substantial, superabundant force by its property of being an exchangeable, sufficient, commodity; capitalism must also be mistaken about the *origin* of its growth, and this mistake is fatal to it.

Is this the dissimulation of force [*puissance*] in order? No. Is it the same thing that we wanted to show in signs; the sensible sign, that of exchange-value, dissimulating the tensor sign which would then have to be confused with use-value; and the reverse? Not the slightest chance. Use-value belongs to the system of sensible signs just like exchange-value, it is not external to it. That this is so, is nevertheless what Marx says, with specific reference to the use-value of *labour force*. For its exteriority, its heterogeneity is responsible, he thinks, and solely responsible, for the introduction of events into the system: if capital is threatened, thinks the prosecutor, it is because it cannot, at the same time, reduce working time to a minimum (v) and continue to reap a profit from the exploitation of this force, the growth of the organic composition c/v ceaselessly lowering the rate of profit and the incentive to invest. Capital captures force and turns it into a means of social labour, countable as time regulated by the clock: it 'binds' force.

One could bring out a sort of homology between this schema and Freud's: something undermines the 'psychic apparatus' or capitalism, an excitation which proceeds from the pulsional 'X' or from force, and in relation to which the 'apparatus' or the system reacts not only by *binding* the disruptive effects that result from the introduction of this force into a circuit of regulated tension, but by modifying, and in particular by heightening, the capacity of the tension regulator, without which the system cracks up. This is because capital for the procurer consists at least in a turning-away of funds, in the capture of force and the putting into circulation, regulated by the law of value and under the form of accumulated labour or 'death'. Living force is the pulsional source of the event, capital is its death as its binding. Nevertheless Freud distributed these roles in the opposite way: what produces the event in the system is the *death* drive, the Eros of life is what produces the system.

Of course, this inversion of signs enables us to discover an 'optimism' in Marx and a 'pessimism' in Freud. But this, in its turn, conceals the essential since the Marxist dialectic is fulfilled entirely within the interplay of force and system, the action, as indirect as one could wish, of the former on the latter is what carries it to its point of rupture. With Freud on the other hand, the opposition between the lethal pulsions and the erotic organization is neither dialecticized nor dialecticizable (subject to an action of the cure); of course the latter binds the former and, in a sense, 'benefits' from it (the famous 'secondary benefit'), but the former are not external to the regulated apparatus, they rather inhabit it, and this unthinkable cohabitation of the regulator and deregulation in the same signs is properly the dissimulation or dissimilation through which every intense sign appears as a coded sign, and some coded (but inassignable) sign conceals an intensity. Even if Freud himself gets this wrong, for example, interpreting the death drives as aggression in *Civilization and its Discontents*, therefore reestablishing a sort of pulsional binarism, it remains that his invention of 1920 gives rise to a dissimulatory monism: there is no equivalent in Marx, too much of a Christian for that.

One first entirely decidable 'effect' (and it is 'original') for this androgynous Marx, is the *splitting* of force into living force and dead force. Living force gives more than it takes, consumes less than it produces, a little meta-economic miracle of the extravagant gift which would be the forgotten origin of all wealth creation. What is killed in reproduction is this absolute, improbable, negentropic excess. It is a matter of the true *origin* of capital, the immutable event which always underlies the process of growing accumulation and which must give rise to its death sentence. The force of labour, conceived in this way, a force which *gives out* more than it *expends*, fully satisfies the petition formulated by Bataille for expenditure and consumption. What is this force, if not the return to 'critique' of an element indispensable to the model of the sovereign gift? Force consumes itself and it is this very consumption which enables the accumulation of capital. Such a model is set up against that of exchange. You believe that there is exchange, says the Little Girl Marx, but under all exchanges of equal value there is an original gift, an irreversible relation of inequality, making all equalities and equalizations illusory. Labour-force is *exorbitant*, or at least beyond value, inasmuch as the origin of surplus-value escapes the whole system of valuations at the same time as it renders this possible. With the result that this is not even a *general* wrong done to it, but a *meta-wrong*, a wrong which is not economic but ontological. Between the value that this force comes to add to those of the means of production employed, and its 'true' use-value, the split is inestimable. That does not mean that they cannot be fixed, which in fact takes place through the continual discussions, dialogues and disputes which surround the definition of salaries and conditions of labour. But, if the cost of force in its donatory function can only be arbitrarily established with regard to what is worked out for other commodities, it is because it *is not* an object, because it remains *beyond value*, and this is why this price may be fixed only in an extra-economic context, beyond the value system, in the context of class struggle. Wherever force escapes the economic approach, for instance: in its originary function, is where, what's more, it is trouble and disorder, and to evaluate it necessitates that one resort to conflicts or institutions of dialogue, which would no longer appear to arise from the regulated body of capital, but from the disparate, uncertain, equivocal, troubled socio-political body. The transcendence of the system by force is marked therefore in the referral of its definition from the field of reproduction to that of struggles.

Prostitutes getting organized to fight the domination of the pimps. The 'political' consequence follows smoothly, in the Marxist's eyes: if it is to obtain a better percentage on rates per lay, one remains within the denaturation of force, one is inscribed into the system, confining labour-force in its entirety within it, consequently comparable to a commodity. In this way *economism* will be denounced in the Leninist critique of union demands. The good fight aims on the contrary to emancipate the venal bodies from the bargaining of their alleged procurers (when it is the former who support the latter) and to reestablish everywhere the magnificent transcendence of the *One who gives* (force), which masks the infamy of the *One who receives* (capital). The hope of the young political woman is simply that the prostitutes become fertile virgins once more, members of a pure (in)organic body which they form *in reality*. And their gift should be distributed amongst them, in proportion, in short, to their respective needs, exactly as is the case, Marx thinks, amongst the organs of a healthy organic body. Capital or prostitution, disease of a social body, one part absorbing the forces of the whole, altering the relation of the given and the taken, reversing the relation of the donor and the donee, the 'boss' appearing to provide labour and sustenance when it is the worker who enigmatically provides the surplus of force; this latter in its rage turned back into the self-styled 'wisdom' of the concerted regulation of jobs, salaries, prices. The emotions of hate or despair which may seize leftist militants or the most infuriated workers when they see the 'proletariat' accept, after renegotiating, the rates for its prostitution, do not of course have economic motives, as in fact the leaders of companies, unions and parties (all good pimps), complain, they nourish themselves on the passion for an *elsewhere*, for an organic body hidden beneath the abstract body of capital, for a force lodged underneath or *outside* power relations.

Now, this idea of a transcendent exteriority of force to the system, which would be at the origin of surplus-value and therefore of profit, would appear to be dangerously threatened by the actual state of capitalist production. Marx himself knows this, as a text from the *Grundrisse* testifies,[59] where he states clearly that the individual labour-force in its immediate use *ceases to be the source of wealth* in proportion to the development of large industry, in proportion, therefore, to the fact that 'the totality of knowledge becomes an immediate productive force'. A remark which, on this decisive point of the accusation that the prosecutor is charged to bring against capital, to ascertain the exploitation, or, as he says here, 'the theft of working time from labour of the other, the present basis of wealth', cannot but make Little Girl Marx despair. For this basis is only present, and although the poor for a long time may hope to reap vengeance for this theft by a reversal (by a revolution) which would finally allow labour-force to be recognized in its unalienated transcendence, it is the very development of capitalism that sticks them away *'in the margins* (*neben*) of the production process, of which they were previously the principal agent'. Thus, more overworking as a condition of the development of wealth in general; more need for the extravagant generosity of a force to ensure growth.

It is true that Marx, worried, soon substitutes another 'master pillar of the production of wealth', 'the social individual', that is, 'the intelligence and mastery of nature by the whole of society', for this poor, marginalized subject. How can we understand this social individual? Is it a society become the *subject* of production in its totality? Is it a group of individuals by which, incredibly, *socialization*, that is 'the artistic, scientific, etc., development of every individual' thanks to the reduction of working time to a minimum and to the extension of its leisure time, will be increased? The formulations of the wise prosecutor belong to this hesitant subject; but this hesitation is not important here; what is important is that Marx, placed before the perspective of a production without the exploitation of the immediate labour-force and therefore without a proletariat, still sees in it the promise of a labour-force, an anonymous and triumphant labour-force, however: 'Man's appropriation of his own universal productive labour force', such is the new social subject, conscious, knowing and able. Is it still the same unified body craved by the love of little genital Rhénane?

No, it is no longer an organic body, it is a fleshless body, a machinic body obeying an immense head. Machines *are the instruments of the human brain created by human hands*; they are the materialized force of knowledge'.[60]

Now, will this body be socialist or capitalist? Marx writes: 'With that, production based on exchange-value breaks down . . . ' And more strongly: 'Capital calls to life all the powers of science and of nature, as of social combination and social intercourse, in order to make the creation of wealth independent (relatively) of the labour-time employed on it . . . [These] are the material conditions to blow this foundation sky-high.'[61] Why this blowing sky-high? Because capital 'wants to use labour-time as the measuring rod for the giant social forces thereby created, and to confine them within the limits required to maintain the already created value as value'. And such is the 'moving contradiction': 'To reduce labour-time to a minimum, while it posits labour-time . . . as sole source and measure of wealth.'[62] So my friends, if capital must burst, it is from counting all wealth in terms of working time, it is because the standard and the basis of value is and remains labour-force measured in hours and minutes. But who says this? The basis of value, meanwhile, is not capital, which does not want to and cannot know its origin, but the bearded, bitter prosecutor of its *causes*; this 'contradiction' is only as mortal as the depth of his hatred, of course.

As for the measure of values, the capitalist has his answer ready: we do not count in working time, we take any unit whatever capable of ensuring a minimum of consistency in the facts in our system (which is production for production's sake); such that the machinic body crowned with a huge abstract head, which we call the social subject and the universal productive force of man, is nothing other than the body of modern capital. The knowledge here in play is not at all made by all individuals, it is separate, a moment in the metamorphosis of capital, obeying it as much as governing it. And today's salaries, the defender of the bourgeois masters and bureaucrats will continue, don't they contain indistinctly the price of the selling of labour time and a fraction of the redistributed surplus? And the formation of additional capital, you are well aware that it has become impossible legitimately to impute to it the metaphysical difference between the use-value and the exchange-value of an alleged labour-force, a difference which alone would be at the origin of surplus-value; but what if in general it would require simply an inequality or a difference of potential somewhere in the system, a difference which marks its frame at the same time as it attests that this system could not be isolated, what if it must ceaselessly draw from new reserves of energy in order to transform them *into more commodities*. Perhaps it 'had to' draw initially on human energy, but this is not essential to it, and it can survive exploitation quite well, in the sense that you, the prosecutor for the poor, understand it, and requires, like every other complex natural system, only an irreversible superiority in its metabolic relation with the bio-physico-chemical context from which it draws its energy. Hence its exteriority, which is not at all transcendent, but simply natural. Do you not say yourself, prosecutor: 'Intelligence and mastery of *nature* by the whole of society?' What is this nature, prosecutor? An 'object' as opposed to a productive social 'subject'; or the (natural) context from which an *equally natural* system draws its energy? And if this is the case, where is the guilt?

Tautology

If the system of capital is, when all's said and done, *natural*, and Marx himself is not far from admitting this in many confessions, a supreme betrayal of the cause which he is supposed to defend,[63] a great many oppositions, stemming from the *desire to cleave* the givens, ought to collapse. It would be opportune enough, for example, to ruin the opposition of 'fixed needs' *versus* artificial needs;[64] let us be content to draw out the consequences of the elimination of the couple-value *versus* use-value.

To determine the former seems to require only two things: the definition of a standard of quantification applicable to all commodities entering into production, and rules of proportionality for the redistribution of products in diverse branches of production. This is how Piero Sraffa understands it when, postulating a regulated body of capital *in a self-replicating state* [*en boucle*], he constructs what he calls a commodity standard as a composite entity formed from n branches of production redistributing the totality of their n branches according to a law of proportionality which will allow the previous distribution of products to be reestablished, and production to start again according to the same methods.

Take a body of production composed of two branches or enterprises, one (**W**) producing wheat, the other (**I**) producing iron; all the wheat produced by **W** must be redistributed between **W** and **I** as subsistence means and means of production (supplying the workers); the same for iron. Value, Sraffa says, will be the proportion in which x hundredweight of wheat is exchanged for y tons of iron in such a way that each is completely redistributed between **W** and **I** as they were at the beginning. Take, for example, the following system of production organized into two branches:

(**W**) 280 *cwt* of wheat + 12 *t* of iron − 400 *cwt* of wheat
(**I**) 120 *cwt* of wheat + 8 *t* of iron − 20 *cwt* of iron

There is only one *value* of the relation iron/wheat which allows homogeneous reproduction, here 1/10. In fact **W** employs 280 *cwt* of wheat for its reproduction per 400 products; it sells the difference to **I**, that is, 120 *cwt*, required by **I** for its reproduction. Conversely, **I** will sell **W** (20 − 8) = 12 *t* of iron, which **W** employs for its reproduction. Therefore, on condition that 120 *cwt* of wheat is exchanged for 12 *t* of iron, the compositions of means of production for the two branches will be thus reconstituted in their initial state. *Value*, says Sraffa, is therefore the equal relation of 10 *cwt* of wheat to 1 *t* of iron.

It is indeed a question here of a standard measure, for 'there is a unique set of exchange-values which if adopted by the market restores the original distribution of the productions and makes it possible for the process to be repeated . . . '[65] The commodity standard or system standard will be, in a complex group, this single set of exchange-values allowing the return of the body of production to its original proportions. 'From such values', Sraffa adds, 'methods of production flow directly', a formula aimed, of course, at neo-marginalism and all theories of value based on demand and subjective utilities; but which no less affects Marxism and the theory of value based on quantity of work. For such a calculation completely excludes the distinction between the 'phenomenal form' and the substantive reality of value, a distinction which, by contrast, is indispensable to the Marxist doctrine.[66] With Sraffa, we abandon cleavage and theatricality. And this is because this *anchoring* in a presystemic exteriority is abandoned, a role played by force in Marx's economic critique, and by the (in)organic body in his philosophical approach.

Sraffa starts with the facts, as does Marx, but not the same facts: Marx's fact is and remains, from one end to the other of the romantic prosecutor's career, the alienation of property, of capital, from labour, which is not therefore a primary fact, but something which makes reference to a still more archaic and hidden 'fact', the lost instantiation of labour and needs, through an immediate mediation, in a social nature or a natural society: a nihilist fact giving cause for *interpretation*. Sraffa's fact is the system of capital as the producer and consumer of commodities: a positivist fact, to be constructed. Here there is no *authentic* point of origin, nor is there any *derealizing* finishing point; there is closure, commodities transformed into other commodities, and salaries as profit are taken as variables, dependent on one another of course (profit = 1 − salary), but as observable givens, which have no need to be explained or interpreted; what must be explained, that is to say constructed, on the other hand, is how, with the 'methods of production' (quite close to 'organic compositions') differing according to the branches, the system can nevertheless maintain itself in equilibrium, that is to say remain a system. Value is simply the set of the rules of transformation for all commodity-products into commodity-goods of production. The entire system of these transformations can be taken as a unit (= 1), and the exchange-value of each commodity will be expressible in terms of this 'composite commodity standard', that is to say in an absolutely *closed* manner; a closure then at the level of the *system* of branches: 'The exchange ratio (of a basic product[67]) depends as much on the *use* that is made of it in the production of other basic commodities as on the extent to which these commodities enter its own production.' And at the level of *each branch*, there is a feedback [*boucle*]: 'In the case of a basic product the prices of its means of production depends on its own price no less than the latter depends on them.'[68]

Such feedback notably implies that, in order to determine the value of a commodity, one does not analytically take into consideration a quantity of substance included in it (labour-force, for example), but its exchangeability as an amount (that is, the relation of its quantity with that of its means of production); and downstream (the relation of its quantity with that of all the commodities that it puts into its production). It is only within the entire set of circuits (at least of basic products) that value can be read; it is clearly read there, not by a return to source, but by the construction of a totalizing theoretical model and by a setting-out of the givens. The meta-economic opposition of use-value and exchange-value, or rather of use-value and value as such, completely disappears here: there are only use-exchange-values, prices in mutual interdependence, or the quantitative relations of commodities.

What, when all's said and done, are we dealing with in Sraffa's approach? Strictly speaking, with a theoretical discourse, expelling from itself every recourse to an exteriority and to a dialectic of the reversal of economic reality, putting only disparities regulated by the laws of transformation into play between terms none of which has a referential privilege, on the contrary, any commodity at all from the system may be taken as the standard, and the composite commodity just described being, in the theoretical model, only the most saturated equivalence of what effectively regulates exchanges in the domain of reference or the empirical system. This is a type of discourse analogous in every way to the one which Saussure elaborated for language, the same epistemological bias (in linguistics, langue rather than parole, in economics, the system of commodities rather than of subjects or goods), and has therefore the same concept of value as *regulated referral*, replacing that of signification-designation. A fully syntactical perspective.

Compared to Sraffa, Marx's attempt and failure to make the system (and his book on the system . . .) self-replicating can only appear illegitimate, whatever the Althusserians may say: what prevents Marx from making a 'scientific' description, is that he must fulfil the function of the prosecutor assigned him by his desire for an integration of goods, means and persons into a single body, his desire for harmonious genitality. Sraffa's 'body' is as elusive as the body of capital, commodities are themselves only evident there as the limits of an endless metamorphosis; which suggests the congruence of capital's operation with that of a theoretical system. It follows, of course, from such an approach that every catastrophic perspective is excluded: the death of capital cannot come to it from within, from some contradiction, there is no contradiction, there are at most disequilibrium states, there is no death through disruption.

In the vocabulary of Little Girl Marx, Sraffa defines the proper field and the strategy of the group of great procurers: an economist's ideology concealed under cover of the harsh prostitution of people and things in the pimps' interests. Is this what we are saying? In Baudrillard's terminology, the accusation brought against fetishism completes this structuration: the occultation of castration and ambivalence in the position of the anonymity of neutral goods. We are not even saying this. We say: here is a structural syntax of the language spoken by commodity exchanges; it is, so it seems, one of the strictest of its kind (but we are not economists enough to make a judgement on this . . .). Does it leave something outside itself? Do we reproach it, as S. Latouche does,[69] for confusing the heterogeneity of the commodity force of labour with every other commodity? This would be to retrace our steps, to seek an exteriority once again, a substance, to continue theology (whether humanist or atheist). On the contrary, we love the coldness of the system and its absolute lack of eloquence: the body of capital speaks only, in a sense, as *ratio*, banknotes and accounts, tautology.

If anything flaws Sraffa's description in this regard, it is the same thing that underlies it, the libidinal instantiation on this *ratio*, the incandescence obtained by the segmentation of the continuum called the ephemeral skin and tautologically interchanging the resultant segments, and ultimately: enjoying *value*, that is to say postponement and its algebraic cancellation. Theoretical discourse is no less *jouissive* than any other; what it enjoys is situated in this same coldness of the model which it constructed, and which, *ex hypothesi*, is a model of *equilibrium* (static or dynamic), that is the estimated *maximal binding* in the object of which it speaks, but primarily obtained in fact through its strict arrangement as discourse. Speech without viscosity, fastened to itself by the nuts and bolts of an infallible axiomatic, tending therefore towards an immobilized or immobilizing body of language, a body which could be for ever debated as to whether it is death or life, this being undecidable.

But even this assessment of the positivistic discourse of closure remains somewhat imperfect from the libidinal point of view. The instantiation of desire on the tautology is far from being the most important of the formations of desire in the capitalist *dispositif*. There is the strange operation which Marx calls increased accumulation, and which poses the problem of so-called growth for economists. The difficulties it presents to economic theory in its tautology would appear to be exactly those that can bring about the presence of a surplus of value in a homeostatically regulated system. How can a system obtain, at the end of a cycle, more than it consumed during the production process? Basically, the answer to this question has always been of the type: *the system is not isolated*, it deducts or receives energetic supplements *outside* itself, which it transforms, integrates into its circuits, and which still allow it thereafter to retain its specificity. The physiocrats call this exteriority nature, Marx calls it labour-force, many Marxists or Keynesians call it the third world or unequal exchange.[70] But in any case the concept of a *borderline* must be introduced, putting the tautological system in contact with an external reserve of energies which can be drawn on.

A *dispositif* of conquest, and therefore of a voyage beyond the rules of tautology, which must not be imagined as the obvious outsides of military or commercial imperialism, but much more subtly and more interestingly as the conquest of time. For the conquest by itself is not a process proper to capitalism, the great despotic States have always practised it, and doubtless the nomads as well; but, for these latter, it cannot be threatening, since it was only the pillage of transient energies, a discontinuous withdrawal [*prélèvement*], a regulated-regulator; as for the former, it has by contrast always been fatal to them because it created a disparity between the quantities of energy conquered and the assimilable quantities of energy: always too much or too little of the first relative to the second. Capitalism includes, on the contrary, in the name of increased accumulation, growth, development, etc., a *dispositif of the regulation of conquest, a dispositif* of permanent conquest. The speciality of this *dispositif* lies in a certain use of currency, which is a game with time. The *libidinal function* of this use must be grasped; the examination of mercantilism, and trade first of all, will allow us to approach it.

Notes

1 M. Rubel shows this in his introduction to Volume II of the Pléiade edition of the *Oeuvres*.

2 This is Böhm-Bawerk's classic critique. See Eugen Böhm-Bawerk, *Critique of Marx* (London: Merlin, 1975). See also Piero Sraffa, *Production of Commodities by Means of Commodities* (Cambridge: Cambridge University Press, 1960), and S. Latouche's discussion of these theses in *Epistémologie et économie*, (Paris: Anthropos, 1973), pp. 539–51.

3 See F. Fourquet's text, 'Généalogie du Capital II—L'Idéal historique', *Recherches*, 14, Revue de CERFI (January 1974), especially ch. IV.

4 See n. 3; here we encounter the discoveries made by Patrice Loraux in a study in progress.

5 Karl Marx, 'Notes to the Doctoral Dissertation', in *Writings of the Young Marx*, ed. and tr. by Loyd D. Easton and Kurt H. Guddat (New York: Doubleday, 1967), p.64.

6 Jean Baudrillard, in *Le Miroir de la production* (Paris: Casterman, 1973); hereafter cited as *Le Miroir . . .*), tr. Mark Poster as *The Mirror of Production* (St Louis: Telos, 1975). But, of course, also in *Pour une critique de l'économie politique du signe* (Paris: Gallimard, 1972), tr. Charles Levin as *For a Critique of the Political Economy of the Sign* (St Louis: Telos, 1972).

7 According to Godelier, or according to Poulantzas (*Pouvoir politique et conscience de classe*), he had also done this in order to provoke Baudrillard's anger. This was our object in studies from two or three years ago.

8 Baudrillard, *Le Miroir . . .* , p.38 (English translation, as well as in the above, in *Jean Baudrillard: Selected Writings*, ed. Mark Poster (Oxford: Polity/Basil Blackwell, 1988; hereafter cited as *Selected Writings*), p.116.

9 ibid., p.38 (Baudrillard's emphases) (*Selected Writings*, p.115—tn).

10 ibid., ch. II.

11 Marx, 'Contribution to the Critique of Hegel's Philosophy of Right' (1843), in Karl Marx, *Early Writings*, ed. and tr. by T. Bottomore (London: C. A. Watts, 1963), p.58.

12 Baudrillard, *La Miroir . . .* , p.113.

13 Michel Leiris, *L'Afrique fantôme* (Paris: Gallimard, 1934), pp.342–475.

14 Pierre Clastres, *Chronique des Indiens Guayaki* (Paris: Plon, 1972), pp.252–61.

15 Sophie Podolski, *Le Pays où tout est permis* (Paris: Pierre Belfond, 1973), p.104.

16 Pierre Guyotat, *Tombeau pour 500 000 soldats* (Paris: Gallimard, 1967).

17 Mina Boumedine, *L'Oiseau dans la main* (Paris: Pierre Belfond, 1973), pp. 152–5.

18 ibid., p.61.

19 Carlos Castoriadis, *La Société bureaucratique*, Vol. I, 2 and *L'Expérience du mouvement ouvrier*, Vol. I, 2 (Paris: UGE, 10/18, 1973).

20 Bruno Rizzi, *La Bureaucratisation du monde* (Paris: 1939).

21 *Socialisme ou barbarie*, 35 (January 1964).

22 i.e. dialectical materialism and historical materialism.—*tn*

23 Didier Deleule and François Guéry, *Le Corps productif* (Paris: Mame, 1972), especially part 1, 'L'Individuation du corps productif', by François Guéry.

24 ibid., pp.37–9.

25 ibid., pp.23–4.

26 Jacqueline de Romilly, *Histoire et raison chez Thucydide* (Paris: Les Belles Lettres, 1956), pp. 180–240.

27 J.–L. Nancy, *La Remarque spéculative* (Paris: Galilée, 1973), in particular the commentary, on p.52 ff., on the addition to p.462 of [Hegel's] *Encyclopaedia*.

28 Jacques Lacan, 'La Direction de la cure et les principes de son pouvoir', in *Ecrits* (Paris: Seuil, 1966), pp. 585 ff.; tr. Alan Sheridan as 'The Direction of the Cure and the Principles of its Power', in *Ecrits, a Selection* (London: Tavistock, 1977), p.226 ff.

29 On this dialectical function of negation in the unconscious, see Jacques Lacan, *Le Mythe individuel du névrosé* (Paris: CDU)

30 G. W. F. Hegel, *Hegels theologische Jugendschriften* (Tübingen: Nohl Ed., 1907), p.258; quoted by B. Bourgeois, *Hegel à Francfort* (Paris: PUF, 1970), p.59.

31 Bourgeois, *Hegel à Francfort*, p.43.

32 Karl Marx, 'Auszüge ans James Mills Elements of Political Economy', *M.E.W.*, Ergänzungsband I, p.461; hereafter cited as 'Auszüge . . . '. Translation modified.

33 Ludwig Feuerbach, 'Das Wesen des Glaubens im Sinne Luthers. Ein Bietrag zum "Wesen des Christentums"', in *Gesammelte Werke* (Berlin: 1970), Vol. 9, p.411.

34 Karl Marx, *Economic and Political Manuscripts of 1844*, tr. Martin Milligan (London: Lawrence & Wishart, 1973; hereafter cited as *1844 Manuscripts*), pp.165–6.

35 Marx, 'Auszüge . . . ', p.455.

36 'Protestant hypocrisy took the place of Catholic candour': this, writes the author of the *Umrisse zu einer Kritik der Nationalökonomie* (also published in the *Deutsche-Französische Jarbücher* at the end of February 1844), is the change introduced by Adam Smith, the 'Luther of political economy', into this 'science'. Marx develops this point in the *1844 Manuscripts*, p.202; see also Marx, ibid., pp. 128–9.

37 Karl Marx, 'Precapitalist Forms . . . ', in *Grundrisse der Kritik der politischen Okonomie* (hereafter cited as *Grundrisse*), tr. Martin Nicolaus (Harmondsworth: Penguin, 1973), p.488; the text dates from 1857–8.

38 ibid., p.485.

39 ibid.

40 Karl Marx and Friedrich Engels, *The German Ideology*, Vol. I (London: Lawrence & Wishart, 1970), p.68.

41 Which Poulantzas says in *Pouvoir politique et classes sociales* (Paris: Maspero), pp.25–6, 134.

42 Marx, 'Precapitalist Forms . . . ', *Grundrisse*, p.489.

43 Karl Marx, *Contribution to the Critique of Political Economy*, tr. S. W. Ryazanskaya (London: Lawrence & Wishart, 1971). This theme of indifference is developed largely in the manuscript entitled 'Sixth Chapter. Immediate Results of the Process of Production', which was to become a part of Book I of *Capital*; tr. and introduced by Dangeville as *Un Chapitre inédit du Capital* (Paris: UGE, 10/18, 1971), especially pp.222 ff., 231 ff., 241 ff; this manuscript dates from 1863–6.

44 Karl Marx, *Capital* Vol. I, tr. Samuel Moore and Edward Aveling (London: Lawrence & Wishart, 1974), p.81.

45 ibid., pp.81–2.

46 ibid.

47 ibid., pp.82–3.

48 Karl Marx and Friedrich Engels, *Manifesto of the Communist Party*, in *Collected Works*, Vol. 6 (London: Lawrence & Wishart, 1976).

49 Marx, *1844 Manuscripts*, p.133.

50 Karl Marx, *'Reading Notes'* (Winter 1843–4; Fr. tr. in Pléiade II, p.11).

51 Marx, *Grundrisse*, p.163.

52 Georges Bataille, 'Madame Edwarda', in *Oeuvres complètes*, Vol. III (Paris: Gallimard; hereafter cited as *OC*), p.26; tr. Austryn Wainhouse as *My Mother/ Madame Edwarda/The Dead Man* (London: Marion Boyars, 1989), p.155.

53 Marx, *1844 Manuscripts*, p.167.

54 ibid., p.134.

55 See Marx, 'Precapitalist Forms . . . ', *Grundrisse*: 'Capital proper does nothing but bring together the mass of hands and instruments which it finds on hand. It agglomerates them under its command. That is the real stockpiling' (p.508, fn.).

56 Bataille, 'Madame Edwarda', *OC*, Vol. III, p.21; Wainhouse, p.150.

57 Marquis de Sade, 'Français, encore un effort . . . ', in *La Philosophie dans le boudoir* (Paris: Pauvert, 1972), pp. 215–17.

58 Pierre Guyotat, 'Langage du corps', in *Artaud*, Colloque de Cérisy (Paris: UGE, coll. 10/18, 1973), p.173.

59 Marx, *Grundrisse*, p.702 ff. The text has been summarized and discussed by Herbert Marcuse in *One-Dimensional Man* (London: Routledge & Kegan Paul, 1986); by Paul Mattick in *Marx and Keynes: The Limits of the Mixed Economy* (Boston, Mass.: Porter Sargent/Extending Horizons Books, 1969); by Naville in *Le Nouveau Léviathan*, Book I.

60 Marx, *Grundrisse*, p.706.

61 ibid., pp. 705–6.

62 ibid., p.706.

63 'If one wanted to pretend, like certain sentimental adversaries of Ricardo, that production as such cannot be the goal, it is because one had forgotten that the formula: production for production's sake, signifies simply: the development of all human productive forces, therefore the development of the wealth of human nature set up as its proper goal. If one opposes the individual's well-being to this goal, so that for example one must never make war because in it individuals would be killed . . . one does not understand that . . . the superior development of the individual can only be achieved through a historical process to which individuals are sacrificed. Not to speak of the sterility of these considerations, since in the animal as in the vegetable kingdom, the advantages of the species always triumph over those of individuals. Ricardo's brutality was not therefore honest only from a scientific point of view, but rather scientifically imposed by this point of view. In consequence, it matters little to him whether the development of productive forces kills landed property or the workers . . . .' Karl Marx, *Histoires des doctrines économiques*, Fr. tr. (Costes), Vol. IV, p.11; quoted by Latouche, *Epistemologie et économie*, pp. 569–70.

64 Marx opposes to Stirner, in a passage from *The German Ideology*, taken from the section 'Saint Max', the natural fixity of desires, that is to say of nutritional and sexual needs. E. Fromm quotes this text in 'Marx's Concept of Man', his introduction to the *1844 Manuscripts* (New York, 1960). R. Kalivoda takes up the whole discussion again in a long note in his *Marx et Freud*, Fr. tr. (Anthropos, 1971), pp. 81–4.

65 Piero Sraffa, *Production of Commodities by Means of Commodities* (hereafter cited as *Production*), p.3.

66 As Marx repeats in his 'Notes on the Treatise of Adolf Wagner', (1880), in Marx and Engels, *Collected Works*, Vol. 24 (London: Lawrence & Wishart, 1989), p.554.

67 The product is said to be basic when it enters, directly or indirectly, into the production of all commodities. Only such products as these belong to the composite commodity which can serve as a standard. See Sraffa, *Production*, p.8.

68 ibid., p.9.

69 Latouche, *Epistémologie et économie*, pp. 547–50. S. Latouche is the French translator of Sraffa's book.

70 It is again on this point that S. Latouche (pp. 550–1) breaks with Sraffa: the latter, the heir to Ricardo and to 'a certain Marx' (he indeed who enjoys by means of postponement, according to us), omits, 'forgets' the necessity, in order that the system may grow, that he experiences of the 'preliminary outlets'. It is necessary therefore, declares Latouche, to return to unequal exchange.

4

Trade

Nicomachean Erotics

Let's not wait for the historians to validate the following event (all the more because they may have already done so . . .) in order to make it a core of questions that preoccupy us, we libidinal economists: the *méson* that Détienne, Vidal-Naquet, Vernant and Finley place at the empty centre of the ancient Greek collective of warrior-talkers, this place for depositing all the plundered loot, this tribunal at the centre of the civil world, this geometral plan of the *isonomia* of the citizens, this hub where all the political radii are instantiated and all the diameters of exchange are neutralized, in sum, this zero, well, it's the same one that Aristotle institutes, under the name of money, as the judge of economic exchanges. Its distributive justice consists initially in *annulling* the terms of the exchange and the exchangists themselves, inasmuch as one wants ('desires', needs, fancies, is motivated to acquire, is interested in) what the other has. Marx, rereading the texts of the *Nicomachean Ethics*, will induce from them the conviction that a theory of exchange, which notably remains tied to prices and to needs, is incapable of understanding why two chairs, and not three, will have to be offered against one table. And he will say: an objective value is necessary, a measurable element common to both terms, we must descend beneath the scene of the market, and in the basement we must find the totally objective and necessary machinery of subjective and contingent exchanges. By so doing, he evidently and intentionally *devalues* the place of the price, by turning it into the surface, the *skin* of the economic body, almost an illusion.

Now, if we start again with the zero of the money-judge, with its function of annulment as Aristotle understood it (without concerning ourselves, we must repeat, with knowing how, and much less why, the figure of the isonomic warrior-politician circle is or is not displaced into the economic sphere—or better: how and why in the Aristotelian world, instead of men bearing arms and words, there will be tradesmen and commodities), we take this skin of the body utterly seriously, precisely because we realize that in libidinal economy, there is nothing but skin on the inside and the outside, there is only one monoface surface, the libidinal body is a Moebius strip, and a *dispositif* like that of the *méson* is not an underground machinery beneath the plateau of the stage or the wings, quite the contrary, it commands certain instantiations of libidinal impulsions on the body-band, the blockage and exclusion of other regions: so the chattering warriors and pederasts don't even show their arse to women, slaves, metics, children, foreigners, nature, but their *profile*, preoccupied as they are with the mad accumulative circle of internal debts of deaths and lives, of productions and words, fascinated exclusively by the balancing out of all that, its compensation and maintenance at the regulatory zero, no longer harnessing any 'external' force insofar as it will be able to find its expression, its place and its neutralization in the world of citizen-calculators.

Thus the 'political' order and, in the narrowest sense of the word, the mercantile order, that of the market where exchanges using payment money take place, is not taken by us as the expression of *something else*, for example, of hidden relations of production, of a subterranean order to be deciphered, no, we take it as a modality, as a figure, a *dispositif* by means of which the pulsions running across the surfaces of the 'bodies' of the young and old, male and female, Greeks and non-Greeks, are to be found driven back towards this centre where they congregate, combine, conspire and must always ultimately be annulled; that is, they are primarily driven back 'to the outside'. This entails, and not metaphorically, many things; for instance, this: the citizen's 'body', the famous Greek body, is a tiny fragment of the polymorphous ribbon (the monoface band), and the city, the *politeia*, consists in only rendering useful, utilizable, a tiny fragment of the band. The harmonious, voluminous totality of the athlete is a prejudice as regards the pieces of the libidinal surface. What is a citizen-body? The pulsional investment of the penis and the logos. But the shank and language are here *diverted* from the charge points offered them by the configurations of other societies.

Far indeed from reserving his semen for the female womb and therefore for the propagation of the species, the Pythagorean homosexuals apportion it out. They will of course impregnate their women, this will simply be the price to be paid for providing the city with young people to educate, arm, introduce into and annul in the homosexual circle. One part sperm for propagation, one part for masculine commerce.[1] They strangely reverse the terms of a *dispositif* that one used to be able to think of as natural; it is when they go to bed with their women that they prostitute themselves, for the prostitute transforms the client's *jouissance* into money and therefore phlegmatically converts the perverse libido or simply its use, the surplus of pulsional energy scattered in society, and dangerous to it, deadly because it is capable of setting it off in every sense[2] without any regard for its organic unity—it converts therefore these perversions or diversions of energy into money, and then into commodities (into capital indeed), thereby taking care to safeguard the social whole, assuming the sacred malediction of genital sterility, but simultaneously bringing about the return of these 'lost' expenditures into the circuit of social exchanges. The prostitute therefore redeems perversion (the diversion of the pulsions) by replacing its product, not semen exactly, but its equivalent, money, not in the entry to her uterus which is necessarily closed off while the penile clientele frequent her, but in the entry to the goods market, and therefore to society. But our warrior, when he makes children with his woman, behaves just like the prostitute when she makes money from society through her client's perversion. And just as the client pays money for the fruitlessness of whatever *jouissance* he may derive, thereby paying homage to the social Eros, so the citizen pays by the semen he deposits in the woman's genitalia for this truly sterile *jouissance*, only obtaining his satisfaction elsewhere in civic homo-eroticism. What happens here then, is not the harnessing of deadly energies in a monetary form, but their regulation under the genital form; but this latter would then appear—and this is the great Greek reversal—as the new and genuine prostitution, prostitution turned inside out; from now on every woman, and no longer insofar as she is *sterile*, but insofar as she is *impregnated*, like a machine that transforms sperm into a child, into a potential warrior—every woman would therefore appear as a detestable but necessary appendage for the one authorized function of *jouissance*, which is here the production of a society of loquacious citizens, homosexuals and warriors. It is propagation which becomes prostitution for them, that is to say the indispensable redemption of the sterile intensities of homosexual *jouissance* by means of the reproduction of children. They pay in semen for perverting semen. They have, therefore, two penises, one for this payment, the other for civic *jouissance*.

Now where is this civic *jouissance* on the inside of the circle of men, apart from payment at its frontiers? What is exchanged here, if not more children, that is to say, the means of reproduction? How are the the connections of libidinal body-strips in the circle of warriors organized? The absolute identity required of the members of this circle, called the equality of citizens, *isonomia*, equal distance from the centre, from the *méson*, the fact that they are all apparently males and speakers of the Attic and Hoplite tongues, that each of them can come to the centre, into this empty tribunal which nevertheless no-one must be able to occupy and appropriate on a long-term basis, the fact that the words of political decision must follow the singular rule of the *tetralogos* (I speak, you respond, I respond to you, you respond to me), after which it is resolved (*bouleusis*)—all these character-istics make the *politeia* a strange *dispositif* for the *annulment of differences*. This annulation is operative from the outset, since it is required only of males in this circle of citizens; and it operates as the rule of all rules of political administration, the rotation of offices, the eligibility of officials, the revocability of appointments, public deliberation on all decisions, the counting of votes: in every case, return to the zero, neutralization by the zero. This democracy, it will be said, rests on the obfuscation of both sexual difference and that of labour. But it further and essentially implies the geometrical formalization of pulsional bodies, and still more it requires an algebra of the pulsions, their comparability, their exchangeability and their annulability by means of some neutral element.

The impossible, dangerous liaison of Alcibiades with Socrates (at least as recounted by Plato in *The Symposium*) not only proves that Eros is at work amongst the citizens, which we know already, it teaches us rather that the circular organization of the desiring bodies in the *politeia* necessarily inscribes them into an equal exchange, equivalence. Alcibiades offers himself to Socrates so that the latter might take pleasure in his youth and beauty, but in order to obtain in exchange the secret of the Old Man's wisdom. There is a market, it supposes therefore the exchangeability of terms which are here the penis-anus region on the one hand (Alcibiades), and on the other (Socrates) the discursive oral region. It is necessary to see in this business proposition a particular sort of amorous advance. Enjoyment, in its political economic perversity, counts on a revenue and discounts what it advances: expenditure with the greatest profit and the least loss. Alcibiades is counting then, and Socrates, justifying his apparent refusal to enter the market, in fact provides the theory of every market (in the simple mercantilism that is politics), which is that there is *nothing to be gained*, that every exchange and the balance of every account is nil. My wisdom's worth in gold, says Socrates, is zero. Such is the *virtu* required by the *politeia*: to remain staunchly within the zero of impulsional exchanges, to live without having lost or gained, to regulate the circulation of libidinal energies at the *minimax*, at the minimum of losses and the maximum of gains allowing the partners a *zero sum game* (the exchangeable quantities are constant) and a game of *complete information* (each knows what the other will ask at the centre): a draw at chess, for example.

Hence the sterilization of penises, and compensation in semen; and also the limitation of the number of exchangist citizens, and again the eroticization of the speech through which, in these political games, essential *announcements* are made. The city is made therefore from completely working over the 'bodies' which enter it, from a squaring-off by which they are reduced to a few useful organs, all the other organs banished, all vaginas, all foreign tongues, every hand which cannot kill, but only work, all speeches delivered somewhere other than *in the centre*, and doubtless many more besides . . . Far from being a complete man, the *kalos kagathos* is a section from the pulsional body-band, a piece of the surface where the libido's investment and its flowing towards discharge are strictly restricted. But more astonishing even than this, is that discharges from one body to others must be compensated for, therefore that the entire coursing of the pulsions across the circle must cross the central zero and that after each cycle, the *quitus*—that is to say the *quies,** the quiescence of nullity—may be pronounced by the group of exchangists. So not only the parcelling-out of the citizen-body, which is not original in itself since the pulsional body has never been and will never be united, unified with itself, and no social organization can anchor itself in its impossible totality—but the instantiation of the useful segment of this body on the zero-centre. Annulatory perversion: annulling through movement, on the ring of the city. Concentration [*circonversion*].

**Quies* (*L*): rest, repose; absence of disturbance, motion, anxiety, aggression; non-participation in a conflict.—*tn*

It is, in particular, in the very institution of the cleavage between use- and exchange-values that one assists with this political operation. If the bodies at work in the *politeia*, and, in Aristotle, the goods and needs in play in the *koinonia*, can be exchanged according to the law of the final zero, it is because they have first undergone the strict libidinal 'education' which will entitle only those segments of the band where *jouissance* will be instantiated convertibly to remain in place on the *agora*, on the market. Market equivalence is the double of political homosexuality: signs of more and less can be applied to these pieces of the body and to the fluxes which cross them, because they are quantitatively calculable, having been set down as homogeneous. What Aristotle, the first of the political economists, will call need, *chreia*, is what becomes of the pulsional charge, pressing towards discharge [*poussant à jouir*] in one segment of the isonomic, concentrated body. And the use-value of a good, which is its value in terms of *jouissance* in these conditions on the circle, will be the capacity of this good, being plugged into the segment of the desiring body, not only to lead it to discharge, but to render the resultant product capable of being turned back once again onto the market, and annullable in the final balancing out of losses and gains. Use-value is, consequently, immediately subordinated to exchange-value, which is already a *jouissance* in the economists', rather than the erotologists' sense.

This is not to say that it doesn't exist, that it is illusory, or alienated. It is nothing of the sort, and, conspicuously, we turn our backs on this old critique. Once again, to sustain it, we would have to be able to speak of a total libidinal body, of a band or collection of organs which can be invested at every point, capable of discharge [*apte à jouir*] everywhere without exemption, in comparison to which every *jouissance* instantiated in one place or another would be so only at the price of a genuine amputation. We recognize this old image, we libidinal economists, it is not so much *jouissance* as phantasm (an entirely sad and nihilist idea), but the make-believe of totalization, of an Eros without a death drive (or, Marcuse, reconciled with it), of a unity without loss. An idea not far removed from *mechanism*, as strange as it may seem: for absent from this and from every physical theory of movement *ex hypothesi*, is the principle that an inclimin-able, irrepressible disorder might at unexpected moments and according to inevaluable modalities, come to disturb the organizations of movements and bring about the dismembering of mechanical bodies. But the death drive of which Freud speaks, and which underlies our own libidinal economism, implies on the contrary a tremendous *chance* (not in itself, but due to its indiscernibility), and if he called it the pulsion of *death*, it is because this chance inevitably involves the disorder of the *dispositifs* at work, their lethalization, just as the 'proper' functioning of these *dispositifs*—for example, that of the *isonomia* of citizens and commodities —stifles beneath its harmonious music the grating and the cries of all the segments of the body-band removed from the circulation of the libidinal fluxes, dehydrated, sterilized, rebellious: subversives beyond concentration. If use-value is from the outset instituted with exchange-value in the geometry and the algebra of the city and the market, it is because it is nothing without this exchange-value and this *isonomia*, and one would be unable, as Marx did, to appeal for one against the other, as what is authentic against what was wrongfully assumed. Everything is false and everything is true. Utility and its 'value' are cut-ups [*découpages*] of bodies, corresponding to exchange and its equilibrium. All this is just one *dispositif*. Use and need are not exteriorities, naturalities, or references from which one would be able to criticize exchange, they are a part of it.

'Everything must have its money value fixed, because then there will always be exchange, and if exchange, association. Strictly speaking', adds Aristotle, 'things so widely different cannot become commensurable; but in relation to need a sufficient degree of accuracy is possible. So there must be some one standard, and that on an agreed basis (*ex hypothesi*) (which is why money is so called), because this makes all things commensurable, since they can all be measured in terms of money . . . It is this that has led to the introduction of money, which serves as a sort of mean (*méson*) . . . but by a convention need has come to be represented by money.'[3]

Strictly speaking then, the terms of the exchange are not exchangeable, *every segment of the libidinal band is absolutely singular.* By convention, however, under the name of need, the pressure from the strength of desire on whatever points of this band will become measurable, and by convention one will contrast it, under the name of a good, for plugging in and discharge, with a proportion of another body or product of that body. Who is this one? The *dispositif* of the *politeia-koinonia*. And as regards money, it is the standard as accounting money and the neutral element as payment money: the convention of conventions of need. The need is what is utterly dissipated by means of money. Money is the zero of need. But it is because the need was first the median site of desires, the reabsorption of intensities as measurable intentions, just as the isonomic citizen was obtained through the repression of heteronomies and anomies. Need is desire maintained within the canons of identity, it is exchangeable because it is not different, or indifferent.

'What money does for us is to act as a guarantee (*egguètès*) of exchange in the future: that if it is needed now, it will take place as the need arises . . . '[4] This zero of money is therefore something else still: it is a temporal instance, the eternal present of possible exchange, and hence of need and possible need. It is the 'for all time' of the market and the community. Money introduces an omnitemporality, that of the economic cycle and that of thought insofar as both are instantiated on the mean. The zero of money is the region of annulation, potential, always possible: I am hungry, I buy, I eat; where there was exteriority of a need and a good, nothing remains (need satisfied, good consumed) but the zero of the money paid, passed into the hands of the seller. The latter experiences no need, this zero in his hands assures me, assures us all (who are on the circumference) that he will *put it back* into circulation against some of our goods. This zero of exchange's past which makes us quits, is at the same time the zero of a deposit against future settlements. Between the need, this political-economic form of desire, whose essential characteristic is solubility, that is to say possible resolution or suppression through money, between the need and this suppression itself, the zero of money *opens up* duration and the durable, permanence. The soluble need, is, in itself, equally predictable. And everything that there is on the periphery of the mercantile political circle finds itself then instantiated on the *possible*. But nothing is more unknown to the pulsion hooked onto its little segments of the two dimensional film, than the possible.

Thought begins with the possible. This is why the *logos* begins with the *politeia* and the market. It is as if the voice or writing, the production of signs with a view to exchange, monopolized almost all the libido of the citizen-merchant bodies. But I am not saying that the body that speaks, writes and thinks, does not enjoy, it is a segment of the flat body of the pulsions, rather that its charge, instead of taking place in singular intensities, comes to be folded back not only onto the need of the market and the city, but onto the zero where both are centred, onto the zero of money and discourse. Nihilism brings this with it: needs, one will say, and therefore the bodies who are supposedly their bearers, needs and their proprietors, the talking mouths, create nothing but ceaseless transition, and there is nothing actual, death alone is immortal, this empty *méson* around which the members of the *koinonia* gravitate.

Ulysses, a commodity in transition from form to form, returns to Ithaca. Ulysses, the speaker and the liar, all his words are annulled, whether true or false, in the final recognition, all his proofs in the final identity. Ulysses is Hegelian spirit, the domination of the possible, the devaluation of all affirmation in favour of a nothing, Hegelian scepticism already arrived at its empty plenitude. A circular voyage, for nothing. This is the voyage of money metamorphosing through all its incarnations, but it is none of them, they are only the moments of a something which is *nothing*, money. But it is also the voyage of the concept, seeking, by trial and error, to exchange itself according to the rule of logic (*determination*), and reducing the affirmed-affirmative singularities to representations or forms of itself, just as money reverses everything in its *possible* specifications.

To die/not to die. In this oscillation of the yes and the no (which is expressed perfectly in French, according to A. Culioli, by the interrogative-reflexive infinitive: *voyager . . . ?*), the linguist sees the modality of the possible, which, once again, he calls the *notion*. One might think that, beneath superficial differences of expression, it exists in every language, but what the *dispositif* or figure of which we speak does for the Greeks, is to make this modality predominate over others—the predominance of the *negative*: the *no* in parity with the *yes*, negation with affirmation, affirmation affirming itself only on condition that it determines, excludes. Socrates' labour, the binary analyses of the later Plato. But desire as displacement of forces over the libidinal body knows no 'no'. None of these exclusions of certain regions, blockages of certain routes, none of the stases which result in quantities of energy being invested as kinds of channels irrigating such zones, not one of these operations is a negation or a denial, each proceeds from the investment of the libido alone;—and it is only, pulsional jealousy excepted, in the body with a memory, instantiated on memory, on permanence, in fact therefore on the concept of its life (its survival), it is only in such a body and in relation to it, in relation to its alleged totality, that one will be able to say that the instantiation of the forces of *jouissance* in such 'regions' as these is accompanied by a disaffection of others and in consequence by a sort of denial focusing on these latter as objects unacceptable to the former.

We must take Freud's metaphors quite seriously here, that is to say *we must not take them as metaphors*, or take them just as they are, those by which with the help of images of foreign towns or countries, such as Rome or Egypt, just like Piranesi's *Prisons* or Escher's *Other Worlds*, he suggests an

entirely affirmative unconscious, simultaneously accumulating investments in the most perverse appearances (for the logos) on every point of
the libidinal body. What Freud makes us consider through these arrogant
violations of the rudimentary rules of space-time, is precisely the affirmativity of these occupations of libidinal terrain. Nihilism indeed comes from
Socrates, doubtless not in the way that Nietzsche thought in his slightly
naïve faith in dualism in *The Birth of Tragedy*, but instead from the model of
the talking homosexual warrior-citizen which the early Platonic Socrates
demonstrates.

When Plato puts the *nihil* into Socrates' mouth, when the latter rejects
Alcibiades' bargain, it is not (for once . . .) the *nihil* of a transcendence, of
an affective state or a state of thought which would be kept out of reach,
placed in another region: it is the negation of this region, it is also therefore
the negation of hypostatized place, the affirmation that there is no site of
discourse and knowledge other than that of trade, which could be gained
by paying the highest price, it is in this way that philosophy's words are
suddenly put back in their place, in annulatory exchange, and thus
committed to annihilation like all exchangeable objects; and, on the other
hand, these objects are from now on established to be immediately
annihilable, that the body's desire takes possession of them, grabs hold of
them as positive extensions, these objects are fated for annihilation by the
zero of book-keeping at exactly the same time as they are desired. If the
worth of my knowledge in gold is zero, says Socrates, it is not because it is
nothing, but because it is money, the vehicle of exchanges and the means
of the annulment of 'debts', that is to say stases of forces [*puissances*] halted
on the libidinal body, *illusions* and *errors*.

Nihilism reigns then on the interior of the circle. The predominance of
the *notion* (in the linguists' sense), that is to say of the concept (in the
philosophers' sense) or of money, not only affects bodies by transforming
the displacements of energy into needs, it not only affects objects by
transforming their plugging into use-value for purposes of discharge, it will
also affect the talking mouth by so imposing on him that he can no longer
enjoy the production of narratives of destiny, the henceforth popular
imagery of myths or the henceforth artistic staging of tragedies, that is to
say in simulacra homogeneous to the libidinal body, in that they count in
terms of the extreme intensities which they convey, making those so-called spectators weep, rejoice, cry, these spectators who are violently plugged
into these simulacra to pump up and pour out their pleasure-pain—no, the

citizen-mouth will have to enjoy the policed political exchange of arguments, in the fastidious *Face to Face* and *Equally Armed* of Isocrates, Lysias, and all analogous plaintiffs, the Peyrefittes and the Marchais, in fine tones, in an evenness of tone and temper, and in the rhetorical regulation of divergences of tone and temper. Instead of arguments, discourses about arguments. The mouth *will have to* enjoy in this way, which is not to say that this will come about—Plato complains often enough that it does not, and that all democrats are rabble, that Callicleses do not speak so as to gain the minimax, but to eliminate the adversary, and that the tyrannical city is like a body sectioned off into incredible polarities. Nevertheless, for want of good (nullifying) politics, philosophical discourse will emerge from this exigency, as dialogues with a neutralizing function, where the result of words will end with a notion on which all the protagonists agree (squared-off citizen-bodies) and by means of which, consequently, the reasons for pursuing the discussion will in the end disappear. This notion, this concept, is a word which will enable the players' mutual debts to be discharged, it will be money from new mouths, the *nihil* in which they will always be able to annihilate the libidinal forces (*puissances*) that move them. And as the citizen-body rejects the uterus, manufacturing hands, barbarous phonemes and syntaxes, so the citizen-mouth will consign the cries, all the signs of its belonging to the libido, to the dungeon of Dionysus' *nocturnes*. First enclosure: night, the first prison, from the point of view of the beautiful zerotic sun of the Apollonians. Its black a-market.

Lydian Eulogy

Herodotus says: 'The Lydians were the first people we know of to use a gold and silver coinage and to introduce retail trade.'[5] In the previous line he remarks that the only difference between the Greek and Lydian money-makers and retailers, is that the latter delivered their daughters into prostitution. This libidinal consistency must be admired. Payment money is the zero installed *ès méson*, centred, with the *koinonia* of men (merchants this time), on this zero, and homosexual perversion established in the market in the form of the homogeneous normality of exchanges and exchangeable goods. This normality is perverse in the sense that it is *sterile*, all past exchanges achieving annulment. Far from aiding propagation, this normality inserts it into the impasse of an unproductive algebra.

The instance of the market, centred on the zero of *all things considered*, can only beat time according to the pulsation, from now on regularized, of 'needs' arising here and there on the circumference of the mercantilist circle, in the bodies of those called buyers. These latter come therefore to the centre, to the market, and collate what each can (wants to) give with what each wants to (can) receive. Goods are balanced out here and there, as are needs, necessarily, as marginalism shows: for every exchange from A to B is at the same time, for A himself, an exchange, a comparison between what he has and what he desires to have. In this way a proportionality of what is offered and what demanded, of the actual and the possible, is established. Thus the famous 'humpbacked curve' will be established, the inscription of diverse choices on the axes of 'utility', which are otherwise encoded in Morgenstern and Rapoport's matrices, of which we will say more later on.

If the game is zero sum, if all that A can gain is lost by B, if therefore there is no *exteriority* to the circle of citizens' exchanges, and if they remain in the zero of the *milieu*, it is clear that the system remains utterly infertile. This society of merchant-men is a quite singular libidinal *dispositif, a dispositif* of the libido's conservation in a sort of pulsional treasure constituted by the members of the *koinonia*, the wealth of which circulates from one to the other without ever leaving the circle and without any libidinal supplement ever being introduced into it. Therefore, not only is it a very selective *dispositif,* but a very conservative one, in the pulsional sense: for the zero of annulments of exchange is, understood in terms of intensities, the sign that the merchant citizen society completely follows the dictates of a regulator of tensions itself programmed on a unit of tension which is the sum of intensities present throughout the circle. If these intensities are entered into a ledger, it is because they have already passed through the filter of the *politeia*, which excludes, as we have said, enormous pieces of the labyrinthine band of the libidinal body. In this case, this market or this city functions as a stable, homeostatically regulated whole, the zero marking the simple return to a state prior to the excitation of exchange. The economic (but doubtless just as much political and erotic) cycle is thus determined by the instantiation of all operations on a mean, or *méson*, or *Mitte*, or medium, or *minimax*, in which differences are annulled. But differences can be annulled there only because they are simultaneously annulled in the constitution of the citizen-merchant-lover-partners, identical bodies where desire, deprived both of its errancy, by means of strict localizations, and of leaps of tension by rigorous educational adjustments (the *paideia*), will be exchangeable against itself in equal quantities.

Here then, the zero of *all things considered* is at the same time the sterility of the *koinonia*. When money functions solely as payment money, it ensures that *nothing happens*, to such an extent that society can no longer reproduce itself. Hence the fringe of women and workers which provide it with young exchangists and fresh goods. But this fringe functions only, let's repeat, on condition that the women are impregnated by homosexual citizens, who then prostitute themselves in reverse: if homosexual perversion has become the model normality, fertile heterosexuality will only be able to be carried out by means of the extreme devaluation which in principle accompanies prostitution. In fertilizing his wife, the Greek citizen diverts a part of his emotions from the circle of the *politeia*, he devotes them to something other, having no civic rights; but this something, the uterus, will, in the form of the child, provide the city from which the child is excluded with what this citizen penis, diverted from its noble pederastic function, has conceded it in semen. But the prostitute, or her proprietor, also turns back onto what is called the *social organism*, in the form of the money she has gained by making a career from her body, the unusable, perverse *jouissance* of her clients. This is all a very Hegelian alienation. Meanwhile, in the 'standard' case of prostitution where it is the woman who is prostituted, it is not her womb that forms the useful section of her body, but any segment whatever (according to what the client demands). As such (indifferent), the she-prostitute is therefore just as much a he-prostitute. The turning back, the *return* to the 'community' of the social body cannot take place in the form of children (since it is this which the client, the pervert, fears and which he goes to her arms in order to avoid), it must therefore take place in the form of an equivalent to children: money.

When the Lydians prostitute their daughters, they take an immense step forward over the Hellenes. The latter only prostitute their penises, the time to ensure the reproduction of citizens, that is to say the return, through the mediation of the uterus—*pudenda par excellence*—of a proportion of their pulsional expenditure. This is prostitution because first of all, it is the diversion beyond the civic institution of the pulsions which belong to prostitution; and because, in the second place, it is also the *return* to this institution, in children, of these diverted pulsional quantities. In all that, a simple calculation of survival and homeostatic regulation. Basically, homosexuality pursued through the vagina and the uterus (just like the prostitute and her pimp: wealth pursued through the perversions of the clientele).

But the Lydians of Herodotus the gentle dreamer, who are doubtless equally forced to pass this way, in other respects suddenly *extend the market*. For to prostitute their daughters—and not their wives who retain the aforesaid reproductive function—is on the one hand to commit them to sterility and on the other to make them enter into the circular game of the exchange market as goods and proprietors of goods (there is no difference) that can pass from hand to hand. The homosexuality of the Dorian warriors is lacking here its characteristic trait of *isonomia*. The genuine merchant exchanges as much with one 'sex' as with the other. He stops conceiving of and practising with the female body as a reproduction machine, he can plug it into the circulation of *jouissances*, but always under the (perverse, homosexual) condition that this body remains sterile, that its 'natural' fecundity is barred, and that for it is substituted a capacity for the reproduction of money. The Lydian citizen does not impregnate this woman (his daughter), he *indemnifies* her, or her proprietor, he pays her, and this payment money is the same as that in circulation on the goods market. By paying her, he can, having consumed her, annul her consumption (pay off his debt to her), since this money will return to the centre in one way or another, when the daughter or her proprietor, having some need to satisfy, will come looking for the complementary good from him. And so nothing will happen.

This *dispositif*, which we will call 'Lydian', taking Herodotus at his word, 'anticipates' capitalism, and this is why it is even more interesting than the aristocratic circle of the Attic pederast killers. It 'anticipates' capitalism in two ways. First it extends the possibility of being counted and measured to other segments of the pulsional body-band. The Greeks left at least women out of *isonomia*; they did not invent a-sexism. The Lydians affirm that the female (sexual) apparatus may provide an opportunity for a *jouissance* very similar to that obtained in homosexuality, as well as sterilization and the comparison of this apparatus with some other segment, on condition that it is quantitatively balanced out. You understand that what is in question here, is, at the infinite limit, the introduction of all the parts of the 'entire' labyrinth of the pulsional body into the circle of exchanges, it is this whole warped, coiled, stretched surface, the immensity of which we will have some idea of if we succeed in making a plane projection of it—but a 'complete' projection which does not avoid any coil of intestinal mucus, any valve, any roughness, useful or useless, of any duct, any light texture of the slightest epithelial envelope, any fissure of the cortex, any hardening of the soles of the feet (an impossible cartography, but obviously so, next to which anatomical illustrations look like academic records), and in which, to begin with, the distinction of the exterior from the interior would no longer even be looked for, suspected, or revealed, any more than that of masculine and feminine—so, in this way the whole labyrinthine surface of the pulsions presents itself as a candidate for mercantilization when the Lydians prostitute their daughters. For if, by the mediation (*Vermittlung*) of money, you can find a taker for a vagina in the same category as for an anus, then it is because you envisage that each parcel of the great labyrinthine band may be turned to cash in the *Milieu* (*Mitte*). *And it is precisely this which is at issue today in universal capitalism.*

But obviously this can only be possible, even for the Lydians, if each of the segments of the pulsional body capable of being exchanged for money on the market as opportunities for *jouissance*, has itself already been weighed up and balanced against some other segment, so that the *proprietor* of this segment, its procurer (given that the *normal man* is, in these market conditions, the procurer of all the possible regions of his body, that he exists only as the instance of location of the libidinal investment of one or the other of these regions, such as his 'culture' or his education, for purposes of *solvency*), so that this proprietor, then, has himself already weighed up, estimated, evaluated, favoured (all this not at all consciously, of course) some other region, in a sort of impossible labour of comparison. Impossible because this latter necessitates what the pulsion cannot do: nullify itself, make itself possible, whereas it is affirmation without modality. Its ubiquity, the fact that it is invested here and there on the labyrinthine body, clitoral *and anal* excitability, for example, or indeed a headache and genital disturbance, has no relation whatsoever with a modalization or modulation of the 'if . . . then' type, nor with the type 'may be', nor the 'either . . . or'. For languages with a similar conjugation to French, the infinitive, as has already been said, was not sufficient even to situate the pulsional investment, for the infinitive is always accompanied, as its shadow, by its negative: to be/not to be, insofar as it restricts what is thought, the notion excludes from it everything that *does not* belong to it, in the mode of the *Verneinung*. And it is because one is by then already in the process of thought that such a determination has the positional value of the possible, what is thought always being collated on the basis of what is left out of thought as its opposite and as what differs from it.

In saying that the dream or schizophrenia treats words as things, Freud was underlining precisely the proper way in which the pulsional signals its presence even in the order of thought, producing effects in it which are intellectually intolerable, of the *figural* in the sense of paralogisms, aporias, *petitio principii*, vicious circles, errors, omissions, inconsistencies, meaninglessness, and finally the extreme *delirium* by which the pulsional rises to the point of parody, becoming indistinguishable from the organization of rational thought, in a gigantic effort made in order to plunge us into a kind of terror situated well beyond scepticism: can one think, that is to say distinguish?

But the pulsion occupying the hollow of the hand and the folded armpit of which Bellmer speaks, is, at the same time as it invests the vulval lips, lodged here and there without having to be *instantiated* here rather than there, heedless as it is of ever unifying what it runs across by consuming it. That's why comparison, which requires the annihilation of the items compared for purposes of unification, already exerts the crushing pressure of unitary order on the pulsions and their singular investments. It is essential to show, and this is what the Lydians make us understand, that this unitary order is in reality a *nullifying* organization. For on the band of the pulsional labyrinth, unity will come about only on condition that each investment is made compatible with another, and calculable in proportion to it, comparison and calculation requiring the annihilation or possibilization of what, as libido, is always invested affirmatively. Therefore the *unity* of the organic body, which we approach to the extent that the fortuitous seizures of the libido which crush and block regions of the band are released and removed, is in pulsional economy dependent on a sort of annulment of investments for purposes of equilibriation. The subject on the circle, the subject-merchant-citizen, is contemporaneous with a species of *negotiation* over scraps of the labyrinthine band.

Psychiatrists, having the good humoured naïvety in outlook of all agents of order, describe the normalization of the hysteric in these terms: clinical repetitive *conditioning* [*matraquage*], constraining the patient to abandon his compulsion, but which also forbids him from falling into *doubt* with regard to his compulsion (that is to say to abandon himself to delirium . . .). Therefore, neither pulsional investment, nor delirious investment: he must (as psychiatrists always say . . .) be led to an affective zero, and since this is unbearable, something like a transference onto the doctor will be obtained in the end, that is to say the opening up of a possible communication . . .

This is how the *paideia* is described. For on the libidinal body, with its beatings, education blocks this and opens that route, provides comparisons, introduces *interest* where, pulsionally, there is no consideration of revenue. If the doctor happens to speak of a *profit*, of a libidinal *benefit*, if Freud, in regard to Dora's cough, happens to suspect a primary profit from the illness (which would be the *saving* of effort, the profit that a crippled worker gains from his becoming immobile) and a secondary benefit also, comparable to alcoholism, which, according to Freud, the injured worker will not fail to spend the proceeds of his begging on (one should hope so)—these comparisons introduce the most serious, the most pernicious confusion into considerations of libidinal economy. They pose the problem in reverse, they thematize the pulsional labyrinth of Dora as if it was managed by a finance minister or a banker, or even by an unemployed proletarian, that is to say by entities all of which, despite their extreme social inequalities, have in common that they belong to the circle of political economy and to its central zero, and that they exist only as the power to calculate utilities and to choose. So the *acephalia* of the great monoface labyrinthine band is suppressed, the psychiatrist or the psycho-analyst substitutes a *homo oeconomicus* for it, capable of comparisons and ratios, a head full of this negative which one German philosopher ended up daring to say that it is this that does all the work, meaning: all the trade.

This substitution is what the Lydians require, with their prostitution and their money. The comparisons and ratios over the pulsional body will take place by means of money, and so the body will cease to be this impossible landscape swept by libidinal influxes, it will be exchangeable piece by piece, part for part, it is centred on its own zero, it makes itself capable of playing rational games with itself, of simulating investments so as to be able to measure them and work out the most profitable *combination*. With the installation of the zero on the body, obtained inevitably at the price of the elimination of entire regions, we are dealing with the institution of the I. This I is the proprietor of the libidinal fields which from now on are defined and controlled, and it can venture into the mercantilist circum-ference to offer and demand certain fields and sections of fields. On the Lydian circle, everything is marketable, the commodity develops from universality, the I is its procurer.

A narrative by Vera Schmidt, concerning the institution of trade:

> The children start to collect flowers. While collecting flowers, Wolik (3 years and 3 months) set down his little boxes not far away in the grass. Genja (2 years and 10 months) drew close to take them; Wolik cries to her from a distance: 'You have no right, they belong to me!' Genja whimpering: 'But I want these little boxes.' I say to her: 'You see, Genja, it doesn't make you happy when

Wolik doesn't want to lend you the little boxes; and indeed, it didn't make him happy when you didn't want to lend him your wheelbarrow. Next time, give him what he wants and he will give you what you want too.' Wolik approaches and listens attentively. When I had finished, he held his little boxes out to Genja with his mind made up: 'Hey Genja, I'll lend you, all right?' Genja is delighted, she takes the little boxes and is already about to escape when she suddenly changes her mind and asks nicely: 'Wolik, d'you want my wheelbarrow?' 'Oh yes, yes!' replies Wolik, rejoicing. Genja runs to her wheelbarrow but it has already been taken by Wolodja (2 years and 10 months) . . . She is caught up in her game and doesn't fancy giving it up to Wolik. Genja remains still and ponders something, eyebrows knitted in a fixed gaze. Then she takes a step towards Wolodja. 'Wolodja, do you want two little boxes?' Wolodja agrees, and gives the wheelbarrow over to Wolik. Everyone is happy: Genja has one little box, Wolodja two, and Wolik has the wheelbarrow.[6]

And Vera Schmidt has her social body.

Institutive Prostitution

This is not all: the Lydians extend exchangeability to segments left fallow, that's one thing; another is to underline that, *in so doing*, they extend perversity. For it is true that from now on, potentially, as we know and as the Lydians have 'always' known, every segment of the sensualist body can, on condition that it is concentrated, take its place as a 'good', that is to say as an object convertible according to the 'nothing' (money), on the circle of exchanges, and it follows that it is at the same time torn from the illusion of a natural functioning and hence prepared for a polymorphous perverse use (but under the stated condition). Polymorphous, since it is from the impossible whole of the band where the pulsional fluxes course that each arbitrarily withdrawn segment must be able to come to find its place within the circuits of trade, which consequently offers, with its central nullity, an unprecedented opportunity for libidinal economy to manifest itself in the infinite, or at least the very great number, of possible investments. On condition therefore of metamorphosis, a very great polymorphism. This formal condition of commutability lying heavily on the unconditional as regards contents (significations, values, codes, beliefs, that is to say all the stable and exclusive arrangements of groups of parts of the body-band) is 'always' that of capitalism. It is also that of mathematics and its logic. When we say that this one or that one always works *in extension*, we are not simply saying that they disregard the point of view of comprehension, comprehension is just as extensive as extension, it is its indispensable complement, the interior of its exteriority, as use-value is to exchange-value. No, we mean that what is abandoned on principle is *intensity*, which is the *incomparable*. For all trade and politics rests on comparability. And the latter necessarily requires the proportionalization of intensities. This proportionalization is to intensities what the *squaring-off* of the early Florentine perspectivists would be to the plastic intensities of the ancient Chinese water-colourists. Every measure of intensities is a species of excessiveness (which in its turn will not fail to gain a high intensive force: intensity in relation to the zero, to the impossible, to consciousness and bad consciousness). This excessiveness is called reason. This latter is obtained through the search for a mean or *proportional mean*, or *minimax*: all instances *regulating* the circulations of intensities, therefore disintensifying or overintensifying them, according to the case, so that exchange can take place 'expediently'.

We have a very fine model of this excessiveness of concentration in games theory, the so-called 'marginal utility' in political economy. A. Rapoport recounts *Tosca*: Scarpia, the chief of police, holds Tosca's lover Cavaradossi prisoner. He is prepared to release him on condition that she gives herself to him, i.e. Scarpia. Here is Scarpia's reasoning: if I play the game, I would save the life of a hated rival, but I would possess Tosca; if I don't play the game, I could win on both counts. For her part, Tosca does her sums: giving herself to the horrible Scarpia, she saves her lover: equal score; the best thing would be to obtain mercy for Cavaradossi without having to give in to the policeman's demands. Each of them, on their own account, therefore has much to gain from cheating; Scarpia taking Tosca, and killing his rival, Tosca escaping the cop once Cavaradossi is safely hidden away. As Rapoport says, 'no argument addressed individually to Tosca or to Scarpia will convince them that they would do better to respect the market (= to play the game sincerely) than to betray the other. Only an argument addressed to both together would be strong enough. Only collective reasoning will be able to help them to avoid the trap of a double betrayal.'[7]

Very wise conclusion, very Aronian, very Aristotelian: *prudent* and *democratic*. Who or what will address this argument to both players? A zero instance, a mediator, a middle term, a unit of calculation, an empty centre. Anyone at all can take on the function of a conciliator. The important thing is not the judge, but the criteria for the calculation of losses and gains, damages and interests. Rapoport proposes the following matrix:

TOSCA			SCARPIA		
S **T**	Sg	Sb	**S** **T**	Sb	Sg
Tg	+5	−10	Tg	+5	+10
Tb	+10	−5	Tb	−10	−5

where **S** stands for 'Scarpia', **T** 'Tosca', **Sg** 'Scarpia in good faith', **Sb** 'Scarpia in bad faith', **Tg** 'Tosca in good faith', etc., and which summarizes the calculation of the two interested parties.

We will see, by going over these sums again, that Rapoport's matrix admits a *floating of prices* according to the nature of the exchange: so for Tosca, the situation of shared good faith (**Tg.Sg**) gives a score of +5, one can infer from this that **Tg** (going to bed with Scarpia) costs Tosca −5, and that **Sg** (Cavaradossi's life saved) gains her +10. But then, under the hypothesis (**Tb.Sg**) where she tricks Scarpia, if the prices remained the same, she would have a profitable balance of +15 (+10 for Cavaradossi and +5 for having escaped Scarpia's clutches). If Rapoport only counts to +10, it is because submitting to Scarpia is in fact disagreeable, but not submitting to him is simply worthless. (**Tb.Sg**) equals therefore: 0+10, and not +5+10.

Is this relatively sophisticated evaluation really fair? This is undecidable. What can be said is that the interest from a decision (**Sg.Tb**) for Tosca, assessed at +10, is at the same time *high* enough to make it interesting, and modest enough to leave Tosca hesitant (+15 would arouse an immediate preference). Without doubt this reasonable and at the same time profitable feature, obtained by writing down 0 and not +5 for Tosca's successful escape from Scarpia's bed, could also force Tosca to cheat. It is in any case this same apparent moderation which, the other way round, will incite Scarpia to have Cavaradossi shot while he's getting what he desires from Tosca. And in fact he would be right, if it didn't enter the young woman's mind (?), having been tricked twice, to kill him, which is not accounted for in the matrices, and which is generally excluded from the circle of partners in the *politeía*. If one of them must be put to death, it is from the standpoint of the central *zero* that it must be contemplated and defined: Socrates.

Here we see how the negotiation of investments on the pulsional body-band *produces* the negotiating subject. This latter *is not* the negotiator, but the unstable result of an interminable negotiation. *Neg-otium:** end of the leisurely fluidity of the influxes. Should I lend my intimacy to the cop's hands and genitals so as then to be able to reserve it for my darling bandit? But suppose I do this, would I not be conned anyway, a slut, since I will have paid for this possibility with exactly that which must be *exorbitant* for my lover? How could he feel comfortable to have in his arms, under his lips, his fingers, his eyes, sheathing his penis, these bits of the body from the very moment that—not that they had been shared with the cop and given back to him like the left-overs of a previous feast, which would be in itself rather pious—but from the moment that they had been traded off, placed in proportion to *jouissance*, my lover's and mine, from the moment that I, in short, prostituted myself? How would Tosca get round this uncertainty? *She is a subject*, that is to say a question, *only insofar as she is a prostitute*. If she pretends to abandon her charms while she is with Scarpia, it is so as to keep Cavaradossi alive and to keep herself alive for him. Suddenly the incomparable investments which would connect together (so we imagine) certain points of the anonymous band with certain *jouissances*, and assemble the love of the young woman and the bandit, these investments are suddenly dissolved, removed, instantiated on nothing, on a permanence which is necessarily impossible since it is destroyed by the same moment of release [*relève*] which operates it. To keep oneself alive or reserve oneself for a subsequent *jouissance* is to instantiate these intensities on the zero of a temporal continuum, and to flatten them into money. When Klossowski speaks of an 'exorbitance' of the 'phantasm' (in his sense of the word), he means precisely that the high or low intensities obtained by the connecting up of partial organs to the polymorphous perverse body which is called the labyrinthine band, that these intensities are disproportionate, and therefore that one should never be able to take advantage of having paid too dearly for their scaring passage. Now Tosca really ought to discount and count up these intensities, no more no less than a prostitute who with her profits has to bring up her kid in the provinces. Tosca counts up income and outgoings, input and output, and this is already prostitution, which makes her exist as the procuress of

---

Neg-otium: *otium (L.)* means 'leisure'; the prefix *neg-* indicates the 'end of the leisurely fluidity . . . '. *Negotium* itself means 'trivial matter'.—*tn*

charges and discharges. Always the zero instance, that of revenue: from the compound, the continuous, another tense, the tense of the subject.

From here we see the question: is there any *jouissance* outside this keeping of accounts, beyond this instantiation on the zero? Lacan says: *jouissance* is 1/0, the interminable oscillation of desire between the institution of a unitary subject (1) and its instantiation on the non-being of reference (0). Is this not the same as what Klossowski says, this time in terms of libidinal economy, when he implies that extreme *jouissance* always brings this aporia with it: how does one compare the incomparable? How does one evaluate the exorbitant? Is it because the phantasm according to Klossowski, which is not at all, like Freud's, a substitution formation, but a rigid, incliminable and repetitive plugging-in of partial organs, nevertheless draws its force, not from all the libido, Eros and death together, flowing there, in this channel, but rather from the vertiginous comparison between the alleged being of a *person* (the victim or the torturer, according to the case), that is to say of a unity with universalist tendencies on the one hand, and on the other, the stupid drivelling pettiness, the murderer of all that presents itself as a totality, from a small *singular* pulsional *dispositif*? And if this comparison is necessarily implied in *jouissance*, isn't it because this latter finds itself always already localized by the negotiatory thought which is about to snatch up and understand as a relation, instead of being it, like an incomparable affirmation? We must then say that Lydian prostitution (which is also to say—with all the accuracy we can muster—capital), which, just as Tosca is the *burden* [*poids*] of the unweighable [*hors-de-poids*], is also all that can be said and felt at the same time concerning *jouissance*. And abandon even the project of a libidinal economy, instantiated on the one intensity at least: thinking being money-making, he who thinks of matters of the passions is necessarily a whore.

But let's go over this again, it's not so simple: in minting coin, the Lydians, as we have said, did not content themselves with regulating intensities on the *méson* of all mediations, they also prostituted their daughters, and so they have vulvas, clitorises, breasts and their nipples, full buttocks, hair, soprano and contralto cries of pleasure, the smells of vaginal secretions, seed squeezed from skins, hairs from the insides of arms and thighs, different colours of hair, of irises, different muscular textures, different bone structures, different positions and couplings; they have all these enter into the circle of transferable goods. They extend the quantity of parts of the labyrinthine band that can be evaluated and exchanged. And at the same time they not only remove the woman's (or at least partially: the girl's) alleged *nature*, but they expose (*prostituere*) her to all the denaturations that can be devised and carried out within the merchant circle. But these denaturations are innumerable, since they are all sanctioned in principle, on the sole condition, as we have said, of isomorphism or proportionality between the goods exchanged. If such a pricing implies the devaluation of pieces of the libidinal body taken in their intense singularity, it can give rise to a sort of new impetus in the circulation of the influxes: for these latter find themselves opening new routes on the immense band of bodies, and therefore the polymorphism of the *jouissive* connections amongst them is increased, as is the libido's errancy. Imagine all these unheard-of, erectile pieces of the surface where charges will be able to accumulate in order to flee from a shock. It is not enough to see them condemned to the law of the *minimax*, we must also see what new concentrations of desires, even if this is in the one authorized form of goods, they will be able to provoke and *satisfy*.

And this authorized form of goods is not, moreover, as we might think, a *useful* form. On the contrary, with this Lydian prostitution concomitant with the monetary institution, we see that utility in its current sense of use-value has simply no meaning, that it can be determined only in relation to the rule of exchangeability, that the Lydian daughter's body does not exist as a thing with a natural predestination and therefore requiring a specific use, but on the contrary that it exists only as the empty negotiatory instance supposed by the comparative evaluations of pulsional regions, like the body-zero with its capitalist function, whereas its alleged *use* is never anything but the blow-by-blow bargaining of exchangeabilities between organs. We must not even say that this body is then perverted or perverse, since it never *is* anything at all (but it *is this nothing*), and therefore cannot be *diverted* from any predetermined use. It is in fact concentrated, inclined to fall back onto the empty instance of the mercantile permanence of intensities which, here or there, explode and die away like stars in the universe.

The prostitute in particular, that is to say the modern business 'woman', who is just as much a 'man'—and the same goes for him—has not had and must no longer have any relation with fertility. Should she occasionally produce children from the *jouissances* she procures, then it would signify that she had received impregnating semen into her womb; but she must be able to receive only money, and this in her purse. For—first argument—this money is convertible on the market, the child is not necessarily so. It will be a long 'time after' the Lydians before the child itself is incorporated into the economic cycle, that it will cease to be perceived as a gift received (from somewhere else), before the woman who consents to bear children is paid (first in the form of child benefits, soon as the right to the withdrawal of labour, later, no doubt, simply a salary), and therefore a long time before the mediatory void undertakes to administer its *own point of view*, that of always annullable equivalences, the introduction and the circulation of new pieces of the labyrinthine body-band in the circuit of trade, onto which child-bodies are concentrated. Oddly enough, it is the last in terms of its date, for the most part still to come, while these are obviously the most affirmative bodies and the most discontinuously perverse, the most intense because the most uncommon in the exploration of connections of *jouissance*. But an understandable delay, if we care for their innocence, for their inability to instantiate the present emotion on a permanence which soon makes it possible to trade, if we care for their libidinal non-subjectivity.

And the second argument: all the struggles we transsexual libidinal economists know and lead, in order that, as was said, women may have the *free use* of their bodies, in particular the free decision to bear or not to bear children, are Lydian consequences. How we love the Lydians and their daughters! In reality, it cannot be a matter of free use, of any *use*, free or not. What we (and capital) desire is that what is called a woman be made genuinely able to benefit from commercial status, in its two aspects: every erection and detumescence of whatever small area of the body-band that is attributed to her, should first of all be possible, and could then be marketed. Therefore the abolition of erotic prohibitions; and her release from the automatic nature of propagation.

At the same time the right to perversion and the right to trade. That is to say the *politeia*. A child, yes, but then the object of a market, the stake in an exchange which will in principle have to annul the charge that the child represents, in libidinal terms the intensities of the affects that it is going to absorb. Therefore the abolition of mothers and wives who have only ever been, since the warrior-pederasts, the mothers of the children that were given them. This is not a free use, since use, the category of a natural goal, would keep, even if 'freely', the woman under the concept of this reproductive finality, her liberty restricted to choosing the moment of and the partner in impregnation. This is the extension of exchangeability onto the alleged feminine body, that is to say the injection of unknown pieces of the band into the exchange cycle and marginal calculations. Those we call women can only attain full civil rights by attaining sterility and polymorphous perversion, monetary properties. It is the very figure of the circle in the process of extending itself to all the fragments of the labyrinthine band which institutes abortive measures, because it wants all eradications.

If the woman's body ceases to be the earth or something like it, an element, a receptacle, so correspondingly the partial prostitution of penises would disappear. Masculinity must no longer be cleft as it is in Greece, between its annulatory *jouissance* and its task of impregnating wombs. The symmetry of the abortive measures, freeing the female body from its reputedly natural destination, is for the man of the *politeia* (?), con-temporaneous with the institution of sperm banks: 'The freezing processes for human sperm in liquid nitrogen today allow the preservation, for several years, of an important production of spermatozoa whose impreg-nating capacity is normal.'[8] Several conditions must be met in order that your sperm allow of concentration [*soit circonvertable*]: you must be less than 40 years old, you must be the father of at least one normal child: the quality side of the product. The practice of eugenics and selection is denied, and it is thereby affirmed how pressing the analogy with Nazi medical practices is. The familial, institutional side, to keep up appearances: you must be married and must inform your wife. But it is the logic of the product which will win the day, have no doubt of it: its quality is inevitably independent of the wife's consent and whether or not they go through the bureaucracy. Nevertheless, few are fond of it, it appears. Is this because the donor isn't paid? (And why are they not paid, if not because of the fear of the irresistible attraction over many young unemployed people that the new profession of sperm-donor would exert, and the excess stock of the manufactured commodity?) No, it is said, the principal factors of opposi-tion are: 'The masturbation necessary for the collection of sperm, the adulterous character of the act (often therefore resented by the wife), the fact of being barely aware of the development of human semen.' As for the fear of adultery, the retort is immediate: the donor should not be married. As for the anxiety (base, need it be said?) of being a father without knowing it, this still derives from the institution of the family in which father and mother see themselves yielding all rights of property over their child as if it was a product. Finally as for the last obstacle, we suggest that the sperm bank makes sure of a preference for the participation of onanists: an excellent illustration of how, in all likelihood, in the great trade of capital, all the little *dispositifs*, all the connections are marketable, to the point that the *dispositif* which, for a very long time, as we know, has not only *everywhere* endured the censures of morality, but has also had to suffer the contempt of free spirits, indeed revolutionaries: to come by tossing off—might, *precisely by reason of the irremediable sterility* of its result (scattering sperm in the soil), become the privileged means (because it is utterly *indifferent*, substitutable and negotiable and can be postponed) of fertile propagation in the mercantilist system. At the same time as the mothers disappear, we are also rid of the fathers with their concern for sperm-revenue in the form of their sons and daughters: this is what Lydian prostitution will soon imply, extended to new regions of the libidinal band, thanks to the expansion of capital. But we will not be free from the great Zero, for all that, quite the contrary.

Outlet Payment

Does this zero take us into the vicinity of Sadean theses? Will the force of the *philosophe scélérat* come to include this mechanism of the circle and rotation? One might think so to hear him, in the pamphlet inserted into *Philosophie dans le boudoir*, justify homicide in the name of an entirely metamorphic conception of nature:

> If the eternity of beings is impossible in nature, destruction therefore becomes one of her laws. Now, if destruction is so useful to her that she absolutely cannot do without it, and if she cannot achieve her creations without drawing from these destructive masses that spell her death, no more annihilation will be recorded; what we call the end of the living animal will no longer be a real end, but a simple transmutation, the basis of which is perpetual motion, the real essence of matter and which all modern philosophers admit as one of nature's primary laws. Death, according to these irrefutable principles, is therefore no more than a change of form, an imperceptible passage from one existence to another, and this is what Pythagoras called metempsychosis. Once these truths are acknowledged, I wonder if one will ever be able to contend that destruction is a crime . . . All that we are doing in indulging in destruction, is simply carrying out a variation in forms.[9]

Now let's ascertain how *jouissance* is instantiated *on the circle*. The naturalism displayed by Sade refers to Pythagoras and to metempsychosis, and just as much again to the Tao and to Spinoza's *Ethics*, we presume. But beyond this naturalism, well known to philosophers, which is a large step in the direction of the dismantling of the subject, of the unified body, there remains or can still remain a philosophy, there remains a means by which the intensities denied individual subjects, are folded back onto an immense hyper-subject which will be in general nothing other than the same central zero that instantiates the peripheral *jouissances* of the citizens. Now Sade clearly says that the death penalty is an infamy because it is a law, that is to say a regulation of intensities, whereas murder, if it is passionate, would be no more a crime than is orgasm. And he provides as a guide in this matter Louis XV's judgement upon meeting an assassin: *I am showing you mercy, but I will also show mercy to whomever should kill you.* This metempsychotic nature is also therefore, or also wants to be, the pulsional band itself: not the reasonable and happy issue of irrational passions, but the circulation of these passions and the coursings [*mise en cours*] of intensities.

Here *two* models collide, *two* paradigms, since here we must introduce *another* zero, a second death, which is no longer that of the centre, but that which will circulate on the circumference and twist, crush and stretch it so as to bring it as near as possible to the labyrinthine body-band. As long as the zero is situated only at the centre, as long as the Greek organization of the *méson* forbids all heteronomy and heterogeneity, but requires, as with trade, compensation for the pulsions and the constitution of the proper body as the cash box for this compensation, one is in rationalization and friendship, deintensified homosexuality, the regularization of the tensions. Thus according to Bataille, in the margins of this circumference certain kinds of channel will be found which point towards the exterior, towards the alleged exteriority of the circle, and by which the non-liquid intensities in the circle, the non-erectile scraps of the body in the conditions of trade, will find an outlet.

This is an apparently common *dispositif*; sacrifice, prostitution, psychoanalysis, are a few amongst a hundred instances of it. In all three cases, it was a matter of valves allowing for the evacuation—under diverse names: the offering, 'having it off', transference—of libidinal charges inexchangeable in the instituted circuits. In all three cases, it is of course *jouissance*, because it is deadly, because it is vain expenditure, that it is a matter of leading astray, outside the cycle. But let's direct our attention to a neglected but nevertheless very interesting aspect of these institutions, that is, the linking up of the medium of exchangeabilities (the goods which serve to *pay* the sacrificer, the prostitute and the psychoanalyst) onto the otherwise forbidden fulfilment of this *jouissance*. In Indian sacrifice as it is described in the ancient Vedic texts,[10] the *daksina* constitutes the payment of the officiating priests. Co-present therefore, are the offer as such, small vegetable or animal fragments, which a fire carries away to the skies, towards the nostrils of the divine—and the species of salary, gold, clothes, horses, occasionally women, which the Brahmin receives from the sacrificers. (It is often the case that the payment of priests is much more important than the sacrificial offering.) Now this ritual involves this remarkable clause of purification: that the sacrificer, he who offers the sacrifice to the divine, must not only be divested, for the duration of the sacrifice, of his profane body, which he will regain only after the event, but also that this divestment consists of the dismemberment of this body, the donor saying to each of the priests in turn: to you I give my arms, to you my belly, to you my eyes (or so I imagine). This new body, very closely related to the aberrant band of the pulsions, is the body of *jouissance*, and its 'institution' makes the sacrifice appear as *jouissance* and the time of the sacrifice as the 'time' of *jouissance*.

In the same way, of course, if we are still following Bataille and Caillois, the ingredients of the offering are consumed as pure loss (here the Indians are really quite parsimonious . . .). Again it will have to be said that the fire and its wreaths also belong to the effects of libidinal irreversibility: for the ashes will not even be *remains*, and if one wishes a fatal discharge without residue, then one will have to *burn*—as the Indians (and the young people in secondary schools) well know. Here therefore, no profit can be calculated; even if it is discounted, if the sacrificer expects an effect of return from the sacrifice, a divine grace. If he calculates a profit, it is in an order where calculation, according to this hypothesis, cannot operate because it is concerned with infinite quantities. It is no more a calculation than Pascal's wager can be a true wager, because the objects to be traded are incommensurable on either side. Pascal didn't mean to say wager, he meant a paradox in the Kierkegaardian sense, which is something else altogether, and once again makes reference to an alterity of *jouissance* from which every reality of revenue, of profit, is in principle excluded.

But side by side with this useless torching, the Brahmin priest is given a tip. And why is this? Because he who gives without return, must pay. The time of *jouissance* is bought. The time of his ravaged, broken, jubilant, sacred body is converted into cash (and it is expensive). When the *daksina* has been paid, then he will recover his organic, unified body, which will be able to start afresh in the closed cycle of exchanges (cosmic this time, we are not in Athens), and this is why this payment is made under the sign of Amaya, the god of mortal men. The payment returns him to the law, into the cycle, that is to say into reality, which involves death, but the death of the organic body, this death instantiated on the cosmic central zero, which is the death of nothing but an episodic and evanescent subject, and which in reality is only metabasis. Such is life.

So: by means of the offering, death through *jouissance*, and by means of the priest's salary, death through order. The same immeasurable time of irreversibiblity is deduced as the labour time of the priest. Where the sacrificer risks going up in smoke and not coming back, up into Nirvana, there, precisely, the men of the central zero and their exchangeability withdraw their portion and manufacture the general from the singular. Sacrifice is a crime of passion, the *daksina* is the accepted price of its expiry in the circuit of minimaxed intensities. The zero of the release is plugged into the zero of input-output matrices. Did it go up in smoke and flames? It must be turned back into goods convertible into cash. It ejaculated? It will impregnate.

From this point of view, it is the same plugging as controls prostitution: the diversion of libidinal energy into perverse *jouissance* is set up by paying for the venal woman, who returns a part of it, in the form of her fees, to the circuit of exchanges. Thus the singularity of the phantasm and the irreversibility of the emotions it procured find themselves paradoxically negotiated as the cost of a lay. If the lay is an exchange [*Si la passe est une passe*[11]], it is because the time opened up by the quartering of the client-sacrificer body closes up on itself, and so he must *come back to himself*, return. They simply undergo the annihilating incandescence. It has to stop, that is to say recover, start again. It is this relief which is assured by the price. One recovers from *jouissance*-death. One has *put aside*, on the hearth of the prostitutes' hotel, the banknotes that settle the brief, mortal *coucherie*.* Such is the *daksina's* function, such, in the last instance, is the analyst's fee.

But in the analytic situation, the relation is more complicated, the solicitation of the passions will take place even further afield than prostitution. Of course the analyst, like the prostitute, must not enjoy, that's the rule of the control of counter-transference, and also, like her, he neutralizes the other's *jouissance*, he mediately instantiates it on the zero of exchangeability, and this due to payment. You will enjoy by investing your desire in me, you will have me play all the roles of the characters that you have been able to invest (that is to say in fact all the pieces of the body-band on which certain connections were able to *procure* some intensity for your Ego-zero, pieces you will call the names of those with which they

---

Coucherie: a 'one-night stand', occasional sexual commerce.—*tn*

were associated, but they don't really belong to anyone, for a person is nobody)—it is no longer the psychoanalyst who says this, on the contrary, he continues: from your couch then, you will be able to enter horizontally onto the stage where these circulations take place, and carry me along there with you, endow me with the functions of each in turn, of a great uncle, a young servant, a rich mother, a younger sister and an old friend, and I will go along with all of it, as the Brahmin priest goes along with setting fire to these living things, grasses, flowers, flesh and bones, the sacrifice. Yet while I go along with all this, I will rid you of your connections, I will treat them as symptoms, as phantasms, as illusory feelings, the same ones that Socrates took it upon himself to extract from the heads of the mistaken young Athenians, I will therefore deliver you from all this. But what does 'deliver' mean here? It means to render the singularity of investments convertible into cash. Not to limit the moment of *jouissance* thus invested to a *lay*, to a time of sacrifice, to a *session*, but, albeit under the name of phantasma, day-dreams, symptoms, rather to seize hold of the circulations of influxes and passages of intensities in order to convert them into cash, this time into that currency which is no longer exchangeable goods, but intelligible *words*. For things will have to be be said, from the great twitching and awkward labyrinth there must issue a comprehensible voice, in the analyst's office unpredictable violences of pulsional excursions must give way, little by little, repeatedly, from session to session, sacrifice to sacrifice, to the return.

Now it is obvious that this so-called 'working through', which is inevitably a labour of the institution of an instance to which to refer the pulsional metamorphoses, and which in its turn will be able to transport them as words and even as amiable feelings, an instance which is exactly the same whether one calls it individual, or Ego, or social being, or whether on the contrary one insists on its nullity, its absence, its zero quality—it is clear that this *working through* is different from either prostitution or the sacrifice. The session is indeed a sacrificial offering and a prostitutive settlement, but it lets political economy penetrate, if I may say so, still much further than they do, into the libidinal, since it is the affect itself that it wants to extract from the labyrinthine body-band and place on the circle of exchangeabilities. Now in Freud, the affect is well and truly the name borne by energy itself in its investments and displacements when it operates on 'representations'. Should Dora cough, should she have an asthma attack, Freud desires that *she say what she is coughing*, and consequently say *what she is choking back*; and how will he be able to recognize that she has said it? (In this case, moreover, he was unable to recognize it, that is, in relation to his own desire to speak.) He will recognize the wish that this oral or respiratory symptom should be instantiable on genitality, that is simply to say on the reproductive body. Therefore not only speaking of intensities and thus beating them back onto the currency of words, but referring them to the organic body, pinpointing them on the cartography of the physiology and the chemistry which is also that of propagation. Not only to pretend to *acknowledge* Dora's Ego-zero which M.K. forced on her against her will in the closed shop, that is to say to exchange this connection of a curiously intense terror, this stasis where fluxes passed and were immediately and completely dissipated and maintained in labyrinthine 'time', but further to propound the hypothesis that her asthma, her cough, her oral and respiratory symptoms proceed from a displacement of the sensation of oppression experienced by the young girl because of the erect sex of M.K. pressed against her stomach while he pulled her to him, displacement in the direction of the thorax and the respiratory system: pressed-oppressed, which conversely implies that the respiratory (or oral) region may only be invested, according to Freud, by *substitution*, and consequently that the only true intensity is genital. Such is the other meaning, almost proper, to be given to the words *to deliver* [*accoucher*].[12] One could take the doctrine of stages and find the same closing down; were one to multiply these stages, were one to add the 'mirror stage', the 'breathing stage', it still remains the case that it is at the very end, when the so-called 'partial' pulsions are finally captured and drawn together under the sign of genitality, that everything works, that *ça va* . . .

There is a direct correlation between the conversion of the time of 'dereality' into cash, of the time *consecrated* to the 'real' at the time of the session, and on the other hand the instantiation by means of speech of all the partialities—the advances of perverse, divergent influxes, unforeseen blockages of some corner of the libidinal surface—on the body of genitality, that is to say, of reproduction. This correlation enables us to see the proximity and the distance of the two cycles, that of money and that of the propagation of the species. If one pays the analyst, it is because in the session there is a risk of being carried away into *jouissance*-death without return, which is already that which the ritual sacrifice of the Indians, and in general every paying of the sacrificer, guards against; if one pays in money, in cash, it is because one is in a monetary system; finally, if one also pays *in words*, it is because here the sacrifice obeys the complex *dispositif* of

Judaism and scientificity: a scientificity which has it that all of language is thought in the category of exchangeability, or that all things, including affects, pulsions, displacements, charge trips, discharges of loss and *tutti quanti* are supposed to be thinkable in the category of language: we have some good examples of this in contemporary philosophical and scientific literature, one need only stoop to gather them up; but Judaism, by contrast, which has it that words are important only on condition that they do not operate as significations, but as gifts, not as exchangeable units, but as courses on the surface of language, draining the fluctuating liquidities of affects; rather therefore as prayer than as reason. There are the two *dispositifs* in analysis, the lead being given now to the side of neutralizable signs, now to the side of emotional debt. But as far as the body is concerned, in any case, it is annulled as the immense crumpled band, and instituted as the bag of organs, each of which is entirely susceptible to falling ill (to being disrupted by causes, exteriorities) whereas all the erectility of this body is supposed to be fixed on vaginas and penises. We are poles apart from the prostitute's body, which is a negotiating body, capable of annulling all the clientele's perversions into money. Here, in the analysis, the whore is the analyst (in that he gets paid to absorb the patient's inexchangeable *jouissance*, and also to transform it into a concept), and the patient is not only his client, he is also his pupil, if the educator-analyst wants to obtain a 'normal', sexed body from the client. A courtesan-pedagogue, a venal Moses. So that in analysis the connecting up of intensities onto the circuit of exchanges in reality takes place three times: the first when the patient pays to reactivate *jouissance*, so as to metamorphose it into money; the second when he speaks or attempts to speak desire, so as to commute it into concepts; the third when in this case a labour of solicitation and instantiation on the sex is supposed to come to institute a normal body, where the libido will be sex and sex genitality, that is the promise of reproduction.

War of Silver, Currency of Death: Mercantilist Politics

The instantiation of intensity on the circle of equivalences gives a first, approximate idea of what *jouissance* in capital might be. To what extent it has to do with money as a libidinal fragment or pulsional force, according to its complexity or rather according to a *primary and manifest dissimulation*, we would choose to discern through the magnifying glass of *mercantilist politics* in the classical age, embodied by the couple Louis XIV–Colbert.[13]

Here we capture a remarkable *dispositif* of double instantiation, which allows us at the same time to confirm the impression that the mercantilist economy of which Marx speaks as the premisses of capitalist economy is a sort of unstable entity, almost impossible, a construction from a theoretical model; and to grasp that what is lacking in the approach of the economist or even the historian of mercantilism is precisely any consideration of another mode of the enjoyment [*jouissance*] of money and commodities than what we currently call *interest*.

Take this letter from Colbert to the King:[14]

> . . . The good state of Your Majesty's finances and the augmentation of his revenues consists in increasing by all available means the amount of silver converted into money which is continually circulating in the realm, and in keeping in the provinces the exact proportion of this money that they require . . . augmenting the silver in public commerce by drawing it from the countries from whence it comes, retaining it within the realm by preventing it from leaving, and by giving men the means to draw a profit from it. Since the greatness and strength of the State and the Magnificence of the King are composed from these three points, the expenditures for which great revenues provide the opportunity render State and King all the greater, because they deplete the revenues of all neighbouring States at the same time. In view of the fact of having just one constant quantity of silver circulating in all Europe, augmented from time to time by that which comes from the West Indies, it is certain and demonstrable that if there are only 150 million pounds of silver in public circulation, one can only succeed in augmenting it by 20, 30 and 50 millions at the same time as one removes the same quantity from neighbouring States . . . I entreat Your Majesty to permit me to tell him that since he took on the administration of finances, he has undertaken a war of silver against all the States of Europe. He has already conquered Spain, Germany, Italy and England, which he has thrown into very great poverty and destitution, and has grown rich from their spoils, which have given him the means to perform such great things as he has done in the past and still does every day. Only Holland still remains fighting with great forces: her northern trade . . . that in the East Indies . . . that in the Levant . . . that in the West Indies . . . her factories, her trade in Cadiz, Guinea and an infinity of others in which all her strength consists and resides. Your Majesty has formed companies which, like armies, attack them on all fronts . . . The factories, the canal for the transnavigation of seas and so many other new developments as Your Majesty has created, are so many reserve corps which Your Majesty created and drew out of nothing in order better to perform their duty in this war . . . The sensible fruit of the success of all these things would be that by drawing, by means of trade, a very great quantity of silver into his realm, not only would he soon manage to reestablish

those proportions which must exist between the silver in currency in trade, and the taxations which are paid by the people, but he could even augment each of them, in such a way that his revenues would increase and he would put his peoples in a powerful position to assist him more considerably in the event of war or some other necessity . . .

A declaration which says everything. First, money; it has two functions, or rather two positions: it is a means of payment, of the discharge of debts, Aristotle's *nomisma*. The king's subjects require it to pay off their taxes, the realm itself in order to be free from foreign creditors, should it happen to have any. There appears to correspond to this function of money a new importance accorded to the production of commodities. These are not objects received from nature ('primary' industry), but manufactured from received objects, and thereby bearing the same arbitrary, human mark as does the monetary instrument. Nevertheless, no more than in ancient Greece,[15] they are considered here only under the aspect of the labour that they contain, like products; if they interest Colbert, it is as engines of war, as means to the *destruction* of foreign *clients*. One can acquit oneself with money by payment; one must, it seems, be able to acquit oneself with commodities, by barter or compensation for the balance of foreign trade—but no, the commodity will not essentially have this status, no more than money resolves itself in its role of the balancing of debts.

Money is also, of course, something precious, a treasure, which marks 'the greatness and strength of the State and the Magnificence of the King'. It is in this way that mercantilism is always associated with *metalism*—Colbert will hunt down the bullionists, manufacturers of impure money, seeming wealth; let's not speak of fiduciary forms of money——which is equally associated with *quantitativism*, a strange doctrine to us, which states that in order to be rich one must accumulate *as much money as possible*; which means only if the latter is kept itself as a treasure. This position of silver is what will disappear in the extension and the sophistication of modern fiduciary money, and ultimately in the complete separation of exchange rates with regard to the traditional standard of reference, gold.

The other characteristic of Colbert's political economy is that it implies that monetary wealth is a finite quantity: 'Having just one constant quantity of silver circulating in all Europe.' This is interpreted according to its most brutal political effect in another note by Colbert, where he concludes a small evaluation of the profits made by the Dutch from their quasi-monopoly in maritime trade in the following terms: 'On this supposition, it is easy to conclude that insofar as we are able to reduce the gains made by the Dutch over the king's subjects and the consumption of the commodities which they bring us, we will increase the silver in the form of money which must enter into the realm by means of our necessary commodities in like proportion, and will also increase the strength, the greatness and the abundance of the State.'[16] This is the same position that in games theory is called a *zero sum game*:[17] every gain by one party is paid for by the adversary's loss, as opposed to a non-zero sum game where the possibility is given of a simultaneous gain by both partners.

Let us recall that the games theorists have established that if the partners in a zero sum game have a 'rational' politics, they would communicate between one another all information concerning their intentions (a game of complete information), and would thus achieve the best result that can reasonably be expected in such a game, which is the *minimax*, or the minimum of compossible maximums. In the case of *Tosca*,[18] we see that if Tosca and Scarpia had 'understood' each other, they would each have been able to obtain a gain of five points. Such is the general idea of the dialogue, a perfectly mercantilist idea, it appears, since it aims to equalize both partners' chances of a gain and to share out in an egalitarian fashion, at the end of the game, the quantity of wealth or pleasure to be distributed between them. A politics of the minimax implies that on both sides the stakes are comparable, the outlays commensurable, and even the players are ultimately permutable: apparently we are steeped in the system (or the phantasy) of generalized equivalence, where intensities are eroded in the interests of the quantities instantiated on an arbitrary unity of reference, which, however, is accepted by each partner. And it is doubtless naïve, or rather perverse, of games theorists to believe that *there does in fact exist* such an organic body of reference, a social body, a rational solidarity, a mediator (which of course embodies itself and its paymaster) to which it is in the *interests* of each partner to appeal in order *to be certain* of obtaining the best compossible result. As if the *passion* for the best *incompossible* result, implying, that is, the destruction of the partner and the end of all games, were not also a general pathos of the desire to play.

The exchangeability of the players themselves, presupposed by a 'rational' politics and marked by changes of spatial or temporal position in competitive sports or social games, implies in turn the recurrence, infinite in principle, of the 'parties'. The 'reasonable' view of exchange is that it is interminable, that the game may be endlessly played. This is why it is inappropriate to annihilate the adversary, since he is a partner, without whom the game is not possible. There is therefore a concern for the preservation of the poles of the exchange which is the characteristic specific to trade in general, and which appears to be necessarily associated with the mercantilist transaction. Here money and the commodity are not things, but concretions of exchangist relations, and are also treated as such.

Now what Colbert says to his king is quite the reverse of this: the quantity of metallic money which is 'circulating in all Europe' being constant, and this gold being wealth itself, in order that the king grow richer, he must seize the maximum of this gold. This is to condemn the partner to die, in the long or short term. It is to count the time of trade not up to infinity, but by limiting it to the moment when all the gold in Europe is in Versailles. And it is to identify gold with the traditional form of wealth, with the earth. To draw gold into the frontiers of the realm is the same thing as to extend the frontiers up to the sources of gold. The earth being round, the conquest must in principle close up on itself, the armies progressing eastward ending up meeting those marching westward, and in this closure, establishing the empire of the world. Locking gold up within the limits of the realm is for Colbert the same operation relativized: it is the earth-gold or the golden earth which must come to complete its movement in the king's coffers. In the first case, the realm is displaced over the earth, envelops it and becomes its coffer, in the second the gold which was displaced will become incarcerated in the realm.

That it is indeed conquest which is in question in mercantilism, Colbert does nothing to hide. 'The administration of finances [is] a war of silver', he says, and in this war French commercial companies are 'like armies' assailing the Dutch companies; factories and large structures are 'so many reserve corps', kept on the alert behind the lines. The realm is a camp, the frontiers a front. Protective customs rates are the outworks that protect the French fortress.

As for the principle of this war, it rests on the fancy that the partner is in a state of inferiority, of need. We see then that this idea of need which will make its fortune in economic and social thought, including Marx's, is simply the organicist metaphor of the irreversible and hierarchical dependence of one party on the centre. 'It is the only monarchy that can do without all its neighbours', affirms La Gomberdière; the king of France, advises Laffemas, must be powerful, 'so that our neighbours cannot do without us'. 'The realm has no need to borrow anything from its neighbours', says Montchrétien, 'for France alone can do without all that it has of the neighbouring lands, just as all neighbouring lands cannot do without her.' And La Jonchère: 'The realm can do without all forms of foreign Commerce, but the Foreigners cannot do without her Wines, Wheat, Salts, etc.'[19] In consequence, the terms of the exchange will never fail to be always unfavourable to them. Especially if France were to add to these natural, given advantages—and this is what Colbert is working towards—those which result from the creation of infrastructures and manufacturing industries. She will always be able to *sell without buying*. She will be able to tax, demand gold, and in quantity, for payment. And this is how it will return to and remain in the realm.

Now, to continue the rapid description of this remarkable *political libidinal economic dispositif*, one wonders what this gold is for. It is for almost nothing, it is not mainly reinvested, but consumed in feasts, representations and expenditures of prestige. Versailles, that is to say the stage or the altar of the realm, is made of this gold, and this is where wealth is dissipated, destroyed, treasure squandered in *jouissance*. There is nothing less astonishing than this combination of the commodity, money and manufacture, with vain expenditure. The mercantilist body is a 'monster', part value to maintain, part gold to destroy; part intelligence, part stupidity, like a centaur. And the commodity in mercantilism is, as far as it goes, a being with a triple function: concretion of exchangist relations, the weapon of a war of silver, means of a ruinous hoarding. At the centre of this fortress of protective rates, customs and edicts, there reigns not the nothingness, the hub of capital or the sober *civitas* which redistributes surplus-values or annuls exchanges in endless cycles, but a fire which embraces them and fuels the blaze of heavenly glory of the king and his court.

To take the libidinal measure of the *dispositif*, let's imagine the four libertine masters of *One Hundred and Twenty Days of Sodom* enjoying not only the land rents that Sade supposes them to have, but also mercantilist revenues. Let's imagine that some Colberts, some assistants (there is necessarily here a redistribution of powers between two instances since there are two poles of *jouissance*), are busy waging wars of silver in some neighbouring town (Paris), trading, setting up a fiscal and military administration whose function of course remains essentially pillage, but through commercial bartering. Imagine additionally that Versailles is the château in *120 Days*; that the king and court are these libertines (slightly more hierarchical) who withdraw to it and stand apart from their sources of revenue, the town and the country, establishing the château of pleasure as a place where all exchanges and contributions flow without return; imagine that the provincial populations which form France are these same peasants from whom Sade's libertines extract their rents at the price of unbearable miseries; and moreover that the manufacturers, ship-owners, bankers, the entrepreneurs who arouse Colbert's zeal have no other function when selling their merchandise than to carry further, to lead further afield, to stretch to breaking point the pleasures on the Versailles stage. Are the money and the commodity invested for themselves in this *dispositif*? Perhaps, one will say, by those called the bourgeoisie, the manufacturers and tradesmen; certainly not by the court, for whom they are only means of *jouissance*. But no, it is rather the opposite which must be said: the mercantilists by definition never invest the object for itself, but only for its value, that is to say its power of extension and interest, these mercantilists being Louis XIV and the Great Powers who, just because they restlessly destroy commodities and money, intensely 'love' the first and have to make the second into a perishable thing: which is only a paradox in capital's eyes, not for the extravagant libido.

What is happening then, in terms of intensities? Klossowski shows that the libertines' *jouissance* requires not only the immediate, so to speak, body of their victims, but the larger and indeterminate body of peasants which their stewards exploit: it is not advisable to establish either a metaphor or an analogy between the object of perverse exactions and that of the worst social exploitations, it is really a matter *of the same body*, the body of reference, indispensable to despotic Sadean *jouissance*, a body to destroy, thus very similar to that formed by the victims inside the château which is, in relation to the external body of the peasants, at the same time as whatever one of its parts and as its *representative* on the stage of pleasures. We are going to go back over this cutting-up of theatricality which is so important here, France as a theatre, the king's subjects as the spectators whose contributions finance the show, the Court as a stage where the courtesans act out their tragedy. But first add to this grey body of French peasants, incarcerated within the theatre walls of the royal and stately office of taxes, the still more distant body of the Foreigners, who are still peasants, but who begin to put pressure on the commercial companies and the one-sided contracts imposed by Colbert's agents, through many intermediaries, on their masters. The Versailles libertines must have 'all the wealth in circulation in Europe', and it is therefore from the grey body of the soil of all Europe that Colbert will draw, until it is rendered as bloodless and pale as its pennant, the gold which he collects by means of the weapons of trade.

Here trade serves to extend the range of the body to destroy, the referential instance of a *jouissance* which has its model in Sade. If it is true that pleasure has no price, the torturing and putting to death of all Europe by the silver wars is not too expensive to sustain the glory of the king, that is to say his *jouissance*. *Here we need* the imagination of a *finite* body, of an economic body, circumscribed like an organic body, for it is on this condition that pleasure will be combined with the destruction it needs in order to be intensified. How would one destroy an infinite body? The apparently technical hypothesis offered by Colbert of a constant quantity of money in Europe (a hypothesis which is certainly congruent with the economic 'stagnation' or 'contraction' of the years 1680–1700) is to be attributed to the mercantilist libido. For this latter, and it is a paradox to our capitalist eyes, makes use of trade not for profit-making, but for extravagance. We should not understand the down-curve in commodity-trafficking or in the entry of American gold and silver into Seville between 1600 and 1650, or those of the manufacture of silks and fustians or of sheets in northern towns during the last quarter of the seventeenth century, as causes of the mercantilist *dispositif*. They are pieces of it. Mercantilist desire requires what we call stagnation or shortage, but which is for it the condition of a surplus-*jouissance*. An infinite economic body opens the perspective of an interminable and divisible growth, it forbids in principle the *comparatively* dark pleasure which Colbert promises to his master, the same as was involved in the ancient Persian denomination of the king of kings.

Hume said that *jealousy* is at the centre of mercantilist politics and economics, and through the exposition of these 'contradictory' effects that he hoped to demonstrate the error in it. If in fact a lot of gold flows into one country to the detriment of others, he will say, the former will come to increase its prices, its imports will grow and its exports fall. On the contrary, 'suppose four-fifths of all the money in Great Britain to be annihilated in one night . . . what would be the consequence? Must not the price of all labour and commodities rise in proportion . . . ? What nation could then dispute with us in any foreign market . . . ? In how little time, therefore, must this bring back the money which we had lost, and raise us to the level of all the neighbouring nations?'[20] The reasoning is none too convincing, but the love of balance is obvious in it, in which we will also recognize Lavoisier's pathos and the generalized passion for negotiatory annulment. As for the 'basis', one might as well try to convince the four libertines that their crimes are leading them to ruin, and that it is in their interests, in the interest of their survival, to *return* in some way the wealth which they extracted from the populace from whom they drew a revenue. One might as well recommend to perversion that it become more democratic and egalitarian with regard to its objects. In truth the body of Europe became, in Hume's epoch, at least for the English, a body of capitalization endowed with the properties of the *jouissance*, or *several jouissances*, which capital requires; for Colbert it was also an enjoying [*jouissif*] body, but in quite another way.

The equilibrium of national trade balances, that is to say the law of the zero, is not taken into consideration here. Desire does not indicate its madness here by taking upon itself conditions of infinity, money does not operate here as a *credit* potential [*puissance*], the capacity offered to the partner to *anticipate* his purchases of goods or services; instead of credit, jealousy. Like that of the jealous person, the mercantilist's time is counted backwards: 'Only Holland still remains fighting with great forces . . . ', and it ends up in the pallor of the European body drained of its strength [*puissance*] and in the master of Versailles' crimson tumescence. And the time of this master is itself counted *to death*: 'After me, the deluge'; not a perpetual tumescence, pleasure is not sought in the intensity of a permanence, but in the intensity of a consumption. The capitalist (as previously Hume and his friend A. Smith used to) sees Europe as a body of investment which brings in a profit, Colbert and his master see it as a body of sumptuousness which exhausts itself; no *we* at all, but the *I/they* dichotomy. An organic reference is as necessary to jealousy as it is to perversion, according to Klossowski; it is a life, something to kill. 'Never in history', writes Keynes, 'was there a method devised of such efficacy for setting each country's advantage at variance with its neighbours' as the international gold-standard.'[21] The gold-standard is what remains of the *golden body*, the organic body of reference for mercantilism, right up until the age of fiduciary currency. The gold-standard is the hallmark of jealousy. The money of genuine capitalism is envious, it is not enviable; in its creditory function it is nothing but permission to set up and to profit; and its time is not counted backwards, on the contrary, it is ceaselessly reproduced by an interminable stimulation of debts. The real money of capital, far from being a treasure, a thing of the earth, is a relation, a power relation certainly, since it must have the capacity to *give the right to anticipate* when granting credit, and have the capacity to profit from it by proving itself credit-worthy; but also a relation of the separation of desire from itself, an inhibition and a new impetus of libidinal energies, the schema of which we will attempt to draw up later on. The money of capital is in one sense only a time given and taken back, anticipated and delayed. Mercantilist money is an erotic and lethal thing.

Let's return to the mercantilist theatre. Perhaps its energetic analysis would allow it the better to examine this strange jealousy, which, as we have seen, has no relation to interest, whether clearly or mis-understood. If it is true that classical theatre requires not one limit, but *two*, the theatre enclosure first, and then the stage-setting, the one in which representation takes place, which envelops the stage/auditorium whole, and the other within which the space of the play is restricted, we will see that mercantilist space is of the same configuration. The customs barrier delimits the entry to the theatre which is the realm: the spectators in fact are the king's subjects, acting the audience. On the interior of the French space, the Court circumscribes another limit, that of its own stage, where the Great Powers are the actors. The congruence of the theatrical *dispositif* which then gives way to classical French tragedy, with the political economy of mercantilism, is certain.

However, the double-limit organization is not at all unique to mercantilist space. Ancient Greece provides a good model of it; the limit of citizenship, and on the interior, the limit of the political sphere, the centre (*méson*) where the orator comes to speak of what has been done and what is going to take place, and through whom therefore the city comes to be represented. This schema is only slightly different from the tragic and comic theatre. But the Greek political stage is not the monarchic stage, insofar as this is structurally empty. Every citizen can in principle stand there and speak, and so become the mirror of the city, its reflection. Associated with this republican constitution is quite another regulation of *destruction*: this only ever takes place beyond the city limits, by means of the war against enemies or rebel allies, and also by means of imperialism against the allies. Who destroys here? Not the king, but the warriors' collective. It is just the power (*Macht*) which drives such a city to consume its strengths and riches in wars and conquests of prestige, as we say. But this desire is not instantiated on a despotic figure circumscribing a second closure (the Versailles stage) internal to the political sphere (the nation, the city); every citizen is gripped by it. If, however, the second stage exists even in republics, it is in order to distinguish a treasure of words rather than of riches. If the exclusivity proper to the determination of power and representation fixes its bar anywhere, it is there, on the skin of language rather than on that of goods; the tribunal soon ceases to be an empty and accessible *milieu*, it becomes the theatre where words are amassed and squandered, procuring prestige. It is not enough to see in the rhetoricians' and sophists' linguistic *technè* the symptom of a professionalism affecting speech, it must also be considered as the acquisition and use of an *enunciatory treasure* giving privileged access to the stage of assemblies, simply because these statements are *credi(ta)ble*: the republican tribunal would be a stage where one expends language as pure prestige and loss. As in mercantilism, this does not preclude, but implies, the generalization of commerce (the commerce of words); but, as in mercantilism, circulation, linguistic in this case, must, under the cover of discharging the obligations contracted in an egalitarian fashion among fellow citizens, allow kings, rhetoricians and sophists to speak, so as to ruin their partners' oratorical credit and ensure their exclusive ownership, necessarily consumptive from this point on, of the treasure of speech.

Classical French mercantilism witnessed another generalization of trade, which it begins to extend to labour by multiplying the manufacturing industries (this is still not in the spirit of the accumulation of capital, but of war through commerce); meanwhile at the exchange centre a place without reciprocity is erected, which monopolizes and destroys surplus-values. This despotic state thus requires the mobilization of an important part of the energy at its disposal, for the purposes of constituting the double-closure, and in order to make the impulsional supplements captured outside flow towards the centre and to have them disappear in it. The 'political' space which we know, with its bulimic and narcissistic capital, and its spider's web of police and 'courts', was organized by mercantilism: a profoundly warlike and pillaging empire, where labour and economic enterprise are only ever real or potential weapons in the hands of the despot, where production does not give rise to credit, but to the prince's whim.

Europe, then, is this twin-bodied monster: a mercantilist body, that is, an exchangist circle formed by the concentration of all the intensities of which the great skin is capable, and by their annulment in the medium of the general equivalent; but it is, at the same time, a golden body, a Barbary Coast, a German, Italian, or English coast to be conquered, looted, ruined. A trading body *and* a victim body, made up of clients who are also barbarians committed to despoilment and destruction. One *sells* them something, one *loots* their gold. The protectionist barrier delimits what is barbarian from what is French, who is the client to be annihilated and who is the subject to be preserved. It allows the filtration of the exporting of commodities regarded as of no use to the subjects, and the importing of metallic treasures from wars and feasts. It lets out what the Beasts from the outside need in order to survive, these Beasts who need France and whom France comfortably 'does without'; 'in exchange', it lets in the materials of glory and destruction, the exorbitant, the inexchangeable.

At the moment when commerce begins to institute the reign of the law of equivalences and the minimax, mercantilist politics reroutes its function in an impossible formula: buy your survival from me, says Colbert to the Foreigner, but at the cost of losing all your means of purchasing, and I will represent your agony from here. On the great skin the pulsions continue to run; but a flux of exports only brings to the addressee regions the constraint of having to return a flow of imports of incommensurable intensity. Thus an 'exterior' is formed on the other side of the customs barriers whose only role is to be emptied into an 'interior', an enormous transfer of the energies current on the ambiguous body of Europe, fuelling the incandescence of the Versailles feasts. And at the same time as it is emptied there, it represents itself in self-destruction, since it is never exhausted by the movement of commerce. The apparently aberrant consumption of treasures on the stage of the Court *represents* the *destruction of the Foreigner*. If there are two limits, and not one, in this theatricality, it is because the first determines what on the exterior suffers war and the destruction of silver, the victim of despotic passion, the golden body of backward countries, the barbaric third world, and the second what on the interior repeats this annihilation of riches in a ritual fashion: the monarch and his court represent and are represented by, in the sacred space of the Centre, the deadly force [*puissance*] which ravages the profane space of the barbaric Periphery. Such is the jealousy of the despotism which fuels mercantilism, which this latter could not content itself with taking, and destroying, but had instead to present in itself what it annihilated on the outside.

The entire West will not cease, in its imperialistic conquests, to *import*, that is to say to repeat on its own body, the 'surplus' of which it deprives the body of the earth. But this surplus only appears superfluous insofar as it has been calculated in mercantilist terms, measured by an alleged minimum *value* of life, reckoned up in alleged *needs*, insofar, then, as the body of the earth covered with barbaric Foreigners which 'one can do without' has entered into commercial contact with the Europeans. The libidinal band coils up on itself, with the inclusion, by means of substitution, of what this closure excludes. The return of the repressed, if you like: the Barbarian is the king. But this must not be understood as perpetual substitution for a lack (where is the lack in all this?), but as something following the recurrence of the death drives right in the midst of the organic State in the process of defining itself erotically. Hence the predominance of the tragic and of the Terror, which will follow afterwards, on the central stage.

Money becomes the general equivalent for rendering the outside peoples, their riches ('products'), and their poverty ('needs'), commensurable with the goods which they buy. And as such, it is of course *nothing* other than the concentratory central zero, nothing other than the final zero of every mercantile cycle. It thus determines *prices* because it determines the calculable relations between quantities, offers and demands for goods. Money is therefore exhibited as *ratio*, number. But mercantilism betrays one of its secrets, or rather publishes it: for since it is not only an instrument of Eros contributing to the formation of the viable body of the European, indeed the global, market, but also a weapon of envy, a means of destruction and exhaustion of this very body that it constitutes, it is the suggestion of other surfaces. Not only the land of Europe united and closed up on itself by the law of exchanges; but also scattered fragments, pieces of people suffering the vampire's bite, so the liberal critique of mercantilism will say; something more than the equivalent is dissimulated in the vampire, it is already capital, the Marxist-Keynesian critique will say. We say: in the exchangeable sign, the tensor—and vice versa. In power [*pouvoir*], force [*puissance*], and vice versa. Now, what remains of this dissimulation (almost completely blatant) of mercantilist money, in capitalism?

Notes

1 The French word *commerce*, like, as Marx points out in *The German Ideology*, the German *Verkehr*, means both 'trade' and '(social) intercourse': similarly, in English, we sometimes talk of 'sexual commerce'; 'commerce' is used here in order to retain this ambiguity.—*tn*

2 *Faire partir* . . . : 'to get rid of, remove, to start up, launch, set off, to light'; therefore, in general, to light the fuse . . . —*tn*

3 Aristotle, *Nicomachean Ethics*, tr. J. A. K. Thomson, revised Hugh Treddenick (Harmondsworth: Penguin, 1976), Book V, 5, 1133a–b, pp. 185–6.

4 ibid.

5 Herodotus, *The Histories*, tr. Aubrey de Sélincourt (Harmondsworth: Penguin, 1984), Book I, ch. 94, p.80.

6 Vera Schmidt, 'Rapport sur le Home expérimental d'enfants de Moscou (1921–1924)', French translation by Jean-Marie Matagne, *Les Temps modernes* (March 1969).

7 Anatole Rapoport, *Les Temps modernes* (October 1963), pp. 704–5.

8 Martine Allain-Régnault, *Le Monde*, 14 February 1973.

9 Marquis de Sade, *La Philosophie dans le boudoir* (Paris: Pauvert, 1972), pp. 231–2.

10 Ch. Malamoud, unpublished paper given in J.-P. Vernant's research seminar [University of Paris], March 1973.

11 ' . . . *Si la passe est une passe* . . . '; *une passe* is a prostitute's 'score', her 'picking up a client'; it is also an 'exchange', a passing over, and a 'passing away'.—*tn*

12 *Accoucher* is 'to deliver (a baby)', to produce, bring forth, be in labour; also, by implication, to be lying down, on a 'couch'—Freud's famous couch.—*tn*.

13 Pierre Deyon, *Le Mercantilisme* (Paris: Flammarion, 1969).

14 Quoted by Deyon, ibid., pp. 101–2.

15 J.-P. Vernant, *Mythe et pensée chez les Grecs* (Paris: Maspero, 1969).

16 Quoted by Deyon, *Le Mercantilisme*, p.100.

17 Anatole Rapoport, *Fights, Games and Debates* (University of Michigan Press, 1960).

18 See above, p.174 ff.

19 Texts collated by E. Silberner, quoted in Deyon, *Le Mercantilisme*, p.99.

20 David Hume, 'On the Balance of Trade' (1752), in David Hume *Writings on Economics* (Madison: University of Wisconsin Press, 1972), p.63. See, in the same volume, 'Of The Jealousy of Trade' (1758), pp. 78–82. Quoted by Deyon, *Le Mercantilisme*, p.103.

21 J. M. Keynes, *The General Theory of Employment, Interest and Money* (1936), in *Collected Writings*, Vol. III (London: Macmillan, 1973).

5
Capital

Coitus Reservatus

'Expenditures' are far from being, as we have seen, absolute liberations from the reproductive cycle: the outpourings of pulsional intensities pouring towards an alleged *outside* always give rise to a double process: on the one hand, a more or less important proportion of these libidinal quantities is compensated for by a return, the *daksina*, payment for the lay, for the session, for words themselves, when they concern the small change of language, the concept; on the other hand, this process dissipates an *irreversible* and *unusable* quantity of pulsions as heat, as smoke, as *jouissance*, in any cycle of this type. These are on the circle, then, effects of transmutation, barely interrupted by expenditure as pure loss, i.e. by extravagant *jouissances*. But there still remains the whole question of *what jouissance on the circle consists in*. At most we understand that this *jouissance* is perverse in contrast to those coursing through the sacrificial, analytic or prostitutive offering, just as, conversely, the latter are if the former is taken as the point of instantiation. We have still to seize this *jouissance* affirmatively, the model of which we have given, somewhat arbitrarily, as the mercantile function of the Greek city.

Still using the same winding, inane route as the pulsions follow on the labyrinthine band, we will find something approaching this *jouissance* in classical Chinese erotics. We must stamp out several doctrines, however dear they may be to our Western nostalgia, according not the least credit even to the Tao, even to its admirable doctrine of weakness, rejecting it all as still on the side of nihilism, whatever proud refinement it may signify in libidinal matters.

> In sexual intercourse [*commerce*], semen must be considered the most precious substance. Saving it, the man will protect life itself. After each ejaculation, the loss of semen must be compensated for by absorbing the woman's essence. [To economize on semen], nine pauses must be made after each series of nine thrusts, or again, to prevent emission, a pressure may be applied by [the fingers of] the left hand to the point located on the underside of the member. The semen will then turn back and do good to the organism. In order to absorb the woman's essence, one should give nine shallow thrusts and one deep, alternately. Placing one's mouth on that of the 'enemy', one inhales her breath and sucks up her saliva. What has been drunk will descend to the stomach and there will change the *Ying* essence into the *Yang*. When this has been done three times, nine shallow thrusts will again be necessary, nine by nine, separated each time by a final deep thrust, until the figure of 81, or 9 times 9, has been attained, thus completing the *Yang* combination.[1]

The great theses of Chinese eroticism, essentially Taoist, are found recorded in this *Yi-hsin-fang*. And here a *dispositif* of commutation can be seen at work, a commutation of influxes so different from those we have briefly cast our eyes over that it merits a renewed attention. For, as opposed to the lay, the sacrifice and the performance, all of which have the effect of gathering a portion of the energy expended in perverse *jouissance* into an exchangeable form (money, goods into the salary of the priests, language), leaving the *remainder* to exit, in some way, from the cycle of reproduction and communication, as vain intensities, utterly lost and, so to speak, stolen by the pervert from the social organization—here, in Taoist erotics, the arrangement is such that it will operate in such a way as to arouse in the woman, by meticulous analysis and consideration of the postures and procedures proper to the maximization of *jouissance*, the intense excitement of her *Yin* energy, *with a view to stealing it from her*. While the prostitute, the priest and the analyst were observing, in the face of intolerable impulsions from their respective viewpoints, a strict rule of the minimization of *jouissance* from these latter and the risks they may have run were their venture not heavily ballasted by payment for professional expertise, the Chinese bedchamber is the site of quite another bargaining: as long as the woman, who may here be considered the subject of *jouissance*, if these words mean anything—better: the region of intensity, and again it must be said: as a body entirely and exclusively dealt with regarding its genital section (allowing Van Gulik to praise the 'normality' of this erotics)—as long as this region of erections and emotions, thus localized, is disavowed and subject to substitution (as in the indifference of the prostitute's womb, the sublimation of the offering or the talking-couch, and by means of the described payments), she is sufficiently intensely excited to do whatever she can in the play of hands, of the mouth, of looks, of the man's penis and loins. However much this connecting-up concerns, throughout the nine positions of the *Hsuan-nu-king* or the thirty of the *Tong-hsuan-tze*, only the penetration of the Jade Shaft into the Cavity in the form of seed through the Jade Gates, the fanatical care with which this penetration, its preparation, its course and its issue are surrounded already obliges us to say that this is not at all a matter of what Klossowski or Sade would call a simple operation of the propagation of the species. In particular, whatever the semen's subsequent fate, the Chinese penis does not act at all like the Athenian penis, which is only concerned, when he penetrates the wife's cavity, to deposit its semen there, as quickly as possible, with a view to the utterly basic and general ends of reproduction: in Greece the problem of the female orgasm was not posed, and when the penis becomes heterosexual, this is, as has been said, a quasi-prostitution, because the homosexual community cannot reproduce itself without the intermediary of women.

It would appear to be the same with the Chinese, where men of letters, officials, military men of every rank, governors, princes and the emperor himself (who are certainly not assembled in a circle like the citizens, but staggered in a bureaucratic pyramid like pagoda roofs) could not ensure the simple reproduction of the population by their state apparatus. Therefore, here too, they must employ women. But they do much more than employ them, and the man who devotes himself to copulation, far from momentarily prostituting his civic penis in the service of propagation and without *jouissance*, pursues, in the bedchamber, a strategy and a medicine which, under the name of erotics, gives rise to a whole cosmology and is combined with a whole politics. The useful fragment of the female body is not taken according to its fertility alone in terms of possible children—although it definitely is in other places, as we shall see—it is here taken according to its intensive force, as *Yin*, which is notated by the five signs of the woman, by the five desires of the woman, by the nine spirits of the woman, according to the *Yi-hsin-fang*. That this is a medicinal matter is affirmed by all the Taoist texts (and even the others), even when they restrict its range: the intensification of female *jouissance* reinforces masculine energy, *Yang*. Secretions from the mouth, the nipples, the vagina, are inhaled by the mouth and the *meatus* of the man, they enter into this fragment of the libidinal body, for that is what it is, like a surplus of energy. This is certainly *Yin*, and *Yin* is the still water that all use without ever exhausting it, this is why it threatens the Yang principle, which is fire and therefore extinguishable, and why erotics is also strategic, and the woman is designated the 'enemy'. But the *Yin* excited by the spasms of *jouissance*, is the water boiling, it is already the fire, it can pass to the *Yang* side, it is a transmutation, not only of elements, but of principles, into one another, for in the one is always the kernel of the other, and the expansion of this kernel in the one leads it to become the other. What the woman gives leads to an agonizing struggle and the cry, by means of the innumerable outflows of liquids described in the Treatises, which is nothing more than her water which has been shaken up so much; and this is why the man, who is on the *Yang* side, will be able to be enriched by seizing it. Enrichment presented as convalescence, a therapeutics of minor ills, but also of serious illnesses (with precise prescriptions concerning the postures and manoeuvres likely to remedy them), but especially the enrichment of potential immortality, that is—in the secular or social, indeed Confucian, version—because they can expect to reap the benefit of beautiful male children from this energetic capitalization, that is—when the use of erotics tends towards Taoist mysticism—on which they count in order to attain, through the repetition of these pumpings of *Yin* in full swing, the immortality of the Tao itself by identifying it with the Name-Less which never ceases to transmute itself.

But all this, no matter how we understand and practise it, initially counts, in total contrast to the pagan function of the Hellenic civic husband, only on condition that the Jade Shaft remains erect in its tumescence and that ejaculation has not taken place. Thus, on the one hand, liquids spill from cavities and corners of the pulsional body-band in the eruption called woman, and on the other is a hard penis, drinking open-mouthed these excitatory liquids and conserving them: *coitus reservatus*.

What is this remarkable *dispositif*? To the Chosen Girl, astonished that the man can take any pleasure in restraining himself from ejaculation, P'ong-tsou responds that doubtless the emission of semen gives a moment of pleasure, but not a sensation of voluptuousness: 'If, instead, the man practises the sexual act without ejaculating, his vital essence will be strengthened, his body will be wholly at ease, his hearing will be refined and his eyes perceptive; even if the man has repressed his passion, his love for the woman will be increased. It is as if he could never sufficiently possess her.'[2] From this ambiguous response, there are two lines to follow: first of all a point of departure for the themes of platonic, courtly, impossible and romantic love inasmuch as instead of plugging libidinal energies into organs, into pieces of the labyrinthine body, the retention of sperm will sanction a different plugging in, this time into *persons*, and love for these persons will be substituted for discharge into anonymous regions. Such a displacement requires the production, on the woman's part as on the man's, of subjects, that is to say of unitary and empty instances, which, by definition, will in fact never be sufficiently 'owned', since they are only an instantiating zero of the pulsions. Continuing in this direction, one soon discovers so-called 'modern' problematics, such as are found in Lacan, which highlight notions of the lack of *jouissance* [*manque à jouir*] and the elusiveness of the libidinal object. Let's observe, however, that these problematics are in fact dominated by precisely that which does not, in any way, hang over Taoist thought, even less its erotics: the category of the subject. For if the Tao is important to us libidinal economists, it is not because of its nihilism, but because of its refinement in the search for and the affirmation of mutability, and thereby the non-existence in it of the question of the subject.

Such, precisely, is the other line to follow from P'ong-tsou's response, and it is this that in other respects all of Van Gulik's texts substantiate: the fortification of the man's body, the refinement of his hearing, his vision, his alertness, this something which, after *Zen*, as Cage says, leaves everything just as it was before, except that one is three inches above the ground—all that, obtained by means of the retention of semen and the constraint imposed upon it, by means of techniques, whether mental or physical (like the pressure of the middle and index fingers on the seminal duct before emission), to turn back towards the head—all that comes not from nihilism but from intensification. This man couldn't care less about the woman he is sleeping with. The Great Chinese have gynaecea of a thousand women: hence anonymity. Perhaps, however, the same goes for him. What must he do? Multiply the circulations, the connections, excite the water with the fire burning in his loins, travel [*voyager*] with extreme reserve, within the tiny margin given by the rules of the books of the *Ars amatoria*. These rules in their minute detail must be understood and practised as those that govern the gestural code, the song, the dance and the music of a *Nôh* spectacle: they perform the function of a guide only for apprentices for whom they delimit *a contrario* the field of things not to do. But the great art, as in Taoist erotics, and doubtless as in madness also, consists in turning the whole field they delimit on its head, making it into a sort of *non-place* which they sweep over rather than circumscribe, and where no-one will never know whether this inclination of the torso, this beat of the tambourine, this gesture of the arm, inclines a little to this side or that side of the rule. In completely reversing the relation of the act, theatrical for the *Nôh*, sexual for the Manual of Love, to its measurement, to the point that it is the first which alone determines its immeasurable intensity, one enters at last into the incomparable and undecidable singularity. The rule is no longer a line passing *around* the field where what *must* happen indeed takes place, while excluding what must not take place, but like a turning on itself (and its axial point of rotation displacing itself on the segment to the right which is the rule), like an oscillating rotation rendering what happens elusive and immemorable (whether it be movements of the head, songs, in the *Nôh*, thrusts of the penis, undulations of the buttocks, in coitus), it serves to do nothing more than to engender, by the impossibility of situating the act in relation to it, this non-place or this unthinkable place which is precisely the passage of intensity. A line engendering an evanescent region where emotion flares up, that region is *par excellence* an incompossible fragment of the labyrinthine band.

That this is the function of the scrupulous erotic prescriptions is undeniable. They do not all the same justify the exclusive privilege accorded to *coitus reservatus*. All the passions would seem to be equally capable here of creating the new space of immeasurable singularities. If then the Tao and the whole Chinese tradition restrict the entire intensive function to the retention of sperm, it is because throughout intensification, there continues to appear what Klossowski called an intention, and it is not by accident that semen is required to retrace its path back to the brain. The intention is doubtless not, as one might think, essentially misogynistic; it is said elsewhere that the woman is also, for her part, able to practise an economy of her vaginal secretions, and of absorbing the *Yang* principle at work in her partner. The *Yu-fang-pi-kiue* gives advice on this, enabling women not to expend their entire *Yin* essence in coitus and to postpone orgasm. The Treatise goes so far as to say: 'If a woman knows the way to nourish her force and the way to realize the harmony of the two essences (*Yin* and *Yang*), she can transform herself into a man. If, during coitus, she can prevent the secretions from her vagina being absorbed by the man, they will flow back into the organism of her own body, and so her *Yin* essence will be nourished by the man's *Yang*.'[3] We cannot affirm too strongly that there is no insurmountable sexual difference, that each one potentially contains the other's correlate, and so there is the possibility of its crossing over to the 'enemy'. No, the question is not one of feminism, the intention to reserve may occupy a woman's head just as much as a man's; the Art of Loving draws no distinction on this point. Ultimately, however, a head is necessary, to which something flows back and is reserved. An instance of collection and relief, coupled with the intention to reach one or even several goals. At first, what offers the most mystical and also the most popular goals is immortality, the return of mutability to the void, and the loss of false subjectivity in weakness, which is true strength. 'The multitude has more than enough. / I alone seem to want. / My mind is that of a fool—how blank! / Vulgar people are clear. / I alone am drowsy. / Vulgar people are alert. / I alone am muddled. / Calm like the sea; / Like a high wind that never ceases. / The multitude have a purpose. / I alone am foolish and uncouth. / I alone am different from others / And value being fed by the mother.'[4] The mother is the water, woman, the *Yin*; the wind is the man, the *Yang*: this confusion belongs to coitus as much as to the Tao, and when one is 'there' (there where *I* do not think, as Lacan says), then it is indeed intensity, without intention, without a precise goal, which arises.

But the intention is only slightly displaced or put aside: the intention to 'be fed by the mother' remains. This Mother, the Mother of the Universe, is the Tao; this is what is said of it: 'I give it the makeshift name of "the great". / Being great, it is further described as receding, / Receding, it is described as far away, / Being far away, it is described as turning back.'[5] To be fed by the Mother is to pump up the *Yin* or the *Yang*, it doesn't matter which, to gather together as much energy as possible in order that the endless fluidity of the wave which spreads out and returns to its supreme emptiness[6] be inscribed. Therefore, while you copulate as intensely as possible, you do not forget this slight pressure of the fingers of the left hand between the scrotum and the anus, this suspension of the to-and-fro of the stomach, which, while vying with your partner, will have you take what he-she is giving you (without counting?), and stealing his-her surplus force which has consequently passed into you; just try to capitalize it all in the fluid inanity which is the Tao: 'Thirty spokes / Share one hub. / Adapt the nothing therein [*Fr.: le vide médian*] to the purpose in hand, and / you will have the use of the cart.':[7] which, in the cosmological order, is the same *dispositif* as the mercantile Greek and Lydian central zero. You were on the circumference, and, using an extreme intensity, you calculate to get yourself kicked out of or be injected into the central void, beyond life and death. You trade. Is this coitus a war? This is not important. What is important is that one says: all right, let's be strategic about this. For strategy is the market, death included amongst the possible outcomes. And what just a moment ago passed for the refinement of precepts allowing the non-place of the libidinal band to be singled out, now appears, by the moralization of the affair and the nihilism which restricts its range to the central void, to be the simple maximization of energetic profit. It is not because this latter is allegedly cosmological or ontological that it is less interesting or incredible. There is a Taoist trade. This can be clearly seen in the alchemical interpretation that can be given of erotic texts. Nothing is more commercial than alchemy: a trade of the simulacra of affects, a quantification of the pulsions of death and life, a weighing-up of the sexes, for purposes of enrichment, and even for absolute wealth, i.e. gold. It is no surprise that this *dispositif* is discovered, by means of Lavoisier's balance and its position of equilibrium for *exchanges of body-weights*, in industry. Taoist erotics, strategy, alchemy, ethics, with their central nihilism, these are so many concentrations, profoundly analogous to what presides over generalized mercantilism.

But there is more, that is, more unimaginative and more directly concentrated: if the man (for, ultimately, in the majority of texts, it is still the man who vampirizes) practises the *coitus reservatus*, it is not only to practise Tao, it is also a safeguard, on the other hand, so that all the semen thus *accumulated* produces beautiful boys and girls, when advisedly released. Of course favourable erotic, atmospheric, seasonal, social conditions are necessary; it remains that what he *reserves* by his studied priapism, is not only annihilation on the central zero, it is the best propagation on the cycle of Chinese political economy. And so the head which his unemitted semen climbs towards and collects itself in is not a mystical head, but more bureacracy. For this head is the head of a family chief, and this chief will be all the more powerful the greater the number of male children he has, and they will be all the more numerous and energetic the more he has hoarded his sperm, and his treasure of sperm will be all the richer the more concubines he has, therefore the richer or more capable he will be, a military man, a man of high office, of procuring for himself numerous women. In short, through this the woman totally fulfils the function of an energy source (you could say the sun, soil, labour force, waterfall, wind) from which he must appropriate for himself the force that she can provide, by optimizing her yield and transforming her into another form of energy (children here), which in turn, by transmutation, will give a supplement of energy (in this case a large family, many fine male heirs, enabling the extension of the family and its powers and its clientele over the spaces on which the bureaucratic hierarchy is superimposed). A Confucian perspective on reserved coitus, itself a very reserved perspective, which judges Taoist erotics indecent and will repress it. One can indeed see that, at the same time as it is the decline of the vulgarity of power, it is also the reverse side and the complement of the Taoist search for annihilatory intensities.

The Greeks have never had this point of view on the woman and the child, and it is a point which, for the pulsional economist, permits the strict differentiation of the civic community and 'despotic Oriental' society. What is this Chinese semen? The object of a saving? More: of a capitalization. A saving would simply be the retention of semen in the occasional *jouissance*. The act of saving is reduced to a pressure of the fingers of the left hand on the seminal duct. But Chinese erotics requires many things apart from this act: it wants to *extract* from the partner as much force as possible; therefore introducing into a body, which will be the reproductive body, *new* quantities of energy. Not only is emission, that is expenditure, suspended, which is the saving; but the *augmentation* of forces, for which the penis no longer operates as an escape route for the over-full, but, in the opposite sense, as a drilling channel through which the energetic substances dormant in the folds of the body (of the earth-woman) are gathered up, stock-piled (genitals, spine, head; pumping stations, pipeline, reservoirs), and subsequently put back into circulation as means of production (fertilizing emission of semen; combustion of hydrocarbons for so-called reproductive goals). Again the analogy is insufficient: the mining must be imagined, by itself, through the excitement it provokes in the layers which contact and open onto the enormous reamed glans promised to them, which already multiplies the energy that they contain. Something that is not true of mining itself (of the intromission of the penis into the vagina), but of *cracking*,[8] something like the erotic manoeuvres surrounding penetration.

The maximization of the partner's orgasm here becomes the object of a search foreign to the preoccupations of simple reproduction. What the *intention* of Taoist mysticism or bureaucracy aims at is an *increased* reproduction. A thoroughly misunderstood element of the simple Greek *philia*, of the simple desire for the exchangeability and permutability of goods and needs, is signalled in the *intention of intensification*. This does not result in every attempt at a simple distinction between the libidinal and the political being dismissed. For if it is true that the cold calculation of the intention to reserve will cover over the boiling intensities aroused by the erotics of postures and procedures, it seems to be because, in the *circle of intentional chills*, the chance of new intensities will once more arise. And it is in examining this route that we come to the question: what is this *jouissance* on the circle, and consequently what is this *jouissance* in capitalism itself?

The Concentratory Zero

Who enjoyed this *jouissance* which is at the same time the reservation and the maximization of intensities? Not: *who* enjoyed? but rather: how did it enjoy [*comment ça jouit*], in what place, under what modality is intensity produced, what labour, deformation, special dance, adulteration does it inflict on the great ephemeral and labyrinthine skin? This man who holds back his semen (force) with the fingers of his left hand and turns it back towards his head, what movement is he caught up in? A polymorphous movement of force [*puissance*], a pure insertion into the cycle of metamorphoses, in which there is only the passage from one form to another, not even: from one intensity to another in a labyrinth, not even: in an inumerable collection of labyrinths each resulting in a collision (collision with a beautiful 'adversary' whom one flees, carried away with fear and its force), hence one flight, and another, the incandescence of the *Yang* encountered, abducted, fled from, transformed, lost in another incandescence? Is what this Chinaman carries with him either an intention to capitalize, instantiation on a centre, doubtless empty, indeed non-existent like the Tao itself, but where the mistress of all metamorphoses resides? Immersion in the force [*puissance*] of metamorphoses? Or instantiation on the power of metamorphoses?

This hesitation oscillates between two sorts of zero, and these two sorts of zero are dissimulated in the very functioning of capital. For this latter functioning is not at all the well-oiled machinery which a certain Sraffa attempted to provide a model of, and no more the contradiction-ridden machinery which a certain Marx wishes to demonstrate, in order to provide proof of its non-viability; it is a function instantiated principally on a central zero, on a commodity standard, on a general, structural law of equivalence; guided therefore, by a certain use (accountant, payer, creditor) of money; but there is also, and simultaneously, dissimulated in this use, unresolvably, a convulsive anti-functioning which puts the system of reproduction at risk, in the name of *speculation*, for example, but which is much more than speculation, which is to the productive usage of money what anti-matter is to matter.

There are two uses of wealth, that is to say of force-power [*puissance-pouvoir*]: a reproductive and a pillaging use. The first is circular, global, organic; the second is partial, deadly, jealous. There are two uses of money, but these two uses of money, these two moneys, if you like, must not be confused with the two conceivable sorts of zeros actually operating in the system. Let's start here, by determining (that's right, men of the concept . . .) a zero of *annulment* and a zero of *conquest*, a zero of value or price and a zero of profit or surplus-value. We will then be able to make a distinction between the two sorts of conquest, the one by annexation and the other by looting, dissimulated in capitalist money, that is to say in the zero of profit. This dissimulation is the same one that we are continually talking about, it commands all the intensity there is in the direction of capital. The capitalist (he who exists and does not exist) is a conqueror, and the conqueror is a monster, a centaur: his fore-quarters are nourished by the reproduction of the regulated system of metamorphoses controlled under the law of the commodity standard, and his hind-quarters by looting overexcited energies. With one hand he appropriates, therefore retains, that is to say reproduces within equivalence, reinvests; with the other, he takes and destroys, steals and flees, hollowing out another space, another time. Again the symmetry of these formulas is deceptive. The same signs, monetary or mercantilist, that *always* count as economic signifiers, that is to say as referring to other signs, *may* also count as very different intensities, *jouissances* from destruction. Reproduction dissimulates destruction, destruction may dissimulate reproduction, but above all the labyrinthine times of destruction cannot be deduced from the single time of reproduction.

Let's first return to the zero. There is in every cybernetic system a unit of reference which allows the disparity produced by the introduction of an event into the system to be measured; then, thanks to this measure, this event can be translated into information for the system. Finally, if it is a matter of a homeostatically regulated whole, this disparity can be annulled and the system led back to the same quantity of energy or information that it previously had. Sraffa's commodity standard fulfils this function. If the system's growth were regulated, it would alter nothing of the loop-functioning (*feedback*[9]) model: it is simply that the scale of reference is then no longer u, but Δu. The model is the same as that which Freud had in mind when he described the working of the psychical apparatus, whether this is in the *Project for a Scientific Psychology* or in *Beyond the Pleasure Principle*. Erotic functioning, maintaining wholes. This Eros is centred on a zero: the obvious zero of homeostatic regulation, but more generally annihilation by the *feedback* (that is to say by the repetition of the binding function), of the system's every insignificant disparity, of every threatening event.

Let's stop a while here. We see how the adoption of this perspective on society, that is, the despotic phantasy of the master situated on the alleged site of the central zero and hence identifying himself with the matrix of the Nothing (as Lévi-Strauss might say), can only compel him to extend his idea of the *threat* and therefore of *defence*. For what event does not present any danger, from this perspective? Not one; quite the contrary, since they are disturbances of a circular order, reproducing the same (u or Δu), requiring energy to be mobilized for purposes of appropriation and elimination. Is this too abstract? Do we need an 'example'? It is the same project as perpetuates, in France and in high places, the institution of an operational Defence of the territory, secured from an operational Centre of the infantry, whose speciality is to ward off the 'internal' threat, originating from dark corners of the 'social body', whose administrative staff claim nothing less than to be a clairvoyant head: this clairvoyance is called the national register; the threat then spreads 'in a global sense; it is not simply military, but diplomatic, economic, scientific, it is internal, even cultural';[10] the translation of the event into information for the system is called intelligence: this, 'that is to say preliminary knowledge', is it not 'the key to every decision'? This research, consequently, 'interests all branches of knowledge and the activity of men . . . It spreads to all domains: political, military, economic, scientific';[11] finally the execution of regulatory orders and their inscription on the 'social body', especially when one imagines this as subject to some intense emotion, for example, the fear and panic that shake it up in every sense and in all cases where the threat of a nuclear war is unleashed (meaning also: where there arises some upsurge or other of protest, contestation, civil disobedience, regarded as insane)—this execution requires the assiduous and subtle infiltration of the communication channels in the social 'flesh', as a certain superior officer marvellously put it, 'the police of spontaneous movements'.[12]

Totalitarianism is nothing but the process of domination of the master group over the enslaved group. This process is not transitory, circumstantial, it is not bound to the function of a particular political party (the 'right') or of a particular social class (the 'bourgeoisie'): a left, united or not, possibly operating in the name of the proletariat, will perform the same labour of the detection of threats, of the centralization of intelligence, the distribution of orders, the elimination of events and men or groups allegedly in contact with these latter. The erotic dimension of the left's desire being more marked than in any other group, one may even wonder if it is any more capable of defending against the circulation of energies than any other formation relying on the unificatory power of capital. In any case, what distinction can we make today, more than half a century after the first workers' revolution, between a 'communist' party's state control of economic circuits and cultural thought on the one hand, and on the other the conditioning and training of all the pieces of the social body by the school, the barracks, the mass media, publicity, conformism and the fear of lack, in a country of 'free enterprise'? Small nuances, here and there, in the all-pervasive white terror, from the point of view of the red violence of mutant intensities on the great pulsional skin. Nuances in totalitarianism and the concentratory power.

The important thing is not to decide between the East and the West, one suspects. It's a question, rather, of remarking that totalitarianism which is the very process of concentration can expand only to the extent that new quantities of energy are included in the said circulation of capital, new quantities which will ceaselessly spread over the surfaces involved and multiply the chances available to the partial pulsions to be invested in the 'social' body, rendering the unity of this latter uncertain. This is the movement of integration which ruins the old distinctions, for example, that of the military and the civilian, the political and the private, the economic and the cultural, which divests these once diverse regions of their specific dignity and has them filed away under the same category in the Central catalogue of intelligence and decision-making. And if there is a crisis of political economy, it is primarily (but not only, as we shall see) because in this process of incessant integration which gives rise to the movement of expansion, the said 'science' of course loses its Latin, but first its object: for what is 'wealth', what is 'good', what is 'exchange', what is 'labour', when salary obviously contains surplus-value, when prices are self-determining, outside all debate amongst the exchangists, according to a complex commodity standard that no-one (except a theorist after 40 years of study) will come to define, when speech, knowledge, opinion, aptitude can and must be accounted for in assets, when the decision to invest in capital no longer necessarily belongs to its owners, when the military man becomes an economist, the economist a psychoanalyst, the scientist a military man, the pedagogue an information scientist?

It is space and time that become the objects of intelligence and decision-making, at the level of the labourer's 'body' in Taylorism,[13] at that of the urban map in metropolitan rush-hours, or the national map on days when people are leaving the industrial nations for their holidays. These are the so-called 'motivations', the final protest of needs, whose quantities are recorded and intensities measured, if possible, by market studies and sales monitoring following an advertising campaign. The most lucid sociologist used to complain of (and laugh) being unable to bestow on his office a sheen of scientific dignity. But now every 'discipline' can only arouse the same great suspicion in its own company. The idea of scientificity succumbs twice: under the subservience of scientific functions to those of capital as the great concentrator, or even under the confusion of the one with the other; and under the effect of decompartmentalization which produces, in the instituted fields of research, the passage of capital, this time as the great pervert. So much so that today's science is at first glance merely research into efficiency, that is, into power, and on the second merely the production of strange and efficient fictions. Not only is there no 'economic thing', there is no 'scientific thing', either.

The great concentrator wants stable circuits, equal cycles, predictable repetitions, untroubled accountability. It wants to eliminate every partial pulsion, it wants to immobilize the body. Such is the anxiety of the emperor of whom Borgès speaks, who desired a map of the empire so exact that it had to cover the whole territory in every aspect and therefore duplicate its scale exactly, to such an extent that the monarch's subjects spent so much time and used up so much energy in putting the finishing touches to it and maintaining it that the empire 'itself' fell to more and more ruin as its cartographic blueprint became more and more perfect —such is the madness of the great central Zero, its desire to bring a body, which can only 'be' if it is represented, to a standstill. And such is the madness of political economy, recognized in Sraffa's constructs. But this was already the madness of the Little Girl Marx, the desire for a social genitality, into which all the partial pulsions would be reabsorbed, which would have its unity in itself and where the 'truth' of political economy would finally prevail, in this case a reproduction conforming to nature.

There is in this desire for 'nature', which is a unitary totality, a furious concentrating energy.

Nihilist Theory of the Zero of Credit

Now look at the *other zero*, no longer that which at the centre proceeds, like money in the *Nicomachean Ethics*, to the equitable annulment of the relations between goods and needs, but that which is, so to speak, thrown onto the same circuit of exchanges, appearing to permit the extension of their range and the increase of their volume, enrichment. No longer payment money, the arbitrary standard of annulments, but credit money. Aristotle, in the *Politics*, which Marx ceaselessly reread from 1857 onwards, distinguishes three chrematistics, that is to say, three sorts of procedures for the satisfaction of needs. The first is perfectly organic, it is inscribed on the body of a familial community producing according to its needs, in autarchy, and has no need at all of money; it is when excesses of goods and needs appear here and there that there arises a need for new exchange amongst natural communities, which brings to bear on the goods at stake in it a sort of basic suspicion, since they are no longer intended for the immediate satisfaction of the needs of the domestic body which produced them, but for the satisfaction of the needs of another familial community: their use-value is then mediated by their exchange-value. Nevertheless, says Aristotle, a chrematistic of this type, if it requires money and its political arbitration, is not counter to nature, it never ceases to take as its rule over need and on the *koinonia* the most organic thing possible, the family. This first cleavage between natural economy and political economy, whose range will be dramatically extended by Marx, is on the contrary minimized by Aristotle because on the whole the chrematistic of such exchanges must in his eyes remain limited, finite, measured by the needs of the exchanging parties, which are domestic communities. Imagine, however, the operation of retail trade, of the *kapélikon*; in the morning, the merchant buys some subsistence good, not for any use he might have for it, but to resell it for more in the evening: here, says Aristotle, this is counter to nature, here is a procedure which contains a potentially dangerous *infinity*: here need cannot limit or halt the process, only the quantity of money which the merchant may use to buy and sell; now this quantity increases during the operation itself. ' . . . on the one hand wealth and the acquisition of goods (chrematistic) in accordance with nature, and belonging to household management (*oikonomikè*); on the other hand the kind that is associated with trade (*kapélikè*), which is not productive of goods in the full sense but only through their exchange.' And this latter form, adds Aristotle, 'is thought to be concerned with coinage, because coinage both limits the exchange and is the unit of measurement by which it is performed; and there is indeed no limit to the amount of riches to be got from this mode of acquiring goods (chrematistic)'.[14]

Here then, credit money appears. The retail trader makes himself an advance; he is at the same time his debtor and his creditor; as debtor, he will have to reimburse the money spent on the morning's purchase with that gained by the evening's sale; as creditor, he will retain an interest on the 'loaned' sum, an interest which in this case consists in the net difference between the sum gained and the sum spent. A use of money that anticipates a result yet to come, when its payment function is forced to settle a present or past debt. To this reversal of time responds the reversal of relations between commodities and money: the latter here takes itself as an end, while in inter-domestic chrematistics it was a means to the satisfaction of needs: **M-C-M** instead of **C-M-C**.[15] Isn't this exactly the same reversal that *coitus reservatus* performs by postponing ejaculation, putting wealth into reserve as semen, as Tao intensities therefore (or as a bureaucratic clientele), while on the other hand it excites those regions (the woman) capable of providing it with energy? Doesn't the merchant activate, extend the circuits of commerce, by inciting new exchanges that at first will inevitably seem useless and even unnatural, and doesn't he, like the Oriental erotician, postpone ejaculation, that is to say the use of the goods that he causes to circulate, for the benefit of that which alone can relate them, *financial energy*, energy as money?

Pursuing this description of the autonomization of the mediator (here, money), we soon encounter Hegel of course,[16] the description he made in 1804 of the formation of *Potenzen, Mitte*, from the starting point of *the inhibition (Hemmung)* of desire. Desire in its immediacy, says Hegel, is a destroyer, its fulfilment always annihilates both the desirable object and the desiring subject as such. The means by which he escapes this nihilist fate is the necessary invention of a *middle term* between the object and the subject. Both the partners and their sexual desire would be annihilated in orgasm if the institution of the family (and of the child) don't come to sublate [*relever*] and reserve the force of this desire, otherwise devoted to consumption. In the same way, the pulsion of nomination, if it is also fulfilled in the immediacy of the emotive expression, could only continually disappear in each of its occurrences, incapable of maintaining itself from one moment the next, and would be no less incapable of recognizing the object designated by the sporadic outbursts: here too it is as an intermediary between the locutor [*emetteur*] and the reference that the *Potenz* of the system of linguistic signs comes to interpose itself, language as an institution. Same thing finally in labour where the manufacturing desire would do away with itself at the same time as it would destroy all its matter, if at the same time the memory of the desire-need and the form of the matter to be put to play against that of the object were not inscribed in the *Potenz* of the tool. Thus, Hegel says, the merely nihilist force of desire finds itself shackled, slowed down by its instantiation on the *Mitte* (a medium which is held in the *milieu*: the child as the medium of love, the word as that of enunciation, the instrument as that of labour); and the institution of this requires a return, *ein Rückkehr*, by which the admittedly destructive desire reverses its course, is turned away from its catastrophic realization and inhibits itself by fixing itself in its own medium. Hegel here employs the word which will be Freud's: *Hemmung*, inhibition.

One is tempted to say that what is described under the cover of such an inhibition of the force [*puissance*] of desire, considered destructive, is capitalization. If the downstream and the upstream of the process of production, which is itself a process of the 'annihilation' of all its components—labour-force, materials, equipment—can nevertheless be preserved, is it not due to a similar inhibition of the destructive pulsion in play in political economy? And this inhibition cleaves the objects, things and men, which it preserves, just as designation divides the object into its 'intra'-systemic signification and its 'extra'-systemic representation or perception (sensible, phenomenological, etc.); or as the family splits the partner in two, into a libidinal object and a spouse endowed with powers and regulated rights. The whole Marxist analysis of the *division* of labour into the concrete and the abstract, of value into use-value and exchange-value, belongs to the same figure of the reduction of force [*puissance*] onto the mediator and its institution as *Potenz*. A figure of alienation for Marx as for Hegel, except that, for the first, this latter is not *well founded* in the second. All dialectical thought with its two great functions of intensification on the mediatory instance and of the division (*Entzweiung*, a term which reappears in the writings of the young Hegel) of the mediated instantiations seems indeed to be, from the point of view of libidinal economy, a thought of *inhibition*.

Yet what is involved in this strange action of an *inhibition* of the supposedly destructive force from which power itself would emanate?

(For, in the name of *Potenz*, there is indeed the question of power.) At least two ideas are compounded there. First, power is, as its name indicates, a potential [*puissance*] in the sense of an operational virtuality, which is never without an organization of events into a past and a future and their commensurability, or at least their co-conceivability. Then it is correlative with an inhibition of desire; power is reduced from desire onto a mean or medium; but this is an understatement, as Marx notes in 1843, for, in a thought of synthesis, everything can be a mean; and so everything is a matter of power. We must therefore say that power comes from desire insofar as it is folded back, and nothing more. (And doubtless we must conclude likewise with the Ego in Freud: continually constituted by mourning the loss of objects, and by the concomitant reversals, it is nothing, the pulsion need not come to be reversed onto this supposedly primary 'proper person', it is rather this reversal (inhibition of the pulsional goal, as noted by Green in his study of narcissism) which constantly produces the Ego as the evanescent instance of its fulfilment.) These two ideas of the *order* of events (in the mathematical sense where two terms are ordered into a set) and of the *inhibition* of desire, combine therefore into that of *Potenz* or power.

In this way the inhibition would coincide with the introduction of temporality, which Freud will call secondary, it would coincide with the activation of this time which is the concept for Hegel. For, in postponing its fulfilment ('destructive', let's acknowledge it once again), it would create a reserve or a reservoir of energy at the same time as a lack, awaiting the hour of its suppression. This waiting would open the interval of a future, and become swollen with the inhibited energy in a cumulative process of retention; in this way the secondary chronological order would be constituted. As in the army, the reserve is something which can serve again:[17] it has already served without being exhausted in this previous task, and it can enter into a process of use in order to start this task again or continue it. It is from the past, it has proved itself, it *can* do so again, it is therefore of the future; but of course of that future which is identical to the past, repetitive of the same. Charles Malamoud shows the importance, in both Vedic metaphysics and Indian practices of ritual feeding, of the category of the remainder: a figure of permanence.[18] This reserve would be therefore power as potential, as force retained from immediate investment.

(And here again one could draw a parallel with Freud, when he imagines *displaceable, floating* energy as desexualized energy, that is to say disinvested for him, and put into reserve under the control of the Ego.

Which amounts to saying that all availability—we will see the importance of this for the function of money in capital—all potential belongs to the realist instance, by which I mean: to that which determines what is reality and what is not, exactly as in economic matters the instance of capital is alone realist. Now these floating masses of energy, if they can always be counted as the reserve of the Ego or of Capital in the service of Eros, unexpectedly also turn out to pass over to the enemy, to the Id, to the partial pulsions and to death through excess; and such is their dis-placeability: not limited to the defensive functions their master assigns them, but stretching even to threaten this latter, just as the Praetorian Guard threatened their emperor. The reserve of capital *may* also become threatening, and this is not as a result of any dialectic whatever. But I am jumping ahead . . .)

What then, from Hegel's perspective, would *credit* be? Not the monstrous infinity that Aristotle foresees with the worst apprehension, but an inhibitive regulation of desire, including the reserve and the return of these energetic quantities into circulation. The question implied in the use of credit is that of knowing what exactly the creditor uses to make an advance to the borrower. For example: with what does the banker make the advance in the operation **M-C-M**? Considering this latter not as the act of an individual but as a libidinal economic functional mode, it is with *energetic remainders* withdrawn *before the deadline* that the capital financier becomes the lender. And what he could draw on in the course of the operation under the name of *interest* as the difference between **M2** and **M1** would be nothing but the result of the deduction that the debtor cannot fail to make in his turn, during the repayment period, from his own energetic expenditure. The loan with interest would therefore only be an actual advance of a supplement of energy normally available at a later date. That which gives credit and renders you creditworthy, is, it will then be said, your capacity for prolonged inhibition. What the lender puts money on (to which he will in fact constrain you), is your second degree negativity, the negation of the negation, the force of having to make your return in semen. But, still according to Hegel, there is no risk of bad infinity in the matter; on the contrary, fertility of the reserve and sublation. If the money merchant lends you 100 units today and deducts from you 15 units of value over n years, it is only because he has the power to anticipate a formation of capital (of reserved energy) which will not fail to take place on the crossing-point that you are. The Marxist theory of the origin of surplus-value is no different from this: if labour-force can be the source of a supplement, it is because it can cost its proprietor, the worker, less energy than it gives to its buyer, the boss. And why then, if only the first is capable of inhibiting, at least for a time, its 'unproductive' energetic expenditure (its consumption and the rest . . .), and the second of activating, also for a time, the productive expenditure of the first? Isn't all that is gained in the time and the place of production abstracted from the place and time of 'life', thanks to a terrible inhibition? And if it can be shown that this is not only the act of masters, but must also be that desired by the proletarians, as Reich sometimes does (and as we ourselves sometimes do), this is no great discovery in the eyes of Hegelianism, for the question is not of knowing who represses, but how it (*ça*) can inhibit itself.

The weakness of such an analysis is glaringly apparent: if all interest is only an advance from an energetic remainder yet to come, obtained by inhibition, and if one supposes a *closed system* of energies, capital would not be able to grow at all, but would simply allow, through the game of interest and profit, energetic quantities, shared out at first by chance or on an equal basis in an imaginary primitive community, to pass into the hands of the creditors, with the total quantity of the potential system not increasing at all. If the supplement to be put into circulation is *already there* in some way, if it is enough to postpone the fulfilment of desire to free new energetic resources, then it is because these latter are due only to a *saving*, whether this is through constraint or spontaneous. Aristotle's tradesman, for example, let's call him (**O**), taking more from his buyer (**B**) than he himself gave to his seller (**S**), subsequently constrains the first to reduce his purchases (that is his participation in economic circuits) in order to be able to reestablish the equilibrium (supposedly constant) of his income and his outgoings. Unless (**B**) in his turn had no opportunity to act like the tradesman (**O**), and to recover, as a seller this time, from a potential buyer, a part or all of the energies which he had lost to his previous seller (**O**). But, if the system is closed, the buyer in question is none other (upon completion) than (**S**), who has already gained his interest in the first transaction with the tradesman (**O**), so that (**B**), raising an energetic supplement from (**S**), will come to compensate that which (**S**) had made from (**O**), and the system will be in equilibrium, no doubt, but not in expansion.

Either the saving really is a saving, which implies the thesis of inhibition, on condition that one supplements it with that of a finite quantity of libidinal wealth; or, under the name of saving, it is in reality a matter of the introduction of new quantities of energy into the system, but the important thing is that when the system is not isolated, it finds its supplement of wealth, not by internal inhibition, but by external expansion, by the seizure of 'external' energetic sources. In this second hypothesis, the *jouissance*, or, better put, the intensity, would not be lodged on a mysterious feedback [*boucle*] by which, just before ejaculation, the fingers of the left hand come to press on the seminal duct in order that the sperm in it make a painful about-turn; or at least it would not be lodged exclusively there, unless one could affirm that this localization has no part in the intensification. But it would indeed be more essential to recognize in this, above all, the fact of the irritation that the 'unnatural' erotics or chrematistics arouses in the deposits of energy initially placed in the shelter of the system: strata of *Yin* dormant in the receptacles of femininity, that come to arouse the works of masculine erotics; masses of natural energies (coal, water, petrol, nuclear) or human energies (artisans, unemployed farmers), which lie dormant in the fringes of capital and which the latter comes to seize and exploit. So the intensities of which capitalism is capable are not exclusively associated with inhibition and reservation, but they necessarily are with *conquest* and agitation.

It is in sum a naïvety or a perfidy to believe that, because it rebounds on itself and is postponed, desire opens the space of a reserve on which it is quite at liberty to draw drafts on condition that it reconstitute this reserve in proportion to the repayments (interests). If desire is, as Hegel thought, purely destructive, why would the increase of its negative potential [*puissance*] reverse the nature of its effects? What then is inhibited in the pulsional movement to give rise to the mock-instance of Ego-History-Capital? Is this the destructive force, isn't this its force and nothing besides, its strength? What is withdrawn from the libido and flattened onto the instance? How could the same force going towards its 'end', to its expansion, be annihilating, destructive, bad, and become good by the fact that it makes an about-turn, that it returns to itself and takes itself as its object, that it comes to a halt and that it is in love with itself, that it becomes reflexive and tautological? If you accept this idea of the return institutive of the realist instance, then you inherit with it all of Hegel's Platonism, hence his Christianity, his nihilism. For if there is nihilism, it is time to say so, it is certainly not in the expansive force [*puissance*] of desire, which, far from destroying the poles between which one supposes it stretched, never ceases to invent pieces of the patchwork by being ephemerally invested in them. No, the nihilism is entirely in the idea that the good, the serious and the true, constitute the turning-back, the *Rückkehr*, and the institution of the *Potenz*; in the idea that inhibition changes the nature and the range of the forces subjected to it, and changes them for the better. All political economy constructed on this basis will be identical to the philosophies of consciousness, resting on the sinister 'force [*puissance*] of the negative'. But the question of capital is that of knowing how desire as affirmative force becomes reserve and institution.

The Reproductive Use of Credit Money

The advance of capital money is not simply an early putting into circulation of energetic reserves to be subsequently restored by saving, it dissimulates two almost incompatible libidinal functions, one of increased accumulation, the other of looting; but both functions are of conquest, capture and appropriation of unprecedented pieces of the patchwork. It is because these two functions are dissimulated together in credit money that it is impossible to make the meaning of the two zeros overlap with that of the two moneys, as if one said, for example, that the zero of the central annulment, of commercial concentration, corresponds to account money and payment money (and the regulative power of the cycles), and that credit money, for its part, involves the other zero, which, in the form of an advance (of what?), is thrown onto the same circuit of exchanges, and would enable the circuit's range to be extended. In fact, credit money involves both the accountancy zero and the creditor zero; and it is only in the event of unique, unforeseeable disturbances—'crises', which are like hysterical attacks—that two uses of credit become discernible, one of reproduction and the other of jealousy. It must be understood that this is not a matter of two moneys and two functions, but of two moneys and three functions: the regulative zero not only affects the exchanges in a homeostatic system, it is still present in this advance of capital which enables increased reproduction; in other words, credit money must also be thought of as a payment money regulating the growth of a regime; and finally this same credit money may on the contrary turn out to be a major deregulator of all capitalist circuits. Two moneys then: one of payment, the other of credit; and three functions: homeostasis, dynamic equilibrium, disequilibrium.

Aristotle has said all there is to say about payment money. But what happens when this payment takes place in a growth regime? This question is known by Marxists under the name of the realization of surplus-value.

If there is growth, it is because a supplement of energy (of whatever nature this is, but always in commodity form) is introduced into the system with every cycle. But without becoming unsettled, how can a system regulated by the single axiom of the virtual balancing out of the terms circulating within it (or, if you like, of their annulment, always possible in principle, in a general accountancy) introduce new terms (commodities) which would not have their monetary counterpart, into its core? A familiar question for economists.

Here, libidinals, is what our imagination suggests to us: in the first place, reverse the whole problem, that is to say, don't start with production and profit, but with the bank and interest; understand that if the entrepreneur can effectively capture (and subsequently put into circulation as commodities) fragments of hitherto untouched energetic zones, it is because he is quite free to spend before earning (buying the means of this capture before selling what it produces); understand that it is unimportant, from our point of view, whether he addresses himself rather to bank financing or to self-financing, since the only question for the system is: how can the *means* of the enterprise be purchased when only the sale of *products* will be able to furnish it with the monetary equivalent?

A problem of cyclical, repetitive time: credit is simply the premature constitution, in the form of means which allows one to transact, of the wealth which will only be given after the event as the products of the enterprise. This function of credit money must not be confused with that suggested by Keynes in the *General Theory* . . . Keynes was aiming at a system whose means of production, already given, fell into disuse only after the crisis of the 1930s. His project then was to get things going again. But we ask ourselves how, in a period of expansion, the conquest and putting into circulation of new energetic units can take place: that is, the creation of capital. Now it cannot take place without passing through the form of money, and without putting this to a specific use, which would be a sort of *preduplication* [*préduplication*] or preplication [*préplication*] of the system by itself. The lender advances the borrower something that neither of them, nor anyone else in the system, can have, *ex hypothesi*, that is, a supplement of means. This supplement will be put into the system only if the enterprise succeeds, and by virtue of this. Credit is the advance of wealth which does not exist, made in order that it come to exist.

The system gives itself an advance, this advance is an *advance of nothing* if we think in terms of commodities; it is just an advance, that is, a credit of time. But a credit of time, at the level of the system, has no specifiable meaning: it could have one only if one admits the existence of a cosmic clock, the hours of which would be commensurable with the time of the system. This standard may have a significance when the advance is, for example, that which a landowner makes in seed [*semence*] to his tenant, because it has to be evaluated on the basis of the following year's produce, and because the annual cycle is not determined by the system of agricultural production itself, but by that of the seasons, which is an independent clock. But such is not the case with a developed so-called secondary or tertiary production, which is barely rooted in cosmic time at all. Here the credit of time is only a process of expansive regulation, an arbitrary act by which a power to include new energies in the system is delivered. The capacity to deliver such powers constitutes the power of all powers.

Nevertheless, it is itself subordinated to the condition of production; the creditor says to his debtor: here is a sum **M**, with it you will produce **C**, these are the terms that enter into the system and of course (since **M** will already have been distributed) find their financial equivalent there. It is necessary to produce. This is why the properties of these credits are quite specific: middle- or long-term, investment constraints, interest rates for loans linked to the average rates of profit. We are far indeed from the *kapélikon*, where the loan takes place for a very short term, or even at sight, where interest rates appear extremely unstable, and where there exists no obligation to produce imposed by the lender on the borrower. To produce means here, specifically, *to extend reproduction*, to make capital pass into intact energetic regions, to transform 'objects', which were not previously there, into commodities; enterprise.

It is therefore an advance of nothing, but not for nothing. This supplement of energy granted under the form of a loan of money must be annulled or realized (whatever you like, it's all the same here) in the form of supplementary commodities. It is in this way that one sees that credit money used in this (productive) manner continues to operate as payment money, as the annulatory zero, as an instance of reproduction: in short, it is an increased reproduction, the unit of reference is not constant, but on the increase. Insofar as this use is limited by (re)production, the credit contains no dangerous infinity, in the sense that Aristotle feared. Currency, here, operates basically only as a *sign of something else*, a sign of industrial or commercial invested capital. It is not its own end nor its own limit: these latter are new commodities which will be exchanged against it at the end of the cycle. The unreality of the advance is therefore temporary (provisional), it will be exchanged for the proper 'reality' of commodities. Of course, these are in turn only means, and it is quite certain that for capital there are only means, means of reproducing itself while growing. But it is precisely this function of postponement, of the sign, which endows anything whatever with the status of reality in the system. The nothing advanced by the bank to the entrepreneur is a reality because it will be exchanged for commodities. By making this advance of nothing, credit money in sum does nothing more than complete the nature of the sign in the system, which is nothing other than to refer endlessly to other signs.

As for the temporality at work in this advance, it is the time of reproduction, which is, like the time of structures, basically atemporal. Of course, the quantity of elements put to work in the system is not constant, and in consequence one need not find all their possible combinations identical to each other from one cycle to another. It is of a rigorously cyclical history that B. Russell can write that 'the final state is numerically identical to the previous one', that 'we cannot affirm that this state occurs twice, for that implies a chronological system', and that he ought rather to express this history in the following way: 'Let's consider the set of all circumstances contemporaneous with a determinate circumstance; in certain cases, the whole set precedes itself.'[19] The history of growing capital is only analogous to itself: the new commodities introduced at the time of the cycle $n + 1$ are to the money advanced as those of the cycle n are to the money then in circulation. Credit in its (re)productive usage rests on this analogy: the future it opens up is no different from the past. The one and the other are identical in principle, this is why they are reversible, and this is how the creditor can buy his future.

The Speculative Use of Credit Money: 1921

There are no 'speculators', bad people perpetrating their crimes behind the backs of the honest managers of capital. Capital money is at every moment subject to a use which is strange and unexpected only if one insists with the economists on seeing only the reproductive function of capital. But there is mercantilism. Marx, in order to establish the general formula of capital, is first obliged to proceed to the analysis of currency and to imagine the mercantilist system as an indispensable stage in the formation of capital proper. Mercantilism is in fact constitutive of capitalism, but it is not a formative 'stage' of this latter; lodged in reproduction and instantiated on its very condition, currency form, it is a potential of intensities. Mercantilism is not a system, at the very most it would be an anti-system, incapable as it is of persisting since it entails the death of the body it exploits through exhaustion. Rather it is a potentiality of conquest by plunder and dissipation, probably always present in economic organizations, but whose importance in terms of its effects is drawn from how much *jealousy* (which it is) is exerted on currency, an indispensable moment in the metamorphoses of capital, and so, in consequence, it can seriously alter the circulation of this latter. For speculation is the mercantilism in capitalism; it pursues in capital money the same sort of intensity that Colbert and Louis XIV might draw from metallic money. It is useless to want to induce 'thrusts of speculative fever', as the historians and the economists say, starting from the general state of the economy. One could imagine that it is when the incitement to invest becomes insufficient that capital enters onto the route where the intended interest rates are much higher than in production. But this reasonable description completely ignores the libidinal difference that this displacement of capitals implies. The Stock Exchange is not a better investment then; it is not an investment at all, it is a battlefield and a field of conquest by means of buying and selling. The very sophisticated currency traded here is not concerned with producing, but with taking.

If indeed there are destructive forces at play in history, it is not, or not necessarily, those that produce war.[20] The production of war is a production of war, it is still a production. But destruction is dissimulated in the most peaceful production, death in the accumulation of wealth. We will not even say that it is the destiny of capital to lead, through its process of accumulation, to the ruin of society. That is not certain, this dialectic is still religious in the hope for or the fear of the catastrophe that it promises. Just as the pulsions of death are dissimulated in those of life, the destructive forces are not discernible from those of production. And, just as the lytic or lethal function belongs to no particular pulsional instance, one could not even say that speculation is deadly and production erotic; the contrary is no less verifiable. And the important thing is not even to be awestruck by this ambivalence; it is rather to pinpoint how *jouissance* or intensity slides from reproduction towards looting.

What is mercantilism other than a politics of the *kapélikon* elevated to the level of the State? The infinity of a chrematistic of currency, so feared by Aristotle, is not and cannot be a property of the reproductive use of capital, which is limited by the zero of annulment. The infinity of capitalist growth contains nothing fearful or mortal since it is regulated in principle on a commodity standard. And if it happens that this standard does not regulate it, it is particularly due to mercantilism, due to a use of capital of which one will indeed be able to say that it is not 'really capitalist', because one has the image of a capital which would be essentially a mode of (re)production, but which it certainly is if the looting of wealth goes as far as to put the survival of the 'social' body in jeopardy (as reproduction requires) and becomes a part of the impulsions active in the system, and perhaps indispensable. In seventeenth- and eighteenth-century mercantilism, one produced in order to sell and one sold in order to increase the quantity of currency. Even there, it is nothing if not very capitalist; but what is less so is this: this quantity of currency *is*, substantially, the wealth which one aims to accumulate (and to spend).

Such is excess, the limitless: it is not capital that one accumulates, something that would be put back into circulation according to the rules of cycles and annulments. One accumulates quantities of metals that form the treasure and glory of war; in so doing, one takes them out of the cycles and the measure of exchanges, and one blocks what assures reproduction in principle. 'Bad' infinity comes from this looting, which returns nothing of what it takes, which can lead only to the exhaustion of the reproductive body. Consumptive hoarding creating between one part and the other of this 'body' a more and more overpowering inequality of wealth: creating between one piece and the other of the libidinal patchwork a more and more hateful jealousy with regard to intensities. If Aristotle's infinity is deadly for him, it is due to the fact that this body exploited by mercantilism is finite, and that a process of increasing disparity between the parts of the body must make this latter explode: the *koinonia* cannot support a heavy difference of potential between its organs.

Take the crisis of 1929, one sees the mercantilist machine there on a large scale. Should the powerful impulsions of looting be at work from one end to the other, should the excess of what is without a counterpart come to light, there is the event, there its affirmativity. The same goes for speculation on the currency markets, a very similar event, which today troubles the workings of global capitalism. For this latter, the givens are not established. The crisis of '29 by contrast is today a kind of huge microscope to cast an eye on capital's libido. Here the pulsional duplicity of the use of currency is easily brought out: investment, speculation; and of time: iterative, singular; and of currency itself: means, treasure; and so of intensity: accumulation by postponement, dissipation. The two incandescences are co-present, indiscernible except by means of their effects, each counting in different regions, the same capital currency in two heterogeneous and undecidable space-times, set side by side, but in the same place: *neben*. It is not *because* the functioning of reproductive capital has become impossible or difficult that its speculative functioning is set to work: what is such an *impossibility*? When is the reproduction of a system not possible? To say this is to attempt to turn tragic on the cheap, and to inscribe in a dialectical destiny what was and is a singular episode, an event: if this proves anything, it is *the duplicity of economic signs*, even the most abstract, and, it seems, the most innocent in the economist's eyes. The crisis of '29 attests that the alleged social 'body'—in fact, millions of rags of the patchwork unified in principle under the capitalist, paranoiac law of reproduction—can fall apart, be taken to pieces, and go to pulp for a long time (right up until 1950–5, that is a quarter century counted on the clock of *Weltgeschichte*), and atrociously (millions and millions of deaths, millions of ruins), without any other 'reason' than the frenzied, jealous impulsions which, since the First World War, never cease to cultivate the use of capital in the sense of Aristotle's feared chrematistic.

After 1914, the so-called world market, that is the 'body' that capitalism is continually trying to give itself, was far from its organic ideal. The imbalance of trade between Europe and the United States is deep: $11,000 million trade surplus for the United States in 1922. Here credit money comes to operate in principle in its reproductive function: loans and credits are accorded by America, during the war, to the allied States, to protect the foreign value of their currency: these dollars permit them to redeem their own devalued currency, the sale of which is everywhere negotiated by the Markets, against dollars or gold; and after the war, to the States stemming from the central Empires, to sustain national currencies hit by inflation: the destruction of Central Europe's means of reproduction leads these states to multiply monetary signs in order to face up to their payments and to initiate recovery. For their part, the European enterprises utilize the credit facilities offered them by American industrial or commercial societies in order to make their purchases in the United States.

What happens then in 1921? A sort of crisis which anticipates in certain aspects that of '29. American lenders begin to offer their European clients' bills of exchange at a discount which the Federal Reserve System [FRS], the issuing institution, then buys; it must therefore cede paper money in exchange for the discounted bills. Hence from June 1918 to December

1920 the value of the commercial portfolio of the Federal Reserve System rises from \$435 to \$1578 million. In parallel, the percentage of gold reserves falls; at the start of 1921, it is at 42.4 per cent, when the legal minimum is then 40 per cent.[21] There is a risk of European inflation spreading to the United States. The FRS falls back to 659 in December 1921, and 294 in June 1922. Hence a simple measure of the stabilization of the dollar.

But it suffices to throw the distribution of forces on the 'body' of capital off balance once more, and seriously. The restriction of trade credit brings with it (look, causes and effects!) a fall in the volume of American exports and ultimately of world prices, which in turn discourages all medium- or long-term investment. Inflation will take the familiar turn in Europe: the gold mark counts for 17 paper marks in December 1920, 46 in December 1921, 1778 in December 1922, 45,000 in June 1923, 1 million in August 1923.

Is there something in this we need *to explain*? This is not the libidinal economist's business. Let's highlight two important things: the first is that the United States finds itself in the position of having exhausted the wealth of a part of Europe (centre and east), which speeds to its organic death for want of being able to instantiate its exchanges on a stable unit of reference, gold or the dollar (which in this period was itself indexed on gold). Keynes described, like a true libidinalist, what economists would hypocritically call 'velocity of circulation': 'In Moscow the unwillingness to hold money except for the shortest possible time reached at one period a fantastic intensity. If a grocer sold a pound of cheese, he ran off with the roubles as fast as his legs could carry him to the Central Market to replenish his stocks by changing them into cheese again, lest they lost their value before he got there . . . '[22] Schacht makes the point in this regard that the German word for monetary value, that is, the title or grade of a currency as a standard (for example, in gold), is *Währung, währen* signifying 'to last'. And J. Néré observes: 'The disappearance of duration upsets men's brains and nerves.'[23]

To tell the truth, the Muscovite grocer is, in his disturbed state, in search of a permanent rule, which is cheese: the perishability of this is less great than that of paper money. What is fascinating in this 1921* crisis is that

---

*The date Lyotard gives here is 1929. However, the Moscow grocer is an example used by Keynes in his 1923 *Treatise on Money,* in the context of a discussion of recent economic crises. I have accordingly amended the text to read '1921'.—*tn*

one then enters another, vertiginous time, made of *as many times as there are exchanges*, hence just like the time of our labyrinth. It is a time of flight where, at the time of each transaction, the exchangists, whose paper money expires, run to get rid of it, not so as to be able to tackle a subsequent transaction in the same, improved position, that of the seller, who is on the contrary cursed, but in the hope of constituting a stock (of cheeses) and of reestablishing a unit of reference independent of currency which would be valid as a good currency. Every encounter of the cheesemonger with roubles must be imagined as an unbearable event which he flees, to imagine that his flight never fails to bring him into contact with still more notes along the way, more and more notes. And from one flight to another, there is no continuity. From one heap of notes to the other, there is no identity, not even simple quantitative difference. Every 'exchange' becomes an event, opens up a type of adventure, where death is the stake.

It is not only the power of credit that, in principle, is possessed by the self-abolishing currency in these labyrinths, it is also its power of discharge. For the flight in the face of money reminds us, by the frightening restriction of time limits, that the latter power is itself a case of the former: the paying buyer acts only to give the beneficiary a credit valid over general wealth, that is, over a third party. The increase in the discount rate in Washington produces this vertigo in Moscow, the reversal of **M-C-M** into **C-M-C**, a grocer who wants only cheese and not money, and who therefore no longer invests the credit and credit time involved in paper money. Mortal stasis on a partial organ of the trading body.

One can imagine the equivalent of this disorder in the field of language: the amnesia of a *microlexis*, without going any further; this is a semantic network guaranteeing a meaning standard thoughout a multiplicity of statements. For example, the lexis of the names of colours; Gelb and Goldstein describe it as the amnesia that Cassirer and Merleau-Ponty comment on.[24] The latter writes: 'We can obtain an experience of this type [amnesiac] by having before us a heap of samples in a passive attitude of perception: the identical colours assemble themselves under our gaze, but merely similar colours form only uncertain relations amongst themselves.' And Gelb and Goldstein: 'The heap appears unstable, it moves, we notice incessant change, a sort of struggle between several possible groupings of colours according to different points of view.' Cassirer comments: there is no longer, for the amnesiac, one single language of colours, but several languages, as many as there are chromatic experiences, 'each sensible impression is affected by a "vector of meaning", but these vectors no longer have a communal direction, they are no longer orientated towards principal determinate centres, they are much more divergent than is the case in the normal person'. No longer *a* circle, *the* colour-wheel; but many small circles, none of which communicates with the other.

The second thing to note: there is perhaps the pain of an incomplete amnesia there, retaining the trace of a unitary exigency, just like that of the Russian cheesemonger. One might think that one was reading, in these protocols of experience, the effects of Colbert's politics on his 'clients'. For this same vertigo, under the name of inflation, necessarily affects parts of the 'body' of wealth which had been deprived of gold, even if very indirectly (in 1921, through the intermediary of the dollar). Gold amnesia. It is because the dollar defends itself, that is to say treats itself as wealth, that it condemns Central Europe to the desert of labyrinths.

The FRS of course, is not Louis XIV, the gold supply of Fort Knox is not principally intended to finance court feasts, and the measure of the increase of discount rates is not an open act of belligerence, but also a general safeguard: in short, we are well within capitalism, not in state mercantilist practice. Nevertheless, we can see this in it, the hypothesis of all mercantilism: that the wealth which is displaced towards the American banks was withdrawn from European capital, that the quantity of currency circulating in the West is a finite quantity, and therefore that the accumulation of signs of credit (European bills of exchange) on one pole of the capitalist 'body' plunges all that belongs to the other pole into the immoderation so feared by Aristotle: economic amnesia, *a-metry* [*amétrie*], anomie. And this position of immoderation, which we find experienced by Central Europe of 1921, which will be affirmed by American capital in the years from 1925 to 1929; admit that it has, formally, a direct similarity with the passage of influxes on the pieces of the libidinal patchwork, that it manifests all the characteristics of the pulsional 'disorder' affecting the body of reproduction: the running Muscovite cheesemonger is an effect of partial pulsional motion.

The Speculative Use of Credit Money: 1929

If you now want to see it positively, look at the New York Stock Exchange, not only on 24 and 29 October 1929, but from 1924, when stabilization follows the crisis of 1921 throughout the West. There remains in the United States an important mass of hot money; a flurry of real-estate speculation on Florida land turns out to be a fiasco in 1925–6; the signs of wealth will follow two principal routes: they will serve as substitutes for the economies and working capital of Austrian, German, and even English companies,[25] being lent on the *short term*; they will serve to sustain speculation on the transferable values on Wall Street, there again in the form of short-term loans, even *call loans*. At the start of 1925, the discount rate, as offered by the (Berlin) Reichsbank, for example, is at 10 per cent, that of the Federal Bank of New York at 3 per cent: the investments, made in Europe at these rates, especially when they are short-term, can be said to be 'speculative', although they may also be reproductive. As for those which, on Wall Street, come to finance purchases of American values at below-par rating since the war, for instance, the railways or the public services (in full recession), their destination demonstrates to Wall Street alone that they aim at rapid gains in fiduciary capital, and not at an interest proportionate to the industrial profit that one could expect from these 'unhealthy' enterprises.

The second trait of these investments, then: at first they bear not on the (re)productive value of actions or obligations, but only on the possibilities of net profit that they offer on the Stock Market; the securities involved are *not taken as signs* (of the means of production), but as *things* that will be granted a plus- or minus-value only by the movements of exchange to which they are submitted. There is a given quantity of negotiable securities in the Stock Market; a rush of buying on a security is enough to enhance its value insofar as the purchasers are perceived as a *profit-making minority* which cannot but inspire jealousy, jealousy ends as soon as the tendency is reversed, it gives way to reserve, then to liquidation. What they call the 'psychological factors' of the play of the market consists in this strange 'perversion' (but dare we employ this word?) of the relation to capital: securities become like gold, to gain gold by the jealous game alone. And when we say jealousy, we don't only mean that between subjects, proprietary jealousy; but amongst all libido, this jealousy that parts of the great film demonstrate for those invested with intensity, direct pulsional jealousy, without the mediation of a proprietary limit, making the masses of capital floating on the body of market values *incapable* of equitable distribution, in parity; rather they are ceaselessly displaced on it, producing the greatest disparities in potential. This is indeed mercantilism and the *kapélikon* once again, the excess inevitably associated with the *finite* quantity (the sum of negotiable securities).

And the second characteristic: purchases of real-estate values on Wall Street from 1925 to 1929 take place, to a great extent, 'in the margins', with money borrowed on sight (*call loans*); for the lender then, it is a matter of a highly flexible investment, repayable on demand. The interest rate for these *call loans* in New York climbs from 3.32 in January 1925 up to 9.41 in July 1929; one can only compare it with the rates charged in Europe 'to attract' American capital. But here the period of the immobilization of loaned capital is still less. I imagine that a *broker* has been given a 'tip', and so happens to make a demand for a call loan from some representative of a bank (we will see that it is not even that), who will hand him a promissory note there and then, after receiving the promise that, if the operation planned by the *broker* is profitable, its fruits will be shared out between them in a certain proportion. Credit money circulates here according to a *time* which is not that of productive capital: there is no longer a natural cycle, nor anything comparable. There is no longer any cycle at all, only upward and downward trends and their reversals, which, in a turbulent period, are unpredictable.

This call-loan credit focusing on very short-term purchases implies maximal *displaceability*. This is no longer the cheesemonger chasing cheese by means of roubles, but the lender chasing money by means of securities. This displaceability is once again a characteristic of the *kapélikon*: imagine that the tradesman makes not one, but two or ten **M-C-M** operations during his day. This adds nothing to the productive capacity of his city, certainly; it is a looting of time, or rather it is a time of looting, where the rapidity of displacement is indispensable because it guarantees that one will be the first in on the deal, on lands when one is a nomad of the steppes, on gold when one is the Great King, on securities when one is a great broker. The same temporal vertigo, the same labyrinths, as those into which *galloping* inflation plunges Central Europe in 1921. It is a passionate time, a time of dissipations.

For, even if the securities traders do not hold sumptuous feasts, they are necessarily affected by this strange situation, which is that of the nomad looter: that the simple conquest of a mass of actions necessarily provokes its devaluation on completion, just as the conquest of a territory by the cavaliers immediately implies that they will have to abandon it, and thus delay its exhaustion. Things conquered in this way, looted, are already dead, and must be rejected as quickly as possible. It is in this sense that every conquest is a flight forward, towards other things *not yet* devalued and nevertheless *already* devalued since they are about to be seized. It is in this jealous way that the times of the labyrinth are oblivious of one another; and each to its own in matters of fire and ashes.

But this is not all. Another, apparently 'technical' characteristic of transferable speculation on Wall Street in this period clearly shows the dissimulated, undecidable character of a suddenly intensely jealous use of capital money. The loans granted the *brokers* are not mainly made by the banks, they come principally from non-banking origins. For example, on 31 December 1924, of the $2230 million lent to brokers, only $550 million did not come from the banks. But on 31 December 1927, the numbers are respectively 4430 and 1830; 31 December 1928, 6440 and 3885 (more than half); and, on 4 October 1929, 8525 and 6440 (that is, about three-quarters non-bank loans[26]). As J. Néré shows, funds not coming from the banks *come from the working capital of industrial and commercial societies*. This means that the capital 'normally' invested in its own reproduction through the intermediary of commodities, 'plays' here at being lent at the highest price in order to be exchanged against securities, even though this may involve their liquidation at any moment, at the highest interest rate. So it is not enough to say that there are evil speculators, there is a compulsion to speculate which can affect even the capital earmarked for reproduction; they are the same men, company heads, presidents of industrial and commercial societies who love the postponed and the deferred and who may prefer them to the pleasures gained from this mercantilism in the second or third degree.

There, as Néré says brilliantly, is the question posed by the crisis of 1929: not to ascertain why there had been speculation on the Stock Market; there has always been speculation, the economist will answer; we would add: it is a libidinal instantiation, no more does it accept a 'because' than industrial capitalism itself (which is no less mysterious, isn't this true?). 'The real difficulty comes from the extent of speculation *on credit*—which is not therefore directly supplied by surplus revenues. The question is of knowing how it happens that this speculation on the Stock Market, eminently risky, involved such a degree of working capital from businesses, and compromised the normal mechanisms of short term credit and payments.' And J. Néré concludes: 'There is a lack of basic information to answer this.'[27]

There is in fact no response to the question of a libidinal displacement of inscription. That intensity, that force is then instantiated in the securities trade and considered as exchangeable things, rather than in the production of consumable commodities, is no more explicable than the fact that the libido lodged in the genital zone moves towards the anus or the ear. Call it regression if it makes you any happier. The eroticization (in this banal sense) of the Stock Market is not to be explained, but taken note of. The proportions that it attains in 1929 permit only affirmation: this is one *manner* in which force (*puissance*) may come to be intensified in capitalism and on the part of capitalists—although this *dispositif* could function only in the margins, and even at the price, in the so-called 'normal' modality, of reproduction and postponement. This example is enough for us to think that *we have not begun* to describe the libidinal economy of capital. These few pages were only a minuscule contribution to this description.

Here again you might say: these pages show an *ambivalence* in the use of credit money, there is a credit which inspires confidence and a credit which does not inspire confidence, a credit which acts according to the time of advances and a 'credit' which acts outside the cycle, in the blow by blow of speculative labyrinths. Don't think this. What is important is not this ambivalence, i.e. one and the same investment somehow both repro- ductive and speculative; the important thing is that two indiscernible instantiations are exposed to intensities, and that voluptuousness may vascillate unpredictably between them. Don't replace the optimistic dia- lectic of the one and the pessimistic dialectic of the other (Little Girl Marx, Mattick) with the open secret of ambivalence. Ambivalence is the co-pre- sence of vectors of opposed meanings in one and the same space-time. But the duplicity of this capitalist credit is the co-presence (but present to what, to whom?) of tensors in signs and signs in tensors. But signs and tensors do not belong to the same space-time: signs arise by definition from the system in which they are transformable (commutable, translatable, exchangeable); each tensor opens up its ephemeral time and its labyrin- thine evanescent space.

It must be clearly understood that the jealous hypothesis of a *finite quantity* of wealth, made by every mercantilism (all speculation), is constitutive of the same labyrinths of which we speak. Every intensity is a flight to death, that is to say to exhaustion, in which energy is spent at the height of its force, hence exploiting every reserve, destroying every organized body: the nomads of great invasions, Louis XIV, the brokers of 1929. Should the signs be exchanged between the former and the latter, should land be exchanged for transferable stocks, nothing would change as regards the phantasy of such a 'finitude', and the reality of its *cruelty*. Signs are not taken here as substitutes following truly sedentary habits of thought (structuralist), they are displaceable masses of energy. The nomad's horse is only the earth made more mobile. When they moved from the earth to the horse—which is neither an instrument nor a weapon, but a more important thing: the vehicle—when they moved from the horse to the bill of exchange, and from this to the call loan, they moved closer all the time towards the *greatest possible displaceability*. Towards a time and a space less and less 'global', cosmic, more and more libidinal, labyrinthine, ephemeral. Is there a space-time of speculation which could be plotted out? A geography and a history of the Stock Market? On the contrary, in putting these things into circulation, there is always something savage which puts the space-time of reproduction, i.e. reproducible space-time, in jeopardy.

Another, recent, example. Saudi Arabia, Kuwait, Abu Dhabi, Qatar and Libya have a total population of 9.5 million inhabitants. After the rise in petrol prices which they imposed on their European buyers in 1973, they pocketed in total around $45 million in 1974. Now all of Europe, the France of the Great King included, assumes the character of a needy client and a victim. For, as the mercantilists so clearly understood, there is indeed very little that they can sell in return to their petrol masters, seeing that these latter *have no need of* whatever it is: even all the Arab petrol-selling countries put together (and not only the five we have mentioned) would be unable to absorb more than $20 million worth of annual imports. Let us add that their surplus exports are payable *in dollars*, just as Colbert demanded precious metals. It is clear that as a result European capitalism cannot but collapse soon. (We know that it is not so simple . . .)

Need we say that it is impossible to describe all this commotion in terms of the exploitation of labour-force? But while we face the facts, Sraffa's straightforwardly structural phantasy is also inessential. For the only way to avoid this collapse, as G. Bosquet remarks,[28] would be of course to determine a new complex commodity standard, including both the tonne of petrol and the automobile unit, for example, following Sraffa's views exactly. But the episode of '73–'74 shows precisely that this commodity *does not exist*, and that in one sense it *must not* exist. If it existed, where would these disturbances come from? How could they take place in a reproduction which has itself as its only end? If investment were regulated to make allowances for the reproduction of the system, so many fits and starts would be excluded from it.

Such is the religion included in political economy: it postulates, like the Little Girl Marx's critique, the organic unity of the body of capital, and believes in it. And doubtless the English, French and Italian 'left' believes this much more than does the 'right', which is prevented from belief by the danger, which provides it with its privileges over the handling of capital, of giving way to dissipatory passions. Political economy is the 'left's' illusion *par excellence*.

The influence that the 'feudal' Arabs directly wield over the fate of the oh-so-serious European entrepreneurs, and indirectly (by speculation on gold, for against what would you have them exchange their petrodollars, these poor wretches at the limits of dissipation?) over the fate of oh-so-productive Europe, is not at all paradoxical. There is only a paradox if we believe in the law of value, even in the form given it by Sraffa, whose complex commodity standard, although free from the hypothesis of an *origin* of value, is none the less nourished by the belief in *equilibrium* and the return. This equilibrium is far from being what is essential. There is in the most 'modern' capitalism, under the name of mercantilism, speculation, imperialism, unequal exchange, a force [*puissance*] not of *order*, but of *zeal*: 'jealousy' comes from 'zeal'.

Another fact to examine from this perspective of the *kapélikon*: the lack of constraint on the dollar's convertibility, the unlinking of exchange rates, the generalization of the principle of hot money—all that applies in the sense of a greater displaceability, more productive in principle, but also more enervated, and far from impeding manoeuvres of a speculative or mercantilist (in our sense of the word) nature, merely displaces their possibility (even if it does mean a return, for want of another *wealth*, to ancient gold, as the emirs do). In view of this displaceability, the investment, that is to say the sedentarization, often in the long term, of energies in the means of (re)production still seems to be a thing of nature, cyclical, regular in principle, turning the productive body into a kind of earth: the earth of the neolithic revolution. But speculation or mercantilism have no natural model; even the sinister second law of thermodynamics gives no account of their errancy; instead we require something like the enigmatic hypothesis of anti-matter, very similar to matter, a totally positive energy dissimilated from the energy fixed in matter only by its effects: when it collides with this latter, they are annihilated.

By investing in commodities (including the means of production), you submit to the regulation of metamorphoses: for production is a consumption and products must in their turn be consumed. It is in this sense that so-called 'use-value', as Aristotle already suggests concerning a chrematistic which uses payment money between natural units of needs (families), is an indispensable modality of the system of reproduction. There is a slow, cosmic time there, that of the seed [*semence*] and its fruit, of the chicken and the egg, of gestation, and of dripping honey. With monetary 'signs', we get away from this time and its space. We go crazy in signs: they allow several times, many times, they are accelerators or brakes, just because they are not constrained to (re)production, that is to say to consumption, to nihilism. Their multiplication issues not from their fertility, from the translation of their face-value into productive commodities, that is, from their investment; this is only a concentration of wealth on one pole of circulation, stolen from the other pole; these are only sweeping movements which exhaust the surfaces. These movements are free of the constraints of all productive consumption; they make possible the dissipation of the surfaces they cross.

What, then, did the Chinaman do with his sperm-wealth? Was it a putting into reserve and a capitalization with a view to gaining the metaphysical Centre or Tao, or maybe even the zenith of bureaucratic hierarchy? Wasn't his reserve in coitus also the intensification of energies and their looting to attain their dissipation? Isn't what he arouses on the woman's body, and on his own, the same enervation aroused by the dollar on Moscow's Central Market and on Wall Street? Why doesn't this reserve give rise to a long-term, invested, reproductive credit? Isn't it also a call loan, a speculation without intention, an incandescence of the surfaces swept away with no concern either to reproduce them or to augment them, a jealous zeal and not a conquest of power? Certainly. The utterly immortal duplicity and dissimulation of all capitalization?

Notes

1 *Préscriptions secrètes pour la chambre à coucher*, collected in the *Yi-hsin-fang* (982–4). Quoted by Van Gulik, *La Vie sexuelle dans la Chine ancienne* (Paris: Gallimard, 1971), p.191.

2 Quoted by Van Gulik, ibid., pp. 188–9.

3 ibid., p.205.

4 Lao-tzu, *Tao-Te-Ching*, XX, tr. D. C. Lau (Harmondsworth: Penguin, 1963).

5 ibid., XXV.

6 ibid., XVI.

7 ibid., XI [Lyotard's emphases].

8 *cracking*: in English in the original.—*tn*.

9 *feedback*: in English in the original.—*tn*.

10 General Beauvallet, *Revue de la défense nationale* (August–September 1973). Quoted by G. Dupin in a dossier entitled *La Double Capture. L'Armée contre la constitution*.

11 Lieutenant-Colonel Jean, in *Forces armées françaises* (June 1973).

12 General of the Army B. Usineau, in *Revue de la défense nationale*, (August–September 1973).

13 'Taylorism': after an American engineer, F. Taylor (1856–1915), introduced *c.* 1918–20: a scientific method of the organization of industrial labour by means of the maximal utilization of equipment and the abolition of useless actions, also called the 'Taylor system'.—*tn*

14 Aristotle, *The Politics*, tr. T. A. Sinclair, revised Trevor J. Saunders (Harmondsworth: Penguin, 1981), Book I, ch. 9, 1257b, p.84. Reviewed by Austin and Vidal-Naquet, *Economies et sociétés en Grèce ancienne* (Paris: Armand Colin, 1972), pp. 189–90.

15 **M-C-M**; where **M** stands for 'money' and **C** for 'commodity'.—*tn*.

16 G. W. F. Hegel, *Realphilosophie*, Vol. I (Jena, 1803–4) (ed. J. Hoffmeister, Hamburg: 1967).

17 'The operational defense of the territory rests on the rapid mobilisation of homogeneous regional units. Who better than you', asks R. Galley of the Congressmen and Congresswomen of the National Union of Reserve Officers, 'can assure the defense of a geographical sector and a population which we know well? Who better than you could train a unit of reservists by local recruitment . . . ?' It is once more, as you will have guessed, a matter of formulating the 'police of spontaneous movements' (*Forces armées françaises*, June 1973, quoted in Dupin's dossier, *La Double Capture . . .*).

18 Charles Malamoud, 'Observations on the notion of "rest" in Brahminism', *Weiner Zeitschrift für die Kunde Südasiens*, XVI (1972).

19 Bertrand Russell, *An Inquiry into Meaning and Truth* (London: George Allen & Unwin, 1940), p.102. Quoted by Jorge Luis Borgès in 'Le Temps circulaire', in *Histoire de l'éternité* (Fr. tr. Paris: UGE, 1951), p.226.

20 See Domarchi, *Marx et l'histoire* (Paris: L'Herne, 1968).

21 All this information (and more besides) is borrowed from Jacques Néré's book *La Crise de 1929* (Paris: Armand Colin, 1971).

22 J. M. Keynes, *A Tract on Monetary Reform*, in *Collected Writings*, Vol. IV (London: Macmillan, 1971), p.41, fn.; quoted by Néré, *La Crise de 1929*, pp. 29–30.

23 Néré, ibid., p.30.

24 See *La Phénomènologie de la perception* (Paris: Gallimard, 1942), pp. 222–4; English tr. by Colin Smith as The *Phenomenology of Perception* (London: Routledge & Kegan Paul, 1962), pp. 191–4.

25 Néré, *La Crise de 1929*, pp. 52–5.

26 L. V. Chandler, *Benjamin Strong*, picture reproduced by Néré, *La Crise de 1929*, p.76.

27 Néré, ibid., p.95.

28 *Le Nouvel Observateur*, 7 January 1974.

6
Economy Of This Writing

Economy of the Figurative and the Abstract

What is this discourse? How is it legitimated? Where is it situated? Who authorizes you to speak in this way? Are you the manager [*tenancier*] of the great skin? But how could you be, when it is ephemeral and offers nothing to hold onto or secure? Aren't you concerned with pure imagination and rhetoric? Are you looking for truth, do you claim to speak it, to have spoken it? Haven't you produced just another new philosophy, yet another system? Yet more words? Have these words the pretension to change the world, at least? If not, what? To interpret it, wretch! In truth it is pure imaginary fabrication on your part, the realization of desire on the 'skin of language', as you would put it, aestheticism, elitism.

Reply with questions, tell them: and your theoretical discourse, what is it? All your questions have the underlying reference to this discourse, this true speech. We will not let ourselves be intimidated by this reference, you know nothing of this truth, and will never know anything of it, we know that it is the weapon of paranoia and power, the grip of unity-totality in the space of words, the return and the terror. So let's struggle against the white terror of truth, by means of and for the red cruelty of singularities. And we will answer you carefully, not because of some concern to understand your questions, but because that will allow us to place this white terror (especially when it presents itself as 'of the left', the most repugnant thing) on our ephemeral skin, and at the same time, to displace, to spread our own force on this monoface band.

Oh women, oh young men, oh ageing friends basking in the full bloom of youth, the unkind, the vehement, the barbarous, the superb, oh homos, oh dependants, oh Arabs, oh blood, help us now to endure this last, constant assault coming from detestable truth and intelligence, make us more intelligent than it, give us the stupidity that it has not and spare us that which it has, take us by the arms, undo your flies, get erect, carry us off to meet the Medusa, we will laugh in her face, spread out the red, the blue, let's open out the blue-bistre stalk of the neck springing from the snow-white blouse, spread out the crimson velvet vaginal cavity, opera satin little hard lips, cerise taffeta large crumpled lips, violet blue glans, raw linen concertina foreskin, impenetrable stretches of silver, gold, chalk, hold all of this under the Medusa's nose, that is how she will be answered.

Medusa immobilizes, and this is *jouissance*. Theory is the *jouissance* of immobilization. In this way the disjunctive bar is invested in its proper function of disjunction, since to disjoin is to immobilize this into this and that into that: identities. When disjunction intensifies within theory, this bar is immobilized at the same time in order to separate the this and the that on either side of itself, and is driven by a gyratory motion at such speed that the attribution of the spaces it generates to one thing or another is impossible. Further: it is insofar as it immobilizes that the bar turns, insofar as it distinguishes that it sweeps indistinctly. What gives you a hard-on, theoreticians, and throws you onto our band,[1] is the chill of the clear and distinct; in fact, of the distinct alone, that is, the *opposable*, for the clear is only a suspect residue of the distinct, translated into a philosophy of the subject. Stop the bar, you say: get out of this pathos—this is *your* pathos. Beautiful and paralysing, medusifying in fact, the severe disjunction that suspends.

The disjunctive function is also and at the same time the synthetic function. You say: it is this, it is not that: for inasmuch as it is this, it is not that. An old principle resting on a synthesis, since in order to dissociate one side from another, we must be on both sides at once. As soon as you disjoin, you unify. Everything that the phonologists, for instance, have elaborated under the name of opposition presupposes this synthesis. A very elementary synthesis, but indispensable to the construction of a *consistent* discourse. This discourse requires continuous use: every statement increases in pathos in order to separate the this from the not-this, it therefore moves forward armed with a *cutter*, a double-edge, and it cuts. The consistency it thus secures rests on a previously arbitrarily defined acceptability. You are aware of the formal properties of a strict, that is to say an axiomatized, theoretical discourse: the most elementary of the rules which allow the establishment of these properties is binary exclusion: either a statement is acceptable, or it is not (in a multi-value calculus of statements, this meta-operator of exclusion continues to operate no less).

Ideally, a theoretical text is an *immobilized organic body*: satisfying the formal properties of consistency, saturation, independence of axioms and completeness as regards the domain of reference, if there is one. An organic body is an assemblage (synthesis) of distinct elements (disjunction) called organs; that these organs might be statements, and this body a text, can only trouble asinine materialists, and only proves that everything is material to the libido.

In a narrative discourse, there may also be an organic body, but it is located at the *reference* pole of this discourse: the narrative will produce a body-effect, it will create the imagination of a simple or complex subject from the *story* told by the narrative, and will then pin the events which it unfolds onto a support whose attributes they will become. In theoretical discourse, however, the outline of this body is situated on the text itself: it is not the domain of reference which finds itself unified and totalized by this discourse, it is the discourse itself that becomes a unity and a totality. (Even its referential properties are formal properties.) The formalism of this discourse is, on the skin of words, something analogous to that of a so-called abstract painting. By contrast, the pictorial counterpart of narrative is figuration.

The disjunctive bar is at work in both cases, the place of its work of cutting-up and the place in which it turns are the same: the body of the text; in narration, in the activity of organizing the narrative, the elementary syntheses are carried out on the text, while *jouissance* is instantiated on the referential story, in the beyond of the text, in what it *shows*.

Can we, as libidinal economists, understand these two instantiations? Yes, we can. This is what we say: there is in every figurative-narrative organization a *pole of immobilization*, and we maintain that the intensities that can be procured from a *tableau vivant, posering,*[2] postures from Sadean or erotic narratives in general, realist pornography, figurative painting, certain *underground* films, and perhaps *all* narration and figuration, flash like electric arcs stretched between this pole of the victim's immobilization (the represented body) and a pole of agitation which plunges the body of what we will call the *client*, for obvious reasons, into the most extreme disorder.

Note in passing, within figuration-narration thus polarized, that the suggestion of a link immobilizing the things shown over there is paid for by the occultation of the processes on the text, on the film, the canvas, etc., by means of which this suggestion may be obtained. The *skin* of the medium and its marks is effaced (pictorially or cinematographically, for example, it is treated as if it were a transparent pane of glass looking out onto an elsewhere situated at some distance), it is the skin of the figurative objects that captures the client's emotion. The referential or denotative function, to speak in Jakobson's terms, outweighs all the others. But then, if we rightly take emotion, that is to say pulsional movements, as the main reference, what will we say? Imagine a client fond of *posering*, a reader of narratives, a spectator of westerns, a devotee of pictures; he faces the thing presented to him as immobile or immobilizing, as if he were in front of *prey*. Prey is an organic body prevented from movement: the envelope of live flesh turns silent and numb. The client's *jouissance* of this requires both its organicity and its death. Extreme movement or emotion is instantiated on the client body as frenzied impatience, astonishment, emission of saliva, tears, semen, creeping flesh, hallucinations, stammerings, pricklings, affects place and displace themselves ceaselessly over the fragments of the great skin that constitute 'his body'. These movements, far from sealing this latter in a total volume with both its centre and its unity in itself, split it into heterogeneous, independent zones, prone to autonomous incandescences: they are nothing other than the so-called partial pulsions. Here, then, is the *dispositif*: an organic body, unified and condemned to death through immobilization (the victim), onto which is connected, under the name of the client, and through the intermediary of an effaced, unrecognized medium, the Brownian motion of the partial pulsions.

In an abstract painting, an important displacement takes place: the picture represents nothing, it does not refer to a pole of immobilization situated in the domain of reference. The pole of immobilization is placed on the client body: this sort of picture demands the ligature of the partial pulsions that were in motion in figuration, the concentration of attention or equally the extreme pacification of the faculties, a putting into a state of dependency. It is on the contrary the chromatically marked support-skin (the canvas, the medium, the pigments) that is set in motion: not only because it no longer effaces itself 'behind' what it represents (while in fact it represents nothing), but also because the apparent immobility, insignif-icant for the eye that doesn't enjoy it, of the assemblages of points, lines, planes and colours is precisely what motivates desire. Here we are closest to what we are looking for, the instantiation of intensity in the theoretical text, immobile mobility. Klee, Delaunay, Newman, Rothko, Guiffrey, deceitful immobilizers, create movement by very small disparities of colour, lines, etc. Disparities, not oppositions. Learning to be set in motion by this, by a blue adjoining a blue, by two brilliances of the same white being dissimulated according to the angle of vision, beyond all loquacity and all didactic chromatics.

Because a vulgar abstract operates by system alone, it is theoretical, it works in the other way, towards the paralysis of the chromatic body; but the noble ones tend towards its mobilization. The client becomes the victim of the image (of the text), and this latter is what moves: emotion from colours, from plastic elements. Fascination with the abstract is an instance of *jouissance* proper, Medusa paralyses the client, but Medusa can move. She moves by disparities, the client-victim believes her frozen, petrified in oppositions, he does not see the system, the disjunctive function of this bar, cutting and synthesizing, he is blind to the main issue: this same bar that slips itself between the blue and the blue, the white and the white, apparently to disjoin them and produce the reign of the concept's distinction, turns indistinctly around in an oscillation which is in no way an illusion or a perceptual hesitation, but a dissimulation of energy, its frenzied leap from and onto this place. The skin of this image does not act as a unified totality, just here and there, in corners, in its impossible contacts between colour fields, always segmentedly or partially, like an ephemeral puzzle of fragments of the pulsional skin. The client body collects itself, unifies itself, dependent upon this puzzle. Is this activity or passivity? This unification even provokes an effect of identity, of sub-jectivity and therefore of active attention on the part of the client; but we say just as much that this latter is dependent upon the image, and that, like the hunter, he is being watched while he believes he is on the lookout. He is the prey, the victim body, constituted into a collected totality and thus setting up perverse motions on the part of the chromatic assemblage: the image body is a sadist to the client body by means of the fascination it exerts. Therefore the *dispositif* here is totally different from the one which operates in the figurative: the emotion, the turning around of the bar of exclusion sweep the image, the polymorphous surface to which is con-nected, by the trap of unification, the victim body of the client.

The Theoretical as Libidinal

Let us now return to the *theoretical genre*, which boasts the aforementioned formal properties. Let's recall its pulsional properties: like narrative-figurative discourse, it allows of an organic totality; but this is not situated on a reference, it is situated on the text itself; like abstraction, it requires the immobilization of its client; but it also requires his disaffection. These differences must be described.

The abstract does not act through a simulacrum-effect, but by means of the organization of its material alone. Now this is precisely the merit claimed by theory, that it advances no illusion or ideology. This claim was obeyed by, for example, the strategy of 'material decomposition', which the group 'Support-Surface', in its time, applied to pictorial simulacra: exhibiting frames, canvases, uniform coloured stamps, reels of lightweight wood or tarlatan twisted into the shape of a Moebian band and left lying on the ground, creating in sensible space the exact equivalent of a set of axioms for paintings in the space of language; these were supposed to be nothing other than acceptable statements, as defined by this axiomatic, within its lexis and syntax. And, in fact, Dezeuze and Cane, under the title 'For a Pictorial Theoretical Programme',[3] formulated the theoretical discourse corresponding to those exhibits.

One cannot, of course, say the same for all abstract painters, of whom the 'Support-Surface' group was in any case no less critical than they were of figurative art. Nevertheless, the libidinal *dispositif* is noticeable in every abstraction, and in particular of the theoretical kind, in that it thwarts the client's transference onto a simulated object, onto a reference. Transference can only bear on the material and its arrangement; is this correct? is it authorized? is this statement acceptable? These become the 'right' questions, the same ones you ask us, theoreticians, and which we question in turn. Questions full of the concern for truth, full of justice and guilt. What does the theoretical text offer its fascinated client? An *impregnable* body, like a thief, a liar, an imposter who can never be caught. Everything stated in this text is in principle capable of being derived from its set of axioms. A text which is utterly consistent within its own terms and can be derived from itself by explicit procedures, a wide-open organic body, which the client is supposed to be able to go through without the *solution of continuity*, repeating it or replying to it without error; a body which tolerates no erring, which defines the apparatuses of exclusion and channels of implication. Every statement formed within it has *right* on its side: the client may in principle derive it from the others. Nice tautological body of the theoretical text, without any external reference, without a risky interior region where roads and tracks may be lost, a model sealed up in its blank identity, exposing itself to repetition.

The theoretical text is a model, something to imitate, which has itself its own model to imitate, its set of axioms; and this set has its own, properly formalist, model. And rather than seeking to show that the closure of models is impossible (Gödel's theorem), and that there is always a primary opacity of the symbol, of ordinary language, one would do better to identify this *return to the same* as a *dispositif* of the passions, no more nor less so than the *return to the origin* with which hermeneutics would like to contrast it. In both cases it is semiotic; the operation bears only on the relations between signs. Let's rather comprehend this model according to its force. This force is revealed in its expansion through mimesis. The mannequin (*mannekijn*, little man) presents *collection* models. It transports the jubilation of the repetition of the same, *jouissance* through serial reproduction.

The closed body of the theoretical text gives rise, as a model, to this same *jouissance*. Its tautologous perfection gives rise to the enthusiasm of fidelity in replication. Ideally at least, it goes well beyond biological reproduction, where effects of similarity due to the mixing of genetic codes are not only not excluded, but are inevitable. The organic theoretical body fulfils its mimetic function through parthogenesis. There is an affinity between the theoretical and the *virginal*. The psychoanalysts will say: the theoretical implies the denial of sexual difference. But in our eyes, this difference is suspiciously semiotic. We say: it implies the denial of disparities, of the heterogeneities of stases and distances which energy travels through; it implies the denial of polymorphism. It needs a form, a good and proper form. Such a form has its basis and its origin in a stable synthetic disjunction.

This disjunction works so hard inside the theoretical body that, ideally, it leads to its immobilization. The *paralysis pole* we find in the figurative is found here too, displaced from the reference onto the material itself. It is not what is spoken of that becomes immobilized by discourse, as in narrative; it is discourse itself, a system of acceptable statements within the 'chosen' set of axioms, which strives to *come to rest*. Quite different from the intensive instance in the work of the great abstract painters: in their paintings the still, painted things are set in motion 'on the spot', at the threshold of perception, ceaselessly: they are in motion towards motion.

But theoretical bodies, as such, are in motion towards rest, like the works of bad abstract painters. They have a goal. Medawar says that a scientific hypothesis relieves an anxiety. Theoretical discourses are instruments for fixing and dispersing intensities, anxiety being the generic name given to all the turns of the disjunctive bar, the common name of the emotions. And he also says that the only difference between the invention (here, however, we are not talking about that at all) of a scientific hypothesis and that of a plastic or musical object, for instance, is that in the latter, affective intensities are conveyed, whereas it is the rule of the former that their transmission is in principle disaffected, and that its reception should involve no emotion.[4]

So, the immobilization of the bar into stable disjunctions on the body of theory (concepts) corresponds to a similar immobilization in the zone of contact between the text body and the client body. The theoretical text makes contact with the client only on condition that he is disaffected, neutralized, supposed to be incapable of mobilization, unfeeling, impartial, that is to say having no part in the emotions dissimulated in the text, nor in any others.

This chill is the heat proper to the theoretical. It is not a parody, its libidinal character rather appears in the anonymity which it claims. The famous *universality* of knowledge, generally understood as the *a priori* of theoretical discourse in its communicability, is, seen from the pulsional point of view, an act of destruction of personal identities. Only anonymous fragments of the pulsional band are plugged into theoretical discourse, fragments capable of repeating it without transformation. One need no longer marvel, after Freud, that repetition may provide *jouissance*; it remains to point out here that a *faithful* repetition, such as theoretical discourse entails, proceeds as much from Eros, inasmuch as it affirms a consistent body, as from the death drives, since this repetition passes through the destruction of particular libidinal *dispositifs* already formed on the client body, and their dialysis into anonymity. The *self-forgetting* entailed by theory is already the amnesia proper to the Id.

The paradox, then, of the disjunctive bar, at once motionless and in rapid rotation, becomes less opaque: as disjunctive, it suspends all passage of energy from the client body to the text body and vice versa; in motion, it opens the passage in its same disjunctive function, in the disconnection of the client *dispositif* in relation to the discourse, it makes a connection out of *jouissance* in non-copulation and anonymous repetition. The libidinal band emerges at exactly the point where it is meant to be excluded. Now this disconnection at the very point of plugging-in is equivalent to the internal homogenization required by theoretical discourse in order to form itself as a body. Just as homogenization can be invested with intensity, so the neutralization of the plugged-in bodies can be accompanied by their extreme excitation. Was this what we had to learn: that the movement towards coldness and death is burning hot? that intensities are not tied to 'life', but may be mobile or fixed on no matter what theme or piece of the great patchwork, including those which, like theoretical discourse, demand extreme coldness and dead replication? We are not saying that this is an error, a perversion, an illusion, an ideology. If mimesis gives you a hard-on [*vous fait bander*], gentlemen, who are we to object?

This is rather what interests us. Capital is also mimetic, commodities producing commodities, that is to say, being exchanged for commodities, the same commuted into the same according to an immanent standard, Sraffa's, for example. If 'knowledge' can become a force of production, as Marx said, it is because it always has been, and is, insofar as it is the construction of identities and systems for their reproduction. Capitalist production is this construction of the conditions of repetition-capacity [*pouvoir*]: to produce in order to produce, to sell in order to sell, series, chains, standards, etc. The return obtained through repetition (valid for 500 km and 3 months, the cost-price of your half-price card will be covered after two return journeys) is, after transcription into terms of political economy, this same movement towards paralysis of discourse that we find in theoretical texts. The model makes the series possible, and hence the saving of energetic expenditure.

This saving is not necessarily deadly: redemption implies the lifting of a debt that burdens the displaceability of capital into energy, therefore its enfranchisement, it is free again, it runs to place itself elsewhere. One can thus understand redemption as regeneration: energy fixed in machines and personnel, *situated* [*disposée*], and in this sense very bound (in the body of invested capital), a part escapes from this *dispositif* and will be situated differently. The compulsion to *stop*, in theoretical discourse, has also this function: the circumscription of a field of reference, the production of a model capable of treating it in a predictable fashion, that is to say, according to identity; and the liberation of potentialities [*puissances*]. In the manufacture of theory, as in that of productive machines, the robot is necessarily implied, and doubly: it guarantees the replication of the model, and guarantees the saving of energy. It gives rise to ventures and conjunctions.

We do not mean that theory *comes* from capital, nor the reverse. Nothing comes from anything, nothing is the effect of a cause. But the relationship is close, capital is as old as theory, as old as the West in matters of the determination of identities. Some objections, however: capital does not stop, whereas theoretical discourse tends towards its immobilization; capital is also an elusive, perverse body, theoretical discourse closes itself up into a beautiful organic body: don't these propositions highlight disparities, making the analogy impossible?

On the contrary, they refine it, and we are capable of a certain ingenuity ourselves. Mimesis closes the theoretical text up as a power of statements [*pouvoir d'énoncés*]. The model is what makes and remakes, makes in conformity to the made: that is power. The robot has power, the robot-maker, power to the second power, and the maker of the robot-maker, power to the third power. What has no power is the statement itself, in principle, since it is nothing more than an effect. This is why we fight the thought of causes: of powers.

In this regard, the theoretical is a major procedure of invagination and the closure of the great skin upon itself; it proceeds by repetitions; it transforms unprecedented statements into simple innovations, the great pain of saying something we know nothing about into the little worry over modifying the theoretical edifice by the addition of some axiom or other, or by the derivation, in conformity with the laws of formation, of some expression which, despite being new, must be no less *well formed*. Theory dreams of what an ill-formed expression would be only to dispel the danger. Innovation is allowed only insofar as it will give rise to the repetition of the theoretical model as a self-immobilizing organism. (Just as capital takes new quantities or qualities of energy into account only insofar as it can repeat its axiomatic of equal exchanges on them.)

Nothing enters the system that wasn't there already, that doesn't have its double, that is to say its model. This mimetic relation encourages dreams of the Augustinian *similitudo*. They differ only as metaphor differs from metonymy, as dependence upon a primary model, received, revealed, transcendent, deviates from the condition of possibility (axiomatic) that the theoretician *gives himself* as the transcendental authority judging every new statement. In *similitudo*, authority does not belong to the theoretician, but to those he addresses: the Word alone speaks, the true Locutor is absent; the locutor's word is really only the metaphor for the other; Capitals for absence, lower case for presence; but with mimesis, the theoretician conquers meta-language, that is, not only the statement, but the statement of the conditions of enunciation. That is why every statement has its double, from the basic set to the system, 'before' it has been offered as an *a priori* possibility. Leibniz has said all this before, even if it is in the language of an ancient metaphysics: that *Alea iacta est** is a statement *already* included in Caesar's notion that God is self-creating, and that the fate thus experienced in Caesar's wandering is included in the axiomatic of the divine omni-discourse. Just replace Leibniz's God with the committee of the directors of the world's ten biggest banks, and you will come to see that what you are doing, what you can do, will be able to enter the 'reality' of capital only insofar as it is recurrent. To think something is to have been able to think it, to produce it and reproduce it. There is no first time, repetition is primary since it is included in the very constitution of the element: concept, commodity. If it is not repeatable, equally exchangeable, it is not an element of the system.

This is the *democratic power* in theoretical discourse. It is a power binding intensive forces into repetitive potentialities [*puissances*]; it is democratic since the conditions of formation of these potentialities are universally accessible in principle. Equality is the political figure of theoretical parity. It exerts its constraint over every discourse and all production. The theoretician, the scientist, will complain about a particular discourse (ours?) because he cannot repeat it, at least not quickly. Useless; inexchangeable. Democratic power is the power of facile identical propagation. We have nothing against it, save its terrorism: for whoever can enjoy other than by repetition is excluded from it, in spendthrift duplication and multiplication. As lax as we might be, it is necessary to acknowledge that the exercise of this power of exclusion of every intense modality other than that instantiated on the disjunctive function is not something added to, taken on moreover by democratic theoretical discourse, this would almost be a bad interpretation, providing the hope of more open acceptations in the future. No, its terrorism is consubstantial with it, it is the act of the use of the bar and the constraint of parity.

But let's not be intimidated by deadly theory, let's leave it to the other death, to capital's revolutionary function of agitation, and to arrogant science, which sprang from theory itself.

In the death through repetition which the accountable signs of capital convey, an almost identical and at the same time heterogeneous function operates silently and inextricably: the two deaths are indiscernible, they

---

**Alea iacta est*: 'the die is cast'.—*tn*

are in conflict. But consider for a moment what is called the 'history' of the sciences, for example, that of mathematics: a continual dissolution of the definitions of mathematical objects through new imaginations which not only extend the totality constituted by these objects to new beings, but completely modify the nature of mathematics: one need only compare Euclid's *Elements* with Hilbert's *Principles of Geometry*. How do we understand these displacements from the energetic point of view? Duplicitously. If they form a history, it is in the same way that there is a history of a nation, or of Europe, or of the West: it is a *Bildung*, it is the movement of conquest, the accumulative journey of the self, the voyage of initiation which is also the phenomenology of mind. The irreversibility, quite secondary, of the time of this history, its 'progress', is, as Cavaillès said of mathematics in particular, the very essence of the body of science: it is nothing but the mark, in its own space-time, of the capitalization processes on utterable statements, and of the conquest of statements hitherto mathematically barbarous. This progress is in time what, in the space of imperialism, the extension of frontiers is to the empire: displacement of a *border* (of an anteriority), beyond which, it is agreed, there is *nothing to hear*. The *limes** are hardly fixed than a freelancer, a black hunter, a solitary traveller, returns and says: something can be heard, here's how. This moment can be described as Caesarism and the exploitation of barbarous frontiersmen; this would be to forget the moment of madness, when Lobatchewsky says, 'I do geometry without recourse to the Euclidian postulate of the parallel', when Cantor says, 'I include infinity amongst the operational numbers'. These moments are not ones of permanence, but of discontinuity, not ones of inhibition, but of delirium assumed and carried to its end. They do not reduce the unknown to the known, they make everything one thought one knew unstable in proportion to what one used to know, for a moment one means to speak like a barbarian on the agora; these moments are to science what Beethoven's late quartets are to harmony.

At each moment, death passes over the established *corpus* of theory a deathly tension, where the survival of the whole system is at stake. Here science is *fiction*.[5] It is not content to repeat itself, to appeal to its reserves in order to reproduce something already known, it forges new surfaces of inscription, it adds to the body of knowledge, to the *corpus*, new segments where the libido circulates and invests, creating an imbalance in this *corpus*,

---

**Limes* (L.): 'thresholds', 'borders'.—*tn*

rendering its life precarious, it is obliged by the very abundance of its discoveries to doubt its vocation to the true, it opens its eyes, it no longer believes in anything, space and time become infinitely suspect to it, the concepts it received as *a priori* become obsolete. After Heisenberg and Bachelard, it has become useless to insist on this theme.

But we need not let ourselves be taken in by the expression which Bachelard called the secret thought of this science: the philosophy of the no. To maintain this negativism would be to reduce the range of the 'disorder' of science to a critical function, to the function of criticizing the *corpus* of possible statements. But this is not so important, it is rather that this science is positively productive or creative, or *fictive*, as is art. It is less and less interesting as theoretical critique (which explains the thousands of confused researchers), and more and more as operational delirium. This delirium requires the death of the knowing subject. *Who knows*, in today's scientific knowledge? Absurd question, posed from an environment where knowledge is in principle supposed to be assignable to a subject who could *possess* it. The delirious sweeping of the theoretical field by modern science not only eliminates the supposedly knowing subject, it disqualifies the supposed subject. Every *topology* [*topique*] seems like an outdated ideology compared to the mobility of libidinal *economy* at play in invention. The modern scientist no longer exists as a knower, that is to say as a subject, but as a small transitory region in a process of energetic metamorphosis, incredibly refined; he exists only as a 'researcher', which means on the one hand, of course, as part of a bureaucratic apparatus of scientific power, but on the other hand, indissociably, as an experimenter, indefatigable and not enslaved, with new junctures and combinations of energy; the statements he proposes count only in terms of their novelty.

And in this sense, in his anonymity and errancy, he is no less the man of capital subordinating his labours to the commands of power. Capital is also positive delirium, putting authorities and traditional institutions to death, active decrepitude of beliefs and securities, Frankensteinian surgeon of the cities, of imaginations, of bodies. There too topology [*topique*] has become derisory, because the category of the *topos* points back to an Aristotelian space-time of the event, allegedly stable and 'natural', whereas in this sweeping, intensities have no precise permanence that would permit the fixing of moments and places to them by recourse to a common referentiality: this is not only because all classes or social groups do not live in the same time and in the same historical environment, nor because some may be backward or far ahead in relation with the others, it is because in the most highly developed 'sphere', in the most (provisionally) highly invested of these regions, i.e. branches of industry, research areas, markets, urbanization zones, all the pieces of the supposed social body, the professions, begin to simmer with excitement because they border on this 'sphere'; so *even there, there is no common topos*, inventions even here, conflicts are not resolvable in an institution, recognized or not, in an instance to be found in one locality. Although it deals with only this aspect of capital, almost nothing need be changed of what we have around us in the world, in society or in life, in order to give it its science-fictionesque significance: it no more has a body than science has a theory. What has to be changed? Very little would make all the difference: the conduction of intensities should be able to take place on *all* the pieces of the social 'body', without *exception*.

Bodies, Texts: Conductors

At the core of the theoretical, there is a game to play, a tight game, which would play out a 'discourse' of dissimulation: this game would not seek to paralyse a client of equal rank, capable of repeating new statements identical to those proposed to him; it would not prejudge in any way what the client can receive from the statements he hears or reads, nor the manner in which he will conduct them; it would seek powerlessness [*impouvoir*]; it would let the plugging-in of its uncertain border with that of its client body take place in an aleatory fashion, without bothering to try and control it. It would be the bottle thrown into the sea, but without desperation, without *ultima verba*, without its launch being a last attempt to signal and communicate a message entrusted to it. There would be no message in our bottle; only a few energies, whose transmission and transformation was left and was desired to be unpredictable. Because we believe in forces, we do not force our client to pair up with our discursive model. Do we even have a model?

We would love multiplicities of *principles* of enunciation, to be judged by their effects, like everything else; but in the knowledge that our discourse is not their cause, whatever they might be. Therefore, this would be neither a Treatise, as in the *âge classique*, nor even an Essay or an Enquiry, such as Montaigne or Hume wrote: not only would this 'discourse' not deal with a definite object, it would not even search for this object, nor would it seek a statement suitable to its purpose.—Are you not *seeking* something, in all this? you will ask us.—Yes, yes. But research in theoretical discourse is like the suspension and postponement of its closure; just as frontiers for the great Caesars were only ever temporary notes in the account of a conquest, to be swept away when a fresh wind blows the *limes* beyond the *limes*: more and more totality . . . ! And therefore more and more bureaucratic unity to be constructed on top of them. A discourse of dissimulation would seek something else altogether: not even the dissimilation of the assimilable and the inexchangeability of the exchangeable; but singularities. Not 'innovations' (deducible from a body of axioms), but unprecedented things. This discourse would seek its madness in the wisdom of research; a bewildered Caesar within the conqueror. And no need of the frenzied parodies of a Heliogabalus.

This dissimulatory discourse would no longer be able to delight in the bitter 'modern' satisfaction with the absence of the object and worklessness [*désoeuvrement*]: there are already several reflexive pages on the question of the position of this discourse, they appear to us to be quite prolix enough, not to say superfluous, and we gain no pleasure, only boredom (and we hope this makes itself felt), from writing on our writing. We do not desire to prise from our client some gloomy rumination on the Nothing which forms the *coda* to the very classical structuralist symphonies. The present writing would not be a book; for there is no book that is not the ideal of the immobilized organic body. These would be only diverse pieces, each piece of variable format and belonging to its own time with which it begins and ends—pieces which might or might not find their place here and there, or rather: subject here and there to the incandescence of the rotating bar. If a certain client body is there, that's fine. If not, that's fine too. Not a book, only libidinal instalments (this provides all kinds of watchdogs with the opportunity to treat the 'author' as a fascist, when he is fascinated).

'We must operate penises, vaginas, arses and skins so that love becomes the condition of orgasm.' That is what the lover, the mistress, dreams about, so as to escape the terrifying duplicity of surfaces pervaded with pulsions. But this operation would be appropriation or propriation, as Derrida says, and ultimately a semiotics in which erections and discharges would infallibly pinpoint the pulsional motions. But *it is necessary* that there be no such infallibility, this is our great and ultimate resort against the terror of the true and power. Fucking ought not to be guaranteed, in either sense, neither as proof of love nor as the security of indifferent exchangeability; love, that is to say intensity, should slip in in an aleatory fashion, and conversely intensities may withdraw from the skins of bodies (you didn't come?), and pass onto the skins of words, sounds, colours, culinary tastes, animal smells and perfumes, this is the dissimulation we will not escape, this is anxiety and this is what we must *will*. But this 'will' is itself beyond all subjective liberty, we can only experience this dissimulation *from the side, neben*, like fugitive blind people, since it is unbearable and since there is no question of rendering it pleasant.

In the theoretical, there is the desire to put an end to dissimulation: the solid and reassuring positivity of the so-called labour of the concept makes an appearance. But it is the same thing with fucking; there is no assurance that these labours procure intensities, nor that intensities happen to occupy their work. Theory's pretension is similar to lovers' demands: there ought to be clear signs; they may be equivocal, the demand is that they be legible, even if this requires a double reading. And it is clear that this legibility required by the erotic or the theoretical implies replication: signs are clear when, through repetition, they permit the inference of a syntax and a lexis, when they permit prediction and anticipation. The theoretical pretension is a pretension to power [*pouvoir*], like every sign-based demand for love.

But our demand addressed to skins, to words, cannot be made transparent, our libidinal time cannot become provisional. Our discourse cannot satisfy theory's requirement, there is no assurance given one way or the other: neither theoretical construction nor *deconstruction* will ensure the possession of intensities. Theory demands the same thing as the amorous mistress and the unkind one: only love should erect the penis, only truth should erect the word! Such was Plato's demand, and so it remains, even in apparently cynical, but in fact very religious, modern discourse.

We cannot believe that deconstruction is a better guarantee of intensities than construction. It is only the negation of the negation, it remains in the same sphere, it nourishes the same terrorist pretension to truth, that is to say the association of the sign—here in its decline, that's the only difference—with intensity, it requires the same surgical tampering with words, the same split and the same exclusions that the lovers' demands exact on skins.

Every fixation of a standard answers to the demand for appropriation, it invests the disjunctive bar with its function of exclusion, and gives rise to the confusion of intensities and identities. Political economy or capital is precisely this. There is no law of value in Marx's sense, but if there is a law capable of fixing the composite of the sign and the tensor, then values, by the same token, also exist: these are only intelligent signs taken according to their reputedly intensive function.

We could say: then it is the opposite, then let's look for intensities in the absences of regularity, in vertigo, in elusive tensions, and let's make theory anti-theory, let's create a discourse in which words would not and could not have their expected *charge* guaranteed. But we are not saying that either. If there is a profound failure, an impossibility, of poetry today, it is not because we live in troubled times and that Being has withdrawn from us. This discourse of profound reasons, conforming to religiosity, bores the hell out of us. Nothing has withdrawn, we have not 'forgotten' anything; the ancient Greeks, Heraclitus the in-between of faith and knowledge, are no more originary than Janis Joplin. The failure of poetry is simply the impossibility of anti-theory; the figure is not to be opposed to discourse, as the site of intensities may be to the realm of identities. There is no site for intensities, *no intense genre*; and if it must be said all over again, let us repeat that the strictest theoretical articulation may give rise to vertiginous passages, and capital in its very rigidity may give rise to *jouissance*.

The demand for clarity must be strongly denounced; it requires the power of he who loves, or who speaks, over his intensities. It demands: have power, define the intense. No, we must receive this demand in terror; flee from it, that's all we can do; it is the first imprint of power on the libidinal band. We say we are incapable of guaranteeing the link between our words, our deeds, our looks, and pulsional sweeps. Hence no clarity: sometimes it works, sometimes not. What you demand of us, theoreticians, is that we constitute ourselves as identities, and responsible ones at that! But if we are sure of anything, it is that this operation (of exclusion) is a sham, that no-one produces incandescences and that they belong to no-one, that they have effects but not causes.

Anonymity, force [*puissance*]: there are some words to satisfy your demand for knowledge. Little matter, but at least see what *effects, not causes*, means. You associate them both as the poles of a single relation, causality. But, after Hume, there is no need to insist on the sham of this little arrangement. Therefore, when we say 'effects', it is not a matter of the effects of causes. It is not a question of referring the responsibility for the effect to the cause, of saying: if this discourse, if this face, this music, produce these effects, it is because . . . It is precisely *not* a matter of *analysing* (not even 'schizo-analysis'), in a discourse that will necessarily be one of knowledge, but rather of sufficiently refining ourselves, of becoming sufficiently anonymous conducting bodies, not in order to stop the effects, but to conduct them into new metamorphoses, in order to exhaust their metamorphic potential [*puissance*], the force [*puissance*] of effects that travels through us.

So you see how there is *anonymity*: we can only attain this conduction by disinvesting the channelling and exclusive *dispositifs* called the ego, property, the closed voluminous body. So you see how there is *passivity*: we have neither to judge causes nor isolate effects, energies pass through us and we have to suffer them, we produce a philosophy of sodomists and women, come what may provided you do what you must, Keats said that the poet is a chameleon, and Hofmannsthal that he had no ego, but this is not enough, it is not just the poets who should have this romantic privilege, already attributed to them and to the gods by Plato; let everything go, become conductors of hot and cold, of sweet and sour, the dull and the shrill, theorems and screams, let it make its way over you, without ever *knowing* whether it will work or not, whether it will result in an unheard-of, unseen, untasted, unthought, unexperienced, effect, or not. And if this passage does not in fact entail the addition of a new fragment to the beautiful and elusive libidinal patchwork, why not weep, and your crying would be that fragment, since nothing is lost, and even the harshest deception can in turn give rise to several effects.

So you see how we have a *theatrics of masks without faces*: every effect is a mask, and just as there is no cause, there is no face. These masks mask no lost origin (a scarcely more refined notion of the cause), they become conductors of one another, without it being possible to assign them an order of appearance, without a law of concatenation, and therefore according to anonymous singularities. So you see how there is *no analysis*: not even Freud's, which is, however, the closest to the discourse we seek. Very close because it is *effects* that the so-called analytic relation intends to make happen, it is affects to which it intends to give rise, and it is as a good conducting body that the analyst exposes himself to pulsional connections; and it is just as much to the force [*puissance*] of an anonymous conducting body, available to intensities, that psychoanalysis aims to lead the isolated ego and the superegoic resistor body of the patient. We would like the analytic relation to be this feminine relation, this relation of ductility and polymorphism. But it is not so, it is also the search for causes, responsibilities, the search for identity, the localization of desire, becoming conscious, masculinization, power, knowledge: that is, analysis. We desire the effects of conduction and the conduction of effects. Lysis, thesis.

No bad conscience, need it be said, in our search for these effects and these conductions in language, as linguists. For others, it is through painting, for others, dance, caressing, money . . . Language is not over and above, as a substitution, and no more is it the totality of the transportations of force. Therefore, no bad conscience, nor the feeling of a crushing responsibility, two relations to the text that circumscribe and define the relation to the politics proper to the White man of the left. We deliver no message, we bear no truth, bring no revelation, and we do not speak for those who remain silent. No-one is silent, there is no-one there, silence plays a role in libidinal music.

It's a beautiful thing to produce this book; just finished, it falls from our hands, we are its effect, pushed aside, and to do this, there are a few moments, a dozen moments, perhaps spread over five years, or over three days, in fact all co-present, each is a tensor sign, an idea on fire, an image, the smell of a tear-gas grenade or an intolerable denial of justice, a face, a book, a tensor sign we had to act on, conducting it and letting it course through a few quick pages, rapidly arranging words into sentences and paragraphs, so that this heat and this chill, this force, may pass through. The book, then, is not a selection, a recollection, a testimony or a statement. No need to become prophetic, no need even to parody prophecy, as Nietzsche does. We love only its *speed*. A race against death, against the frenzied night which will strike us down? Not at all, it is not worth the trouble of dramatizing in this dull, still Western way; for which one must flee, if it is disorder that is to be feared?—the ego, the agent. The speed of which we speak is not for protection, it is not narcissistic flight; rather speed *before the advance* of the awful jets of energy that will steer the course of the pen, the onset of thoughts, insight; to run towards that, to catch the pulsions in flight, to steal the words they require, to become a multiple conducting body, a multi-directional polymorphous area. The book would be these fragments obtained by the effects of intensities.

We lay no claim to madness. *Acting the madman* is the most despicable thing: acting the pliant native to the colonial authorities. Acted in this way, the madman is always *the king's* fool; despots need their fools: their justification, the court's representative of what it excludes. Just like doctors and their patients, politicians and their workers. No pretence at madness, just a *search* for it. But let's be careful here; we do not *pursue* it as something like our good, of which we had been deprived by some evil event, like some being which ought properly to belong to us and which would be in flight: so the poor parents search for their fleeing children, and when they think they have them, they forget to look after them. Madness is not a good, and we detest those who cry: Long live madness! Madness is not the conquest of the individual singularity. It is what is intolerable in intensity. To pursue madness would be to become, to make of one's body, to make of language, a good conductor of the intolerable. This would be a discourse being displaced towards excitation and being refined for it; Ilse Barande rightly says that it is this movement, which is nevertheless admirable, that one tries to cover up and depreciate under the name of perversion.[6] A perversion, but one which would escape nosography; one which is not a *dispositif*, but a labyrinth. The discursive conduction of affects on the skin of words would not be continuous/discontinuous, like a logical deduction, an articulation; it would be one, another, and another labyrinthine unravelling from which the force of these effects would, every time, uniquely, shoot out. Disorder, deconstruction, the figure, offer no guarantee of good conduction.

Stop confusing servitude with dependence. We would like a book of complete dependence: these pieces of the ephemeral patchwork would be composed and added to the body, the fingertips, all over the sheets; and these formations would, for a moment, make us dependent on them. If there is no cause, there is no author. Once the libidinal band is open, the sheets of desire extend themselves by the intussusception of one fragment by the other, like a substance into cells, we have only to set up our paper screen, in order that, by printing these movements, they immediately become pieces of the band. So for the last time, stop confusing power [*pouvoir*] with force [*puissance*]. If there is labour involved in adding these few intensive instants to the band, it is an elusive, powerless labour, which opens up to force. Power is an ego's, it belongs to an instance, force belongs to no-one. That force works towards the eradication of all subjectivity is precisely its violence. This is its condition. With the result that, when we say 'Let each go his own way' [*laissez tous passer tout*], it is not a prayer for non-violence, it is violence itself. Stop confusing violence and the white terror. White terror is instantiated, it destroys here to construct somewhere else, over there, it crushes several pieces of the great film, but does so in order to construct a centre. Violence is not constructive, it consists entirely in non-construction, non-edification (uselessness), in sweeping away defences, in opening up routes, meanings, minds. This sweeping-away leaves fresh scars, just like a bulldozer. Violence or red cruelty destroy instantiated appropriations, powers. Is it never pure?

And this 'book', is it always this Harlequin's costume of libidinal fragments, no sooner assimilated than it collapses into rags? Will it neither run its course nor pursue its quarry in the political economics of publishing, literature and thought? Will its red violence not be dissimulated by the white terror? Isn't it possible that it will be taken as a testimony, as a statement of truth? And how in fact could this tension commit itself to the outside of rationality; ductility sheltered from regularity? All speech is endowed with a truth-value, whatever this expression means. Even for we libidinal economists, and not just for you, theoreticians, what is said here *counts as true*. For as soon as there is an *ego*, a *we*, the instance is ready, awaiting its truth, like an old beast awaiting its pasture. Therefore, no surprise, extreme serenity as regards this question. Nietzsche could even be shown to be a Platonist. Insofar as one wants to show something, one organizes the object of which one speaks according to the field of the true and the false, and shows one's 'true' and 'false'. Instead, it is a matter of *not* showing in this sense, a question of *not* making signs in the spirit of the true and the false. Is the *dance* true? One will always be able to say so. But that's not where its force [*puissance*] lies.

We need not leave the place where we are, we need not be ashamed to speak in a 'state-funded' university, write, get published, go commercial, love a woman, a man, and live together with them; there is no good place, the 'private' universities are like the others, savage publications like civilized ones, and no love can prevail over jealousy. Must our fear of sign-systems, and therefore, our investment in them, be still so immense that we search for these pure positions (from the heights of which we would not fail to give everyone everywhere lessons, and it will be a sinister paranoiacs' revolution, once again)! What would be interesting would be to stay put, but quietly seize every chance to function as good intensity-conducting bodies. No need for declarations, manifestos, organizations, provocations, no need for *exemplary actions*. Set dissimulation to work on behalf of intensities. Invulnerable conspiracy, headless, homeless, with neither programme nor project, deploying a thousand cancerous tensors in the bodies of signs. We invent nothing, that's it, yes, yes, yes, yes.

Notes

1 ' . . . *ce que vous fait bander . . . et vous jette dans notre bande . . .* '.—*tn*

2 *posering*: in English in the original.—*tn*

3 'Support-Surface', a group of artists in France from 1966 to 1972; see Jean Clair, *L'Art en France, une nouvelle génération* (Paris: La Chêne, 1973).—*tn*

4 P. Medawar, *The Art of the Soluble* (London: Methuen, 1967), pp. 145–6, and p.155 ff.

5 See Boris Eizykman, *Science-fiction et capitalisme* (Paris: Mame, 1974) (with an afterword by Lyotard, 'Ante diem rationis', pp. 225–43).

6 Ilse Barande, 'Notre duplicité: les "perversions", leur champ, leurs origines', in *La Sexualité perverse. Etudes psychanalytiques* (Paris: Payot, 1972).

Index

Alcibiades, 159–60, 159, 160, 165
Althusser, /L, 95
Aristotle, 94, 102, 156, 157, 161, 162,
    189, 216–217, 220, 221, 223, 225,
    228, 229, 232, 238, 254
Augustine, 6, 7, 8, 9, 13, 46, 64,
    65–70, 73, 74, 88, 89, 251

Bachelard, G., 254
Barande, I., 261
Bataille, G., 56, 63, 77, 105, 133, 137,
    141, 182, 183
Baudelaire, C., 76, 77
Baudrillard, J., 87, 102, 103, 104, 105,
    106, 108, 112, 117, 119, 121,
    122–24, 126, 127, 128, 131, 136,
    148
Beaumarchais, 39
Beethoven, L., 253
Bellmer, H., 2, 171
Bergson, H., 46
Blanchot, M., 76
Böhm-Bawerk, E., 151
Borgès, J. L., 35, 37, 215
Boulez, P., 43
Boumedine, M., 113
Bukharin, 64

Caesar, 45, 78, 252, 256
Cage, J., 50, 206
Caillois, R., 105, 183
Cantor, G., 253
Cassirier, E., 231
Castoriadis, C., 102, 114–116
Cavaillès, G., 253
Chaplin, C., 137
Clastres, P., 49, 108
Clausewitz, 63
Colbert, 187, 188–198, 227, 232, 237
Culioli, A., 164
Cunningham, M., 50

Delauney, S., 32, 246
Deleuze, G., 17, 49, 64
Détienne, M., 156
Derrida, J., 256
Deyon, P., 17, 49, 64
Dezeuze and Cane, 247
Diderot, D., 152

Eco, U., 48
Einstein, A., 109
Engels, F., 96, 97
Escher, 40, 164
Euclid, 253

Feuerbach, L., 125–126, 127
Flaubert, G., 56
Flechsig, P., 53, 55–64, 73
Fourier, 40, 64
Frege, G., 53
Freud, S., 16, 21, 22, 25, 26, 27, 28,
  29, 43, 46, 48, 51–53, 55, 57, 63,
  64, 69, 73, 74, 109, 122–124,
  140–1, 161, 164, 165, 170, 172,
  177, 185–7, 213, 218, 219, 249,
  259

Gelb and Goldstein, 231
Gilson, E., 92
Gödel, K., 248
Goethe, 64
Green, A., 219
Guattari, F., 64
Guéry, F., 118, 127
Guiffrey, R., 246
Guyotat, P., 111, 139

Hegel, G.W.F., 13, 35, 47, 53, 61, 63,
  68, 73, 80, 94, 116, 120, 122–24,
  164, 168, 217, 218, 219, 220, 222
Heisenberg, W., 254
Heraclitus, 258
Herodotus, 166, 169
Hölderlin, 124
Hume, D., 194, 195, 255, 258
Husserl, E., 43, 46, 47, 53

Jakobson, R., 120, 245
Jaulin, 46, 105
Joplin, J., 258
Joyce, J., 25

Kant, I., 46, 47
Keats, J., 259
Keynes, J.M., 195, 199, 224, 230
Khajuraho, 26
Kierkegaard, S., 183

Klee, 12, 246
Klossowski, 7, 25, 36, 62, 64, 69–77,
  81–89, 176, 177, 193, 195, 204,
  207

Lacan, J., 43, 48, 52, 61, 105, 119,
  120–25, 127, 177, 208
Laclos, C. de, 63
Lafont, S., 91
Lafont, X., 60–61, 64
Lao-Tzu, 5
Latouche, S., 148
Lavoisier, 194, 209
Leibniz, G.W., 252
Leiris, M., 107
Lenin, V., 64, 142
Lesnievski, 12
Lévi-Strauss, C., 42, 44, 46, 105, 108,
  213
Louis XV, 182
Louis XIV, 187, 193, 227, 232, 236
Lucretius, 62
Luther, M., 68, 125, 126

Machiavelli, 77, 87
Malamoud, C., 219
Marcuse, H., 118, 161
Marx, K., 5, 69, 87, 89, 94–106, 110,
  112, 115, 116–9, 121, 125–9,
  130–6, 138, 139, 140–4, 145, 146,
  148, 149, 156, 162, 188, 199, 211,
  216, 218, 219, 220, 226, 250, 257
Masson, A., 41
Mattick, D., 236
Mauss, M., 105, 119, 120, 121, 122
Medawar, P., 249
Merleau-Ponty, M., 94, 231
Montaigne, 255
Morgenstern, 167

Nancy, J-L., 152
Negri, E. di, 68

Néré, J., 230–1
Nietzsche, F.W., 16, 25, 28, 39, 40, 50, 53, 64, 70, 78, 99, 165, 260, 262

Pascal, B., 25, 183
Peirce, C.S., 18, 42
Piranesi, 164
Plato, 7, 18, 42, 66, 74, 87, 105, 159, 164, 165, 166, 257, 259
Podolski, S., 152
Poe, E.A., 44
P'ong-tsou, 205, 206
Poulantzas, G., 153
Proudhon, 128
Proust, 25, 28, 29, 49
Pythagoras, 181

Rapoport, A., 167, 174–5
Reich, W., 221
Rizzi, B., 115
Romilly, J. de, 152
Rothko, M., 246
Rousseau, J.J., 106, 125, 127
Russel, B., 53, 226

Sade, D.A.F. de, 37, 61, 62–65, 69, 72–73, 75, 79, 81, 83, 86–88, 113, 138, 181, 182, 192, 193, 194, 204, 244

Saint-Victor, R. de, 48
Saussure, F. de, 18, 42, 104
Schmidt, V., 172–173
Schoenberg, A., 43
Schreber, D.P., 53–64
Shakespeare, W., 133
Signorelli, L., 51
Smith, A., 195
Socrates, 159–160, 164, 165, 185
Spinoza, B. de, 39, 40, 62, 181
Sraffa, P., 145–150, 211, 212, 215, 237, 238
Svyerdlov, 64
Sterne, L., 25, 101

Taylor, F., 215
Tomatis, 110
Trotsky, L., 64, 115

Van Gulik, R., 203, 206
Varro, 7, 8, 9, 64, 65
Vernant, J–P., 156
Vidal-Naquet, P., 156

Warhol, A., 32

Zeami, 50

Question what you thought before

Continuum Impacts - books that change the way we think

AESTHETIC THEORY - Theodor Adorno 0826476910
I AND THOU - Martin Buber 0826476937
ANTI-OEDIPUS - Gilles Deleuze & Félix Guattari 0826476953
A THOUSAND PLATEAUS - Gilles Deleuze & Félix Guattari 0826476945
DISSEMINATION - Jacques Derrida 0826476961
BERLIN ALEXANDERPLATZ - Alfred Döblin 0826477895
PEDAGOGY OF HOPE - Paolo Freire 0826477909
MARX'S CONCEPT OF MAN - Erich Fromm 0826477917
TRUTH AND METHOD - Hans-Georg Gadamer 082647697X
THE ESSENCE OF TRUTH - Martin Heidegger 0826477046
JAZZ WRITINGS - Philip Larkin 0826476996
LIBIDINAL ECONOMY - Jean-François Lyotard 0826477003
DECONSTRUCTION AND CRITICISM - Harold Bloom et al 0826476929
DIFFERENCE AND REPETITION - Gilles Deleuze 0826477151
THE LOGIC OF SENSE - Gilles Deleuze 082647716X
GOD IS NEW EACH MOMENT - Edward Schillebeeckx 0826477011
THE DOCTRINE OF RECONCILIATION - Karl Barth 0826477925
CRITICISM AND TRUTH - Roland Barthes 0826477070
ON NIETZSCHE - George Bataille 0826477089
THE CONFLICT OF INTERPRETATIONS - Paul Ricoeur 0826477097
POSITIONS - Jacques Derrida 0826477119
ECLIPSE OF REASON - Max Horkheimer 0826477933
AN ETHICS OF SEXUAL DIFFERENCE - Luce Irigaray 0826477127
LITERATURE, POLITICS AND CULTURE IN POSTWAR BRITAIN - Alan Sinfield 082647702X
CINEMA 1 - Gilles Deleuze 0826477054
CINEMA 2 - Gilles Deleuze 0826477062
AN INTRODUCTION TO PHILOSOPHY - Jacques Maritain 0826477178
MORAL MAN AND IMMORAL SOCIETY - Reinhld Niebuhr 0826477143
EDUCATION FOR CRITICAL CONSCIOUSNESS - Paolo Freire 082647795X
DISCOURSE ON FREE WILL - Desiderius Erasmus & Martin Luther 0826477941
VIOLENCE AND THE SACRED - René Girard 0826477186
NIETZSCHE AND THE VICIOUS CIRCLE - Pierre Klossowski 0826477194

www.continuumbooks.com